Simple SysML for Beginners

Using Sparx Enterprise Architect

SIMPLE ▶

SysML for Beginners

Using Sparx Enterprise Architect

David Hetherington

Asatte Press

Austin, Texas

Simple SysML for Beginners

Using Sparx Enterprise Architect

by David Hetherington

First Edition

Version 1.0.2

ISBN 978-1-937468-05-7

http://AsattePress.com

Table of Contents

Chapter 1 – Introduction

This book is for beginners. This book assumes that you have just purchased a copy of *Enterprise Architect* and are anxious to get started, but otherwise don't know too much about SysML and don't have much experience using *Enterprise Architect* or any other similar tool. The purpose of this book is to help you get through the initial learning curve and get you on your way to becoming proficient at SysML modeling.

How this Book is Organized

This book is designed to be a tool companion for three books on SysML which are much more comprehensive:

- **Delligatti, Lenny** – *SysML Distilled: A Brief Guide to the Systems Modeling Language*. Addison-Wesley Professional, 2013

- **Friedenthal, Sanford and Alan Moore, Rick Steiner** – *A Practical Guide to SysML, Third Edition: The Systems Modeling Language*. Morgan Kaufmann, 2014

- **Douglass, Bruce Powel** – *Agile Systems Engineering 1st Edition*. Morgan Kaufmann, 2015

Together, these three books provide in-depth coverage of SysML. [1] However, these books show only finished diagrams. They don't cover the steps needed to construct the models and the diagrams. These steps can be remarkably complicated; the sequence of steps needed to construct the underlying model for a diagram is often less than obvious when using a real SysML tool. The goal of this book is to get you comfortable enough with *Enterprise Architect* and the basics of SysML so that you can confidently construct common models.

This book covers all nine SysML diagram types, showing detailed steps to construct simple models that demonstrate key concepts for each diagram type. If you work your way through all of the examples in this book, you should be ready to tackle more complex modeling problems as they come your way.

---

[1] For more information on these books, see the *SysML Books* section on page 371.

This book is organized as follows:

- **Chapter 1** – Introduction. This chapter.

- **Chapter 2** – This chapter will get you up and running with the tool. We will learn how to create models. We will create a few basic diagrams. After completing this chapter, you will have a feel for the basic structure of a model as well as a feel for how *Enterprise Architect* works.

- **Chapter 3** – In this chapter we will discuss the high-level goals and purpose of SysML before we delve deeper into SysML and into the tool.

- **Chapter 4** to **Chapter 12** – In these chapters we dig deeper into each of the SysML diagram types. We will cover several of the most common usages of each diagram type. At the end of each chapter there will be a section listing advanced topics not covered along with page references in the three books mentioned above to go to for more in-depth information.

- **Chapter 13** – This final chapter discusses some of the challenges in helping an organization introduce model-based systems engineering techniques.

The back section of the book contains a number of useful appendices as well as some standard reference sections such as a glossary and an index.

About the Examples

As you work your way through this book, you will find that the example systems presented are simple to the point of silliness. You will encounter a lot of doorbells and coffee makers. Nothing that you encounter will involve more than high school mathematics. No advanced engineering expertise will be needed to understand the examples.

This focus on extremely simple examples is actually something that I have changed in the years that I have been working on this book. Like many other authors of similar books, I have worked on many fascinating and complex systems. As such, my initial instinct was to present some of these as examples. However, in the intervening years I have come to understand that examples involving advanced technical expertise unrelated to the concepts I am trying to illustrate are simply distracting for the reader. Part way through writing this book, I pulled out all the examples about automotive radar, ocean drilling ships, and complex telecommunications systems and replaced them with the extremely simple examples that you will find in the rest of this book.

At this point I would also like to point out that my coverage of the tool will evolve slightly as the book progresses. Starting in Chapter 2, I will show every single mouse click needed to make the tool run. Nothing will be skipped or left as "an exercise for the reader". As the book progresses, however, I will gradually skip explanations of mundane operations explained in earlier chapters. As such, I recommend that you follow the examples in the book in the order that they are presented.

About the Diagrams

The "Show every mouse-click" approach mentioned in the previous section requires a lot of annotated screen capture diagrams. Here I have had to make some tradeoffs to show as much detail as possible while keeping the print version of this book to a manageable size.

For initial study, the best experience will come from reading either the print edition or reading the electronic edition on a larger, high-quality device such as the *Kindle Fire HD 10* tablet.

One of the advantages of the Kindle, iOS, and Android devices is that the images can be zoomed. Simply press firmly on the image for a few seconds and a menu will appear allowing the image to be zoomed and scrolled as needed. This function is powerful enough to zoom way in to see the fine detail of an icon in a screen capture.

Unfortunately, the *Kindle for PC* application displays the book in a fixed format with no ability to zoom the images.

The *Kindle Cloud Reader* is a more flexible. [2] While there is still no zoom function, this reader automatically expands all images to the full width of the column. If you adjust the width of your web browser, the reader will switch into single-column mode while using about 70 percent of the screen. At this size, the images are quite easy to see.

As such, for working step-by-step through the examples, I recommend a dual-monitor arrangement with the *Kindle Cloud Reader* running on one monitor and the tool running

---

[2] The *Kindle Cloud Reader* is available here: https://read.amazon.com/

on the other. Alternatively, a *Kindle Fire HD 10* tablet or similar iOS or Android device combined with a single-monitor PC running the tool should work well.

For more information, please consult the Asatte Press application note:

https://asattepress.com/Downloads/Application_Notes/eReader-Application-Note.pdf.

Downloading the Examples

All of the examples in this book can be downloaded from:

http://AsattePress.com/Downloads/SysML4Beginners.html.

The download file is a standard zip file. Once you unpack the file, you will find that it is organized in a hierarchy that matches the book.

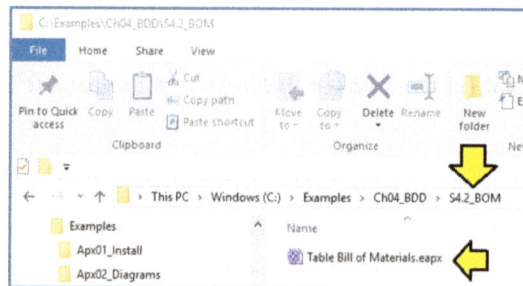

Figure 1-1 – Example file in directory for section of book

Figure 1-1 shows the *Enterprise Architect* file for the table example model from Chapter 4 in the section *Modeling the Bill of Materials* on page 76.

EAPX versus EAP files and Unicode Support

Between version 13 and version 14 of *Enterprise Architect*, Sparx introduced the "*.EAPX" file type replacing the previous "*.EAP" file type. There are also considerations regarding JET4.0 and Unicode support. (See *Unicode Support* on page 365 for further information.) The example files for this book are in Sparx 14 "*.EAPX" and JET4.0 Unicode format.

Tool Version

The screen captures in this book were produced with *Enterprise Architect* version 14. Later versions of the tool may be slightly different. In particular, Sparx has announced the intention to rename the "Project Browser" to "Browser" in version 15.

Permitted Use of the Examples

1) The book and examples are provided "As Is", without warranty of any kind, express or implied.

2) The book and examples can be used freely for all types of individual study and classroom instruction with the following restrictions:

   1) Copyright laws are respected. Students must purchase or rent individual copies of the book.

   2) The book and examples cannot be bundled or redistributed in any fashion without the express written permission of Asatte Press, Inc.

   3) Instructors must direct students to the Asatte Press, Inc website to download the examples.

   4) The examples cannot be stored on a local server and indirectly distributed.

   5) It is acceptable for the examples to be stored as part of the configuration management process for an instructional course as long as this storage is not used as a method of indirect redistribution or re-bundling.

Consultants and instructors at private and public educational institutions are welcome to use this book and the example files for the book in classes including instruction delivered for a fee provided the conditions of use above are respected. In other words, if you are a consultant you are welcome to use the books and examples as part of your paid service as long as you make it clear to your clients where the material is coming from and ask your clients to actively purchase books and download the examples themselves.

For questions about special arrangements, long-term licensing, bulk book purchases, teaching materials, and other uses that don't seem to fit into the conditions above, please contact: SysML.for.Beginners.SparxEA.2020@asattepress.com

Style Conventions

To the greatest extent possible, this book follows United States spelling conventions and *The Chicago Manual of Style* [CMS17th] for style and formatting.

Periods inside quotation marks at the end of a sentence are one exception. This book follows the British convention (periods outside the quotation marks) because the American convention adds periods to text such as variable names that should not include a period.

Customer Support

Please address any concerns about the physical condition of your copy of the book, refunds, or other sales-related matters to the retailer who sold you the book.

Reports of typographical errors and technical questions can be directed to:

SysML.for.Beginners.SparxEA.2020@asattepress.com

Complimentary Printed Book for Typo Submission

Asatte Press has put a lot of time and effort into proofreading and checking this book. Nevertheless, there are probably a few remaining typographical errors in the text. Our plan is to periodically make minor corrective updates to the image used to print the book as well as to any electronic versions. If you find a typographical error, please send an e-mail to the address above pointing out the text that seems to be in error and suggest a correction. If your suggestion is accepted, after the next printing update, we will be happy to mail you a complimentary copy of the corrected print edition. Don't forget to include your mailing address in the e-mail.

Chapter 2 – Quick Start

Ready to start? We are going to dive right in, do a quick pass through the tool, and create a simple SysML model of a doorbell system. Don't worry too much if the SysML concepts presented in this chapter seem strange; we will be back to explain them in more detail in subsequent chapters.

Introducing the Tool

Before we start constructing our first **model**, there are a few routine housekeeping matters to take care of.

Starting the Tool

Assuming that you selected the installation option to have *Enterprise Architect* install a Windows desktop icon, the easiest way to start the tool is to click on that icon.

Figure 2-1 – EA icon

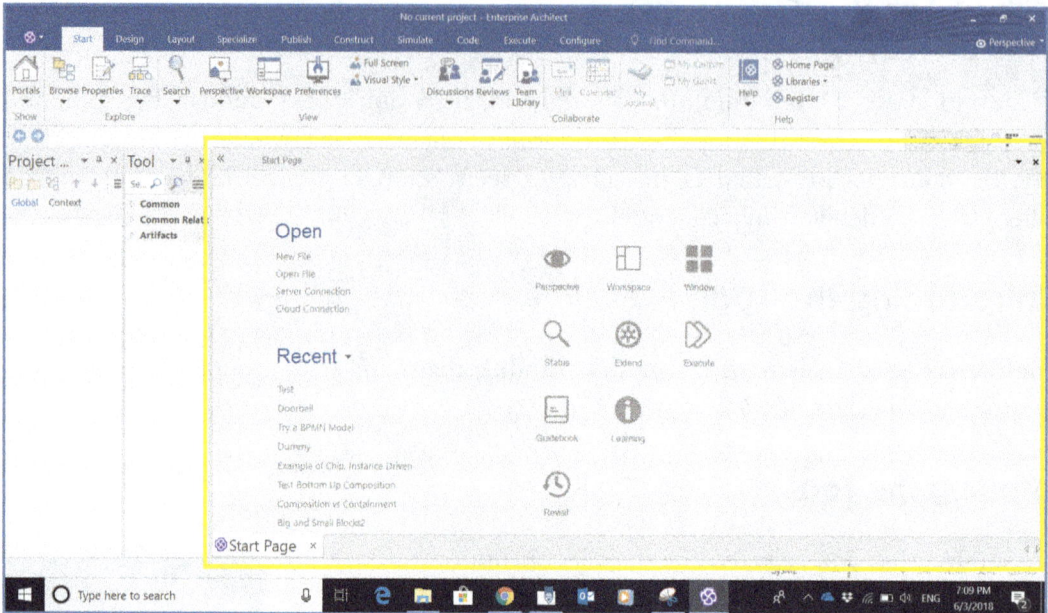

Figure 2-2 – Start Page

This start page presents a list of recent projects as well as some other options. If you find this start page helpful, feel free to use it. Being somewhat old-fashioned, I generally use the standard "File, Open" interface which is supported as well. As such, I usually click the "X" in the upper right-hand corner of the "Start Page" tab to dismiss the start page.

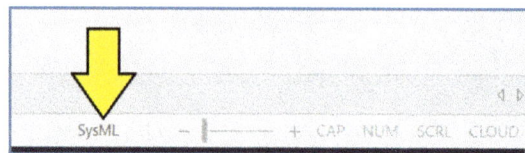

Figure 2-3 – Confirming SysML perspective

Before we get to work creating SysML models, we will want to confirm that *Enterprise Architect* is actually running in SysML mode. Version 14 of the tool has enhanced support for "perspectives". In previous versions, when you created a new model, the tool would ask you what kind of model you wanted (SysML, BPMN, UML, etc...). In Version 14, the perspective determines what kind of model will be created. You can confirm that the tool is running in the SysML perspective by looking for the "SysML" indicator at the bottom of the screen as shown in Figure 2-3.

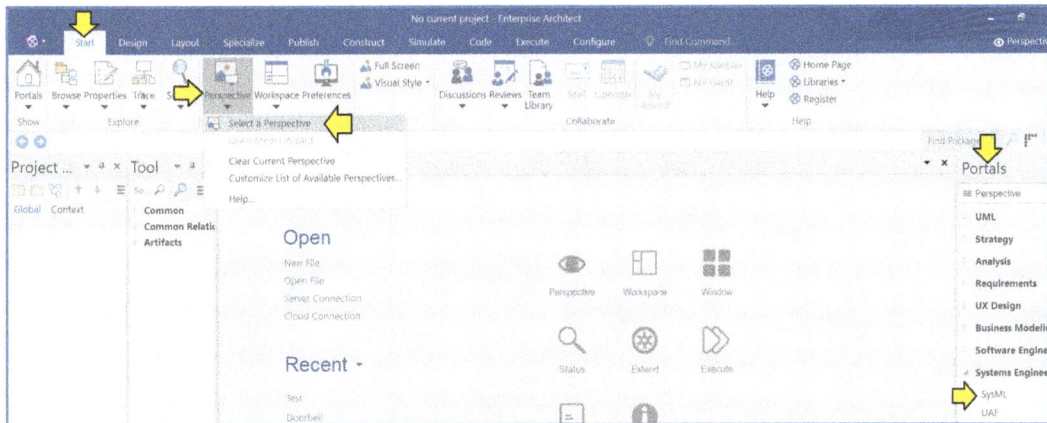

Figure 2-4 – Setting SysML perspective

If the current perspective shows something other than "SysML", the perspective can be set as shown in Figure 2-4.

1) Select the "Start" ribbon.

2) Pull down "Perspective" and select "Select a Perspective".

3) The "Portals" pane will appear.

4) Under "Systems Engineering" click on "SysML".

Backing Up a Model

Enterprise Architect version 14 stores each project in a "*.EAPX" file. This file contains data in a format used by the Microsoft Access JET database engine. It is a binary file, not a text file. The file can be copied, renamed, moved and otherwise manipulated like any other Windows binary file. [3]

---

[3] In versions of *Enterprise Architect* previous to version 14, Sparx used the file type "*.EAP". In version 14, Sparx introduced the new filetype: "*.EAPX".

Likewise, the "*.EAPX" file can be checked into a version control system like Subversion or GIT as a binary file. Note that since the file is binary, you will not be able to use the differencing functions of the source code control system. However, if you are disciplined about commenting each commit, you will be able to track changes in each version of the project.

Creating a Model

Now we are ready to create our first model.

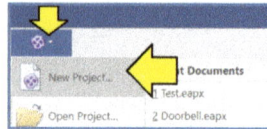

Figure 2-5 – Starting a new project

Pull down the menu in the top left corner of the screen and select "New Project..." to start a new project.

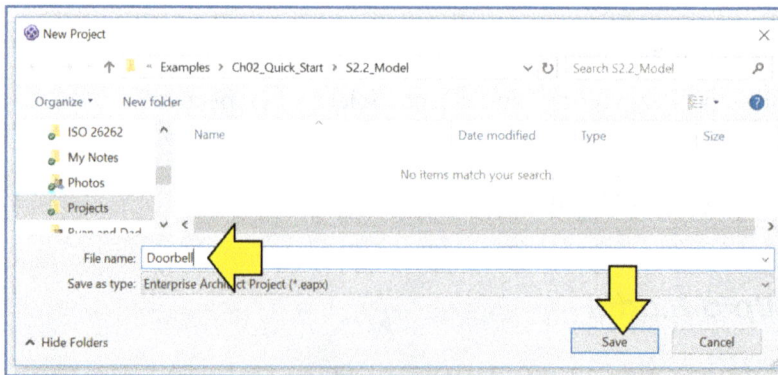

Figure 2-6 – Naming the new project

Give the new project a name. Our first example will be a doorbell system. I recommend that you name the project "Doorbell".

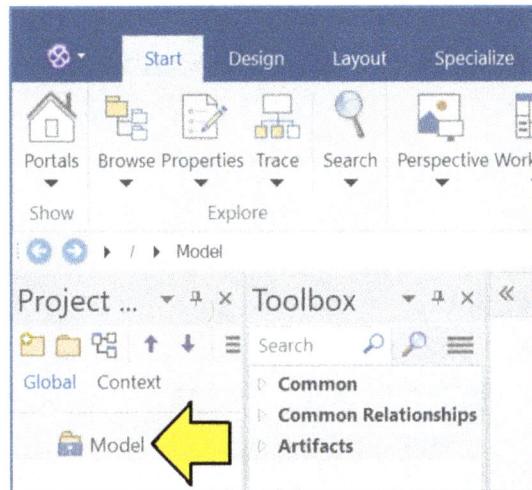

Figure 2-7 – Empty model

We now have an empty SysML 1.5 model. It is possible to use this model as is, but I prefer to give my models descriptive names, especially since we may want to include more than one model in a project later.

In earlier versions of *Enterprise Architect*, you could right-click on the model and rename it. In version 14, there is no such entry in the right-click context menu. However, there is another way to rename the model helpfully pointed out by Sparx support:

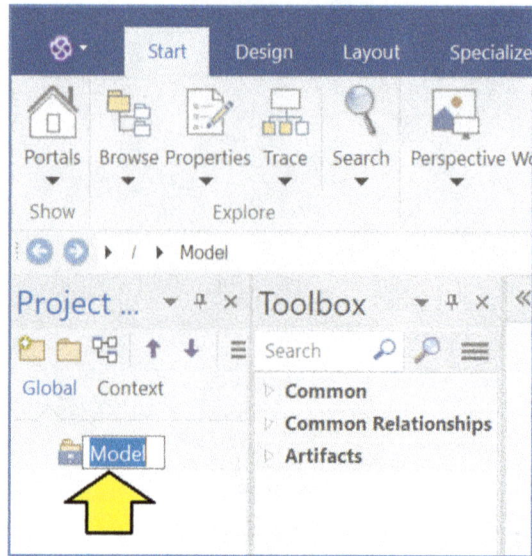

Figure 2-8 – Select model and press F2

Just select the model and press function key 2 (F2). The model will shift into edit mode and you can rename the model. I recommend that you name the model "Doorbell Model" to be consistent with the project.

Adding a Package

Before we can do anything useful with our new model, we will need to add a **package**. Packages are a central feature of SysML models. In fact, the model itself is a special kind of package. You can think of packages as being very similar to directories in the Windows file system. You can name packages freely. You can put packages within packages.

Let's create our first package.

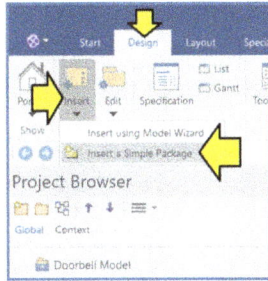

Figure 2-9 – Create the first package

In the current version of *Enterprise Architect*, the first package cannot be created from the right-click context menu for the model. Instead, you have to access the "Design" ribbon, pull down "Insert", and then select the "Insert a Simple Package" option as shown in Figure 2-9.

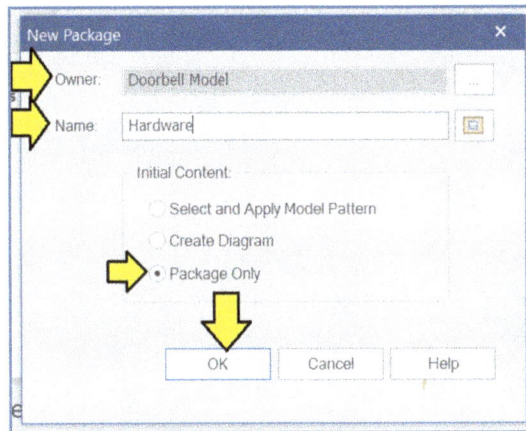

Figure 2-10 – Name the package

1) The "Owner:" field should default to the name of the model.

2) In the "Name:" field, enter a name for the package. Since we will be modeling the hardware pieces first, I recommend that you name the package "Hardware".

3) For the moment, select the "Package Only" radio button.

4) Click "OK" to continue.

Adding a Block Definition Diagram

Now we are ready to add our first diagram. SysML 1.5 defines nine types of diagrams. The first diagram we will add is a **block definition diagram** – the most basic diagram for defining the elements of a system.

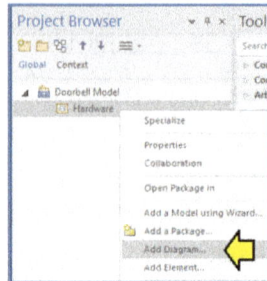

Figure 2-11 – Right-click and add diagram

Right-click on the new package "Hardware" and select "Add Diagram...".

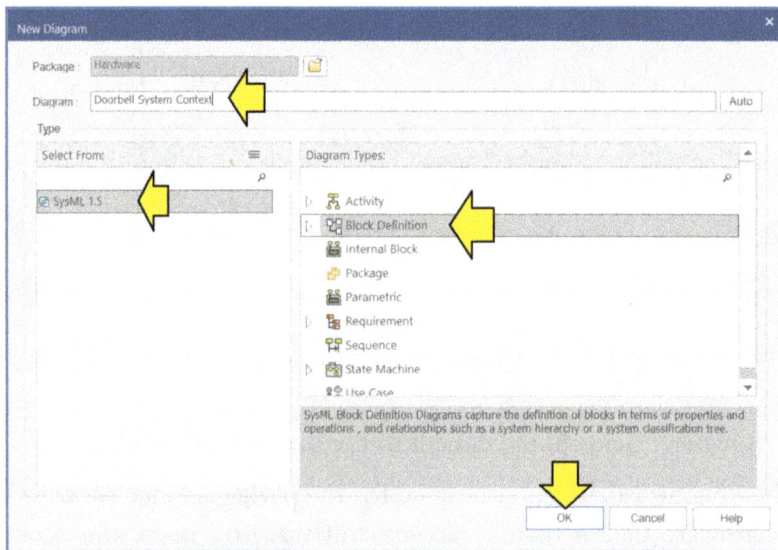

Figure 2-12 – Name the block definition diagram

1)   Name the diagram "Doorbell System Context".

2) Under "Select From:" select "SysML 1.5".

3) Under "Diagram Types:" select "Block Definition".

4) Click "OK".

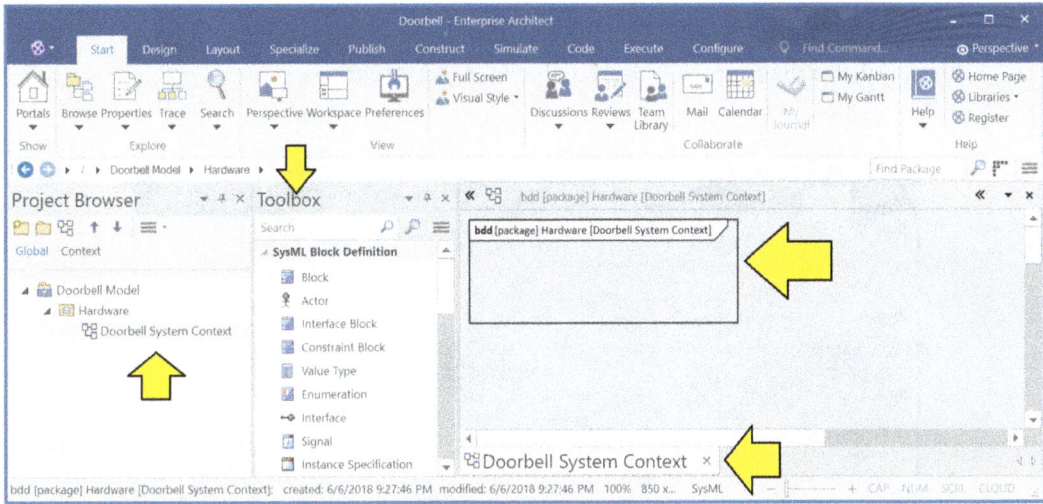

Figure 2-13 – Quick look at the tool

Let's take a quick look at the tool now that we have created the block diagram as shown in Figure 2-13:

1) On the left side of the screen, we can see a pane called "Project Browser". This pane presents a hierarchical view of the model than can be expanded and explored similar to the file explorer user interfaces in Windows and other operating systems.

2) In technical articles, this view is often referred to as the "Containment Tree".

3) In the project browser, we see that the tool has added a block diagram called "Doorbell System Context" in the package "Hardware".

4) In the center of the screen, we can see a pane called "Toolbox". This pane contains icons for different SysML elements that are appropriate for block definition diagrams.

5) To the right of the screen, we see that the tool has created our block definition diagram.

6) The diagram pane is a "tabbed view" layout which can show multiple diagrams as tabs. We can see the tab for our diagram at the bottom of the screen.

7) Our diagram has a standard SysML frame with a header. "bdd" stands for "block definition diagram". This diagram lives in the package "Hardware". The name of the diagram is: "Doorbell System Context".

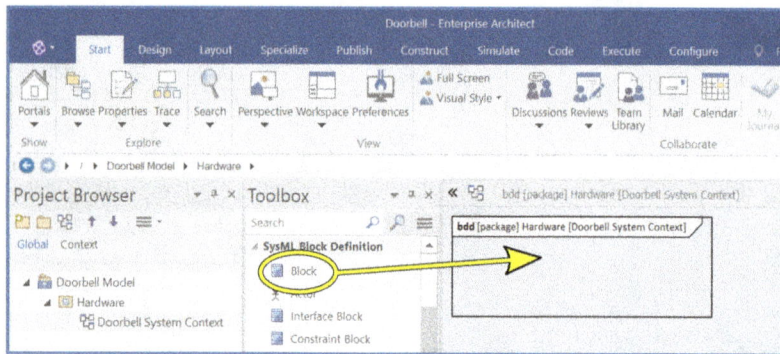

Figure 2-14 – Click on the Block icon and drag it to the diagram

Now we are ready to add our first **block** to our model. In the "Toolbox" pane in the center of the screen, click on the "Block" icon and drag it to the right into the frame of the block definition diagram as shown in Figure 2-14.

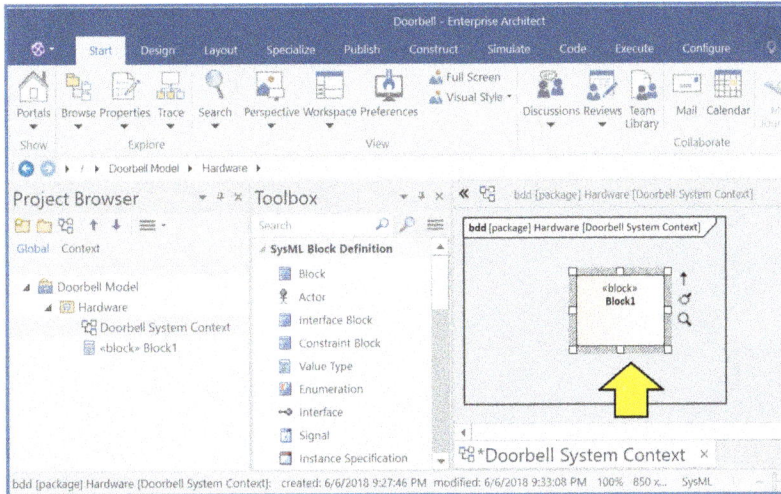

Figure 2-15 – A block will appear in the diagram

A block will appear in the diagram.

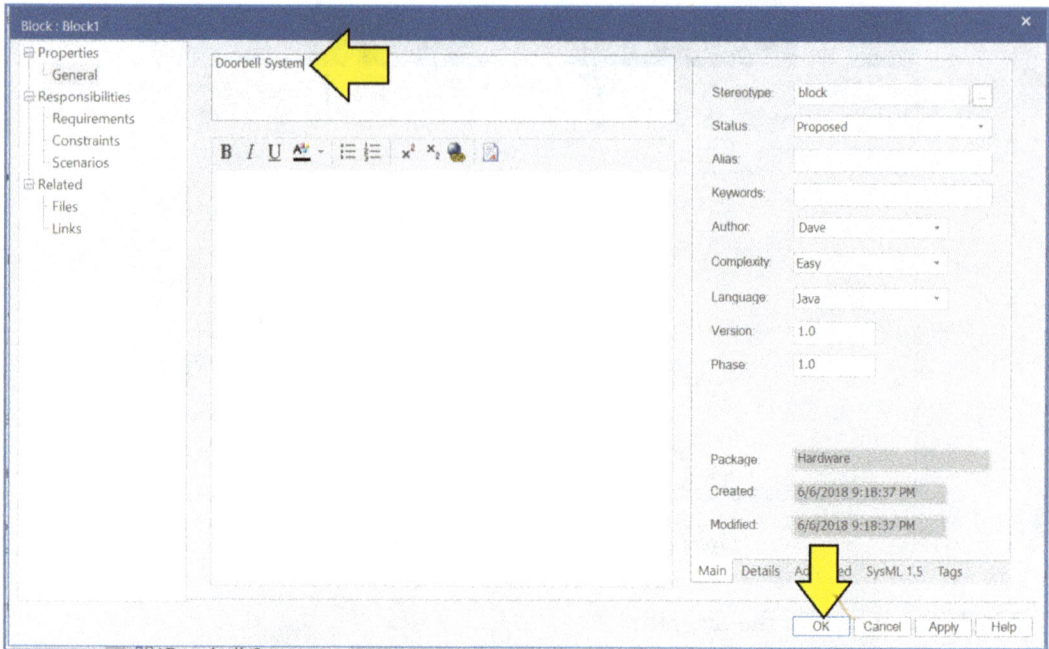

Figure 2-16 – Double-click, name the block, press OK

Double-click on the block. The properties panel for the block will appear. In the top center box, name the block "Doorbell System". Click "OK".

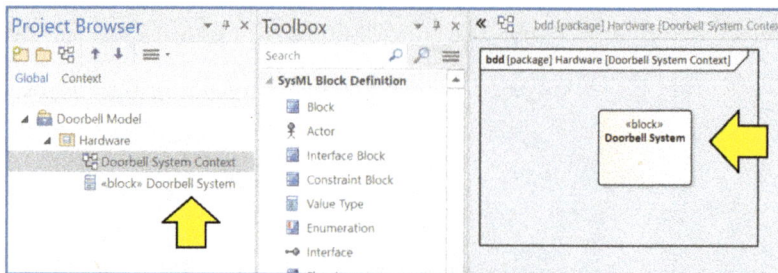

Figure 2-17 – The new block appears in the model at left and in the diagram

Examining Figure 2-17 we see the block in two places. We see the block in the project browser in the left pane. We also see the block in the diagram in the right pane.

Our First Glimpse of Model-Based Systems Engineering (MBSE)

We are at now at the starting line for "Model-Based Systems Engineering (MBSE)". That is, the project browser is showing "the model" and the diagram is just a diagram. We could make two or three more diagrams with the same "Doorbell System" block. In the model there would still be one and only one block. That is, the model represents "the truth" and the diagrams are just views of the model. A model element can be shown in as many or as few diagrams as desired. In fact, you can create a model element directly in the project browser and not include it in any diagrams at all. This flexibility to make many different diagrams including the same element becomes a central feature of MBSE because this technique allows the systems engineer to make many simple diagrams for different stakeholders, each diagram showing only the model elements of interest to that stakeholder.

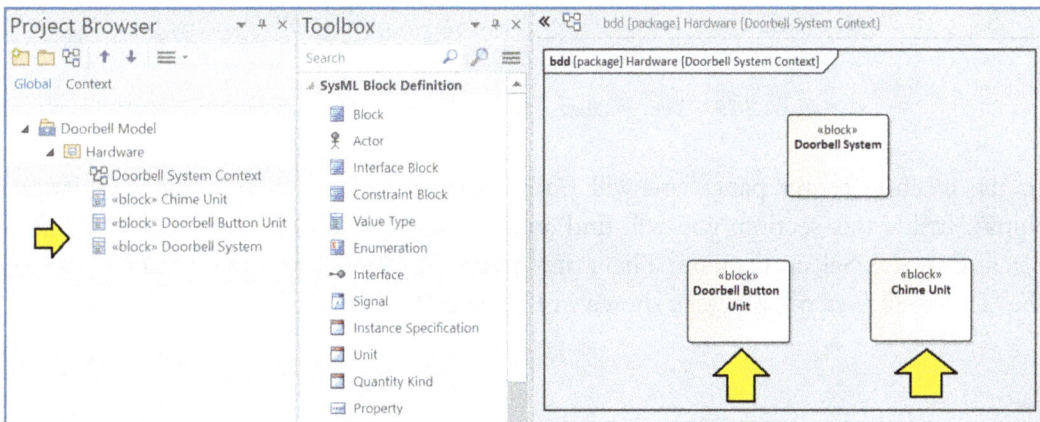

Figure 2-18 – Add two more blocks to the diagram

Using the same procedure, add two more blocks and name them:

•   Doorbell Button Unit

•   Chime Unit

Now that we have the two main units for our system, we are going to introduce a relationship called a **composite association**. This relationship is often referred to more simply as "composition".

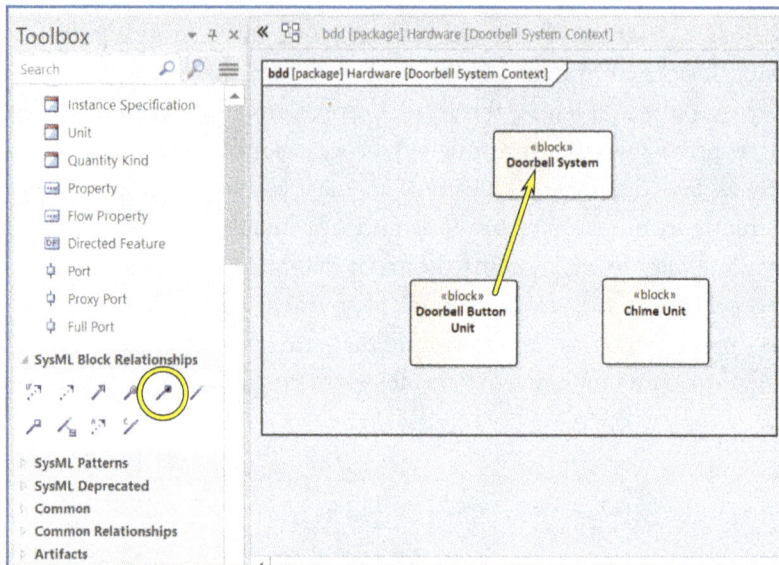

Figure 2-19 – Select the composition relationship and drag as shown

In the toolbox center pane, you will find a section called: "SysML Block Relationships". Inside this section, you will find an icon that is a line segment connected to a black diamond. Select this icon. Then, drag from the "Doorbell Button Unit" block to the "Doorbell System" block as shown in Figure 2-19.

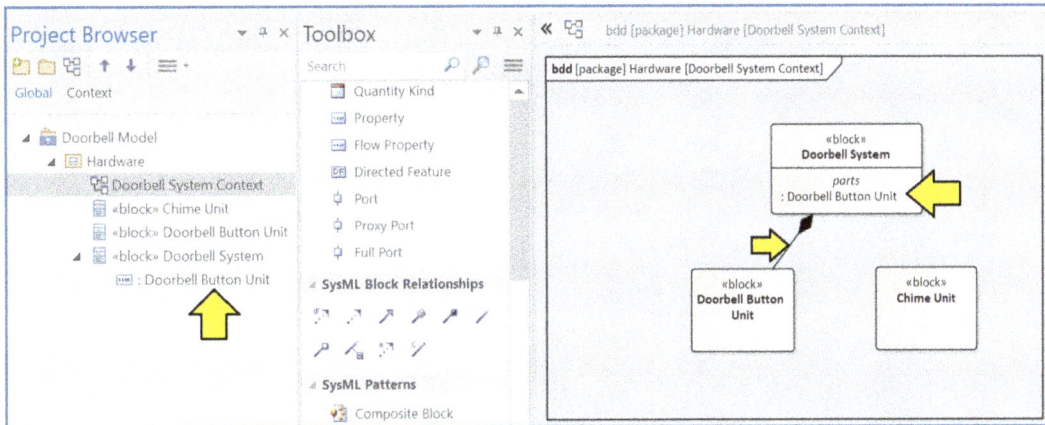

Figure 2-20 – Composition relationship

After you have completed the drag operation to connect the two blocks, three changes will be visible in the tool as shown in Figure 2-20.

1) The block "Doorbell System" now shows a compartment called "*parts*". Inside this compartment is something called: ":Doorbell Button Unit".

2) There is now an arrow whose arrowhead is a black diamond from the "Doorbell Button Unit" block to the "Doorbell System" block.

3) In the project browser, we can see that "Doorbell System" now has something nested underneath it called ":Doorbell Button Unit".

What we have done is modeled the idea that the "Doorbell System" contains a **part** which is a (not yet named) instance of the block of type "Doorbell Button Unit". For the moment, we are not going to worry too much about the differences between "types" and "instances". We will cover that topic in more detail in later chapters.

Before we continue, let's give the part a more sensible name. In the project browser, select the part. Press the F2 function key. Name the part "front". Now we have a part with the qualified name "front:Doorbell Button Unit" which makes a bit more sense. (4)

Draw a second composition arrow from the "Doorbell System" block to the "Chime Unit" block and name the new part "kitchen".

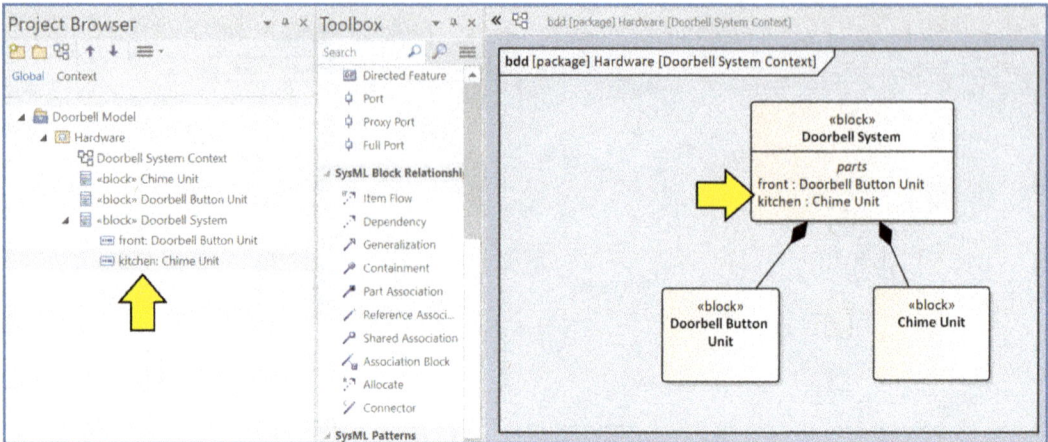

Figure 2-21 – Both part relationships

Your diagram should now look like Figure 2-21.

Next, we will add an **actor** called "Visitor" to the diagram. In the toolbox in the center of the screen you will find an icon for "Actor".

---

[4] Note that part names are actually "roles" from a UML point of view. We will discuss this in more detail in the chapter about internal block definition diagrams.

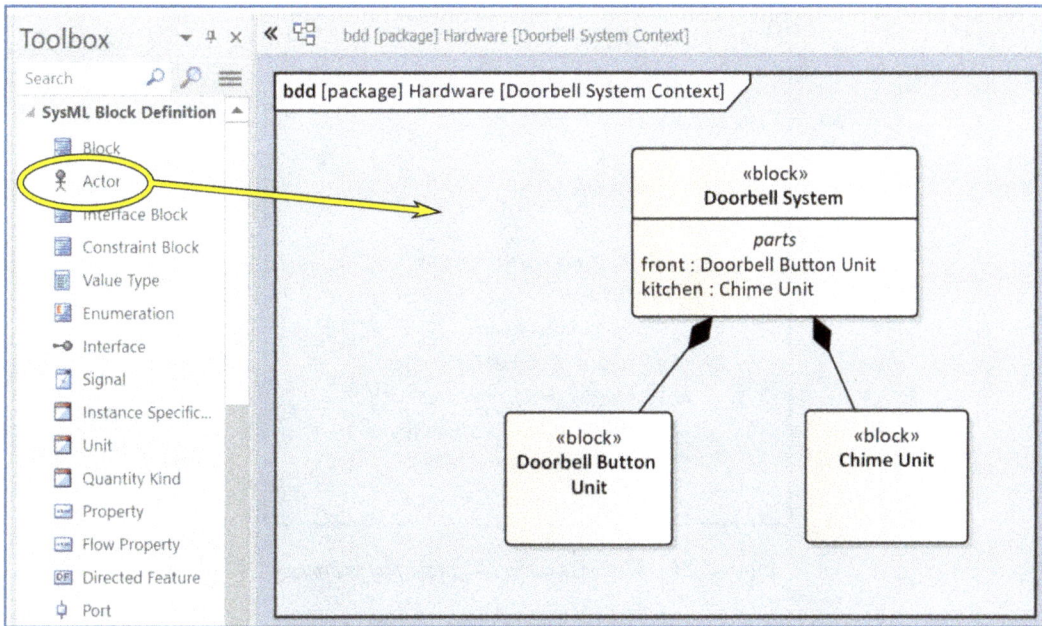

Figure 2-22 – Drag the actor icon to the diagram

Drag the "Actor" icon to the diagram.

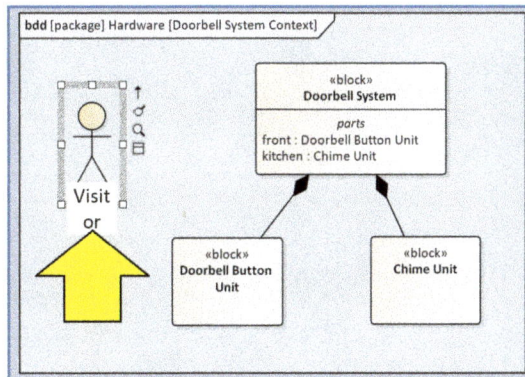

Figure 2-23 – Name the actor

. Name the actor "Visitor".

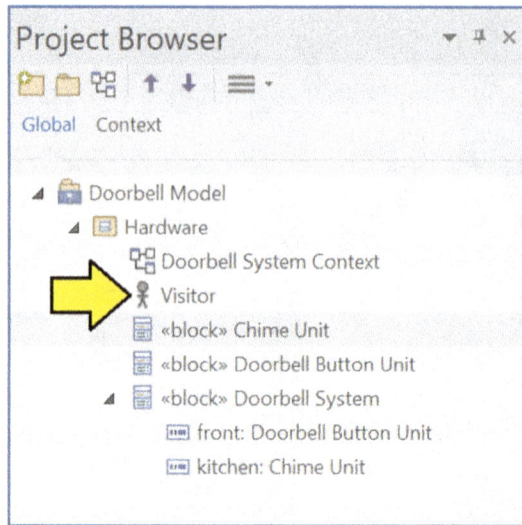

Figure 2-24 – Visitor is now visible in the project browser

We can now see that the visitor is visible in the project browser. However, since our actor is a human [5], we will not want to model the actor as belonging to the package "Hardware". Add a new package to the model called "Actors". (See the procedure previously outlined in *Adding a Package* on page 14.)

---

[5] Actors do not need to be human. In fact, SysML provides an alternate box notation for actors such as cloud server processes that are not humans.

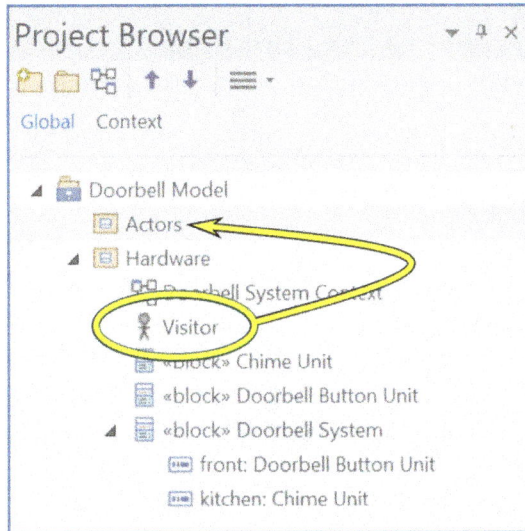

Figure 2-25 – Drag the Visitor to the Actors package

Drag the visitor from the "Hardware" package to the "Actors" package.

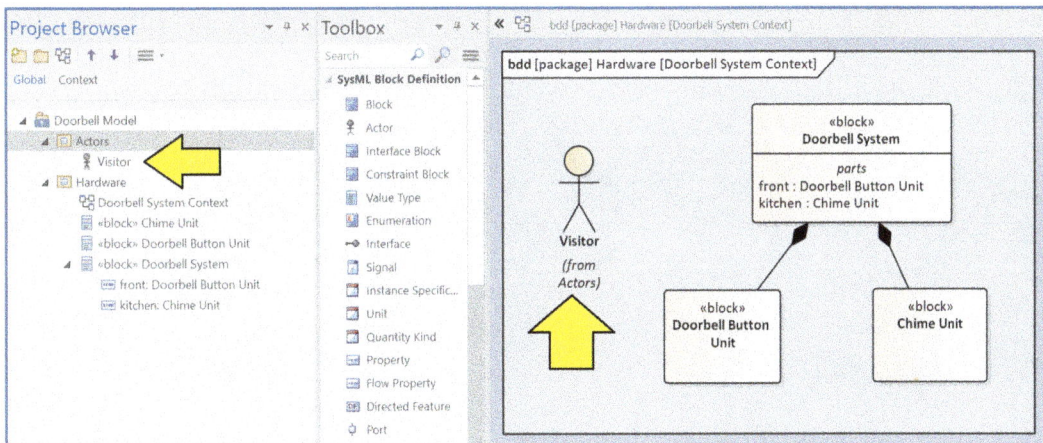

Figure 2-26 – Visitor now in proper package in project browser

Your diagram should now look like Figure 2-26. There are two important points about the diagram in its current form:

- Notice the notation "(from Actors)". This notation indicates that this element belongs to a different package. That is, the diagram belongs to the package "Hardware" and the visitor is a guest from the package "Actors" so to speak.

- Notice also that the visitor is part of the context for the system but is not part of the system itself. That is, the visitor is shown in the context diagram, but there is no composition arrow from the doorbell system block to the visitor. This point is important: deciding which elements are part of the system and which others are merely things in the neighborhood is one of the first steps in a disciplined systems engineering process.

Adding a Requirements Diagram

Now we are ready to add a few requirements to our system. SysML provides a **requirements diagram** for this purpose. The first thing we will want to do is add a package to the model called: "Requirements" (See the procedure previously outlined in *Adding a Package* on page 14.)

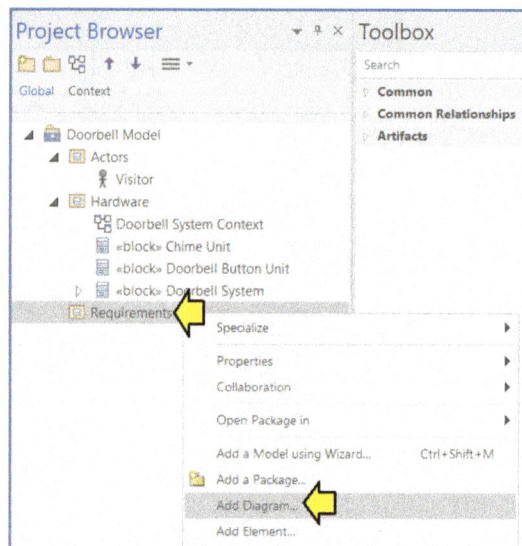

Figure 2-27 – Right-click and select Add Diagram...

Right-click on the "Requirements" package and select "Add Diagram...".

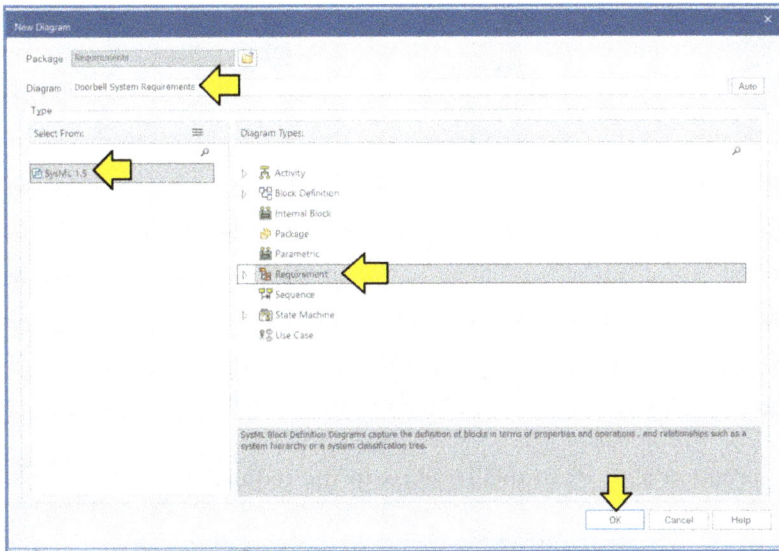

Figure 2-28 – Name the diagram

The "New Diagram" dialog box will appear:

1) Name the new diagram "Doorbell System Requirements".

2) Under "Select From:" make sure that "SysML 1.5" is highlighted.

3) Under "Diagram Types:" select "Requirement".

4) Click "OK".

Now that we have created the requirements diagram, we can add a **requirement** to it. This operation is similar to adding a block to a block definition diagram.

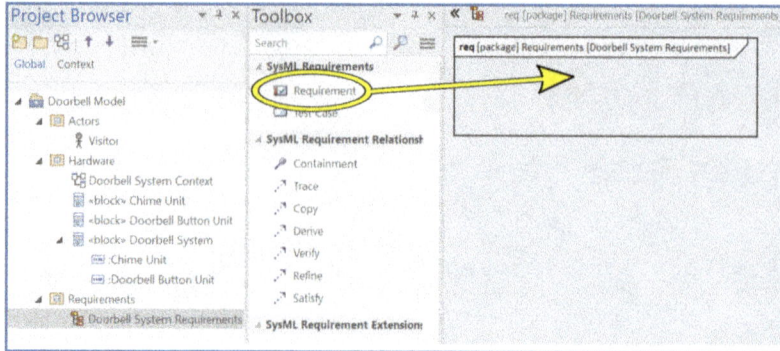

Figure 2-29 – Drag the requirement icon from the Toolbox to the diagram

Drag the requirement icon from the Toolbox to the requirements diagram.

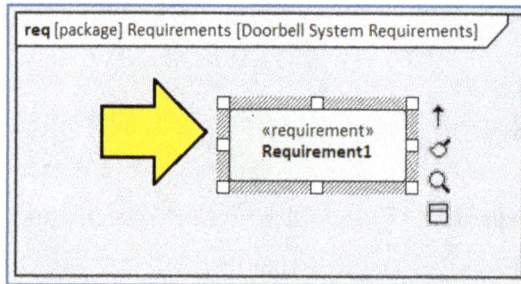

Figure 2-30 – Double-click to open the requirement

We now have a requirement element. Double-click on the element in the diagram to open the properties window for the requirement.

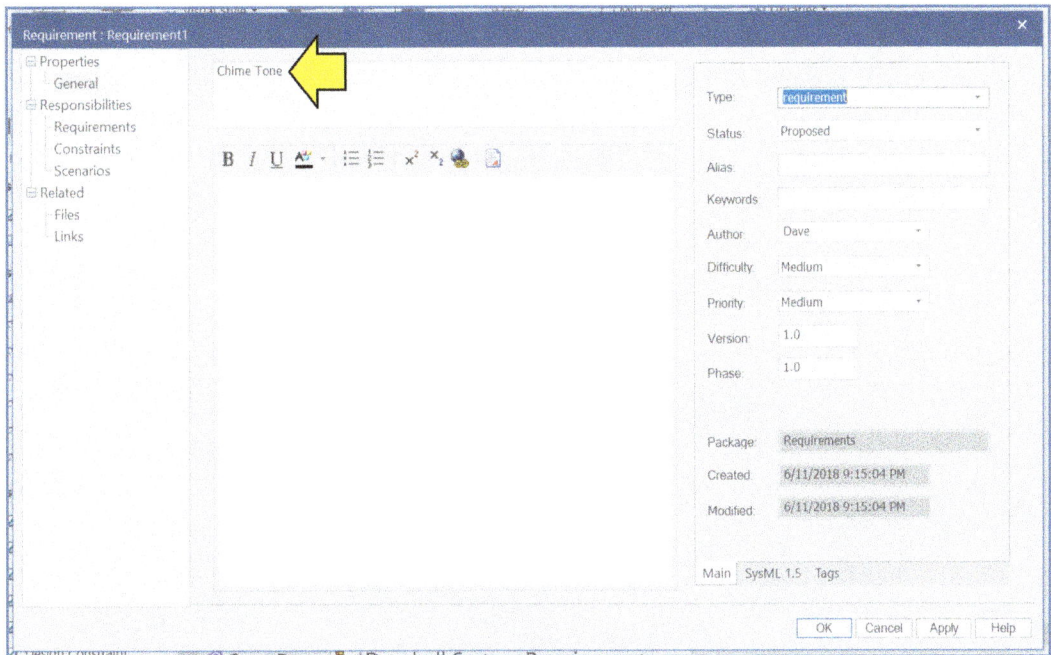

Figure 2-31 – Give the requirement a name

The first order of business is to give the requirement a **name**. Let's call this requirement: "Chime Tone". Enter the name as shown in Figure 2-31.

The next thing we notice is that it is not immediately obvious where the requirement **id** and **text** should go. [6] *Enterprise Architect* is actually older than SysML and was originally designed for UML. Since UML did not explicitly provide for requirements, the makers of *Enterprise Architect* created their own UML extension for requirements and the current SysML requirement feature is built on top of that. As such, the SysML functions appear as sort of an add-on to the original UML extension.

---

[6] An early reader has reported that in version 15 of the tool, the requirements id and text can now be entered directly in the properties panel for the requirement. The steps described here are for version 14 of the tool.

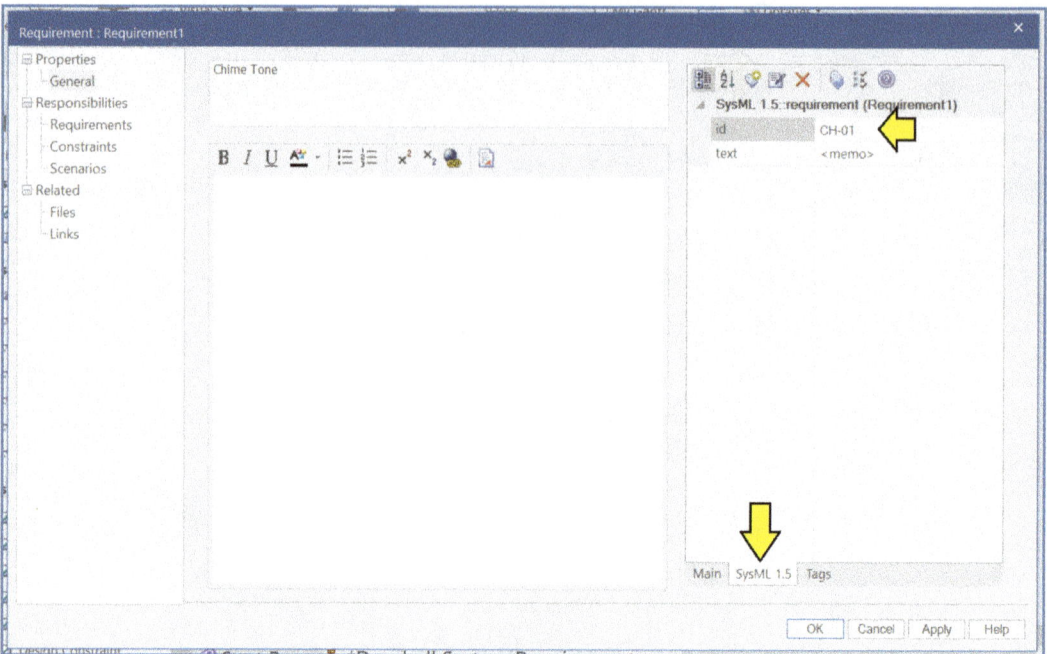

Figure 2-32 – Click the SysML 1.5 tab and assign an ID

In order to set the id and text, first we need to locate and select the "SysML 1.5" tab as shown in Figure 2-32. Once the tab appears, you can enter an id as shown. The id can be any text string. For the moment, let's call this one "CH-01" for "First requirement related to the chime unit".

We have our requirement id assigned, where does the text go?

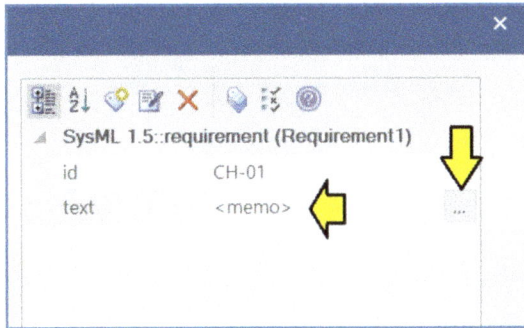

Figure 2-33 – Right-click inside the <memo> field, then click the three dots

1) If you look carefully, just under the requirement id field is another field called "text" that contains the text: "<memo>".

2) Click once to the right of "<memo>".

3) The background of the tag "text" will turn dark and a new small box with three dots in it will appear to the right of "<memo>".

4) Click on the three dots.

5) A dialog box will appear.

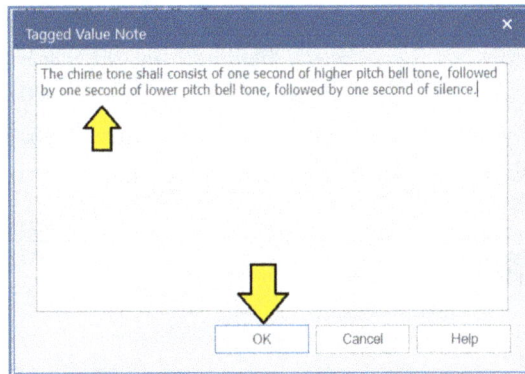

Figure 2-34 – Enter the text of the requirement

Enter the following text:

The chime tone shall consist of one second of higher pitch bell tone, followed by one second of lower pitch bell tone, followed by one second of silence.

When you are done, click "OK".

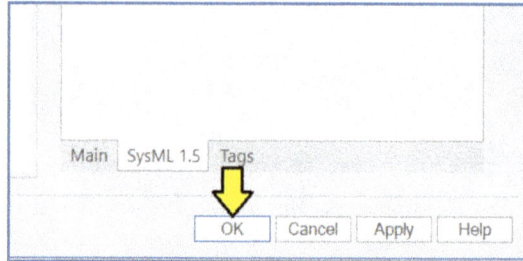

Figure 2-35 – Click OK to finish

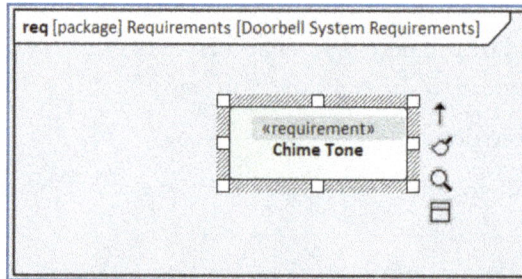

Figure 2-36 – By default the diagram does not show id or text

After you click "OK" your diagram will look like Figure 2-36. Where are the id and text? In *Enterprise Architect* these are not shown by default.

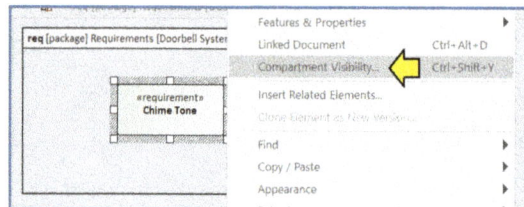

Figure 2-37 – Right-click and select compartment visibility

Right-click on the requirement in the diagram and select "Compartment Visibility...".

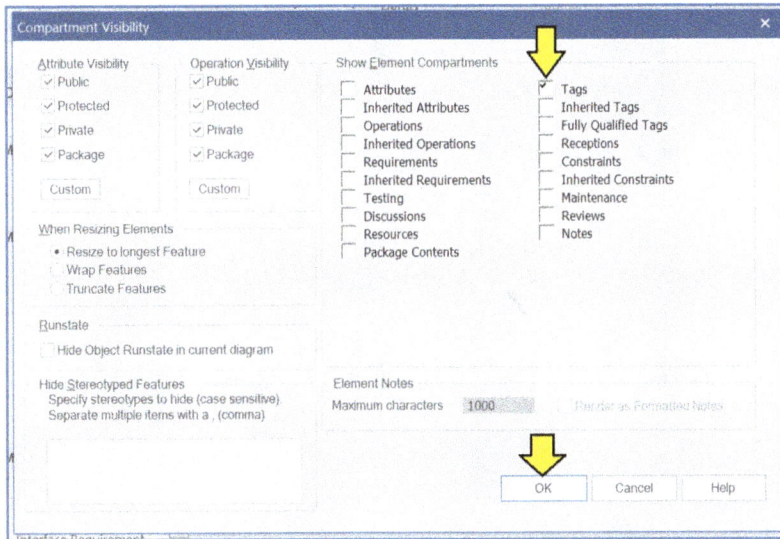

Figure 2-38 – Select Tags and click OK

Enterprise Architect considers the id and text to be "Tags" that have been added to its requirement element. In order to make the id and text show up, select "Tags" and click "OK" as shown in Figure 2-38.

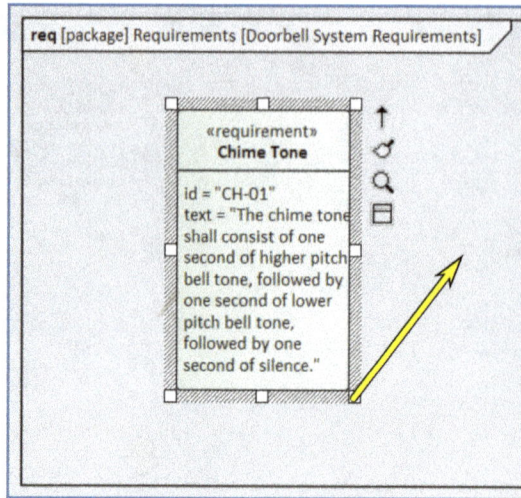

Figure 2-39 – Drag the corner of the requirement box to resize it

After you have set the requirement element in the diagram to display the id and text you will probably notice that the overall shape of the requirement box is probably not ideal. Also, the text may be bumping up against the border of the box. You can simply grab a corner of the box in the diagram with the mouse and drag to resize it. The tool will reflow the text as you resize the box.

Tip - Resizing the Diagram

What if you want to zoom the diagram in or out? You can resize any diagram and zoom in or out by holding down the control key and rolling the wheel on your mouse. Actually, there are three motions (which are common to some other graphical software packages):

- control key + mouse wheel = zoom
- shift key + mouse wheel = move left or right
- (nothing) + mouse wheel = move up or down

Let's add a few more requirements. Have you ever visited someone's house and been frustrated because it wasn't clear whether the doorbell button was really doing anything or not? Our doorbell system is going to solve that problem:

1) As the visitor approaches the door, the doorbell button will be glowing dimly.

2) After the visitor pushes the button, the chime will sound inside, and the doorbell button will begin flashing brightly on and off.

3) When the chime is finished, the doorbell button will return to the glowing dimly state. [7]

In order to save you time and effort in typing, I have provided a spreadsheet of these requirements in the example files in the directory *Examples\Ch02_Quick_Start \S2.5_Req_Diag*

---

[7] The observant reader will notice that we have just created the beginnings of a "user story" for our system. User stories are an important part of almost any design methodology.

ID	Name	Description
CH-01	Chime Tone	The chime tone shall consist of one second of higher pitch bell tone, followed by one second of lower pitch bell tone, followed by one second of silence.
CH-02	Chime Cycle	The chime cycle shall consist of three chime tones.
CH-03	Chime Cycle After Button Press	When the doorbell button is pressed, the chime unit shall complete one chime cycle.
BT-01	Flash During Chime	While the chime cycle is in progress, the doorbell button shall flash.
BT-02	Flash Cycle	The button flash cycle shall be 0.5 second bright illumination followed by 0.5 second of no illumination.
BT-03	Idle Dim Glow	When the doorbell system is idle, the doorbell button shall glow dimly.

Figure 2-40 – Requirements for the doorbell system

Go ahead and repeat the procedure and add the remaining five requirements to the model.

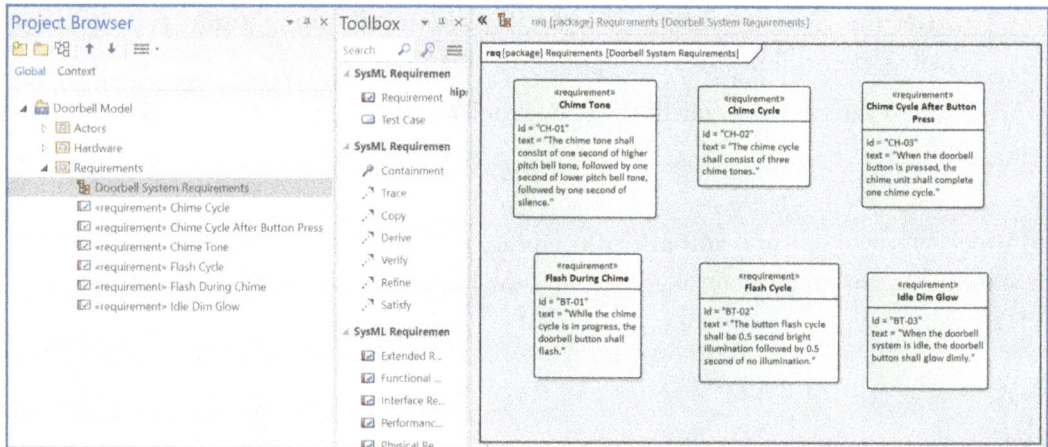

Figure 2-41 – Completed requirements for the doorbell system

When you are done adding the requirements, your requirements diagram should look like Figure 2-41.

So far, we have shown how to get a set of requirements into the system and how to place them on a diagram, but we really haven't yet shown the compelling benefit of integrating requirements into a graphical system model. In order to show this benefit, create a second requirements diagram called "Button Glow Detail".

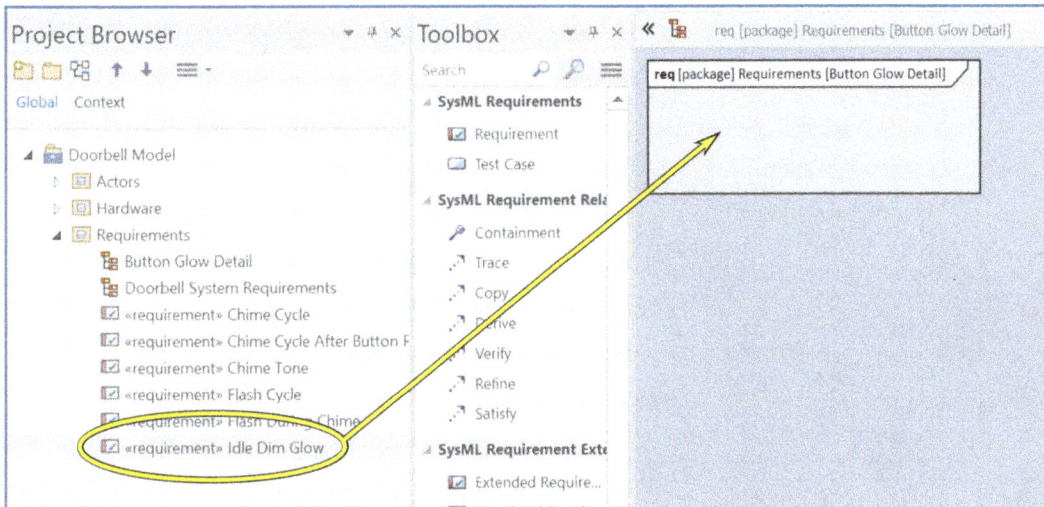

Figure 2-42 – Drag the idle dim glow requirement to the diagram

Drag the "Idle Dim Glow" requirement to the diagram. Select the default of "Drop as Link".

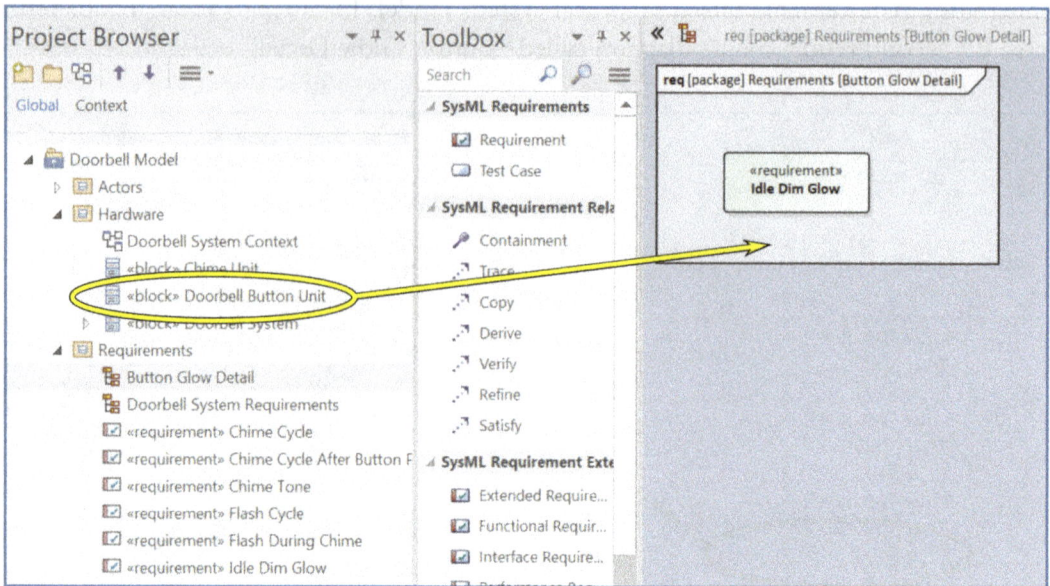

Figure 2-43 – Drag the doorbell button unit block to the diagram

Next drag the "Doorbell Button Unit" block to the diagram. Select the default of "Drop as Link".

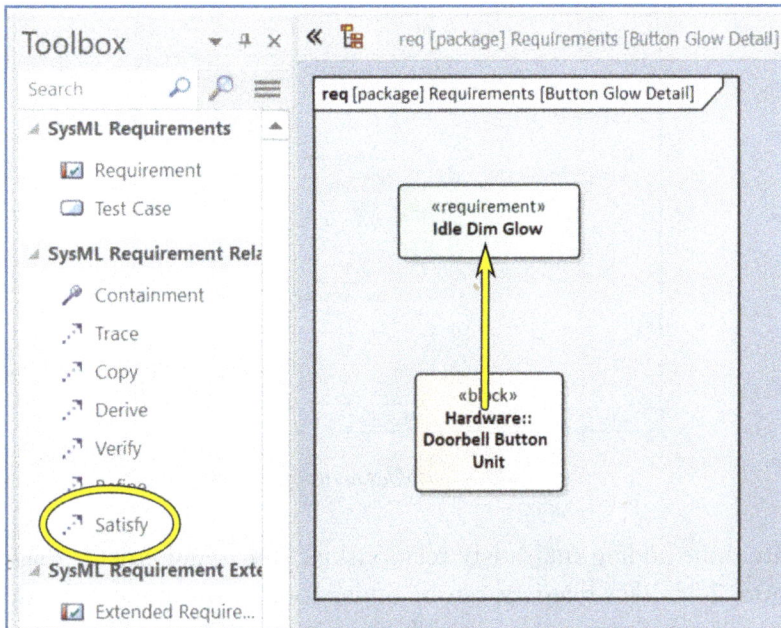

Figure 2-44 – Select satisfy and drag relationship

In the toolbox select the "Satisfy" icon and drag a **satisfy** relationship between the button unit and the requirement.

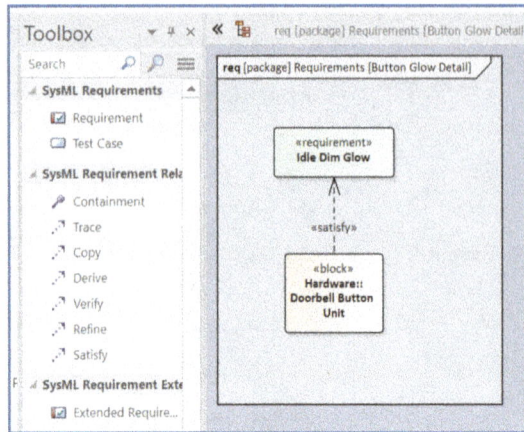

Figure 2-45 – Completed satisfy relationship

When you are done adding the satisfy relationship, your requirements diagram should look like Figure 2-45. This diagram can be understood as meaning: "The doorbell button unit is responsible for satisfying the idle dim glow requirement".

Quickly examining the toolbox, the reader will notice that there is also a SysML element for test case as well as several more descriptive relationships. In the chapter on requirements diagrams, we will go into more detail about how these relationships can be used to make helpful diagrams that help stakeholders understand complex relationships between requirements, system elements, and test cases.

Direction of Arrows

When first shown a diagram like Figure 2-45, many engineers will feel like the arrow is pointed in the wrong direction. Such engineers are used to thinking of requirements as flowing downward from top to bottom. SysML inherits its arrow direction philosophy from UML. One point about UML (and SysML) is that arrows are navigated in the direction that they point. Hence, the requirement relationship arrows are "owned" by the elements that need to satisfy the requirements. This arrangement makes it slightly easier later to answer the question: "Which requirements does this block need to satisfy?"

Adding a Sequence Diagram

In the preceding sections, we have taken a quick look at diagrams for structure and for requirements. The last thing we will do in this chapter is add a diagram that describes system behavior. SysML defines three behavioral diagrams:

- Activity diagram
- Sequence diagram
- State machine diagram

In this section, we will create a simple **sequence diagram** for our doorbell system.

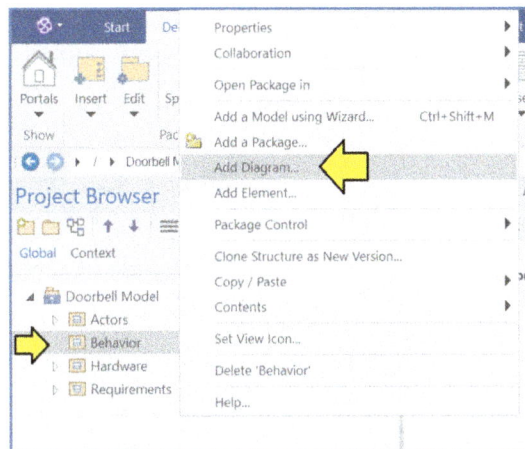

Figure 2-46 – Add a package and a diagram

Add a new package for "Behavior" to the model. Right-click on the new package in the project browser and select "Add Diagram...".

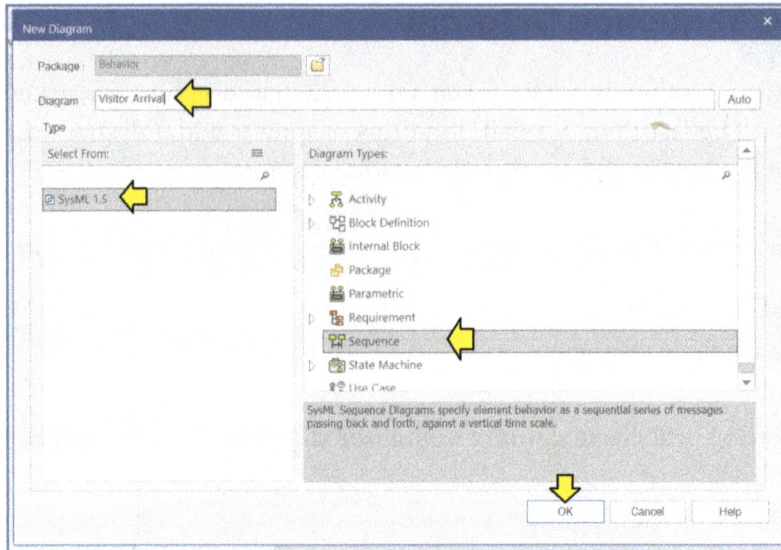

Figure 2-47 – Name and create the diagram

Give the diagram a name. The sequence diagram is actually the internal representation of a model element known as an **interaction**. A such, it makes sense to name a sequence diagram with a noun phrase that represents an interaction or activity. Name this diagram: "Visitor Arrival". Click "OK" when you are done.

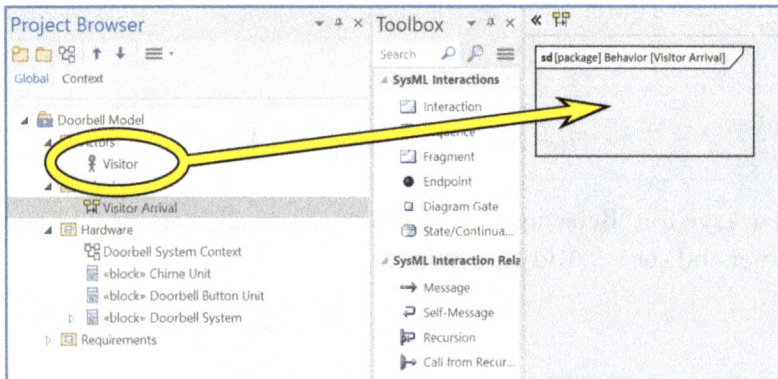

Figure 2-48 – Drag Visitor to the diagram

Drag the visitor from the project browser to the diagram.

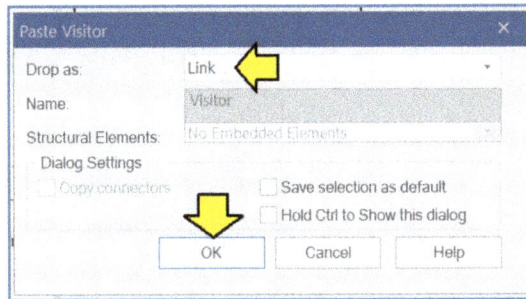

Figure 2-49 – Accept link

A dialog box will appear confirming that you want to create a "Link" to the diagram (as opposed to creating an instance or an object which are not what we want to do right now). Accept the "Drop as:" default value of "Link" and click "OK".

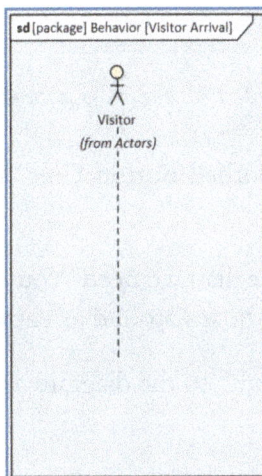

Figure 2-50 – Lifeline

After you click "OK" *Enterprise Architect* will create something called a **lifeline** for the Visitor element.

- At the top is the element itself.

- Underneath this is a notation of the package which owns the element

- Below that is a dashed line. The dashed line indicates the passage of time in the "life" of the element, starting at the top and progressing downward in time.

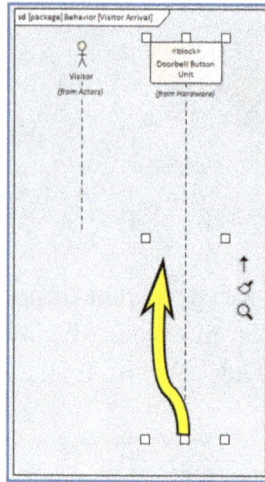

Figure 2-51 – Drag box to shorten lifeline

Next drag the block named "Doorbell Button Unit" from the project browser to the diagram.

Oops! The lifeline is a little longer than we need. You can shorten or lengthen a lifeline by clicking on it and dragging the boxes around as shown in Figure 2-51.

Drag the block named "Chime Unit" to the diagram as well.

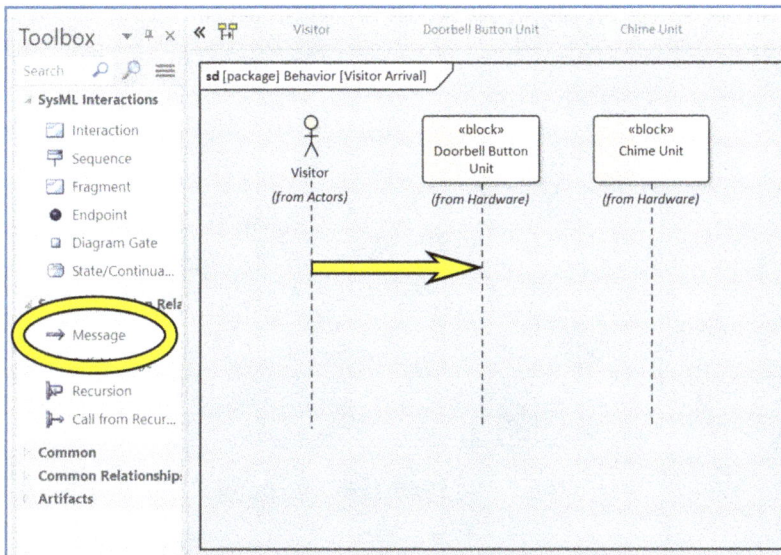

Figure 2-52 – Drag a Message from Visitor to Doorbell Button Unit

We now have three lifelines for three elements. Now we are ready to start creating the actual interaction between these three elements. In a sequence diagram each communication between two lifelines is a **message**. In the toolbox select "Message" and drag from the lifeline for the visitor to the lifeline for the doorbell button unit.

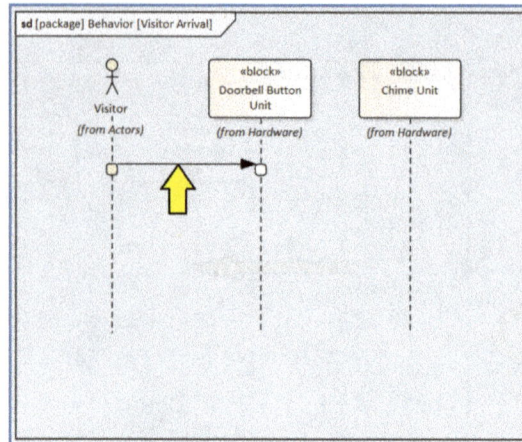

Figure 2-53 – Double-click on the message

We now have our first message on the diagram. However, there are two things we will want to change immediately:

- The message needs a name.

- The solid black line and solid black arrowhead represent the default message type of "synchronous". Unless we expect the visitor to stand with finger attached to the button until the doorbell chime is complete, we probably don't want to model this message as a synchronous message. An asynchronous message will be more appropriate.

Double-click on the message arrow to open the properties window.

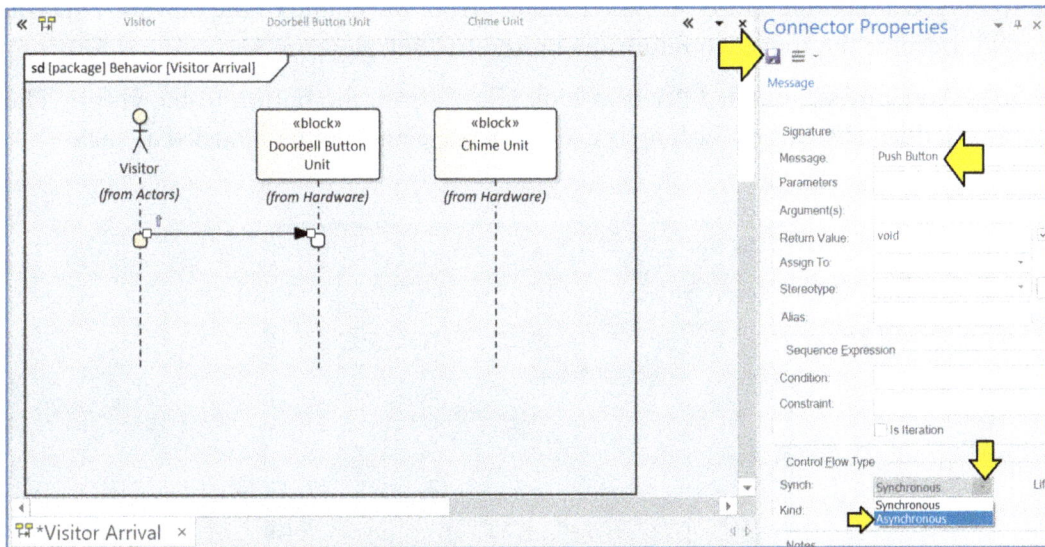

Figure 2-54 – Name message

A window called "Connector Properties" will appear to the right of the sequence diagram. This window is new in *Enterprise Architect* version 14.

1) Name the message: "Push Button"

2) Pull down "Synch:" under "Control Flow Type" and select: "Asynchronous".

3) In order to save your changes, click on the floppy disk icon in the upper left corner of the "Connector Properties" window.

Now let's go ahead and add some additional asynchronous messages to complete the modeling of our story:

1) Add a message called "Button Pushed" from the button to the chime.

2) Add a message called "Chime Starting" from the chime to the button. Later, as we add more detail to the model, this will become the trigger to make the button begin flashing brightly.

3) Add a message called "Button Flashing" from the button to the visitor. The flashing is just a visual indication, but it is a message nonetheless and we can model it as an asynchronous message.

4) Add a message called "Chime Ending" from the chime to the button. This will become the trigger to return the button to "dull glow" mode.

5) Add a message called "Button Dull Glow" from the button to the visitor. The sudden absence of flashing is itself a message and can be modeled as such.

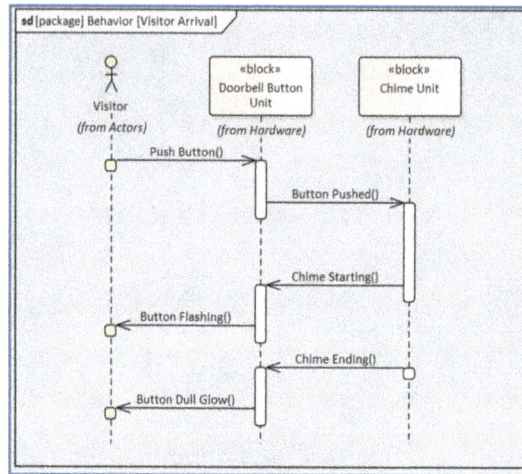

Figure 2-55 – Finished sequence diagram

Your finished sequence diagram should look like Figure 2-55.

This concludes our quick look at SysML and at the *Enterprise Architect* tool. In the next chapter, we will cover some general topics and questions before we start looking at each of the nine SysML diagram types in more detail.

Chapter 3 – Take a Deep Breath

In the previous chapter, you constructed a simple model and familiarized yourself with some of the basic functions of *Enterprise Architect*. In the chapters that follow, we will look more carefully at each type of diagram and extend your familiarity with the tool and with SysML modeling. By the time you have finished the book, you should be well equipped to study and practice the more advanced modeling topics covered in the books listed in *SysML Books* on page 371.

However, before we dive into the details of all nine SysML diagram types, it is worth taking a deep breath and discussing the goals a bit. What is it that we are trying to achieve with model-based systems engineering? How does SysML fit into our goals? If you are in a hurry to get to the details, you can certainly skip this chapter and come back to it later. However, I recommend that you read through it briefly at this point before continuing to the detailed diagram chapters.

The Model-Based Systems Engineering Vision

There really isn't a universal "laws of physics" style, crisp, clear definition of just exactly what "model-based systems engineering" is (and is not). It certainly has something to do with visual diagrams and a central database containing "the model" (whatever that is). Beyond these basics, however, there is plenty of room for disagreement. If you assemble ten distinguished experts in a room, pull out the magnifying glass, and try to define exactly where the border of "model-based" and "not model-based" lies, you are likely to end up with thirteen or more conflicting opinions.

Rather than engaging in that sort of magnifying glass exercise – and ending up deluged by hate e-mails from said experts – I think it will be more helpful to back into the subject by discussing some goals and examples.

Goal 1 – The Shared Vision for the System

The first goal for model-based systems engineering (henceforth "MBSE") is to enable the establishment and maintenance of the *Shared Vision for the System* [8] for a large and complex project. We can illustrate the problem by considering the example of a project to make a "Pay as You Drive Auto Insurance" box. If you drive responsibly, your auto insurance rates are low. If you start driving like a drunken sailor, your rates instantly increase.

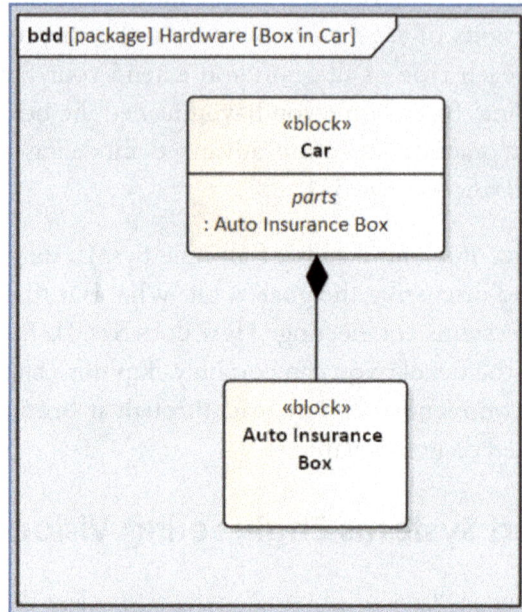

Figure 3-1 – The box mounts in the car

Clearly, we are going to mount the box in the customer's car. Therefore, we can start by modeling a car and an insurance box. We also expect this to be a high-volume product; unit costs have to be as low as possible.

---

[8] In versions 1.0.0 and v1.0.1 of this book, the term used here was: "Single Version of the Truth". That term was widely used in the MBSE community until around 2020. However, the understanding of the community has evolved to recognize that the "truth" is the superset of all information of the system – not something you would want stored on your laptop! The updated term is a more accurate representation of the goal for the content of the system model.

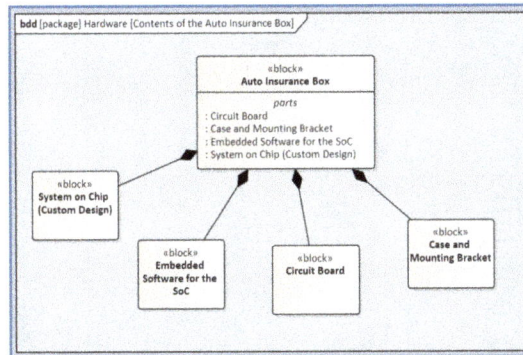

Figure 3-2 – The box contains a number of elements

The auto insurance box will have at least four major elements:

- **System on Chip –** We are going to sell millions of these. We can't pay for a disorganized collection of generic components. We will need a customized "System on Chip" (henceforth "SoC") that sweeps as many of components into one silicon die as possible.

- **Embedded Software –** The SoC will contain one or more processor cores. We will need some embedded software developed to run on the SoC.

- **Circuit Board –** We can't just attach the SoC to the dashboard with duct tape. The SoC will need to be mounted to a circuit board with other components to condition the power, watch for ignition on and off, and so on.

- **Case and Mounting Bracket –** Of course, we can't mount the circuit board in the car with duct tape any more than you can mount the unprotected SoC in the car with duct tape. We will need a properly designed case which protects the components, has the proper thermal characteristics, is built to withstand automotive shock and vibration, and meets other automotive mounting requirements.

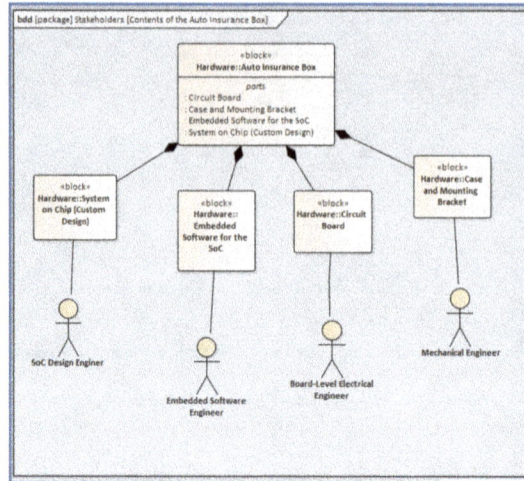

Figure 3-3 – Each element requires specialized design expertise

Each element requires its own specialized design engineer. [9]

---

[9] It is actually worse than this. The SoC alone may require as many as 20 different kinds of specialized design engineer. Also, I have not considered the verification and validation teams or the teams that would handle all of the automotive qualification testing. However, as we will soon see, even this modest underestimate of the number of stakeholders is difficult enough.

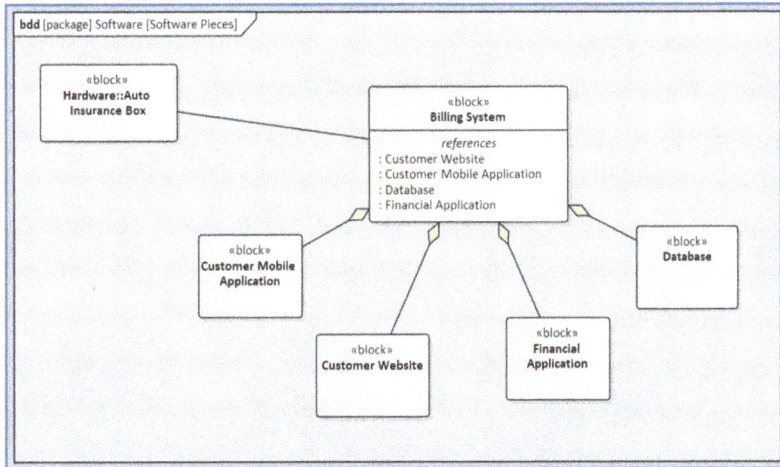

Figure 3-4 – The system will need quite a bit of software

But wait! There is more. The system will need quite a bit of software and this software will require several more development experts:

- **Cloud Application Designer** – Someone will have to design the main cloud-based software pieces.

- **Database Designer** – If the system is going to serve millions of customers, a specialist will be required to design the database.

- **Web Designer** – We need to provide a web portal to help customers sign up and to handle other administrative tasks.

- **Mobile Application Designer** – No one will take us seriously if we don't also provide a mobile application.

This team is just barely sufficient to get the system bolted together. We are also going to need some other specialists for guidance:

- **Data Privacy Expert** – We need to make sure we are compliant with all data privacy laws.

- **Ethics Expert** – What if the system detects that the driver is wildly out of control and barreling directly towards a crowded elementary school? Should the system automatically notify the police?

- **Accountant** – Someone needs to make sure the system manages billing and payments properly.

- **Lawyer** – We might need several of these.

- **Marketing Expert** – What sorts of features should the system offer?

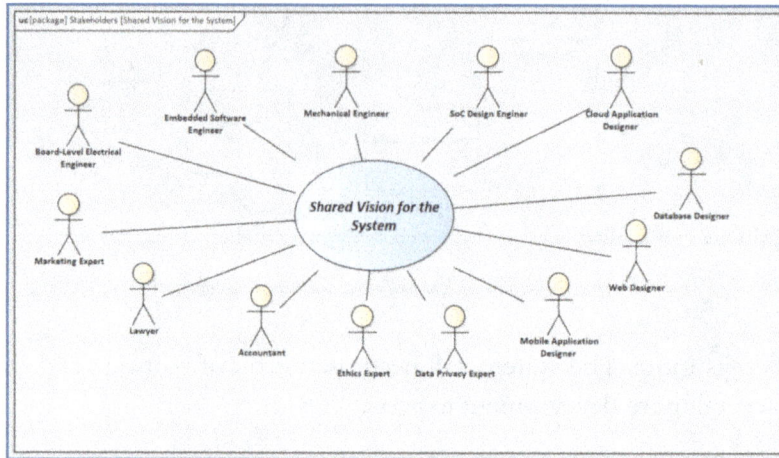

Figure 3-5 – The shared vision for the system

Eventually, all of these stakeholders need to arrive at a common understanding of what the system does and how it works. Obviously, the web designer does not need to know every detail of how the accountant is going to set up the accounting system. However, the accountant needs to know in pretty fine detail what is going to be tracked and what should determine the billing rate. Likewise, concerns from the data privacy expert will have significant impacts on all of the software pieces. Less obvious is the fact that these sorts of data privacy concerns could reach all the way into the SoC and require the chip designer to implement hardware-enforced data isolation between different blocks of memory in the chip.

Creating this common understanding is the key role of MBSE in general and SysML in particular. The goal is to provide a set of diagrams that are semantically precise, but flexible and simple enough to be understood by everyone – from the mechanical engineer to the ethics expert.

SysML does not replace the tools of each specialist

It is important to note that each specialist has specialty tools. The mechanical engineer has multiple computer-aided design tools. Each of the software engineers uses different specialized language and design tools. The accountant definitely has specialized tools as does the lawyer and probably even the ethics expert. SysML does not replace any of these specialized tools. The role of SysML is to create the *Shared Vision for the System* common understanding that enables each specialist to use the specialized tools to deliver his or her part of the overall system.

Goal 2 – Divide and Conquer

So far, I have shown you a goal of getting all of the diverse stakeholders to share a *Shared Vision for the System*, but I have not yet shown a compelling reason why that goal could not be achieved with PowerPoint or Visio. Goal 2 concerns the ability of MBSE to allow you – the systems engineer – to have very focused discussions with each stakeholder, one-at-a-time.

The key here is that true MBSE allows you to make simple diagrams for each stakeholder that focus exclusively on aspects of the problem of concern for that particular stakeholder – while letting the model consolidate all the different perspectives underneath the covers.

Let's take a quick look at a simple industrial coffee maker as an example:

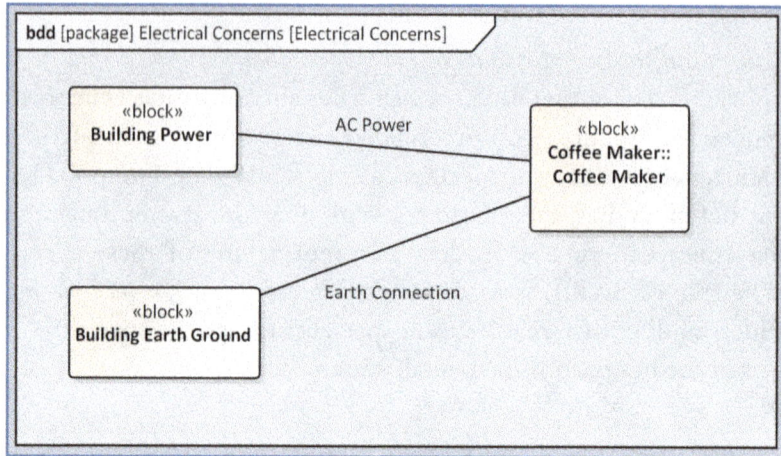

bdd [package] Electrical Concerns [Electrical Concerns]

«block»
Building Power

AC Power

«block»
Coffee Maker::
Coffee Maker

«block»
Building Earth Ground

Earth Connection

Figure 3-6 – Electrical concerns

First up is the building electrician. The coffee maker will need a connection to AC power. The coffee maker will be dealing with fluids and directly in contact with the users. It will definitely need a high-quality connection to earth ground for safety reasons. While we are interviewing the electrician, we make a diagram for the electrical concerns.

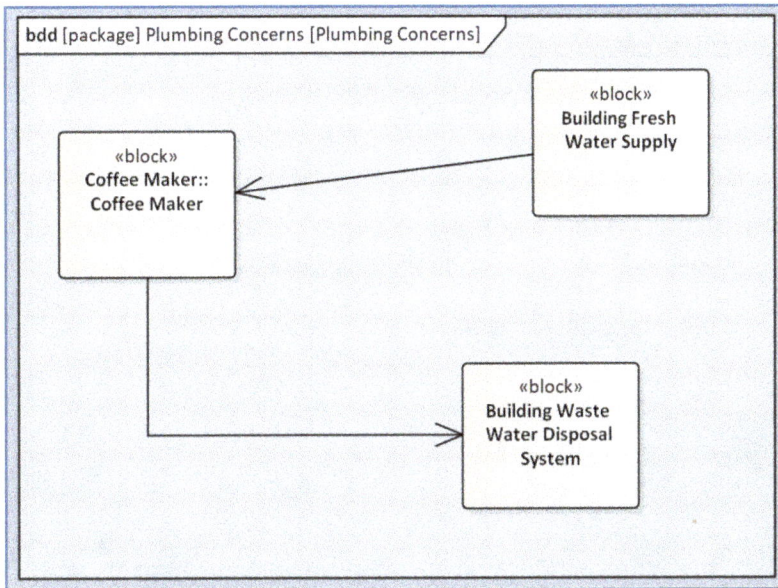

Figure 3-7 – Plumbing concerns

The coffee maker should be automatic. Obviously, it will need a source of fresh water. It will also have a spill tray. The spill tray needs to be connected to the drain. We make another diagram for the plumbing concerns.

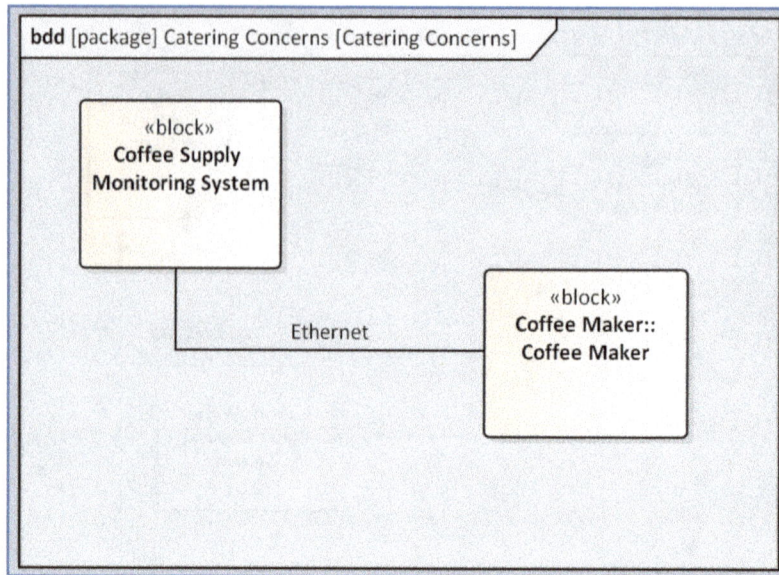

Figure 3-8 – Catering concerns

As we interview the catering department, we find that they expect to have a large number of these machines in operation. They need a central monitoring system to check when specific machines are running out of coffee. At this point, we don't really know the details of how this monitoring will work, but we specify an Ethernet connection for this purpose.

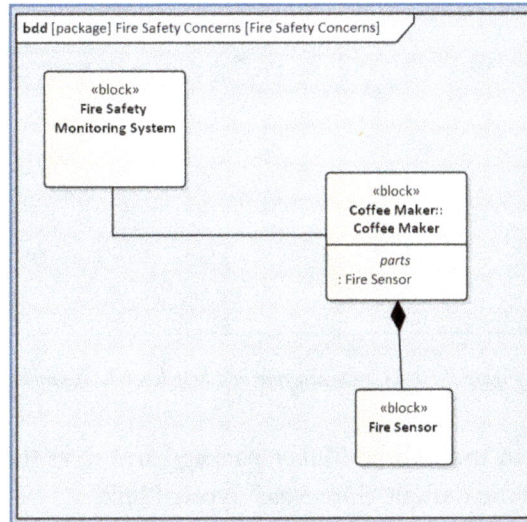

Figure 3-9 – Fire safety concerns

Finally, the fire safety department wants the coffee maker to have a fire sensor and a connection to the central fire safety monitoring system. Initially, we have offered to let them share the Ethernet connection with the catering department, but they are not so enthusiastic about that idea. For the moment, we have modeled an unspecified connection to the fire safety monitoring system.

So far, we have created a diagram for each stakeholder – in line with our MBSE strategy. We can confirm that the model has consolidated all of the stakeholder input by creating a block definition diagram to explore the Coffee Maker block.

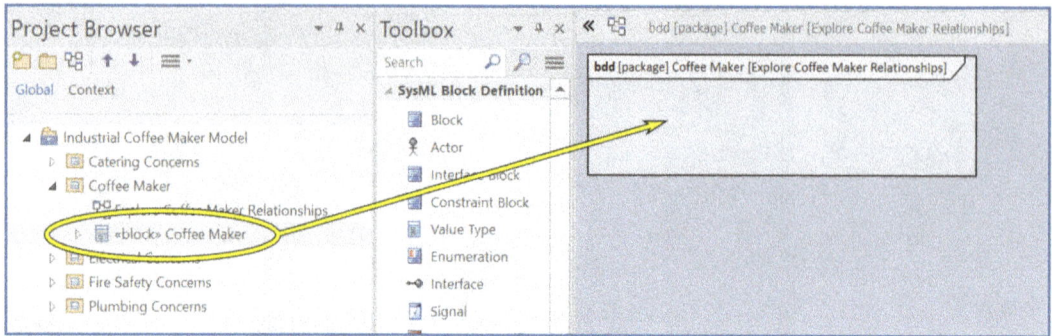

Figure 3-10 – Create diagram and drag block to diagram

Create a new diagram in the Coffee Maker package and drag the Coffee Maker block to the diagram. Accept the default "Drop as:" type of link.

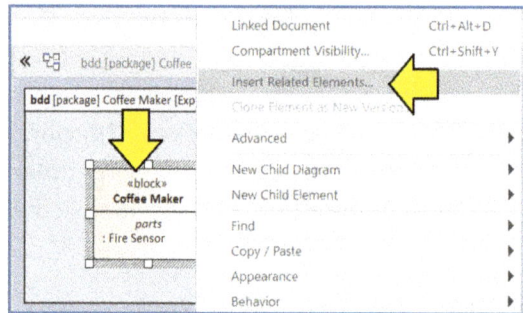

Figure 3-11 – Right-click on block and insert related elements

Right-click on the block and select the menu entry "Insert Related Elements…".

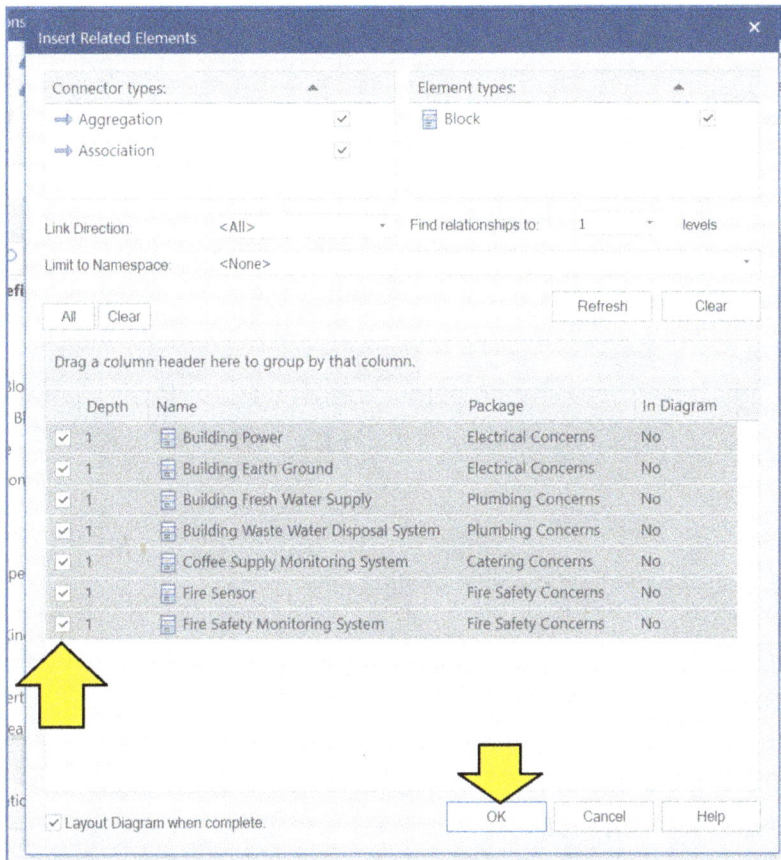

Figure 3-12 – Select all related elements and click OK

A dialog box called "Insert Related Elements" will appear. In this dialog box we can see that the model has captured and consolidated all the information from the different stakeholder diagrams. Click to select all the related elements in the lower pane and click "OK".

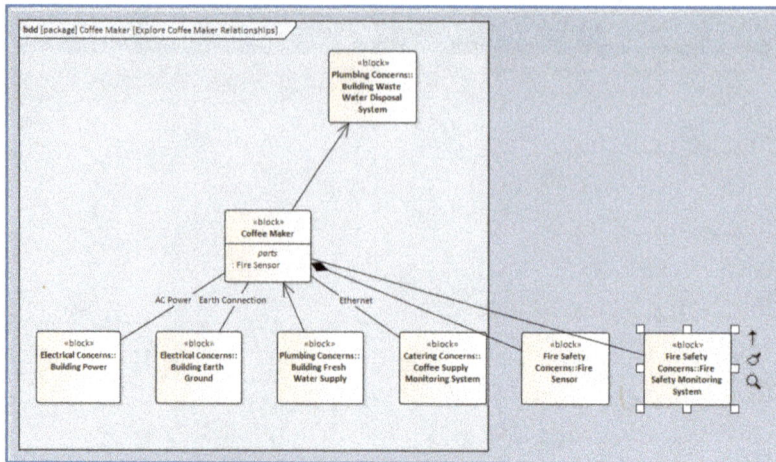

Figure 3-13 – Diagram shows all related elements

The diagram now shows all of the related elements.

The Tool/Model Gets Progressively More Helpful

The ability of the tool to automatically insert related elements gets more and more helpful as your skill improves and you elaborate your model. You will quickly learn how to make new views by dragging certain elements to a new diagram and letting the tool automatically add selected relevant relationships and elements.

Goal 3 – Common Understanding of Diagrams

Goal 3 sounds similar to Goal 1, but Goal 3 is important enough to be worth noting individually. While it is important that all stakeholders buy into the *Shared Vision for the System* it is even more important that the stakeholders **understand** that vision and that all understand it the same way. [10]

---

[10] This goal – making diagrams that everyone can understand – sounds rather obvious. However, it is easy to get carried away and produce diagrams that your stakeholders don't actually understand.

Goal 4 – Simplification

MBSE originated in the aerospace industry. Legend has it that one day, the airplane makers woke up and realized that their specification documents weighed more than their airplanes. Goal 4 of MBSE and SysML is to reduce the dependence on complicated text artifacts in large system development projects.

The ancient saying goes:

> *A picture is worth a thousand words.*

SysML will not completely eliminate the need for text descriptions of things. However, a good SysML model can reduce the need for long blocks of written prose. Not only will the amount of text needed drop, but well-designed SysML diagrams should be easier to understand than the blocks of dense prose they replace.

Goal 5 – Knowledge Management

Used properly and consistently, creation of SysML models can be a great way to extract and codify the tangled "tribal knowledge" embedded in large systems development organizations.

I once talked with a technical fellow at one of the largest defense contractors in the United States. He explained that his company was systematically going through its base of legacy software and modeling the behaviors simply as an intellectual property best practice. That is, code on its own was very difficult to scan and consider for reuse. Good graphical models made it much easier to understand the function and capabilities of the legacy software blocks at a high-level. This improved understandability in turn helped the company manage this legacy software as a library of reusable intellectual property assets.

Goal 6 – Avoiding High-Level Mistakes

Goal 6 is that MBSE should help a team avoid high-level mistakes. Recent studies of companies that have deployed MBSE confirm that the largest perceived benefits are early in the project.

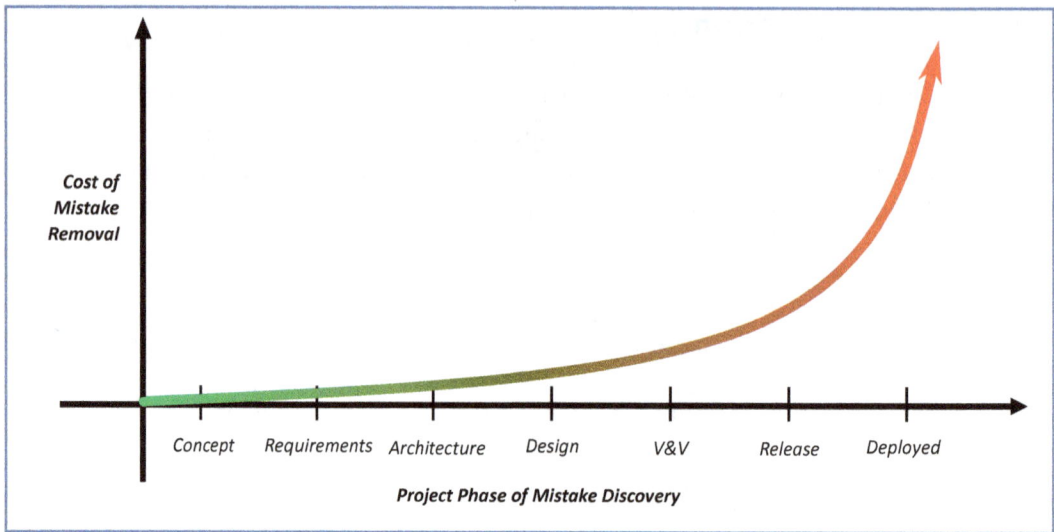

Figure 3-14 – Mistakes are cheaper to remove early in the project

In the software development world, the benefits of removing bugs early in the project are well understood. A bug detected at the requirements or architecture stage is several orders of magnitude less costly to remove than a bug detected after a product has been deployed to thousands of customers. MBSE and SysML are very helpful for moving the detection of fundamental mistakes, misunderstandings, goal conflicts, and other problems towards the left side of the curve shown in Figure 3-14.

Why SysML?

In the previous section, we laid out a series of six goals for model-based systems engineering. In this section, we will go back and review how well SysML meets those goals. We will also look at a few other aspects of SysML along the way.

Does SysML Meet the Goals?

The first question is whether SysML meets the goals. The first three goals are easy to assess.

- **Goal 1 – Shared Vision for the System**
- **Goal 2 – Divide and Conquer**

- **Goal 3 – Common Understanding of Diagrams**

I use SysML on a daily basis in the context of a large organization and I love using SysML to meet these three goals. I run circles around colleagues who are still struggling to express themselves in PowerPoint and Visio.

The next three goals require individual answers:

- **Goal 4 – Simplification**
  I recently completed a safety manual for an automotive semiconductor product written entirely around an integrated SysML model. The total number of pages in the manual was similar to previously written manuals for similar products. However, I increased the number of diagrams by more than a factor of five – with a corresponding dramatic reduction in the number and size of long blocks of dense text. If you focus on this goal, you definitely can use SysML to take some of the dense text bloat out of your product documents.

- **Goal 5 – Knowledge Management**
  Knowledge management can take many forms. I am currently working on projects involving reuse and variants in models and requirements. These are a form of knowledge management and SysML models are part of the team strategy.

- **Goal 6 – Avoiding High-Level Mistakes**
  This goal is more difficult to assess. I certainly believe that SysML can be very helpful in helping teams avoid high-level mistakes. However, proving the absence of mistakes is challenging. As of this writing, SysML is only 13 years old. So far, we do not yet have enough data as an industry to make solid statistical comparisons. Nevertheless, I am personally convinced. I have seen the SysML modeling effort flush misunderstandings between teams to the surface. SysML can definitely help complex teams avoid high-level mistakes.

Flexibility

One of the impressive achievements of the original authors of SysML is SysML's incredible flexibility. The concise set of nine diagram types can be used to model a wide variety of different systems. SysML can be used to model airplanes, ships, automobiles, medical devices, railway networks, semiconductor architecture, and just about any other system that you can imagine.

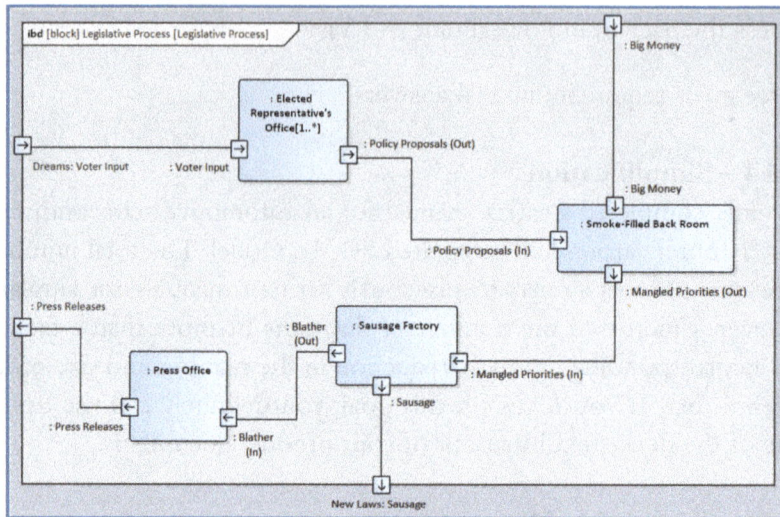

Figure 3-15 – SysML model of a legislative process

SysML can even be used to model political systems!

Tool Supplier Diversity

One of the benefits of SysML is that there are a reasonable number of tools to choose from. There are three major tools (of which *Enterprise Architect* is one) and another 5-10 secondary tools – depending on what you count. Some of the secondary tools offer only partial implementations of SysML.

SysML is also used as a conceptual foundation for other types of specialized tools such as tools for safety engineering.

One of the weak points of SysML is interoperability between tools. SysML can be encoded in UML XMI files and most tools do provide for import and export of XMI files. However, XMI interchange has a number of limitations:

1) XMI itself contains ambiguities and different tool suppliers encode certain specialized structures in different ways.

2) Only the model (The project explorer in *Enterprise Architect*) is encoded. Diagrams are not included. [11]

3) All of the major SysML tools – *Enterprise Architect* included – provide small, convenient, differentiating features which are not part of the XMI standard. Not surprisingly, these small convenient extras do not survive porting between tools. If you have relied heavily on such a feature in your model, the ported result can be unusable.

If future portability of models is a concern, you will want to study the standard carefully and make sure that you use only perfectly standard modeling features. Also, you will want to invest more time in polishing the structure of your package tree to make it easy to navigate as the package tree is what is actually going to get ported.

---

[11] The three major tools also provide some options to directly import each other's models, including diagrams. However, having tested all three, in my experience only the very simplest SysML diagrams port successfully from tool-to-tool.

Chapter 4 – Block Definition Diagrams

In this chapter we will take a closer look at the SysML block definition diagram and at blocks themselves. Blocks and the block definition diagram are really the heart of SysML and form the foundation for the rest of your model.

Types versus Instances

The first thing we need to understand about blocks is that a SysML block does not represent a concrete "thing" but rather a "type of thing". The concrete thing is an "instance" of a block. [12]

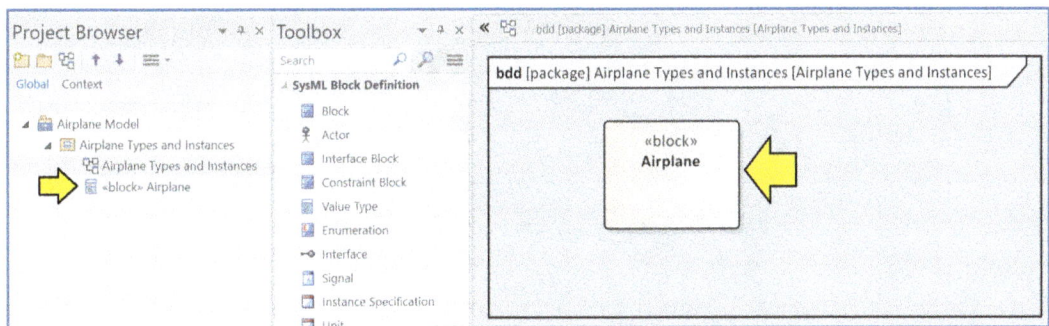

Figure 4-1 – Model with an airplane Block

Go ahead and create a simple model:

1) Name the model "Airplane Model".

2) Create a single package called "Airplane Types and Instances".

3) In the package, create a diagram also called "Airplane Types and Instances".

4) Add a single block called "Airplane" to the diagram.

---

[12] This discussion is going to seem very familiar to anyone who has ever done any object-oriented programming in a language like Java or C++. That similarity is not a coincidence. SysML 1.5 is a profile on top of UML and the "block" is a stereotype of the UML "classifier" which is used to model classes in object-oriented languages.

(If you need to review, the procedure is described starting in *Creating a Model* on page 12.)

At this point, we have defined a type of thing called "Airplane". How do we create a concrete instance of a "Airplane"?

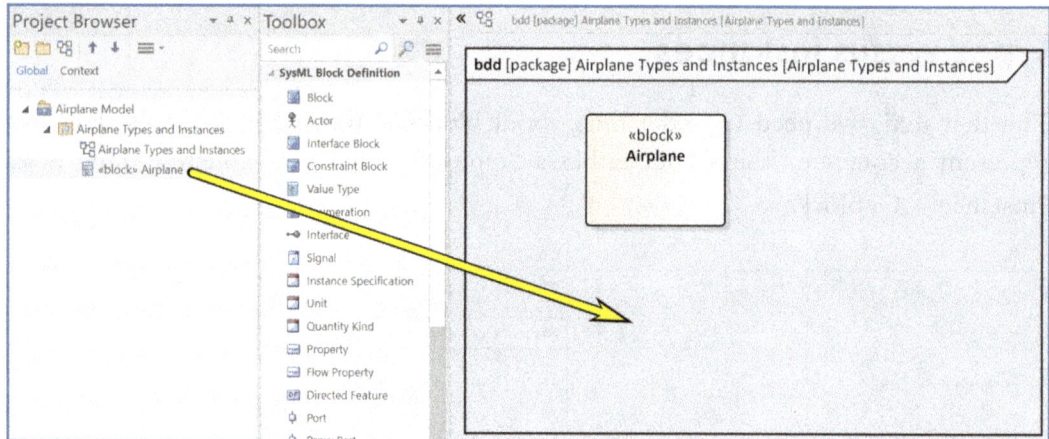

Figure 4-2 – Drag the airplane block to the diagram (again)

Drag the block "Airplane" from the project browser to the diagram (again). This step may seem a little counterintuitive but go ahead and give it a try.

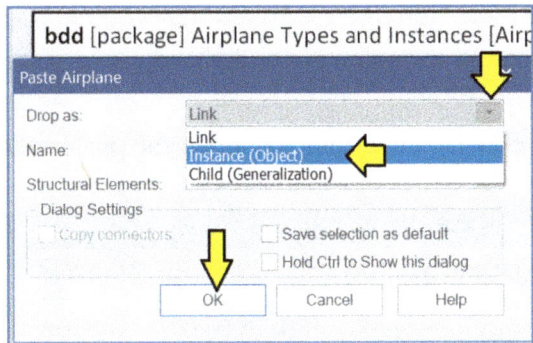

Figure 4-3 – Select instance rather than link

When you release the mouse button to drop the airplane onto the diagram, a paste dialog box will appear. Pull down the "Drop as:" control and select "Instance (Object)". Click "OK".

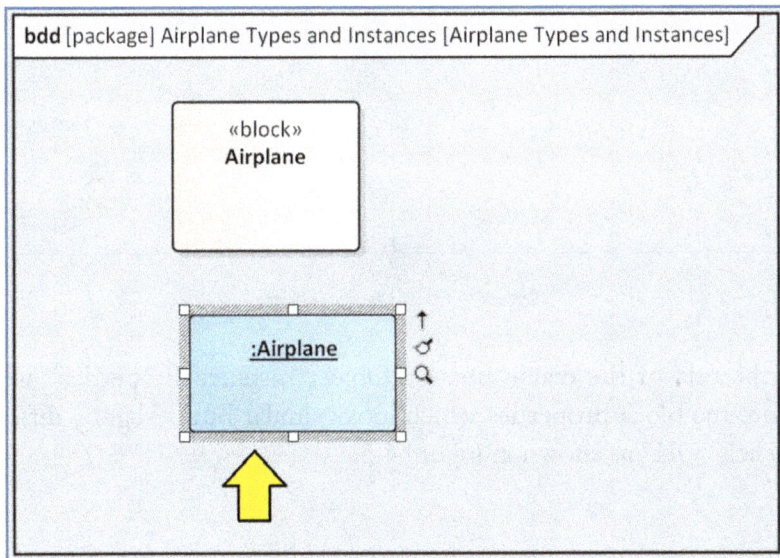

Figure 4-4 – Instance created, double-click to name it

Now we have an instance on the diagram as well as the block definition. They look similar, but there are a number of small differences:

1)   The stereotype «block» is not shown.

2)   "Airplane" has a colon in front of it.

3)   Both "Airplane" and the colon are underlined.

Go ahead and double-click on the instance to open the properties dialog.

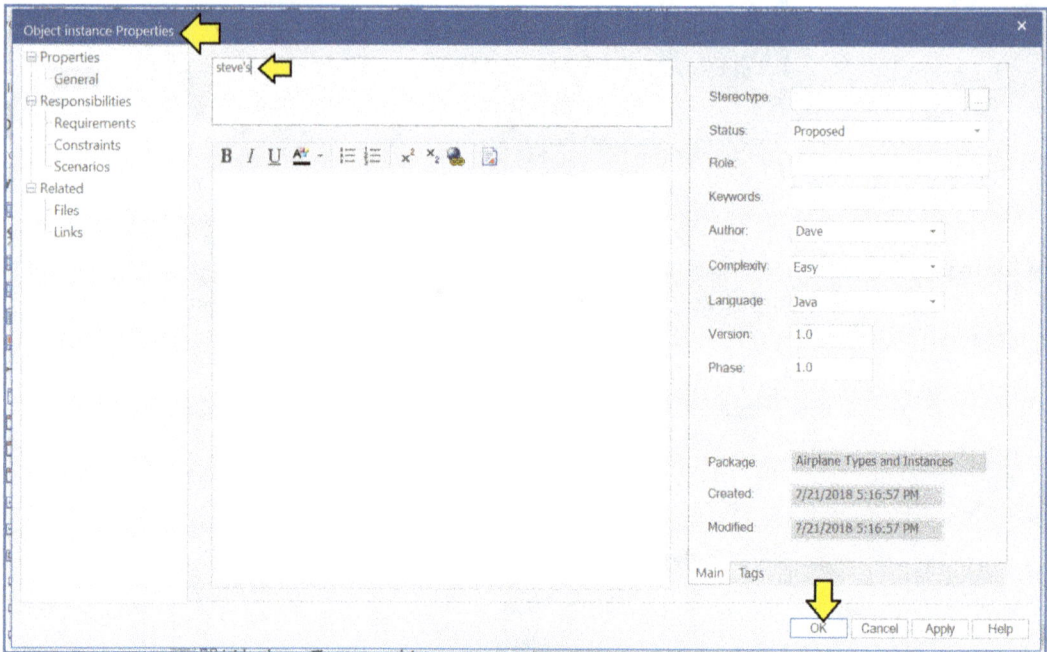

Figure 4-5 – Name the instance

Notice that the title of the dialog box is "Object Instance Properties" which distinguishes it from the block properties which looks similar but is slightly different. Enter a name and click "OK" as shown in Figure 4-5

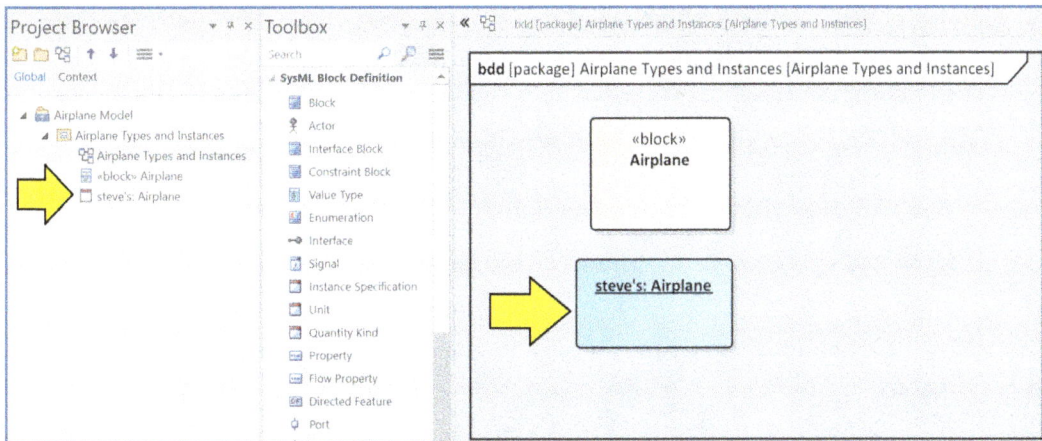

Figure 4-6 – Finished instance in project browser and diagram

In Figure 4-6 we can see and compare the original "Airplane" block and the "steve's:Airplane" instance.

- Both are shown in the project browser, but they have different icons.
- The general notation for instances is "[name]:[type]".

Most of our modeling will be done with blocks, not instances. However, it is useful to understand the difference. Instances also have some potential applications in trade studies. That is, it is possible to model blocks that cover all the options or have configurable parameters and then create multiple instances that have specific values and choices for comparison.

Naming Conventions for Blocks and Instances

The names for blocks and instances can be almost anything, but by convention instance and part names usually start with a lowercase letter and block names are usually capitalized. Also, many modelers avoid spaces in instance and part names. The apostrophe in "steve's" in Figure 4-6 is actually marginal, but it is legal and in this case helps illustrate the point that the name is an identifier of a specific instance.

Modeling the Bill of Materials

One of the common tasks in an engineering organization is to create a "Bill of Materials" for a system.

- What kinds of things are in the system?
- How many of each kind of thing do we have in the system?

Creating a bill of materials is a nice exercise to get a sense of the role of the block definition diagram.

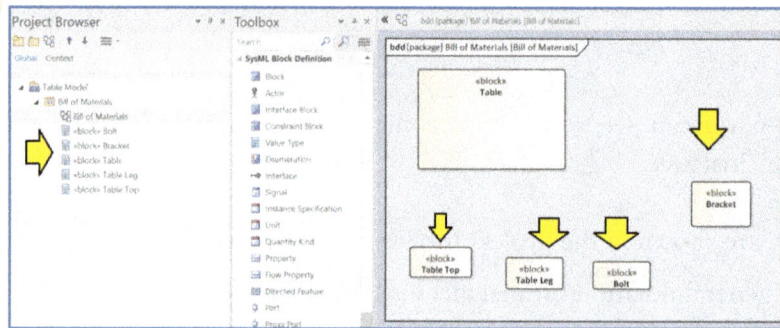

Figure 4-7 – Types of parts in the system

By now, I assume that you know how to create a basic model. Create a basic model like the one shown in Figure 4-7. Add five blocks to the model as shown:

- Table
- Table Top
- Table Leg
- Bolt
- Bracket

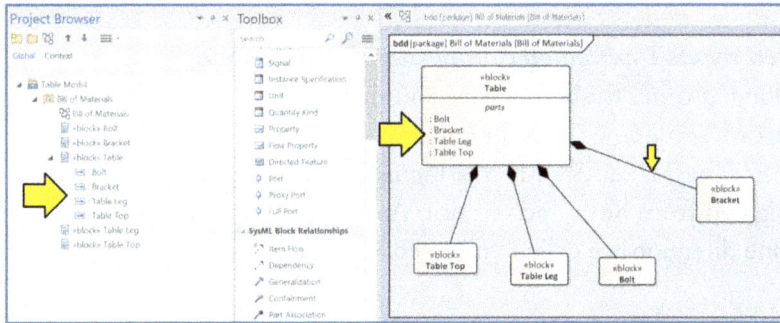

Figure 4-8 – Add composition relationships

Add four composition relationships as shown in Figure 4-8. [13] After you have completed the dragging of the black diamond composition arrows, you will notice:

- Four entries, one for each "part" have appeared in the *parts* compartment of the Table block.

- Four entries have appeared nested under the Table block in the project browser. (You might need to click on the Table block in the project browser to cause these to appear.)

---

[13] See Figure 2-19 on page 22 for the basics of dragging the composition arrow.

Directed versus Undirected Composition/Aggregation

In looking at other SysML books, you may have noticed that the composition arrows sometimes have open arrowheads at the child component end of the line. SysML and UML distinguish in associations whether they can be navigated from both ends or not. Associations that can only be navigated in one direction are called "directed" associations.

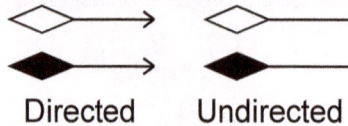

Directed   Undirected

The difference between the two kinds of associations does not usually matter much. However, if you are trying to generate software source code from your SysML model, it might be worth considering.

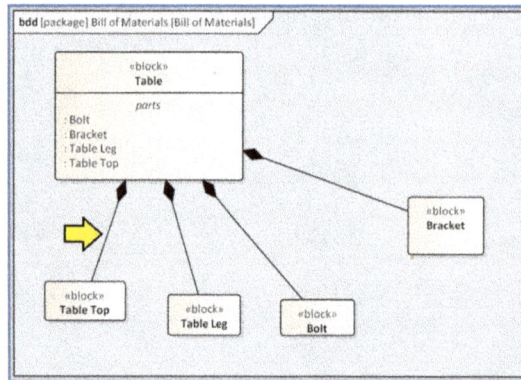

Figure 4-9 – Double-click on the first black diamond composition arrow

Double-click on the first black diamond composition arrow (the one connecting "Table" and "Table Top").

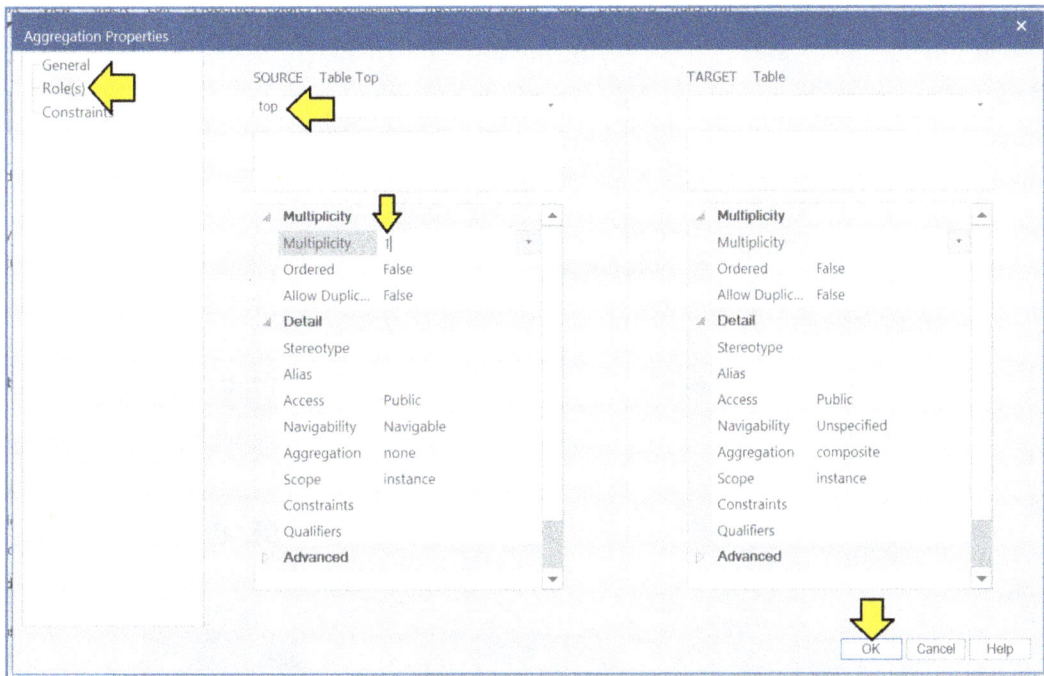

Figure 4-10 – Click on Role(s) tab and set role name and multiplicity

The next steps are a little tricky. After clicking on the black diamond composition arrow, the "Aggregation Properties" dialog box will appear, but it will not look like Figure 4-10 until you click on "Role(s)" in the upper left corner of the dialog box.

Once the roles window appears, we see that there are two columns, one for the "Table Top" end and another for the "Table" end. There is a lot of information that can be configured for each end. For the moment, we are going to focus on the "Table Top" end (that is, the "part")

Set the name for the part as shown. We will name it "top" for the moment. We could also name it "Fred". However, it is important to understand that what we enter here is not really the name of the part but rather the name of the role that the part will play in the context of the Table block. [14]

---

[14] If this description of names versus roles is making your head spin, you are in good company. This unusual naming philosophy is related to object-oriented programming and SysML's origins in UML.

The next thing we are going to set is the **multiplicity** which answers the question "How many of these do we have in the system?" The general format of a multiplicity in SysML is something like: "0..7" which means "between zero and seven". However, multiplicity can also simply be a number. In this case, we will set the multiplicity to "1" which means: "The Table system contains one and only one Table Top". Click "OK" to finish.

Next, set the role names and multiplicities of the remaining black diamond composition arrow relationships as follows:

- **Table Leg** – set the role to "legs" and the multiplicity to four.

- **Bolt** – set the role to "fastening" and the multiplicity to eight. Each bracket will require two bolts.

- **Bracket** – set the role to "mounting" and the multiplicity to four.

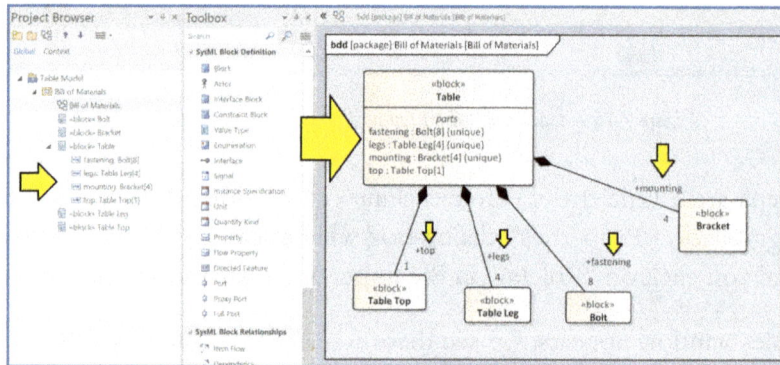

Figure 4-11 – Finished bill of materials diagram

The finished bill of materials diagram will look like Figure 4-11:

1) In the project browser, the role names and multiplicities are now shown for each part. Notice that the fully named parts have the same "[name]:[type]" structure as instances, but they are not underlined.

2) The entries in the *parts* compartment of the Table block have the same format. (15)

3)   Near the part blocks, the role name and the multiplicity are now visible. Note that the initial alignment of these might not be that attractive. You can simply click on them and drag them slightly to adjust their position.

Modeling Similar Types of Things

One of the most powerful features of SysML is its ability to model types of things. That is, if you have seven things, all of which have ten common parts, you can model a type for the commonality and then "inherit" the common features from the type.

Let's start by making a basic model of types of airplanes:

1)   Create a model called "Airplane Types Model".

2)   Within the model create a package called "Airplane Types".

3)   In the folder, create three blocks:

   •   "Airplane"

   •   "Cargo Plane"

   •   "Passenger Plane"

Clearly, a cargo plane is a type of airplane as is a passenger plane. This sort of relationship is called **generalization** in SysML.

---

[15] As we can see in Figure 4-11, after we set a specific multiplicity for a part, a notation: "{unique}" appears in the *parts* compartment. This notation was introduced in the SysML 1.4 standard and pertains to the question of whether given a multiplicity > 1, each part would be unique with no duplicates. In any case, for this sort of detail setting to be usable, a lot more support would be needed to support the configuration of different aspects of this part. In an email on 8 August 2018 Sparx support identified the appearance of "{unique}" in this case as a bug that will be fixed in a future release.

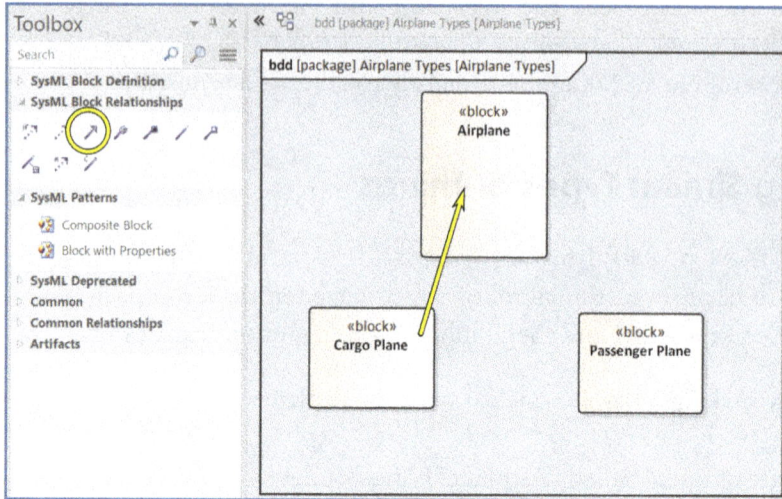

Figure 4-12 – Drag generalization relationship

In the toolbox under "SysML Block Relationships" select the generalization relationship. This arrow has a closed but empty arrowhead. As shown in Figure 4-12 drag a relationship from "Cargo Plane" to "Airplane". Drag a second relationship from "Passenger Plane" to "Airplane".

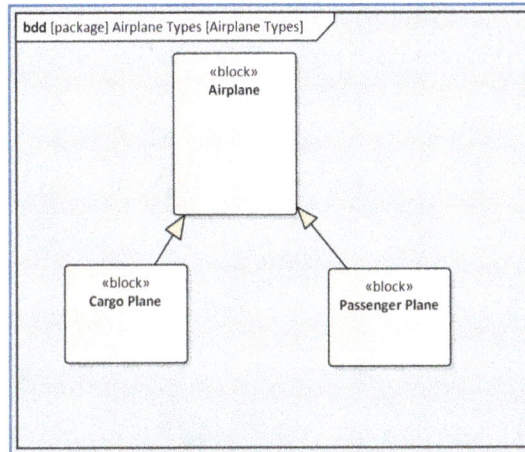

Figure 4-13 – Finished diagram

Your finished diagram should look like Figure 4-13. This type of diagram can be read as: "A cargo plane is a kind of airplane."

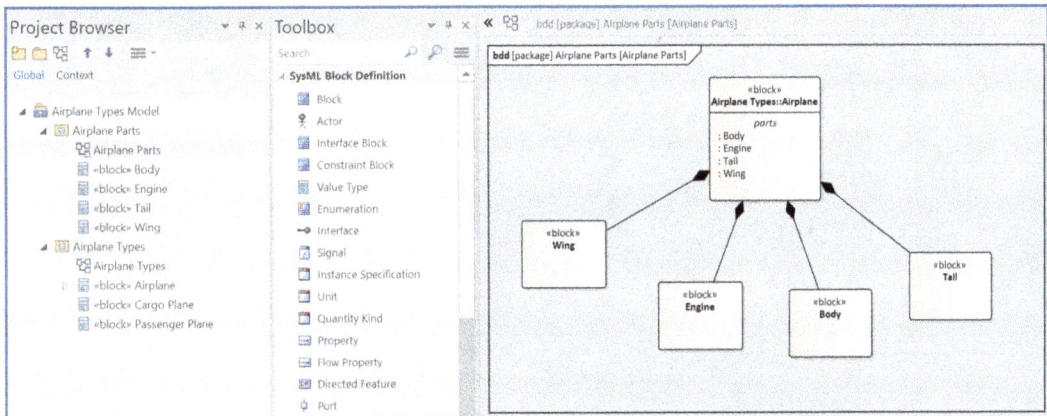

Figure 4-14 – Airplane common parts

Now let's think about some of the parts that are common to all airplanes:

1) In the model create a new package called "Airplane Parts".

2) In the package create a new block definition diagram also called "Airplane Parts".

3) Drag the block "Airplane" into the diagram creating a link.

4) In the package/diagram create four more blocks:

- "Wing"
- "Engine"
- "Body"
- "Tail"

5) Drag composition relationships between the four new parts and the airplane block.

Your finished diagram should look like Figure 4-14.

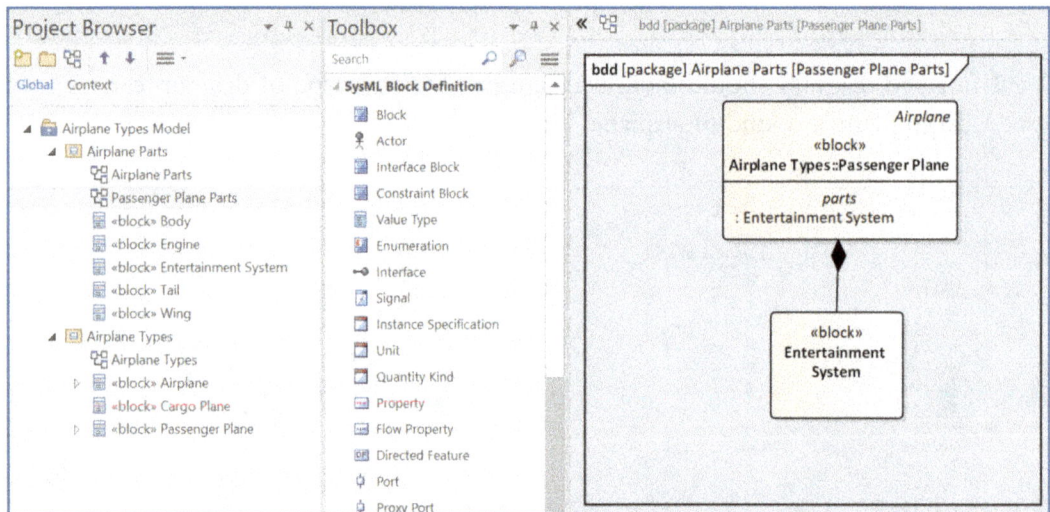

Figure 4-15 – Passenger plane parts

In addition to the common parts, our passenger plane will have an entertainment system.

1) In the "Airplane Parts" package create another block definition diagram called "Passenger Plane Parts".

2) Drag the block "Passenger Plane" into the diagram creating a link.

3) In the package/diagram create a block called: "Entertainment System".

4) Drag a composition relationship between the entertainment system and the passenger plane block.

We have now modeled the idea that in addition to the common airplane parts, the passenger plane has an entertainment system. How can we see this idea in action? Let's start up our factory!

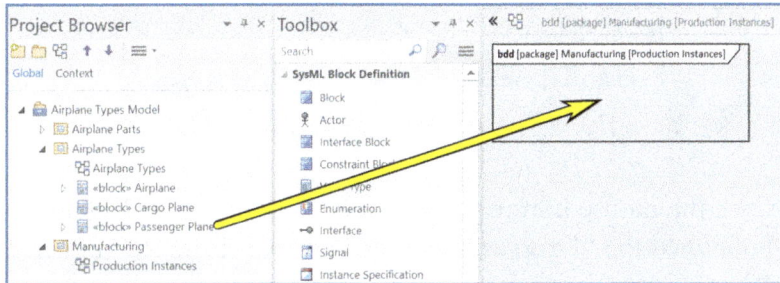

Figure 4-16 – Drag the passenger plane to the diagram

1) In the model create a new package called "Manufacturing".

2) In the package create a new block definition diagram also called "Production Instances".

3) Drag the block "Passenger Plane" into the diagram as shown in Figure 4-16.

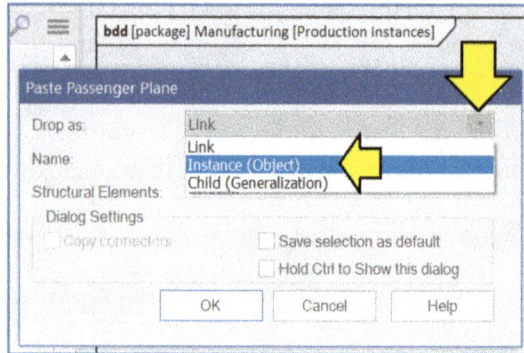

Figure 4-17 – Select Instance

After you release the mouse button to drop the block onto the diagram, a dialog box will appear. Pull down the "Drop as:" menu and select "Instance" rather than the default of "Link".

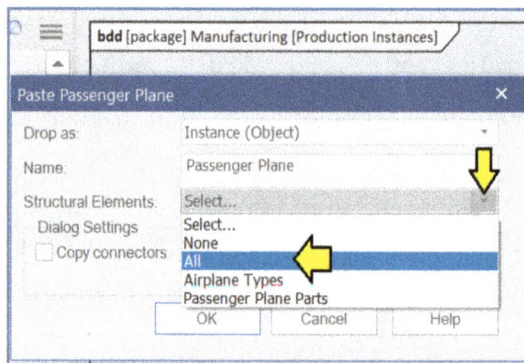

Figure 4-18 – Select All

Pull down the "Structural Elements:" menu and select "All".

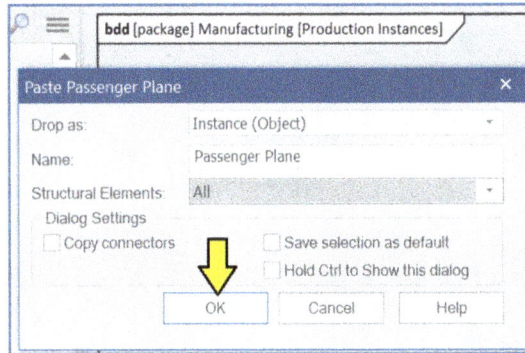

Figure 4-19 – Click OK

Click "OK".

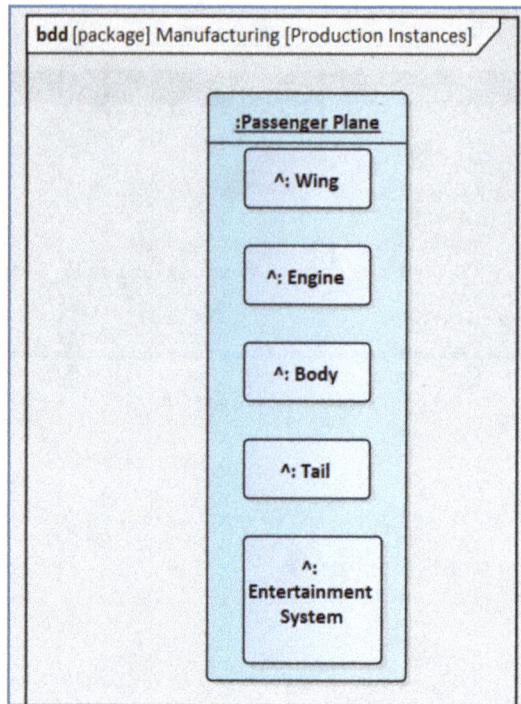

Figure 4-20 – Part instances created

Voila! Your diagram should now look like Figure 4-20. [16] [17] Now we see the mechanism of inheritance in action: not only does our passenger plane instance have an entertainment system, it also has the wing, body, tail, and engine of its parent the (ordinary) airplane.

---

[16] You may need to click once or twice or adjust the sizing a bit to get the diagram to resize itself properly.

[17] Note that *Enterprise Architect* displays the part names with a leading caret symbol. (^) SysML 1.4 was retargeted to UML 2.5 and picked this symbol usage up in the process. The caret indicates an inherited member. For ":Wing", ":Engine", ":Body", and ":Tail" the caret symbol notation is correct. However, ":Entertainment System" is owned directly by "Passenger Plane", not inherited from "Airplane". As such, there should not be a caret in front of this member. Sparx support has acknowledged this as a defect which will be fixed in a future release.

Composition versus Aggregation

SysML supports two general approaches for building something from other things:

- **composition** – building a system from parts
- **aggregation** – building a system from references

We have already seen an example of composition in Figure 4-11: the table is built up from a table top, legs, brackets and bolts.

In this section, we will create a system based on aggregation: a guide of my favorite restaurants in Austin, Texas.

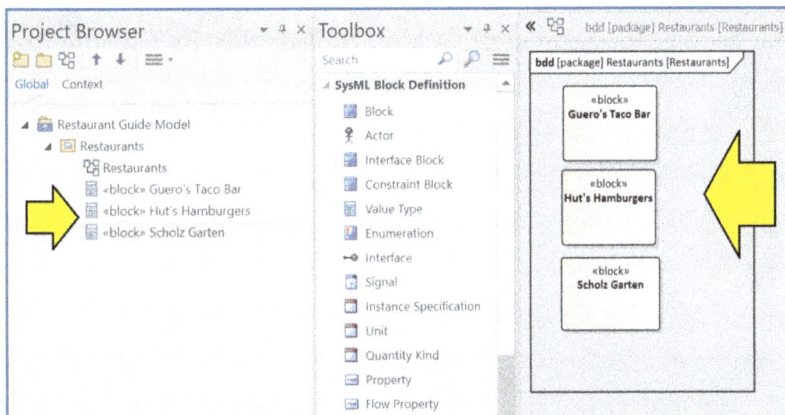

Figure 4-21 – Dave's favorite Austin restaurants

1) Create a new model called "Restaurant Guide Model".
2) In the model create a new package called "Restaurants".
3) In the package create a new block definition diagram also called "Restaurants".
4) In the package/diagram create three blocks for my favorite Austin restaurants:
    - "Guero's Taco Bar"
    - "Hut's Hamburgers"
    - "Scholz Garten"

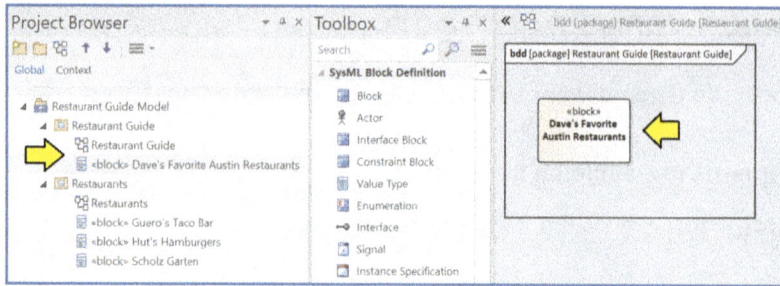

Figure 4-22 – Create guide

1) In the model create a new package called "Restaurant Guide".

2) In the package create a new block definition diagram also called "Restaurant Guide".

3) In the package/diagram create a block called: "Dave's Favorite Austin Restaurants".

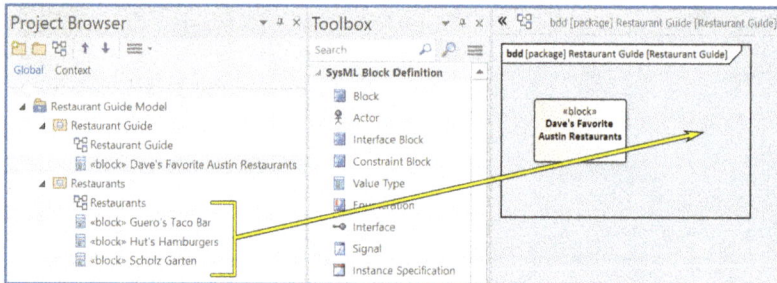

Figure 4-23 – Drag restaurant blocks to the diagram

Drag the three restaurant blocks onto the diagram, accepting the default "Drop as:" value of "Link" in each case.

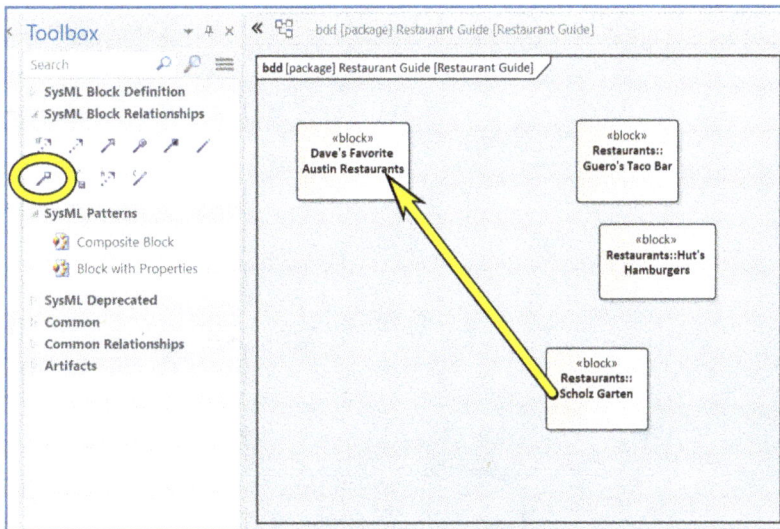

Figure 4-24 – Drag aggregation relationship

1) In the toolbox select the relationship for aggregation. This relationship is a line with an empty diamond as its arrowhead.

2) Drag the relationship from the "Scholz Garten" block to the "Dave's Favorite Austin Restaurants" block.

3) Drag the same relationship for the other two restaurant blocks.

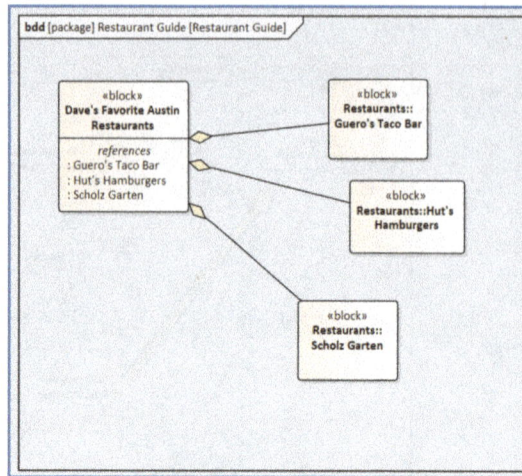

Figure 4-25 – Finished model

The finished diagram is shown in Figure 4-25. Notice that the compartment name is "*references*" rather than "*parts*". One of the key steps in understanding the difference between composition and aggregation is to think through what happens when the top-level block is destroyed:

- **composition** – consider our table example from Figure 4-11: imagine that the finished table is standing in student's room in a university dormitory. Hearing the news that the university's football team has just qualified for the national championships, in a fit of excessive enthusiasm the student and his friends rush the table down the stairs and toss it on the celebratory bonfire. At this point the table is destroyed, as are the table top, the table legs, the brackets, and the bolts. [18]

- **aggregation** – as for the restaurant guide in Figure 4-25, after purchasing the book you might be disappointed and toss it in the nearest recycling bin. From there it would get shredded and made into paper towels, napkins, and various other paper products. However, the destruction of the restaurant guide would do absolutely nothing to the restaurants. They have been around for decades,

---

[18] Strictly speaking, the table is responsible for arranging for the destruction of its top, legs, brackets, and bolts as it is going up in flames itself. This detail, however, is usually only relevant for software objects.

long before the creation of the restaurant guide, and they will be around for decades after everyone has forgotten about the restaurant guide.

Composition and Aggregation Terminology

As you read different books and articles on SysML, you will find slightly different terms for these relationships. Here is a little list of the terms:

- part relationships:
    - The relationship is formally known as a **composite association**.
    - The resulting set of blocks as a **composition**.
    - The activity of putting things together this way is referred to as **composition**.
- reference relationships:
    - The relationship is formally known as a **reference association**.
    - The resulting set of blocks as an **aggregation**.
    - The activity of putting things together this way is referred to as **aggregation**.

Value Properties

We will not get very far modeling much of anything using blocks before we will want to associate data items with those blocks such as "weight" or "serial number". In SysML, these sorts of data items are referred to as **value properties**.

Let's make a simple model with a few value properties. We will start with a simple model of a vending machine that dispenses a beverage called "Tall Cool One" in bottles.

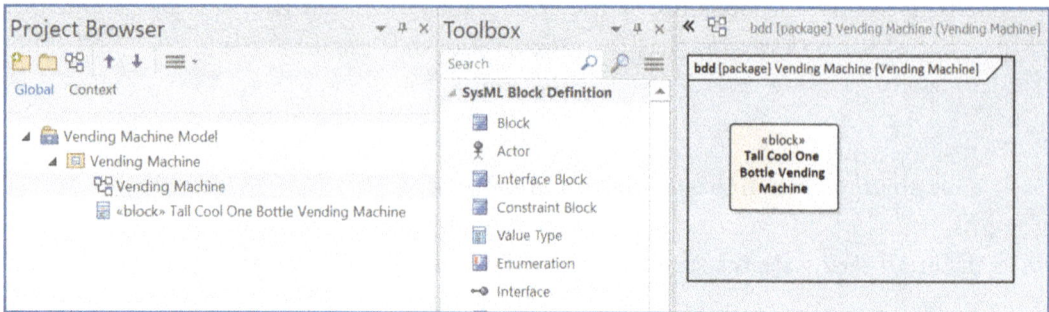

Figure 4-26 – Basic vending machine model

Create a model called "Vending Machine Model" with one package called "Vending Machine" that in turn contains a block definition diagram also called "Vending Machine". In that block definition diagram, define a new block called "Tall Cool One Bottle Vending Machine".

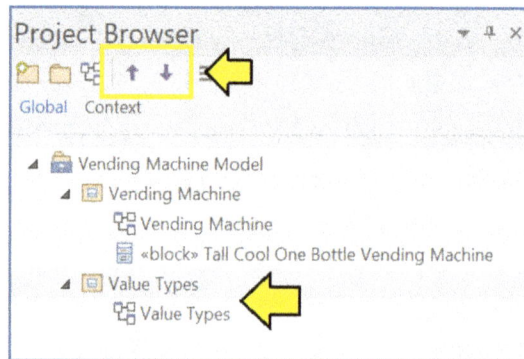

Figure 4-27 – Add package for value types

Before we can define the **value properties** for the block, we are going to need to define the **value types** for those properties. In order to keep the model neat, we will want to separate this type definition from the modeling of the block itself. Create a new package called "Value Types" and inside this a block definition diagram also called "Value Types".

Reordering Things in the Project Browser

You may have noticed when you created the "Value Types" package it ended up at the top of the list of packages in the model, not the bottom. Fortunately, it is easy to rearrange the order of things in the project browser by using the up/down arrows to move things up and down as needed as shown in Figure 4-27.

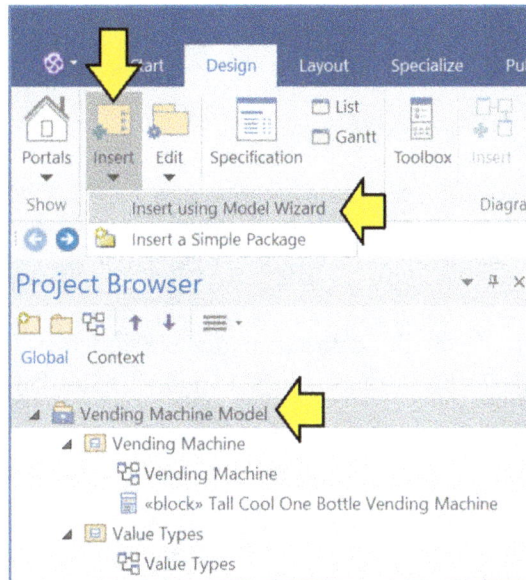

Figure 4-28 – Insert using wizard

Next we would like to bring in the *Enterprise Architect* standard type library:

1)   In the project browser, select the model itself.

2)   Select the "Design" ribbon.

3)   Select the "Insert" and then "Insert Using Model Wizard".

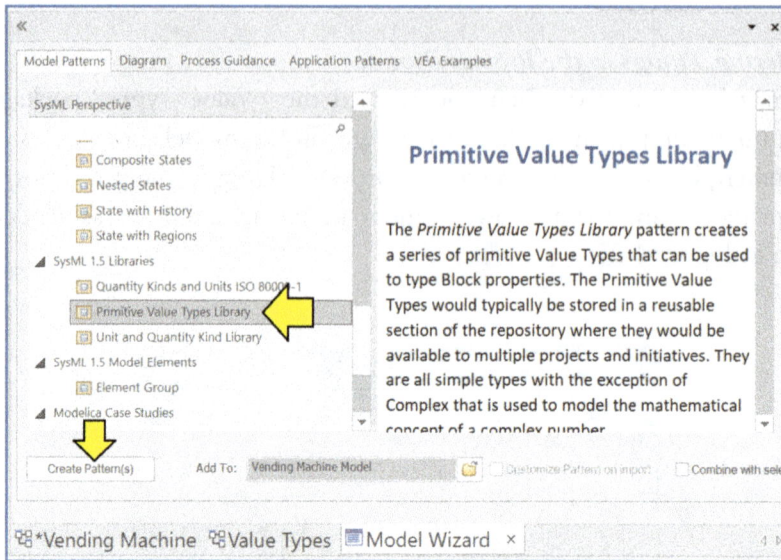

Figure 4-29 – Create Primitive Value Types Library

A model wizard will appear in the diagram pane. Scroll down. Under "SysML 1.5 Libraries" select "Primitive Value Types Library". Click "Create Pattern(s)".

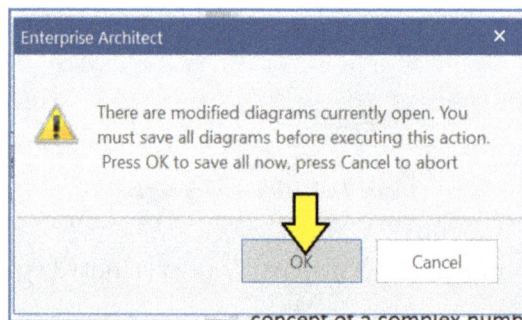

Figure 4-30 – Click OK if warning appears

If a warning appears about saving currently open diagrams, click "OK".

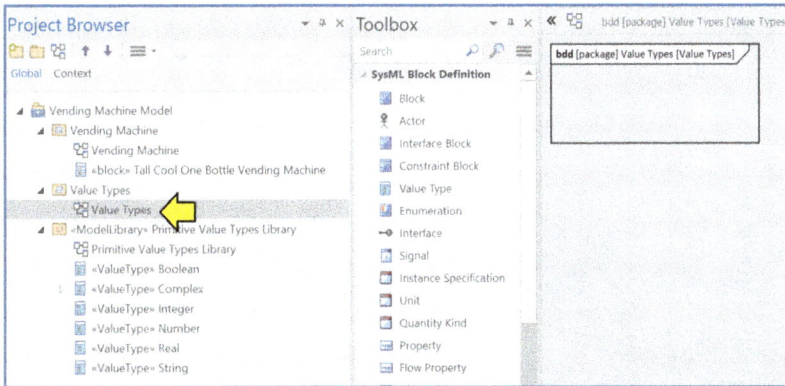

Figure 4-31 – Reopen value types block definition diagram

Reopen or reselect the block definition diagram for value types.

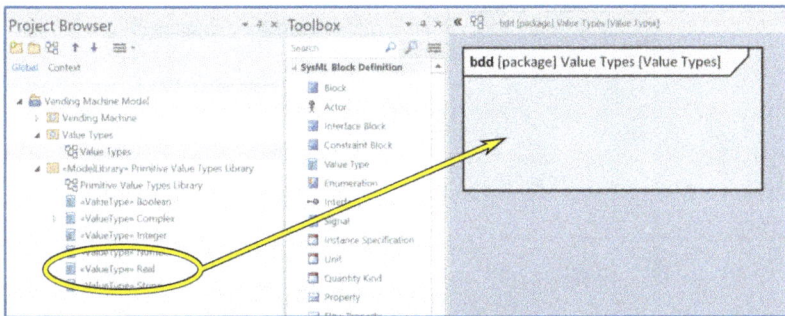

Figure 4-32 – Drag real to diagram

From the project browser, drag the real value type to the diagram.

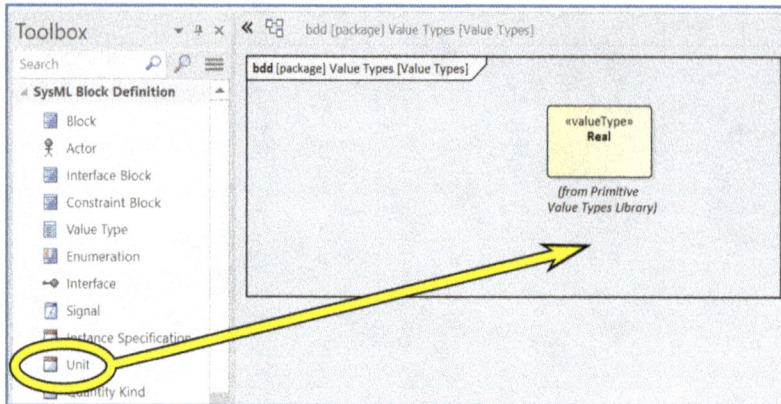

Figure 4-33 – Drag Unit to diagram

From the toolbox, drag the **unit** icon to the diagram.

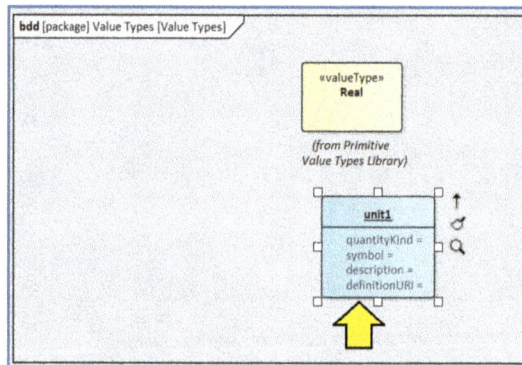

Figure 4-34 – Double-click on unit

Double-click on the unit element to open it.

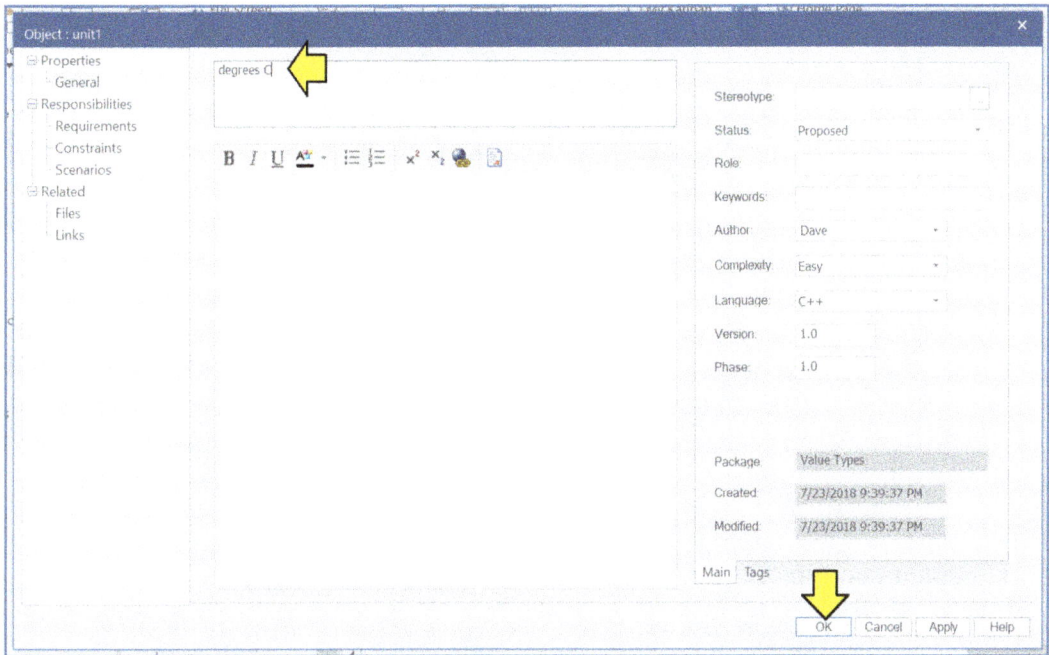

Figure 4-35 – Name the unit and click OK

Name the element "degrees C" and click "OK" to close.

The sharp-eyed reader will have noticed that:

- The diagram symbol for the unit looks a little different than the symbols for the other elements. This difference is because SysML 1.5 actually defines a unit as a sort of instance rather than as a type in its own right. This is a fine point that you do not need to worry about further, except that the distinction causes the next slightly remarkable phenomenon:

- The unit instance seems to have some interesting properties such as "symbol" but that there was not an obvious place to set these in the dialog box for the name.

EA 15 Note: *An early reader has reported that the following sequence works a little differently in version 15 of the tool. In version 15.2, select the unit, press Ctrl+2 to open the properties window if it is not already open, look for a "Run States" tab in the properties window.* [19]

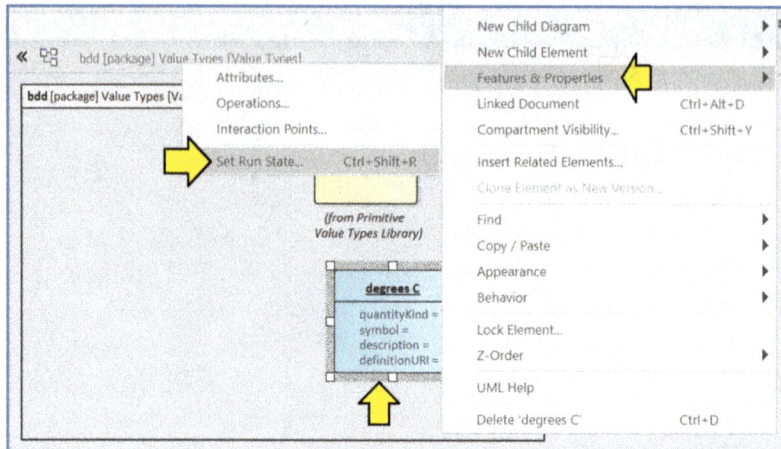

Figure 4-36 – Right-click and select Set Run State

1) Right-click on the unit.

2) Select "Features & Properties".

3) Select "Set Run State...".

(19) See: https://sparxsystems.com/enterprise_architect_user_guide/15.2/modeling/proptab.html

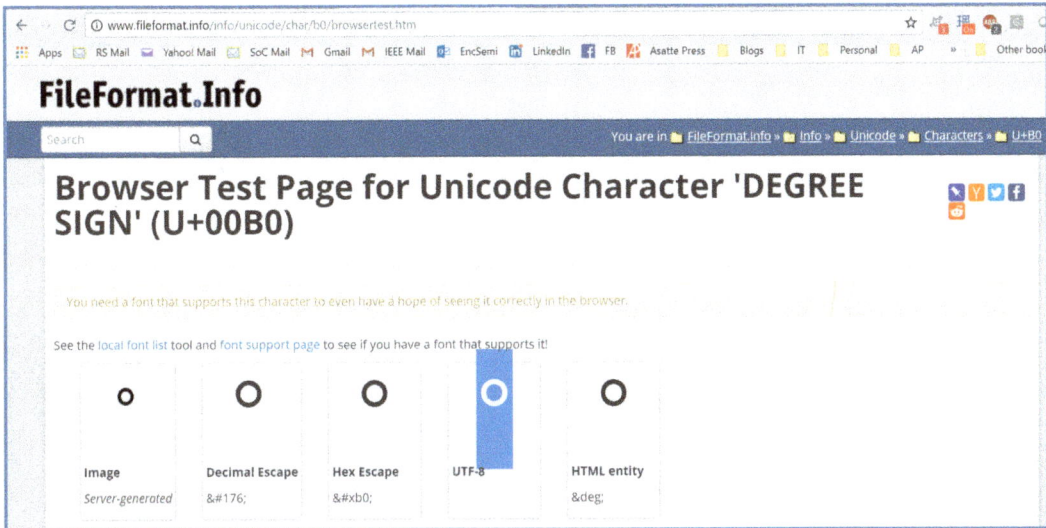

Figure 4-37 – Website with Unicode degree symbol

The easiest way to get the degree symbol is to find it on the internet and copy it. Type: "Unicode degree symbol" into your favorite search engine. A number of choices should come right up. The symbol is actually just a Unicode character. You can select and copy it to the clipboard just like copying the character "X" from a web page.

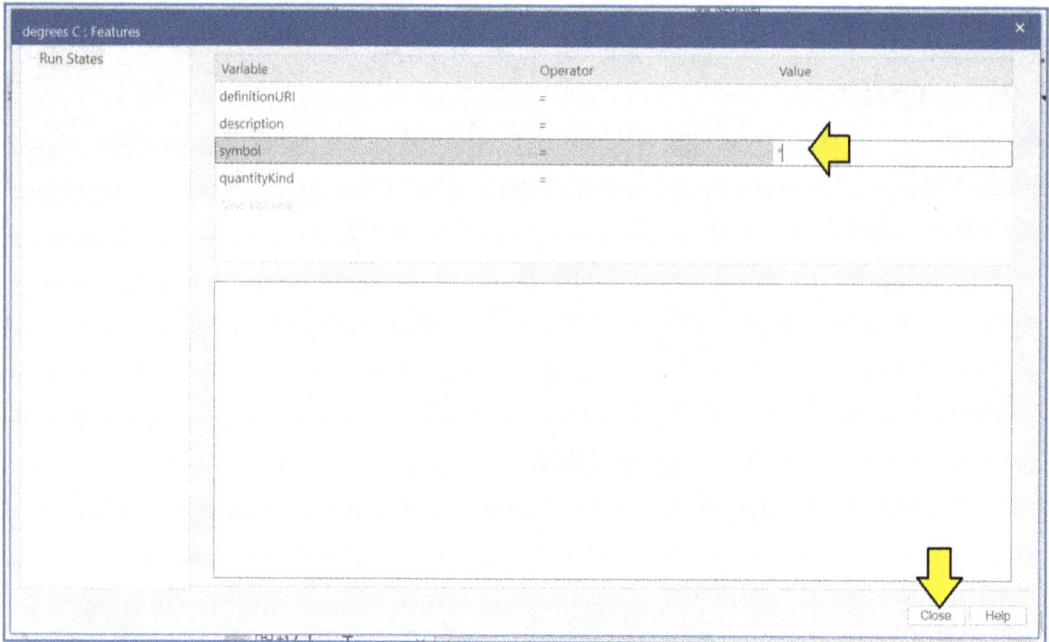

Figure 4-38 – Ctrl-V to paste degree symbol

Use Ctrl-V to paste the symbol into the value field for "symbol". Click "Close".

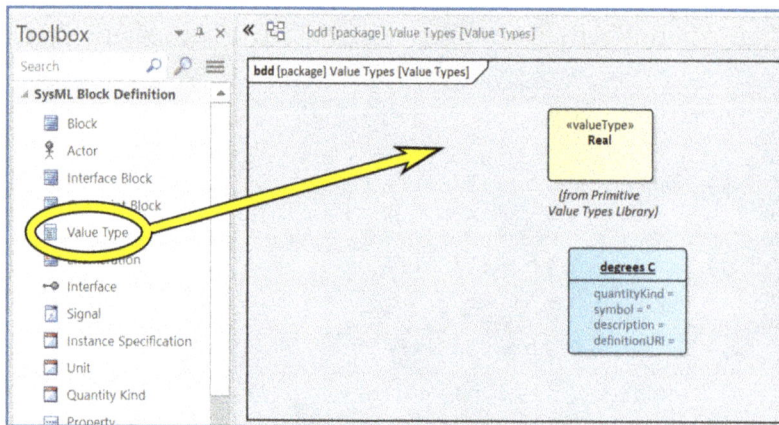

Figure 4-39 – Drag Value Type to diagram

From the toolbox, drag the Value Type icon to the diagram.

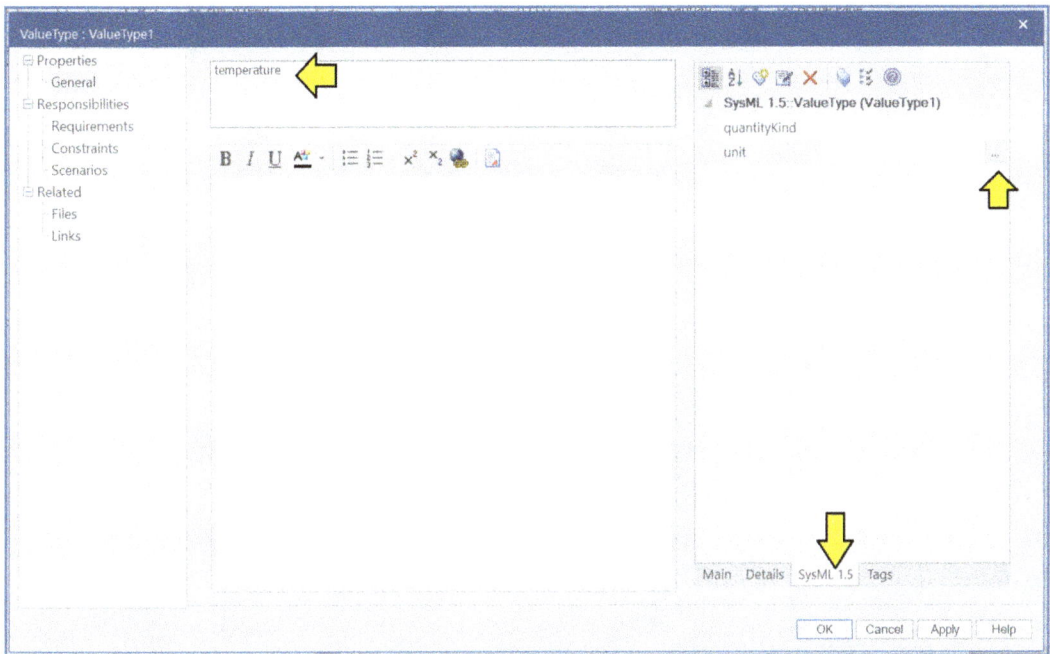

Figure 4-40 – Name the value type

Double-click on the value type. Name it "temperature". Click on the "SysML 1.5" tab. Click on the three dots next to "unit".

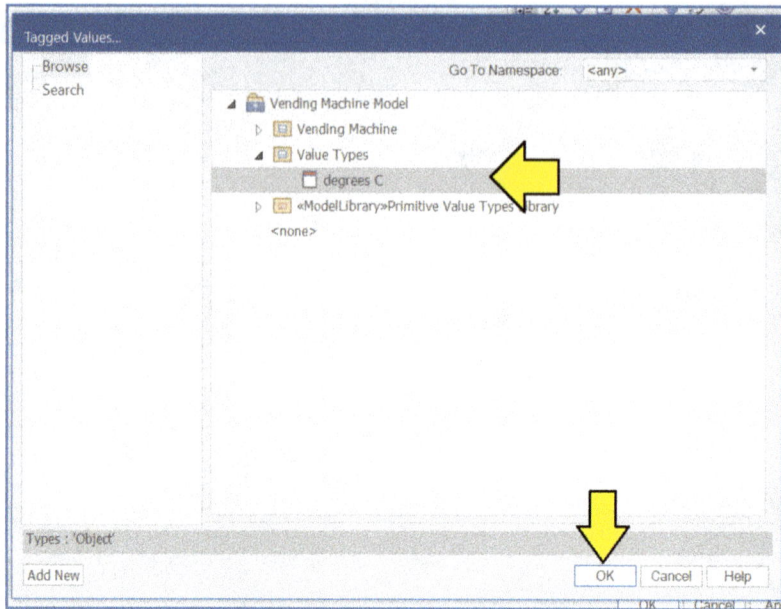

Figure 4-41 – Navigate to degrees C

Navigate to the "degrees C" unit and select it. Click "OK".

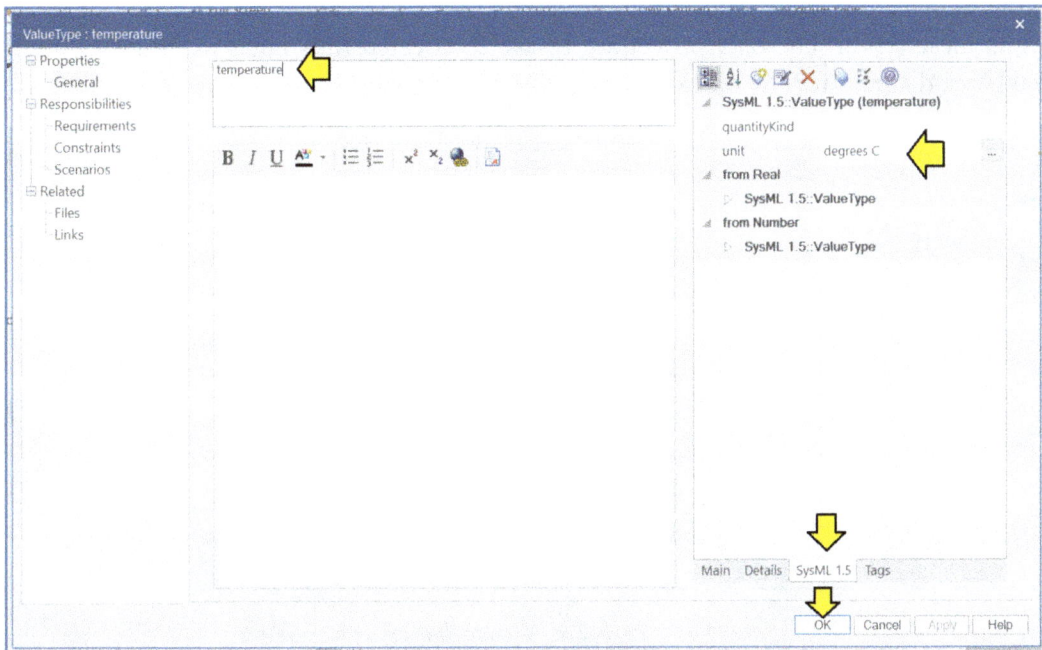

Figure 4-42 – Click OK twice

The temperature value type is now defined. Click "OK" twice.

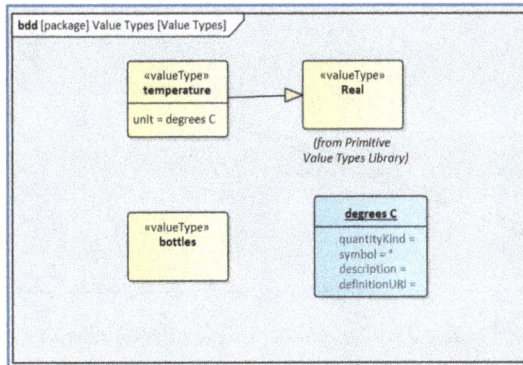

Figure 4-43 – Value types ready

Drag a generalization relationship from "temperature" to "Real" to indicate that the temperature is a kind of real number. Create another value type called "bottles".

Now we have our value types all set up. How do we add value properties to our block using these types? The only procedure I have discovered thus far is to create an internal block diagram for the block and drag the value properties to that diagram.

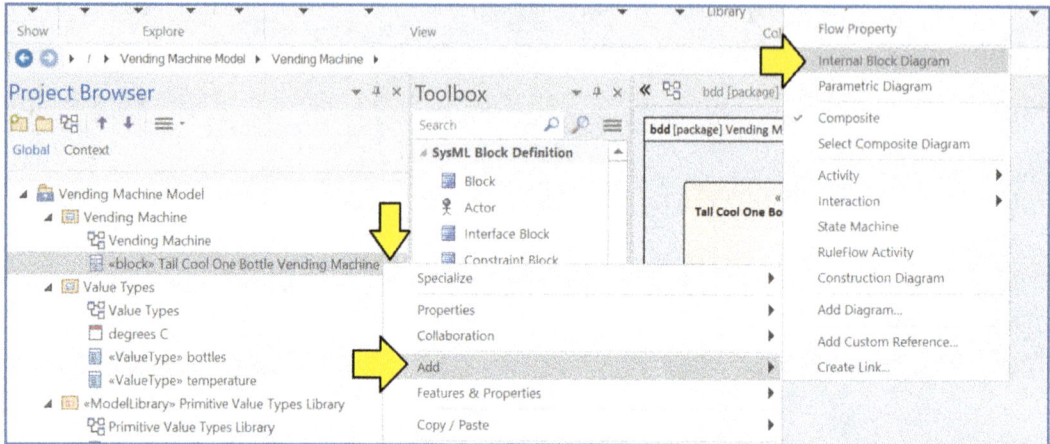

Figure 4-44 – Right-click and add internal block diagram

In the project browser right-click on the vending machine block, select: "Add" and then select "Internal Block Diagram".

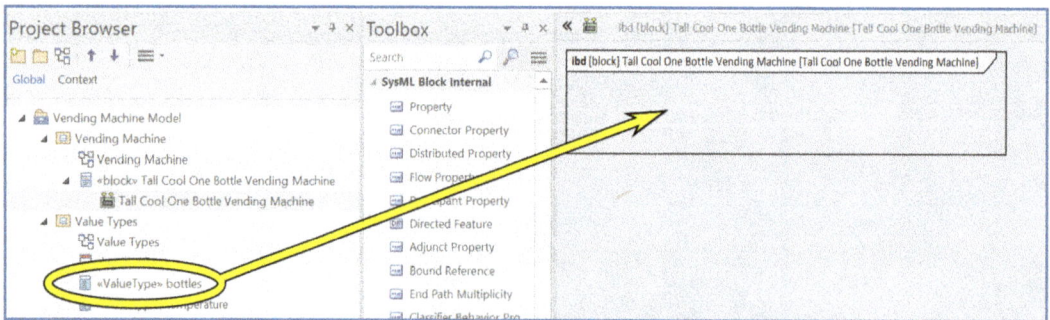

Figure 4-45 – Drag bottles to internal block diagram

Drag the value type "bottles" from the project browser to the internal block diagram.

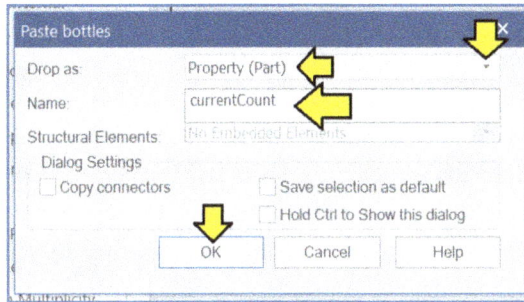

Figure 4-46 – Select Property (Part) and name the value property

When you release the mouse button to drop the value type onto the diagram, the dialog box shown in Figure 4-46 will appear. Select "Property (Part)" rather than the default type of link. Name the value property: "currentCount".

Repeat this procedure to drag the "temperature" value type to the internal block diagram and name the resulting value property: "coolerTemp".

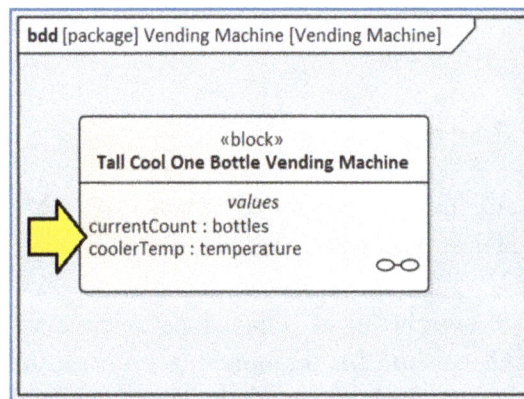

Figure 4-47 – Value properties displayed

The completed value properties should display as shown in Figure 4-47. *Enterprise Architect* has correctly understood that we did not really want to create "parts" but rather that our intent in dragging value types to the internal block diagram was to create value properties. A new compartment called *"values"* is now visible that shows the block's two value properties.

SysML Value Properties versus UML Attributes

UML approaches the problem of adding data items to classifiers using **attributes**. Since UML is designed to model (and generate) software, UML attributes are dimensionless and unitless. It is up to the designer of the software to interpret the meaning of the data. This approach works well for software but is less satisfying for systems engineering in which units and dimensions are a key concern. As such, SysML implements the more robust (and also somewhat more complicated) **value property** concept covered in the section above.

Enterprise Architect can actually handle either approach and you can add UML attributes to a block if desired. However, using UML attributes rather than SysML value properties will cause you headaches later if you want to go on to model complex mathematical relationships using SysML parametric diagrams. On the other hand, if your primary interest is in generating software source code from your model, you might be better served by using UML attributes.

Operations and Receptions

Next we will turn our attention to things that blocks do. SysML defines two types of method that can be owned or performed by a block:

- **operations** – are **synchronous** which means whoever or whatever requests the operation waits around for the operation to finish before continuing on to do something else. Operations are sort of like paying for something at a cashier. You stand there and wait until the payment process is complete.

- **receptions** – are **asynchronous** which means that the caller does not wait for the requested activity to complete. A reception is like dropping a letter into the mail. You don't stand and wait by the mailbox for the letter to have some effect. Each reception is tied to a SysML element called a **signal** which is like the letter that you dropped into the mail.

Continuing on with the model from the previous section, let's add some operations and receptions to our vending machine.

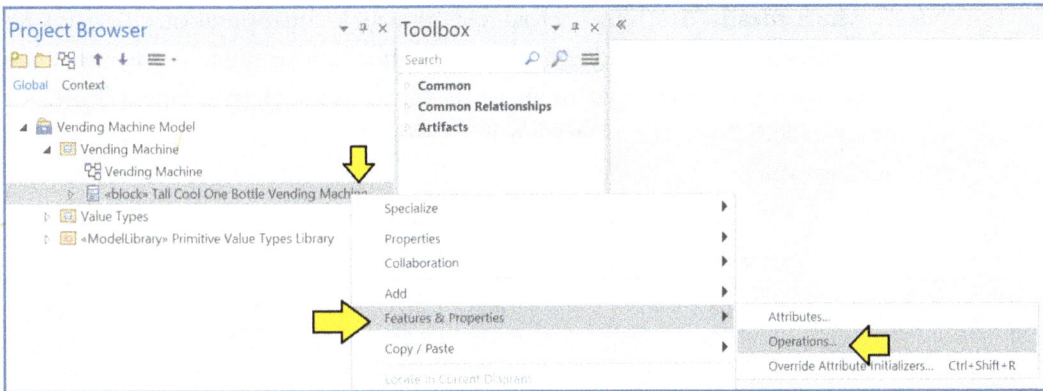

Figure 4-48 – Right-Click and select operations

1) In the project browser, right-click on the vending machine block.

2) Select "Features & Properties".

3) Select "Operations...".

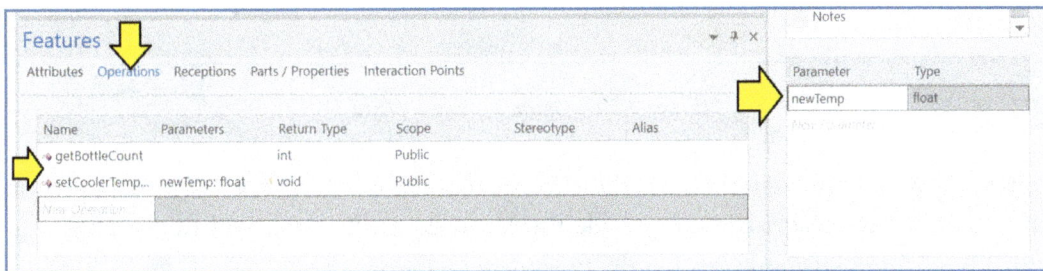

Figure 4-49 – Define operations

A new window called "Features" will appear. Let's define two operations for the vending machine:

- *getBottleCount* – returns the count of bottles currently available in the vending machine. Not surprisingly the return type is "int" for integer.

- *setCoolerTemp* – sets the temperature of the beverage cooling compartment in the vending machine. At this point, we are not far enough along in our design to think about status return codes. For the moment, this operation returns "void" which means "nothing". However, although this operation does not return any information, it needs some information about what temperature we would like the cooling compartment to be set to. As such, this operation has a parameter called: "newTemp" which is of the type "float" which handles real numbers as opposed to integers.

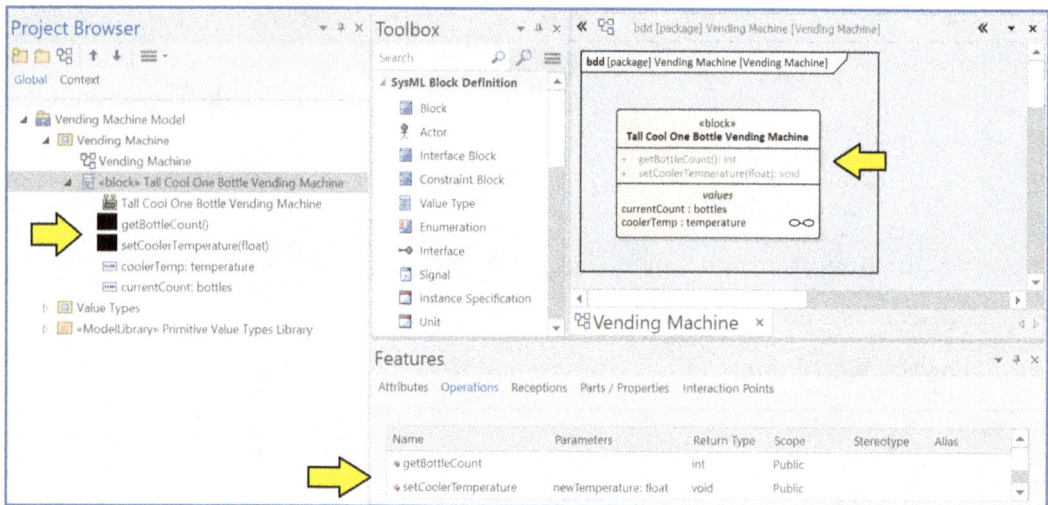

Figure 4-50 – Operations now displayed

After completing the definition of the two operations, we should see the operations in three places: the project browser, inside the *operations* compartment of the vending machine block in the diagram, and in the "Features" window. [20]

Next we will think about a signal and its matching reception. Although we have not modeled the details yet, our vending machine will have a small video screen to entertain customers who are enjoying their bottles of Tall Cool One beverage. Although we have not worked out all the details yet, we know from our stakeholders that we will

---

[20] The sharp-eyed reader will notice that the operations we have just defined are somehow related to the value properties we defined in the previous section.

want to be able to send a signal from a server at corporate headquarters and cause an advertising video to play.

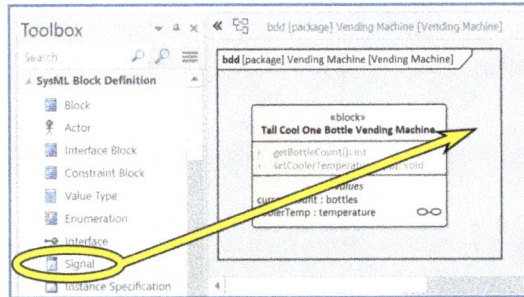

Figure 4-51 – Drag signal to diagram

From the toolbox, drag the **signal** icon to the vending machine block definition diagram.

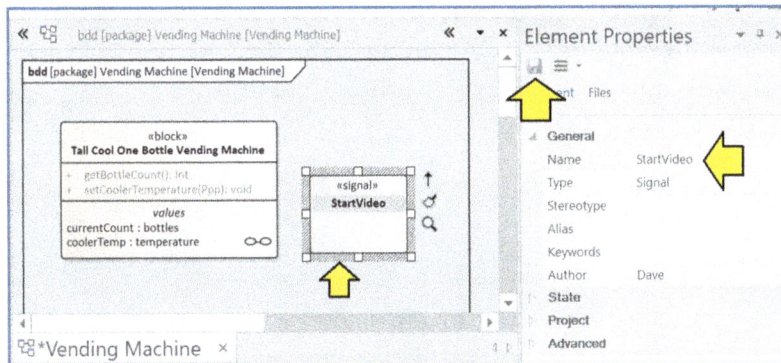

Figure 4-52 – Name the signal

Double-click on the signal and name it "StartVideo". Use the floppy-disk icon to save your changes.

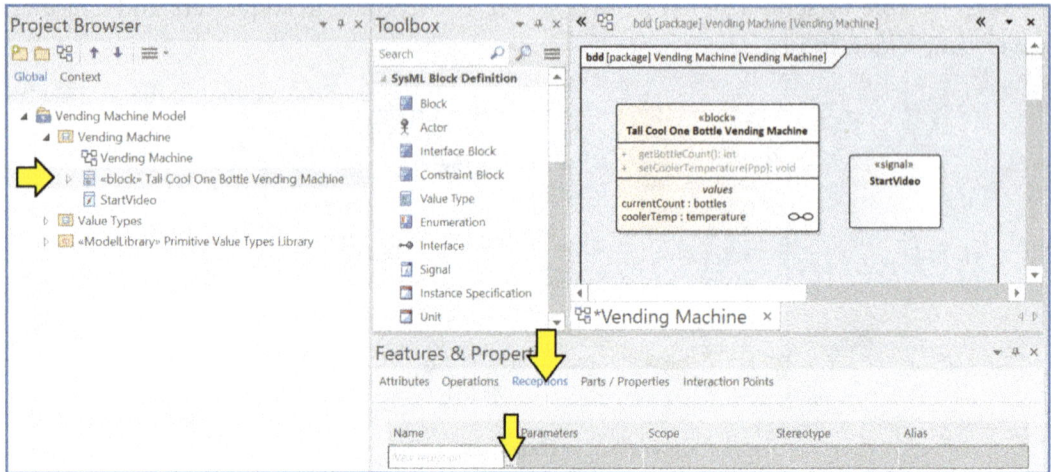

Figure 4-53 – Select block and click on three dots

Reselect the vending machine block in the project browser. If the "Features & Properties" window is not visible, right-click on the block and select it from the context menu. Select the "Receptions" tab. At the right of the "Name" field you will find a small box with three dots in it. Click on the three dots.

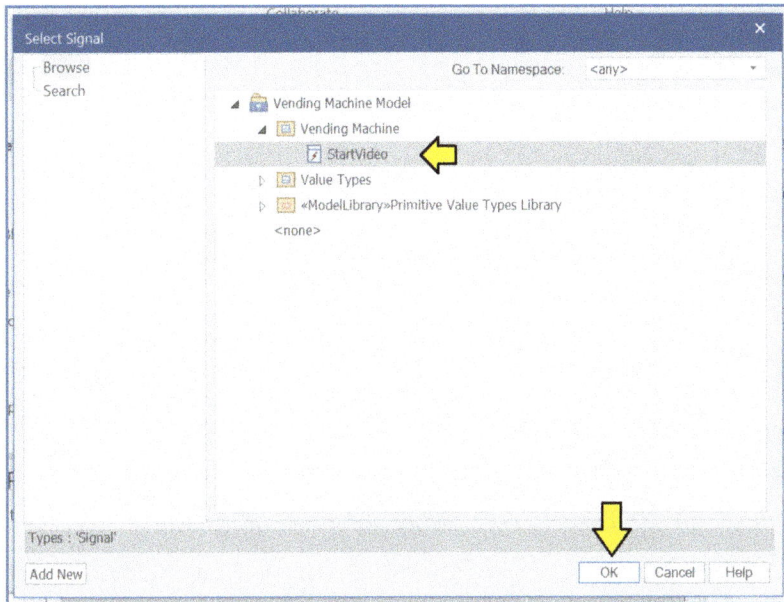

Figure 4-54 – Select signal and click OK

The "Select Signal" dialog will appear. Navigate to the previously defined "StartVideo" signal and select it. Click "OK".

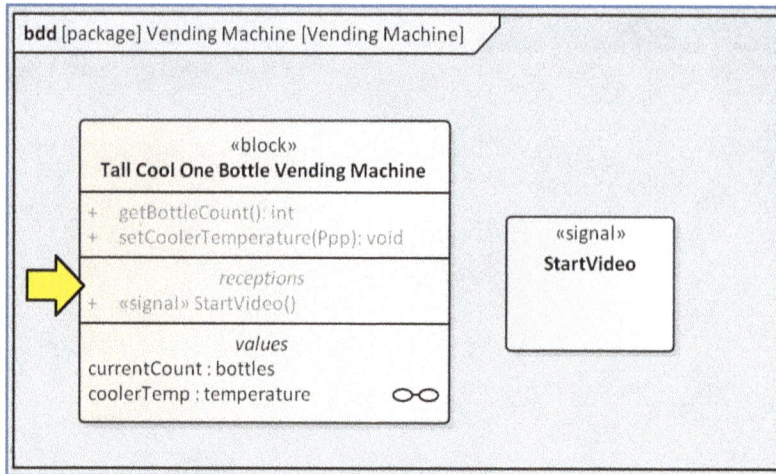

Figure 4-55 – Receptions compartment will appear

We can now see that a new compartment called: "*receptions*" has appeared and the reception for the "StartVideo" signal is now defined.

Ports

The last topic we will cover in this chapter is the definition of ports for blocks. The modeling elements related to ports were changed significantly in SysML 1.3. SysML currently defines two kinds of ports:

- **full ports** – exist on the boundary of a block and are parts in their own right. A good example of a full port would be the ubiquitous three-pronged power connector on the back of most desktop personal computers. The port is a physical part that gets bolted to the case of the personal computer. There are separate connections from this part to the actual power electronics components deep inside the machine.

- **proxy ports** – provide access to the functions of a block. Proxy ports do not necessarily exist as physical connectors on the exterior of the block. An application programming interface (API) would be a good example of a proxy port.

Let's return to the vending machine model from the previous sections and add a few ports to the vending machine block.

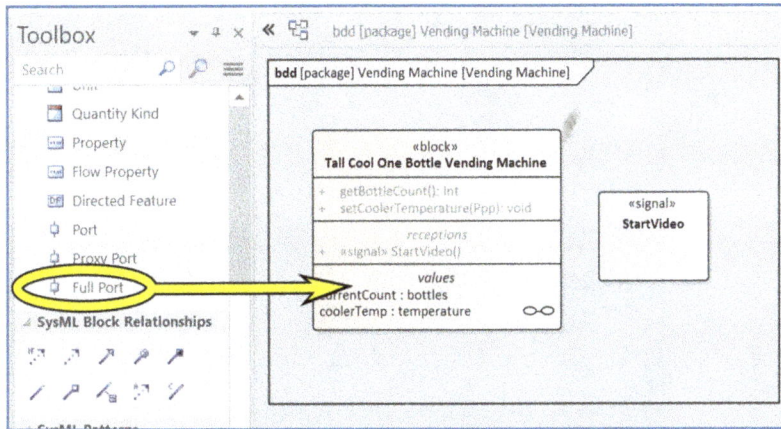

Figure 4-56 – Drag Full Port icon to the vending machine block

Drag the "Full Port" icon to the diagram and drop it on the vending machine block. Note that you need to release the mouse button somewhere in the interior of the block.

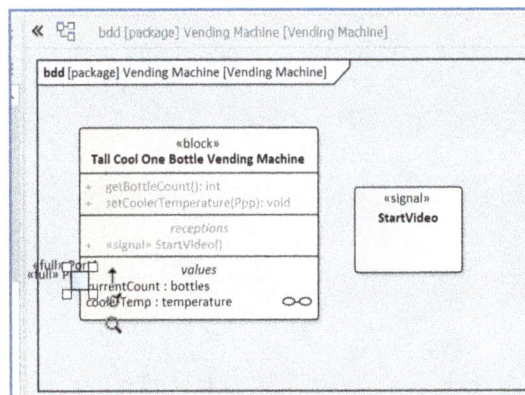

Figure 4-57 – Some adjustment of the formatting will be needed

After you drop the port onto the block, the formatting will usually be a little jumbled as shown in Figure 4-57. You will probably want to drag the block itself slightly to the right to make some space in the diagram. You can also drag the port around the perimeter of the block to position it (top, bottom, left, right) where you would like it. Double-click on the port and name it: "PowerPlug".

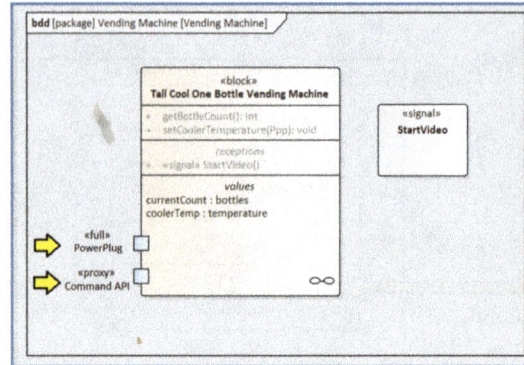

Figure 4-58 – Add a proxy port for a command API

Add a proxy port for a command API as well. The resulting diagram should look like Figure 4-58.

With that, we have completed our initial modeling of the external aspects of our vending machine. In the next chapter, we will learn how to hook things up inside the vending machine.

Further Study

Here are is a list of further topics you will want to study to hone your expertise.

- **constraints** – We will be covering constraints in *Parametric Diagrams* on page 321.

- **operations, provided and required** – Provided operations are provided by the block defining the operation; required operations are **not** provided by the defining block and must be provided by some other block.

    - [Friedenthal] – page 147

- **UML-style ports** – Up until SysML 1.2, ports and interfaces were taken directly from UML. In SysML 1.3, the approach and diagramming were changed significantly. However, most tools still support the UML approach. Also, as of 2018, the OCSMP certification exam is still written around the original UML ports and interfaces approach. For more information see:

    - [Delligatti] – page 38
    - [Douglass] – page 114
    - [Friedenthal] – page 180

- **Value property details** – SysML supports more detailed specification of value properties including static/derived, default values, initial values, and distribution.

    - [Friedenthal] – section 7.3.4, pages 136-137

Chapter 5 – Internal Block Diagrams

In this chapter, we will look into the SysML internal block diagram.

Parts and Multiplicities

One of the first subjects that SysML beginners find confusing is multiplicity. That is, SysML beginners initially think that multiplicity is obvious and straightforward, only to find out that multiplicity and part roles are not as simple as they seem.

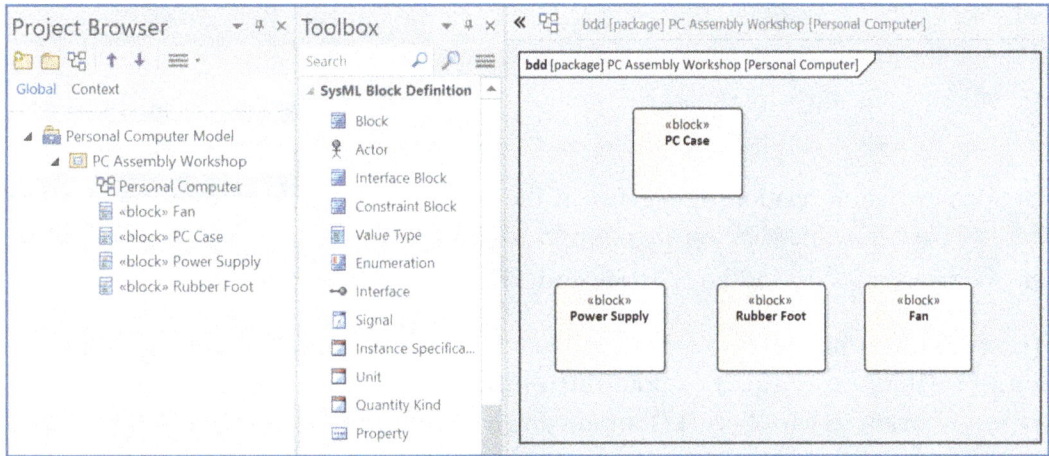

Figure 5-1 – Basic model of a personal computer case

We will illustrate the concept by making a simple model of a personal computer case and some of its parts. Create the starter model for the personal computer case as shown in Figure 5-1.

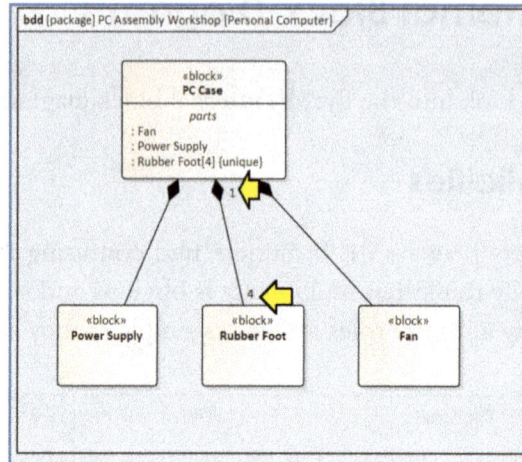

Figure 5-2 – Create composition relationships

Drag composition relationships between the power supply, rubber foot, and fan and the PC Case. Double-click on the composite association for the rubber foot and set the multiplicity to "1" for the PC Case and "4" for the rubber foot. [21]

The rubber feet on the PC Case are rather anonymous things. We really don't need to model anything more specific about them than that there are four of them. However, what if we want to have both a front fan and a rear fan, possibly with different specifications?

---

[21] See Figure 4-10 on page 79 for the procedure to set multiplicities.

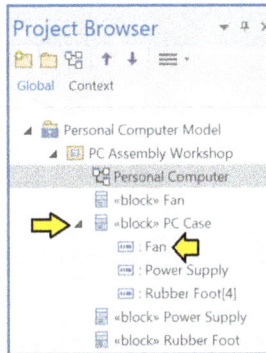

Figure 5-3 – Double-click on the fan

In the project browser, double-click on the ":Fan" part.

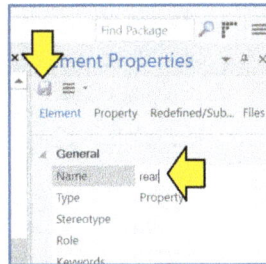

Figure 5-4 – Name the fan and save

The Element Properties window will appear. Name the fan "rear" and click on the floppy-disk icon to save your changes.

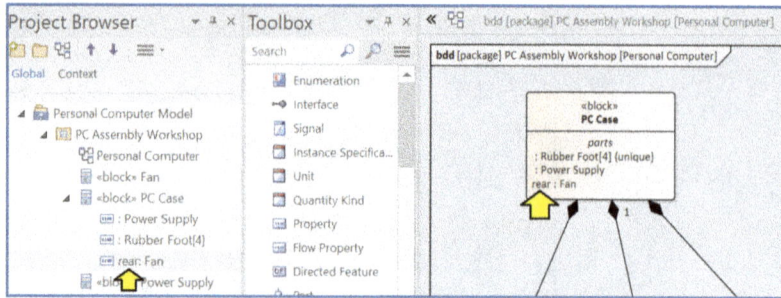

Figure 5-5 – The Fan part is now named

The ":Fan" part is now named "rear". Perfect. Now, how do we add another one?

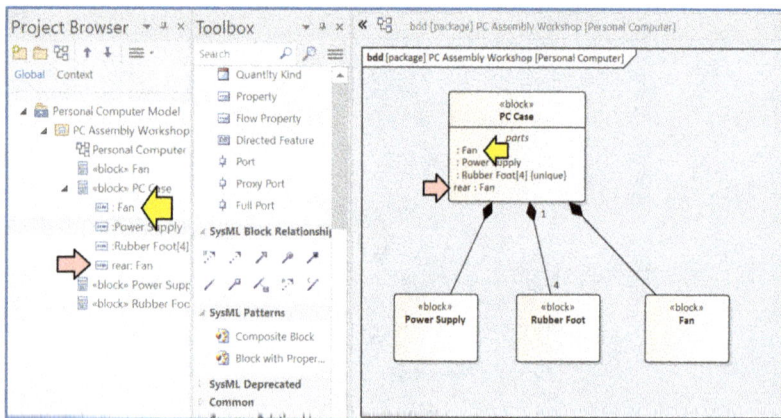

Figure 5-6 – Drag to create second part instance

This step might feel a little counterintuitive but select the composite association icon in the toolbox (again) and drag from the fan block to the PC Case block (again). *Enterprise Architect* will NOT create another black diamond arrow, but it will add another part of type ":Fan" in the project browser and the *parts* compartment of the PC Case block as shown in Figure 5-6.

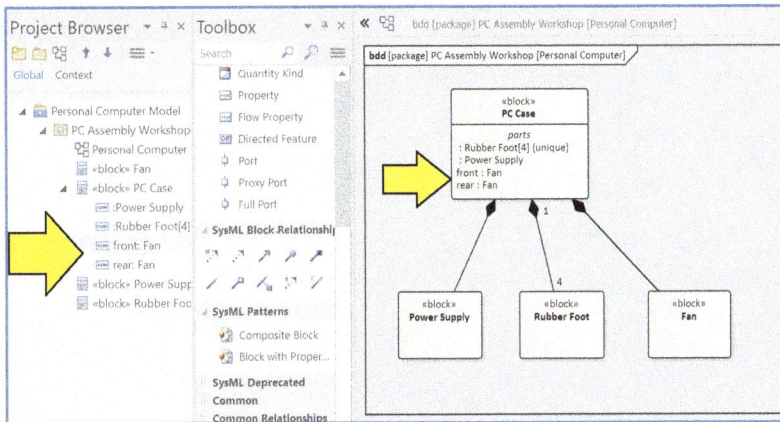

Figure 5-7 – Name the second fan

You can now name the second fan: "front".

One Arrow or Two?

The SysML standard calls for multiple composition arrows when you have multiple parts of the same type with different roles. Strictly speaking, *Enterprise Architect* is out of compliance with the standard on this point. However, I personally found the multiple arrows pretty confusing when I first encountered them. Furthermore, if you need more than two or three distinct parts of the same type, the multiple arrows approach can become unmanageable on the diagram. See:

- [Delligatti] – page 49 Figure 3.20
- [Friedenthal] – page 116 Figure 7.1

However, if you prefer the standard approach, by right-clicking on the first arrow and selecting: "Line Style" and then "Tree Style - Vertical", you can get the standard look.

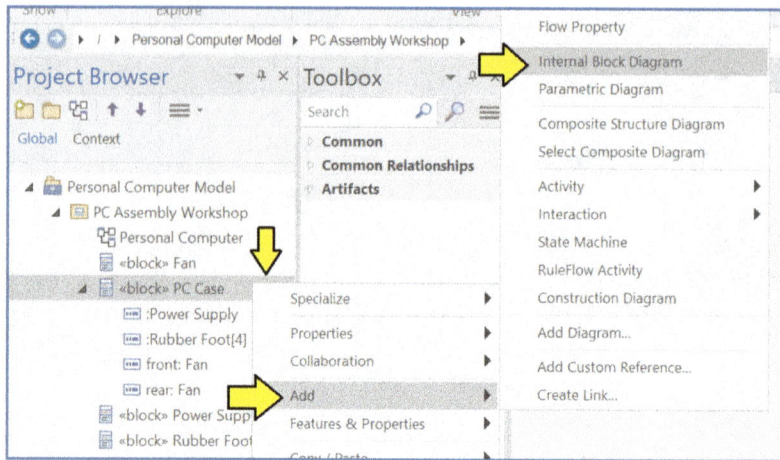

Figure 5-8 – Create an internal block diagram

Now we are ready to create an internal block diagram. In the project browser, right-click on the PC Case block and select "Add" followed by "Internal Block Diagram".

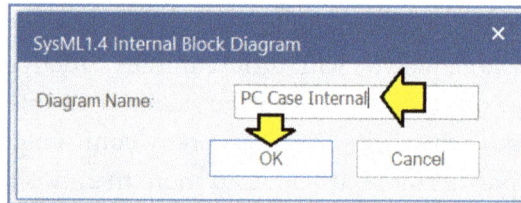

Figure 5-9 – Name the internal block diagram

Name the internal block diagram. I usually append "internal" to the name of the owning block when I create an internal block diagram, but that is purely a matter of personal taste.

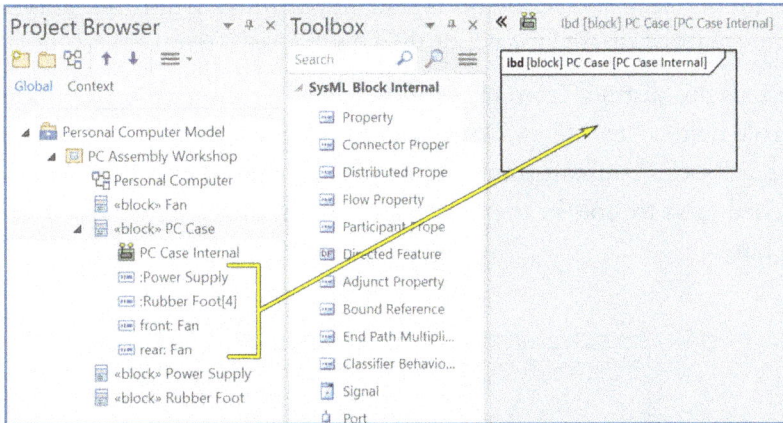

Figure 5-10 – Drag the part elements to the diagram

The internal block diagram will be empty after you create it. That emptiness might surprise you. However, as with all SysML diagrams, you only need to show the elements on the diagram that are relevant to the understanding of the stakeholder who will consume the diagram. In this case, we want to include all of the parts. Drag them from the project browser to the diagram as shown in Figure 5-6.

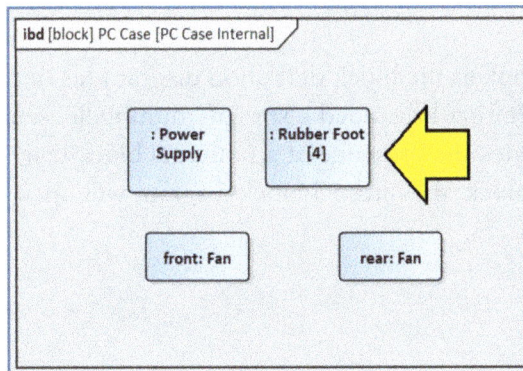

Figure 5-11 – The rubber feet show as only one element for four feet

Now we can see the difference between multiplicity on a single part and multiple parts of the same type:

- The rubber feet are anonymous and not distinct from one another. In fact, they are part of the PC Case, but they don't have a named role.

- The fans are distinct from one another. It is also important to understand that the role names "front" and "rear" actually belong to the PC Case block, not to the fan block. You can think of the sheet metal of the PC Case as having an assigned spot to bolt in the front fan and another assigned spot to bolt in the rear fan.

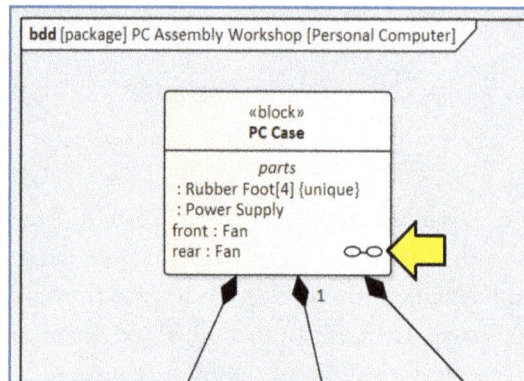

Figure 5-12 – Dumbbell symbol for drill-down

If we now go back and look at the block definition diagram (as opposed to the internal block diagram) we can see that has added a sort of "dumbbell" symbol to the PC Case block. This symbol indicates the presence of an internal block diagram for the block. If you double-click on the block, the internal block diagram will open.

Dumbbell, Rake, and Drill-Down

UML State Hidden
Decomposition Indicator

UML Action Call
Behavior Indicator

UML defines both a "dumbbell" and a "rake" symbol. The UML dumbbell symbol indicates that a state has a hidden decomposition. The UML rake symbol indicates that an action calls another UML behavior. SysML recommends the use of the rake symbol for a number of additional cases of composed elements. See [SysML1.5] Section A.2 *Guidelines* on page 197. *Enterprise Architect* uses the dumbbell (Sparx refers to the symbol as "looking glasses") for state decomposition and the rake for call behavior actions. However, rather than using the rake for the additional SysML composed element cases, *Enterprise Architect* seems to use the dumbbell instead.

Personally, I don't find the SysML rake symbol linking to be very useful. You can only drill down one level and it really does not provide much flexibility. In my own models, I simply insert hyperlinks into the diagrams. These are much more flexible, and they are freeform. If you have three different diagrams that make sense as the next level of "drill-down" you can insert three different hyperlinks and simply drag to make the block (or activity, or whatever symbol you want) large enough to contain three hyperlinks. The example files for this section contain a simple model called "Hyperlink Example" that demonstrates three layers of drill-down.

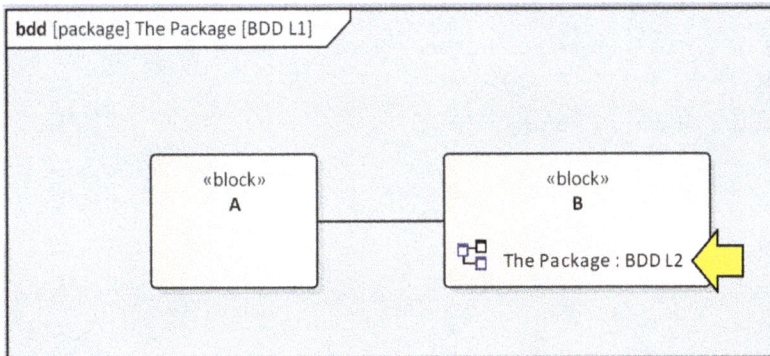

Nested Parts

One of the challenging topics in SysML for beginners concerns nested parts. A beginner will expect nested parts to behave sort of like nested gift boxes: a box inside of a box inside of a box inside of a box. While intuitively appealing, this is not really how SysML works. When you create a composition relationship, you are really creating a sort of "mounting bracket" for the part. That is, when you create the parent instance, you have to separately create and install the part at that time. As such, you really don't know what is inside the part until it is created. A "battery subsystem" part that was defined years ago, when the "appliance" model was created might have been replaced by a plug-compatible battery with a completely different chemistry by the time an instance of the appliance is generated.

In order to demonstrate the ability of *Enterprise Architect* to display nested parts in internal block diagrams, we will create the metaphorically slightly imperfect model of a family with multiple generations. Parents are not actually composed of their children. However, the generation metaphor is easy to understand in a diagram.

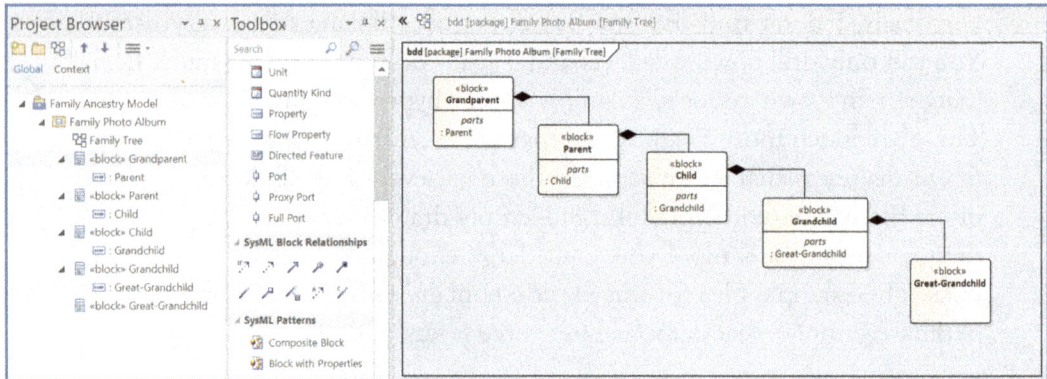

Figure 5-13 – Several generations

Create the basic model shown in Figure 5-13.

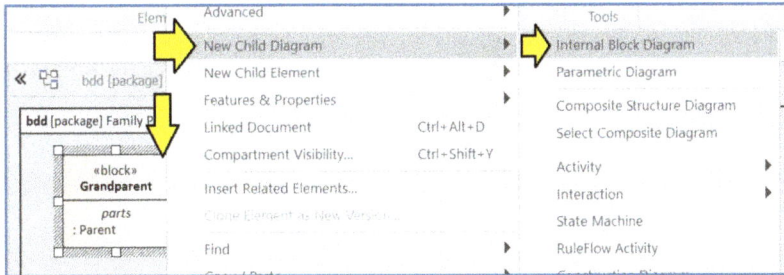

Figure 5-14 – Create an internal block diagram

Right-click on the "Grandparent" block, select "New Child Diagram" and then "Internal Block Diagram".

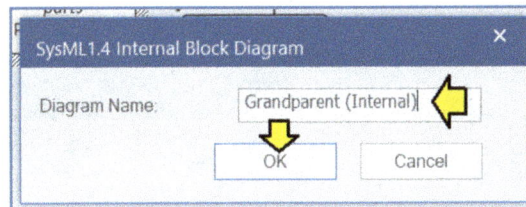

Figure 5-15 – Name the diagram

Name the diagram "Grandparent (Internal)". The created diagram will be empty. Given that the grandparent block definitely has a part of type ":Parent" this default diagram emptiness may seem a bit odd at first. However, all SysML tools that I have encountered behave this way.

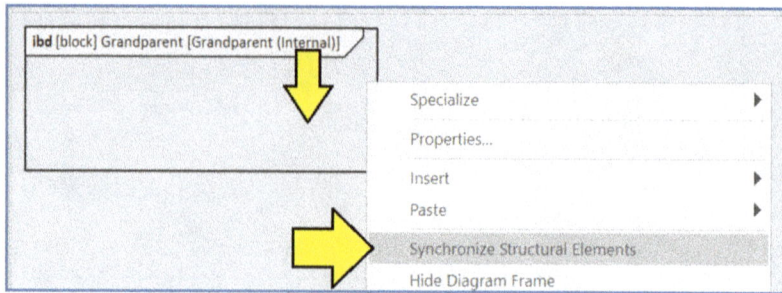

Figure 5-16 – Synchronize structural elements

In order to see the parts inside the block, we need to ask *Enterprise Architect* to synchronize structural elements. Right-click on the diagram and select "Synchronize Structural Elements" as shown in in Figure 5-16.

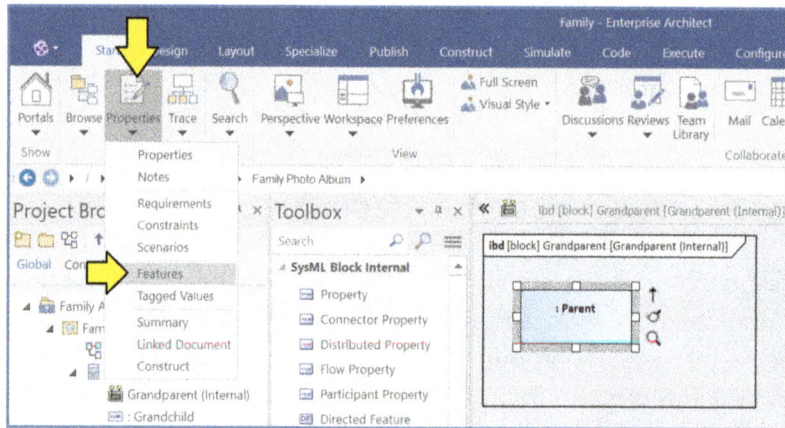

Figure 5-17 – Open features window

We now have the parent within the grandparent. In order to show the child within the parent, pull down the "Properties" menu in the ribbon and select "Features".

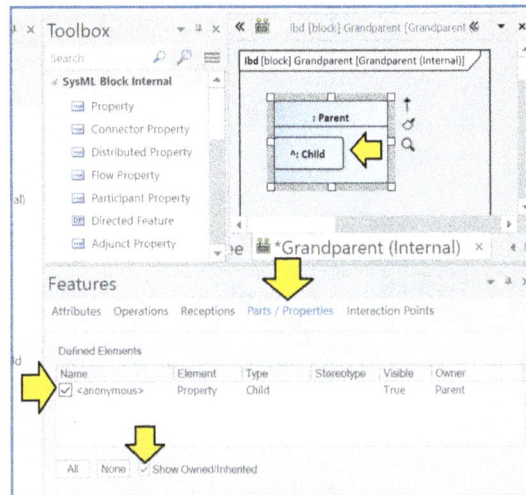

Figure 5-18 – Show child

In the features window, select the "Parts / Properties" tab. At the bottom of the window, check the "Show Owned/Inherited" checkbox. Select the child property. The child part should now become visible in the diagram. [22]

---

[22] Note that *Enterprise Architect* displays this part with a leading caret symbol. (^) SysML 1.4 was retargeted to UML 2.5 and picked this symbol usage up in the process. It is supposed to indicate an inherited member. However, ":Child" is an owned member, not an inherited member. Sparx support has acknowledged this as a defect which will be fixed in a future release.

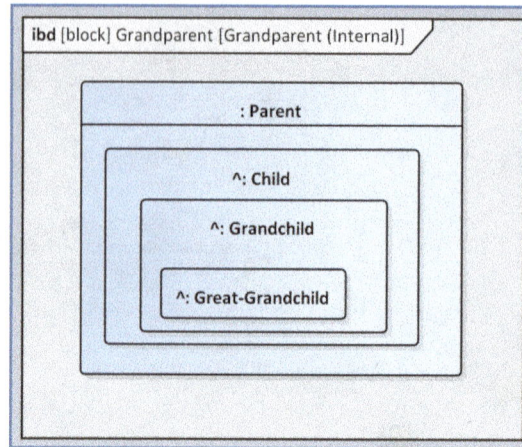

ibd [block] Grandparent [Grandparent (Internal)]

: Parent

^: Child

^: Grandchild

^: Great-Grandchild

Figure 5-19 – Continue to drill down

If you next select the ":Child" element, you can use the same feature setting to show the ":Grandchild" and then the ":Great-Grandchild" elements. The result will look like Figure 5-19.

Connecting Things Together

One of the key roles of the internal block diagram in SysML is to show how blocks are connected together. The overall subject of interfaces is quite large, well beyond the scope of this book. Furthermore, the steps needed to end up with current SysML ports properly modeled on an internal block diagram using *Enterprise Architect* are somewhat intricate. In this chapter we will show two examples:

- One example will cover **full** ports and the other will cover **proxy** ports because the approach to specifying what sort of stuff the port handles is different between the two.

- Both will show the connection of a port on the exterior of the block to a part inside the block. The modeling steps to set this sort of connection up correctly are a bit intricate. If you can model the connection of something external to a block to something internal to the block, modeling more connections inside the block between parts inside the block will be straightforward.

Full Ports

As previously mentioned in *Ports* on page 114, the full port can be thought of as a part in its own right, a connector that gets bolted to the cover of the block. We will create a model of a personal computer case and its power supply to demonstrate this concept. (23)

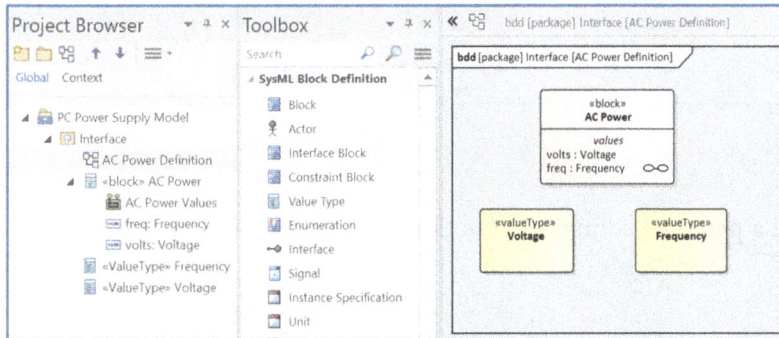

Figure 5-20 – Define something called AC power

One of the key differences between the two types of SysML ports is that full ports are typed by (ordinary) blocks while proxy ports are typed by (special) interface blocks. As the first step in our modeling process, we will model a block called "AC Power" as shown in Figure 5-20 with two value properties, one for voltage and one for frequency. (24)

---

(23) Personal computer "Do-It-Yourself" enthusiasts will notice that the following model is not actually quite right – current PC cases have a cutout which allows the power supply to present its AC power interface directly. However, we will gloss over that detail for the purposes of illustration.

(24) See *Value Properties* on page 93 for the procedure to set up value properties.

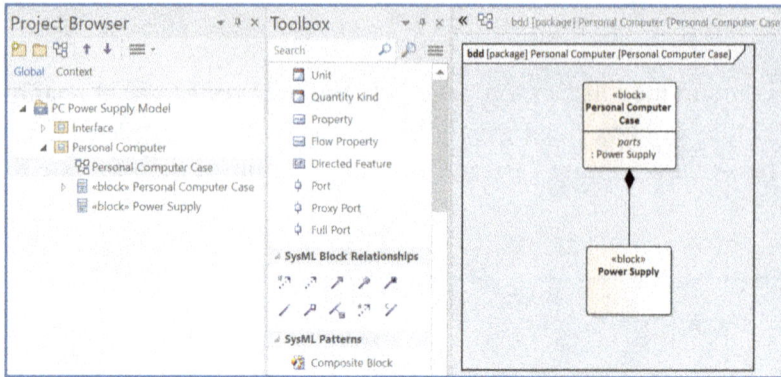

Figure 5-21 – Define the PC case

Next, model a personal computer case that contains a power supply.

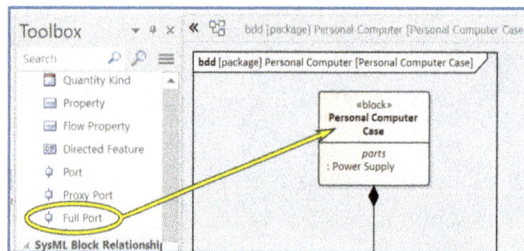

Figure 5-22 – Drag Full Port to personal computer case

From the toolbox, drag the "Full Port" icon the diagram and drop it on the personal computer case block.

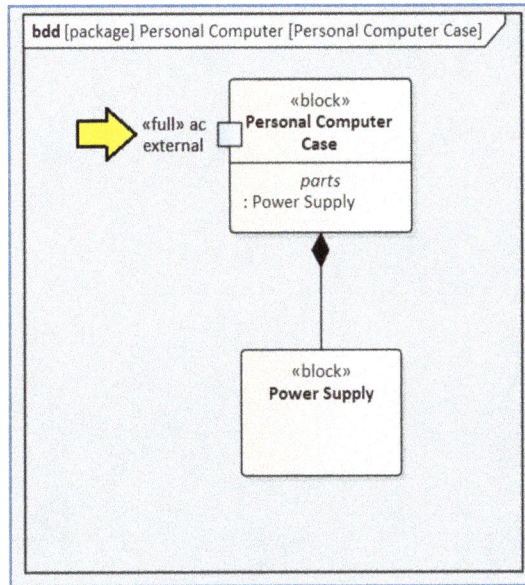

Figure 5-23 – Name the port

Double-click on the port and name it "ac external". You will also want to drag the label around and resize it to look nice.

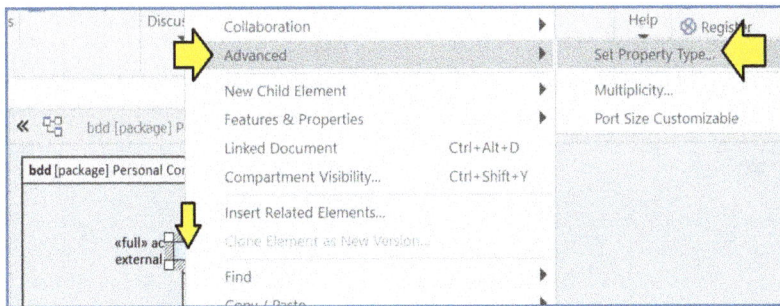

Figure 5-24 – Right-click to set property type

And now for a critical step - right-click on the port and select "Advanced" followed by "Set Property Type...".

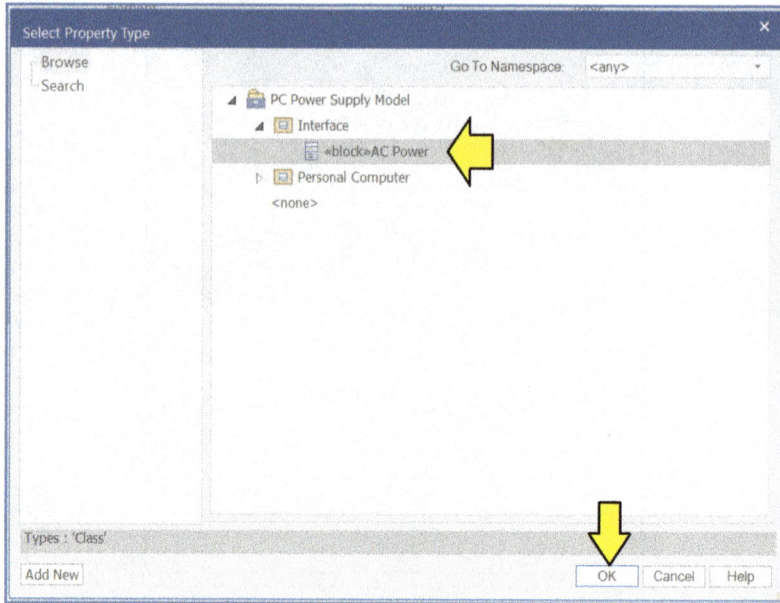

Figure 5-25 – Select AC power

Navigate to the "AC Power" block, select it, and click "OK".

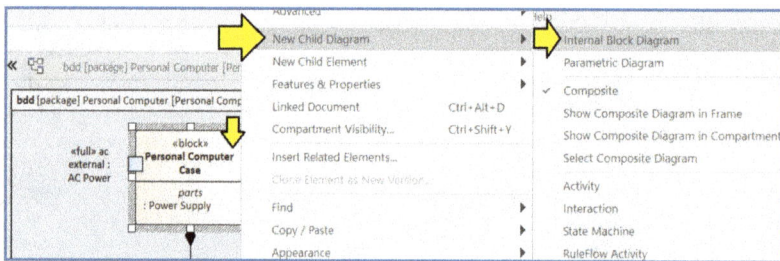

Figure 5-26 – Right-click and create internal block diagram

Right-click on the "Personal Computer Case" block and select "New Child Diagram" and then "Internal Block Diagram".

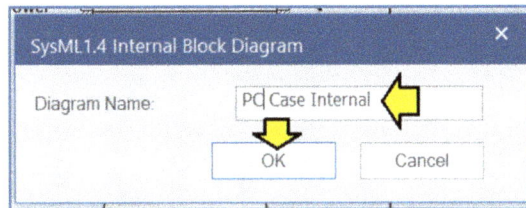

Figure 5-27 – Name the diagram and click OK

Name the diagram and click "OK".

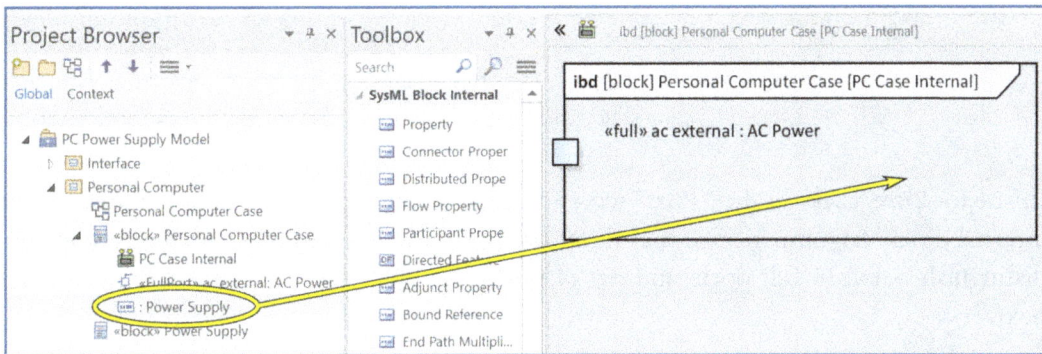

Figure 5-28 – Drag the power supply part to the diagram

In the project browser expand the "Personal Computer Case" block. Drag the ":Power Supply" part to the diagram.

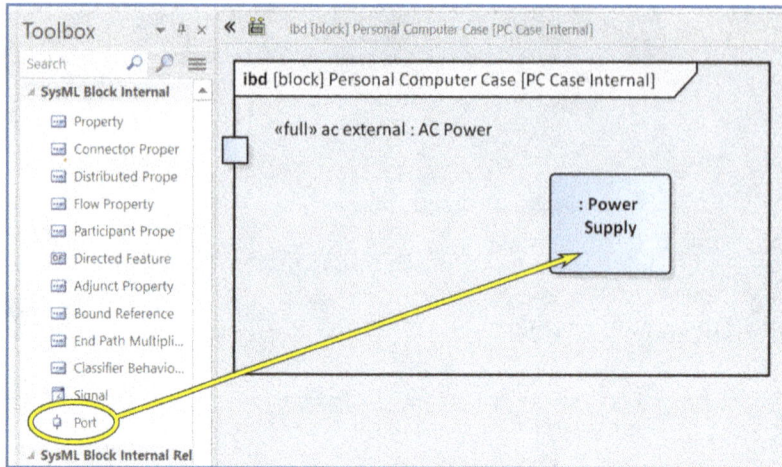

Figure 5-29 – Drag port to power supply

In the toolbox, click on the "Port" icon and drag it onto the power supply block in the internal block diagram. Notice that the toolbox for the internal block diagram does not distinguish between full ports and proxy ports. We will need to clarify that difference next.

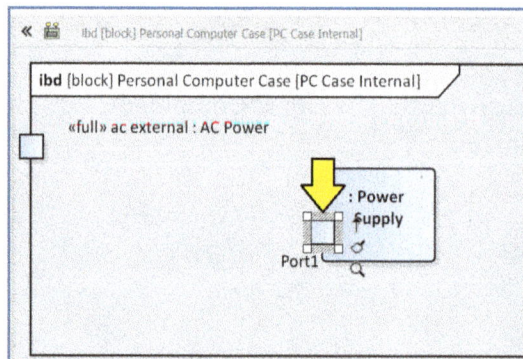

Figure 5-30 – Double-click on port

Double-click on the port.

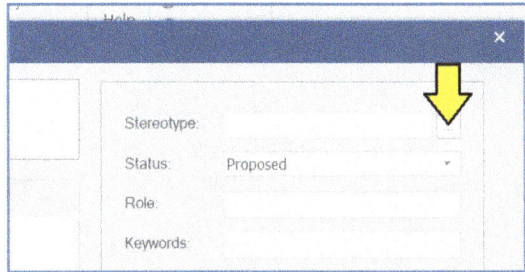

Figure 5-31 – Click on the 3 dots

Once the properties dialog box for the port opens, find the stereotype field. Next to this field you will see a square with three dots in it. Click on this square.

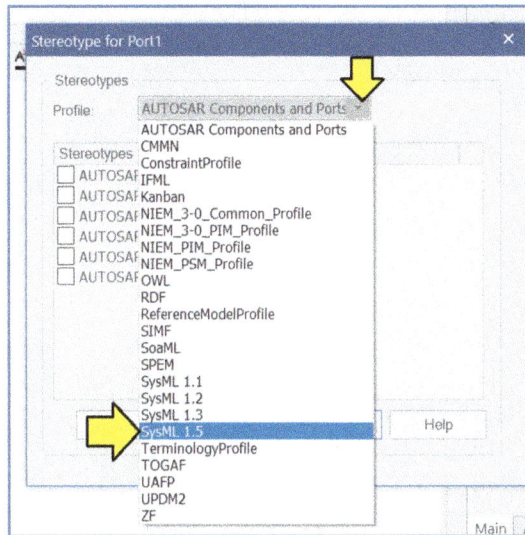

Figure 5-32 – Select the SysML 1.5 profile

Pull down the menu for the profile and select the SysML 1.5 profile

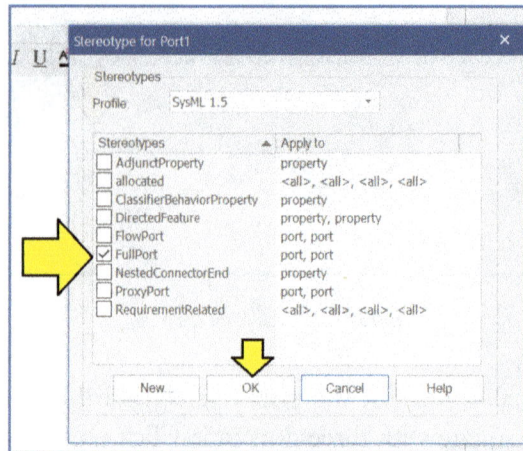

Figure 5-33 – Select FullPort and Click OK

Select "FullPort" and Click "OK".

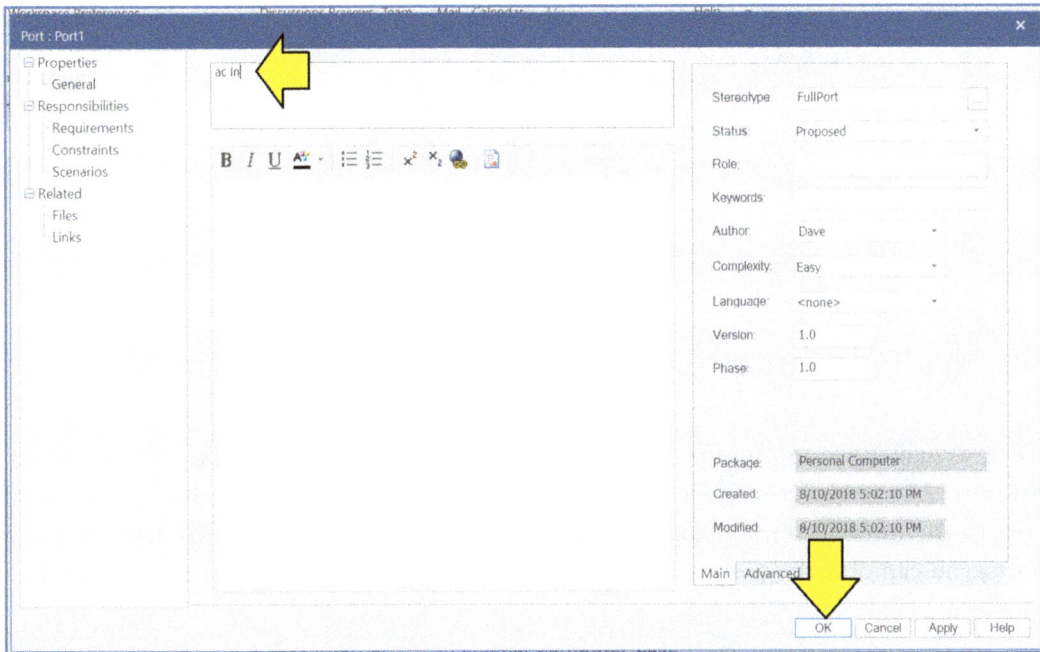

Figure 5-34 – Name the port and click OK

Name the port "ac in" and click "OK". Next we need to set the type for the port.

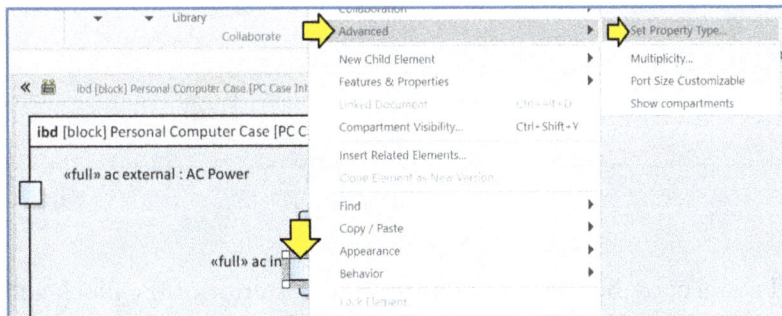

Figure 5-35 – Right-click on the port and select set property type

Right-click on the port and select "Advanced" followed by "Set Property Type…".

Navigate to and select the AC Power block as shown in Figure 5-25 on page 136.

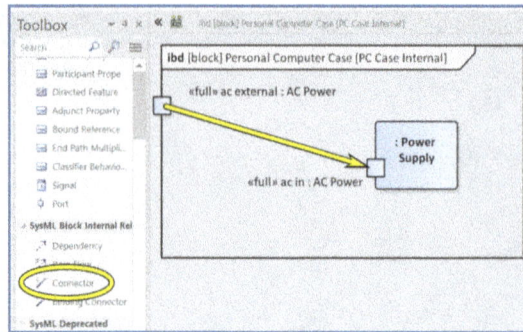

Figure 5-36 – Drag connector from the external port to the internal port

Next, we will use a **connector** to create a connection between the full port to the internal port. In the toolbox select "Connector" and drag a connection from the external port to the internal port as shown in Figure 5-36. After you have connected the two ports, you can drag the corners of the connector around until the diagram looks nice.

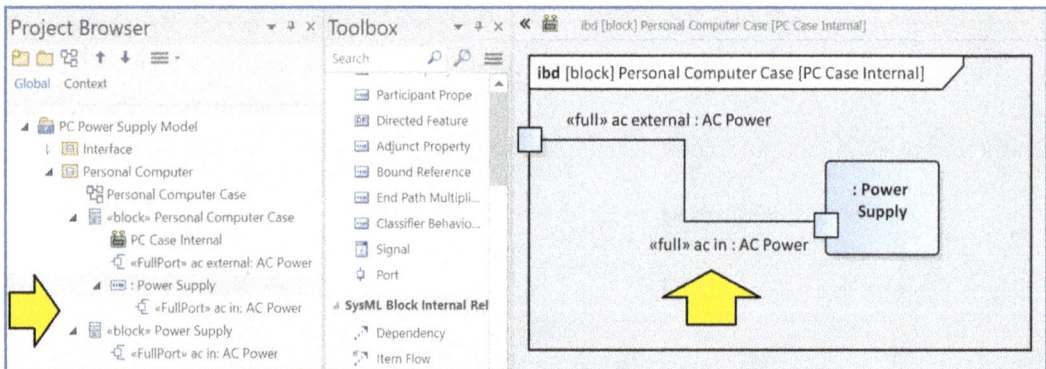

Figure 5-37 – Finished

The finished connection between a full port on the exterior of the block and a compatible full port on a part within the block is shown in Figure 5-37.

Proxy Ports

Next we will turn our attention to proxy ports. Unlike full ports, proxy ports are typed by a special SysML element called an **interfaceBlock**.

In order to illustrate the steps for modeling proxy ports, we are going to develop a model for a special robotic fruit picker. Being the latest in high-tech agricultural equipment innovation, our robotic fruit picker can flexibly pick different types of fruit and create juice from that fruit as it is rolling through the orchard. Our marketing department has decided to call this product the "Robotic Juice Picker".

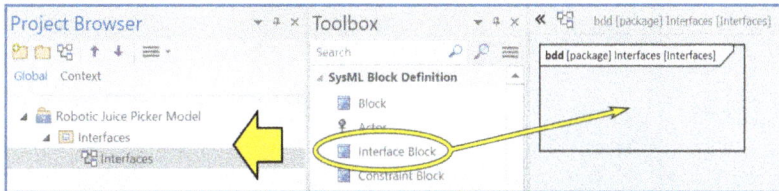

Figure 5-38 – Create model, add diagram, drag Interface Block to diagram

As a first step, create a simple model, give it a package called "Interfaces", add a block definition diagram, and drag the "Interface Block" icon to the diagram as shown in Figure 5-38.

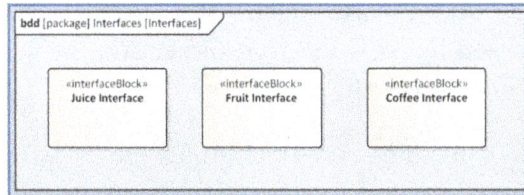

Figure 5-39 – Create three interface types

Create interface blocks called "Fruit Interface", "Juice Interface", and "Coffee Interface".

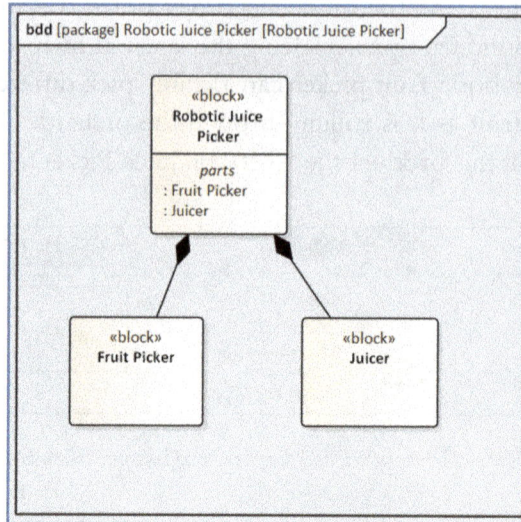

Figure 5-40 – Set up basic hardware structure

Next add a package to the model called: "Robotic Juice Picker". Inside the package create a block definition diagram also called: "Robotic Juice Picker". Add blocks for the robotic juice picker and its parts the fruit picker and the juicer. Add composition relationships as shown in Figure 5-40.

Now we are ready to do something more interesting. We know that the juice has to get out of the robot somehow, but marketing is still not sure whether it needs to come out as a stream of liquid or already packaged in recyclable single serving containers. As such, at this stage in the modeling of our system we are going to use proxy ports at the overall level and on the juicer itself.

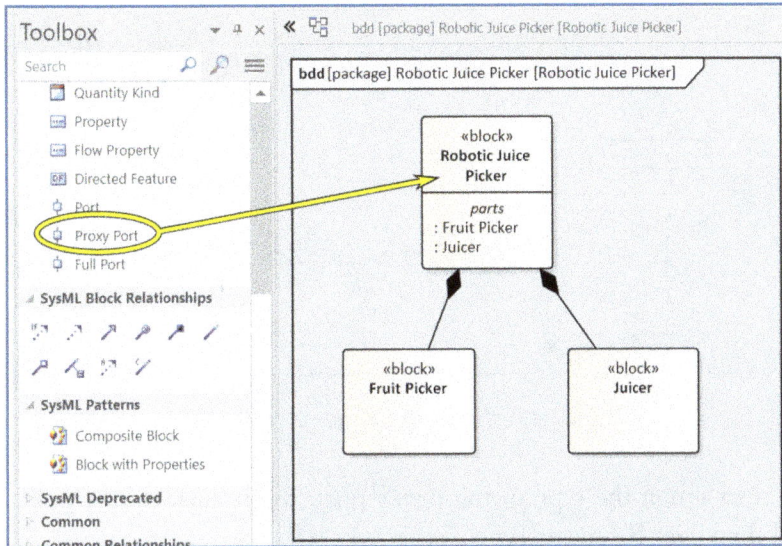

Figure 5-41 – Drag Proxy Port to the block

From the toolbox drag the "Proxy Port" icon to the diagram and drop it on the "Robotic Juice Picker" block.

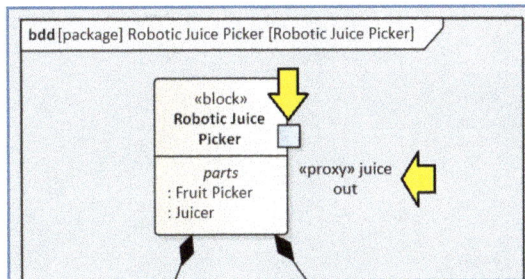

Figure 5-42 – Drag port around border to right, double-click and name

Drag the port around the border of the block until it is on the righthand side. Double-click on the port and name it: "juice out".

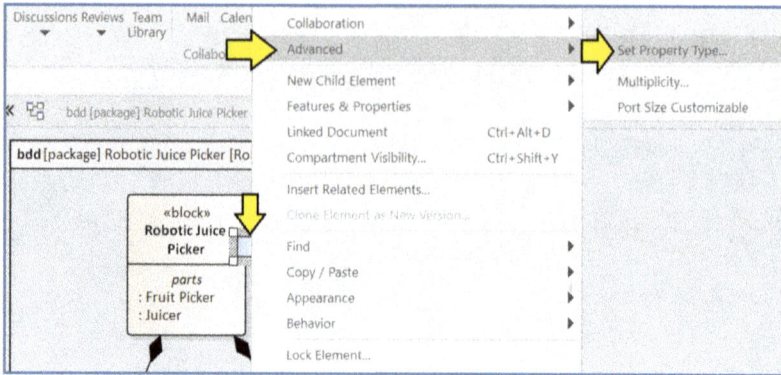

Figure 5-43 – Use context menu to set property type

Next we need to assign the type of the proxy port. Right-click on the port, select "Advanced" and then "Set Property Type...".

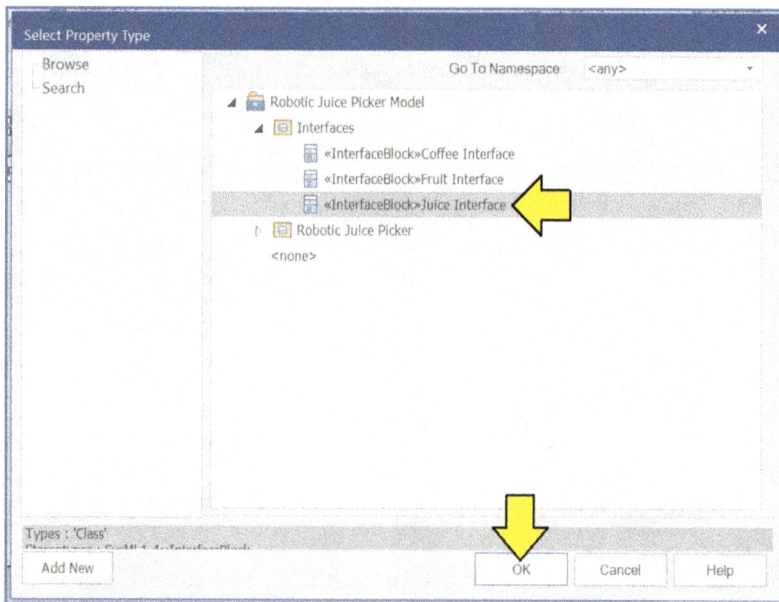

Figure 5-44 – Select Juice Interface

Navigate to the juice interface block, select it, and click "OK".

Now we are ready to create an internal block diagram for the robotic juice picker and connect things together.

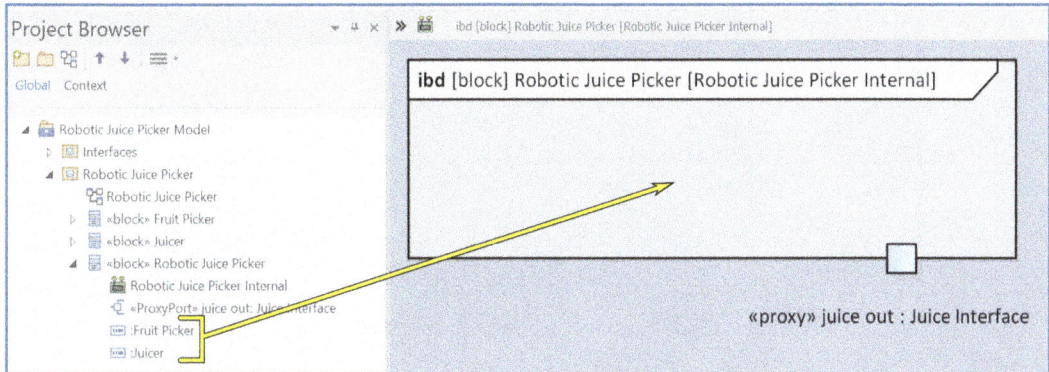

Figure 5-45 – Create an internal block diagram and drag parts to it

Create an internal block diagram for the robotic juice picker block. [25] The new internal block diagram should show the port on its frame, but probably not in a very convenient location. Drag the port around the frame until it located on the bottom border of the frame as shown in Figure 5-45. From the project browser, drag the ":Fruit Picker" and ":Juicer" parts to the diagram. **Note:** be careful to drag the parts from within the "Robotic Juice Picker" block; do NOT drag the blocks that define those parts!

Now we are ready to add ports to the ":Fruit Picker" and ":Juicer" parts. Notice that the toolbox for the internal block diagram only contains a "Port" icon. There are no proxy or full port icons. If we need to, we can use the generic "Port" icon and assign the "ProxyPort" stereotype after we have added the ports to the parts. However, in this case we will use generic (untyped) ports.

---

[25] Right-click on the block in the project browser and use the context menu to add the internal block diagram to the element.

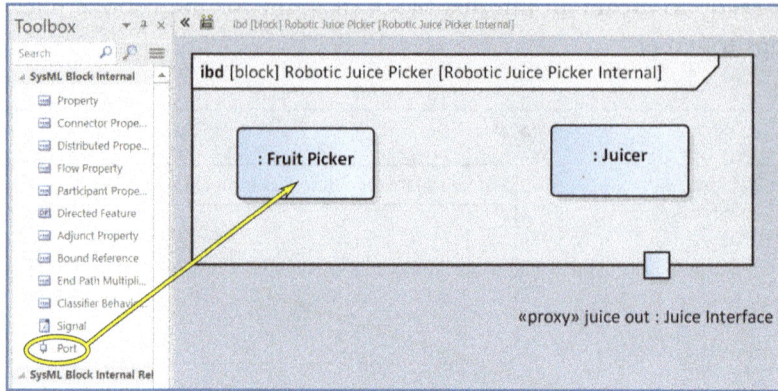

Figure 5-46 – Drag Port to the Fruit Picker

From the toolbox, drag the port icon to the ":Fruit Picker" part in the diagram.

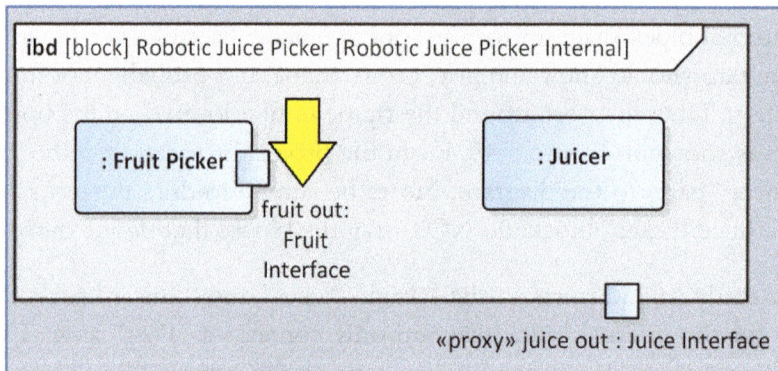

Figure 5-47 – Name port and set type

Click on the port and name it: "fruit out". Use the procedure shown in Figure 5-43 on page 146 to set the type to "Fruit Interface".

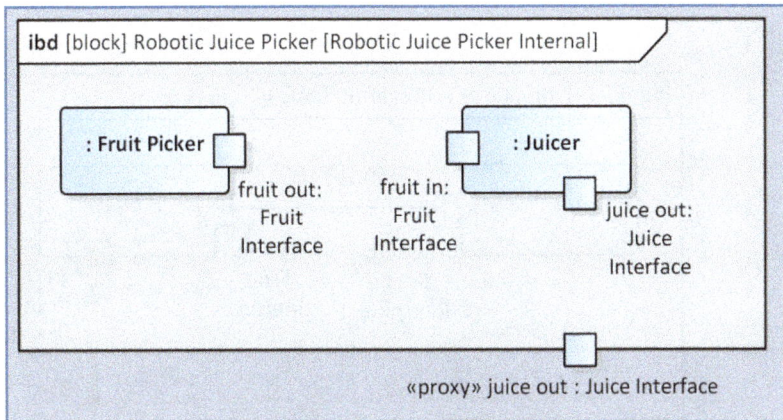

Figure 5-48 – Add remaining ports

Add two proxy ports to the juicer block. Note that the ports on the internal parts do not need to be proxy ports. Here we are using untyped ports.

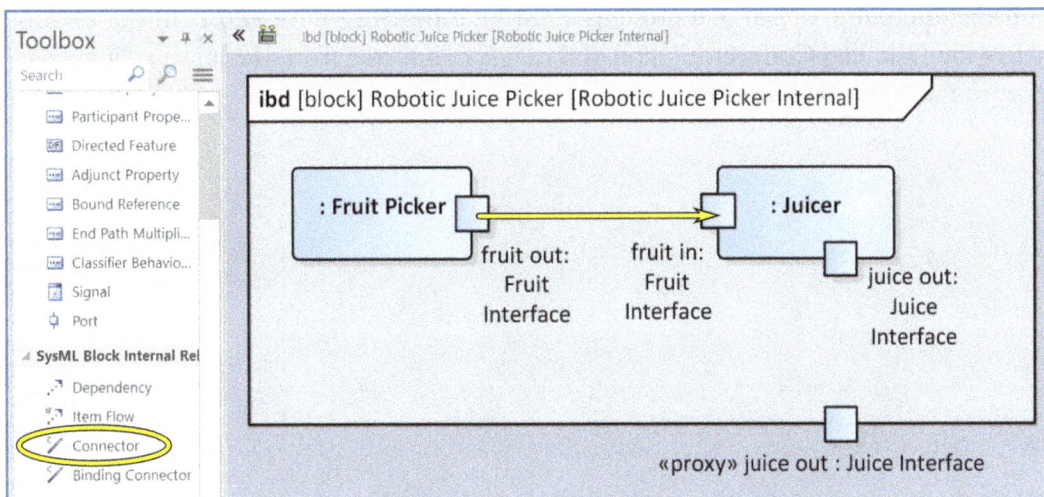

Figure 5-49 – Use a connector to connect the picker to the juicer

In the toolbox select the "Connector" icon and drag a connector from the picker's "fruit out" port to the juicer's "fruit in" port.

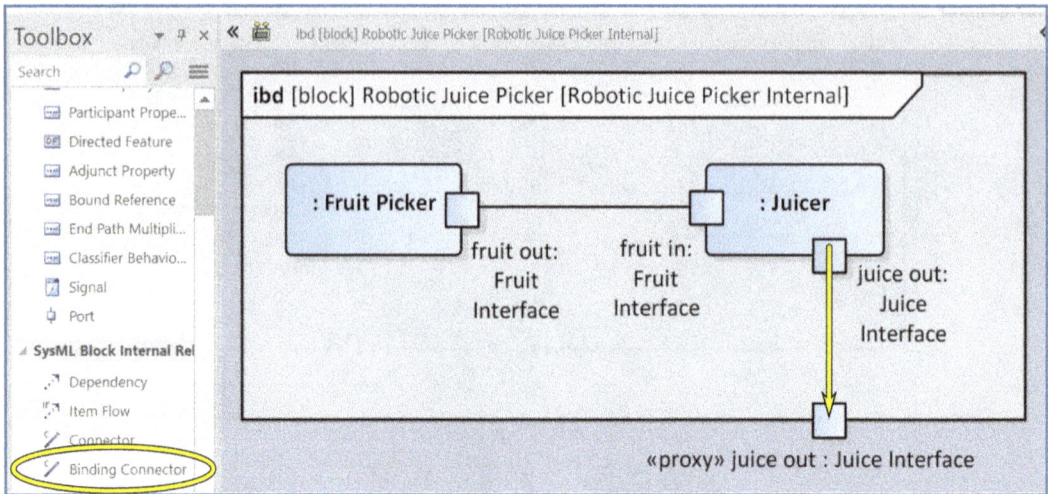

Figure 5-50 – Use a binding connector to connect the juicer to the proxy port

Now, we are ready to connect the proxy port. The connection between a proxy port and the internal part that it represents must be a **binding connector**. In the toolbox select the "Binding Connector" icon and drag a connector from the juicer's "juice out" port to the "juice out" proxy port.

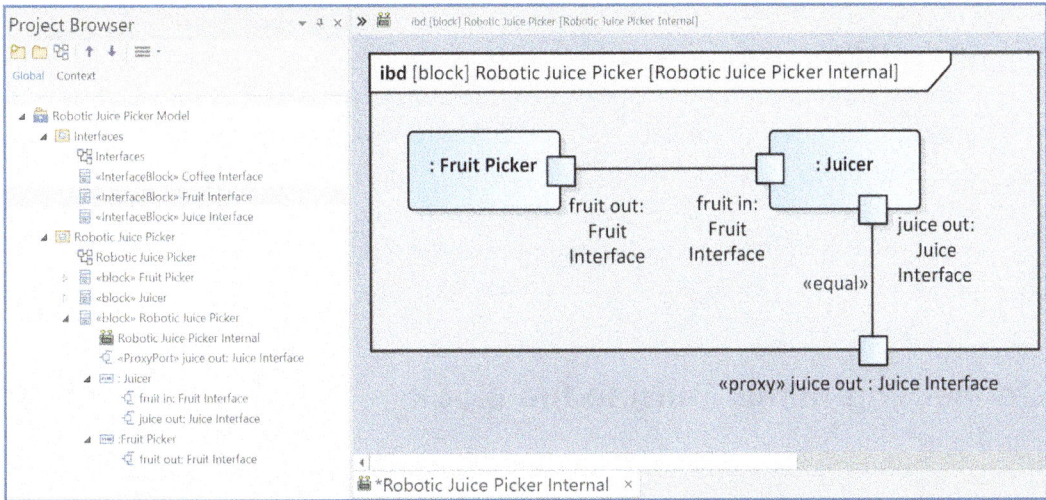

Figure 5-51 – Completed model

Figure 5-51 shows the completed model. The picker picks "Fruit" which might be apples or oranges and passes the fruit to the juicer. The juicer creates "Juice" which is made available outside of the system.

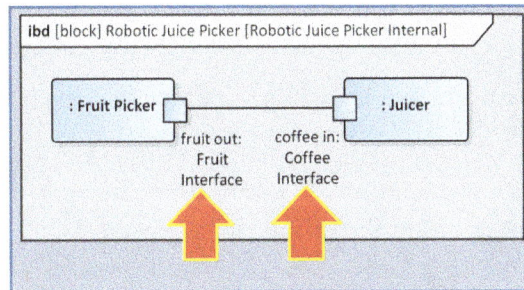

Figure 5-52 – Mismatched interface blocks

Figure 5-52 shows an incorrect model. A port of type "Fruit Inteface" is connected to a port of type "Coffee Interface".

Model Validation

Although it is beyond the scope of this book, on a larger project your team might want to set up model validation to detect consistency problems like this. The ability to algorithmically detect model inconsistences like the one shown in Figure 5-52 is an important benefit of using SysML or other model-based systems engineering approaches on large and complex projects.

Connecting Things Outside the Block

How do I show connections from parts inside an internal block diagram to other blocks that are outside the block that owns the diagram? Such connections can be shown if the block owning the diagram and the external block are connected by a reference association. The external block will show up in the internal block diagram as a box with a dashed border.

In order to illustrate the steps to model such a connection, we will create a somewhat simplified model of the robotic juice picker from the previous section:

- We will only model the robotic juice picker and one internal part – the juicer.

- We will skip the ports as they will just clutter the diagrams we are making for this purpose. [26]

- We will introduce the concept of a remote monitoring system that (somehow) monitors the juicer within the robotic juice picker.

---

[26] **Note:** on a real project you would probably keep the entire model and just make additional diagrams that showed only the elements and the attributes of the elements relevant to the particular discussion at hand. That is the key point of the model-based systems engineering (MBSE) approach. However, this is an instructional text, so I want the example model itself to be as simple as possible. As such, we will just create a new version of the model with only the relevant elements.

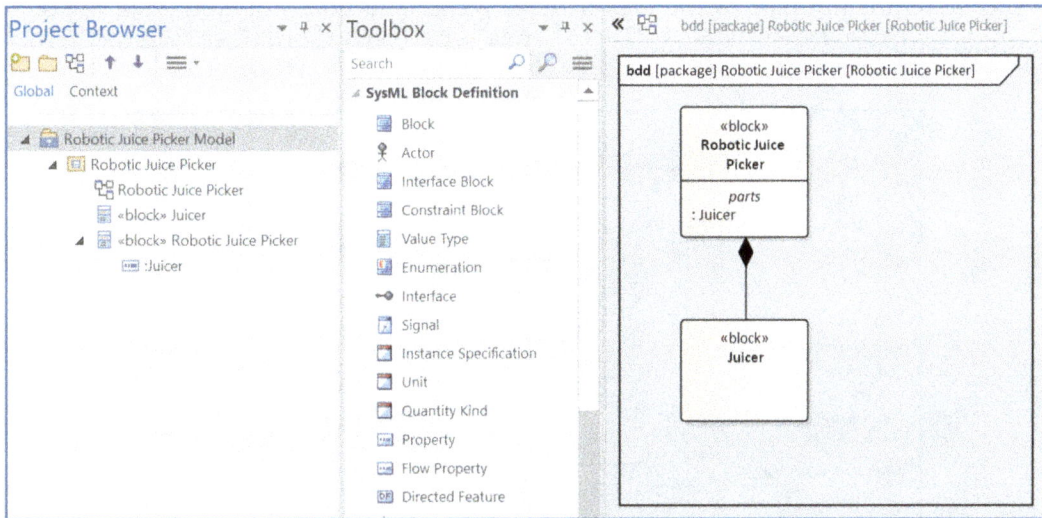

Figure 5-53 – Start with the basic model

Start by creating a basic model as shown in Figure 5-53.

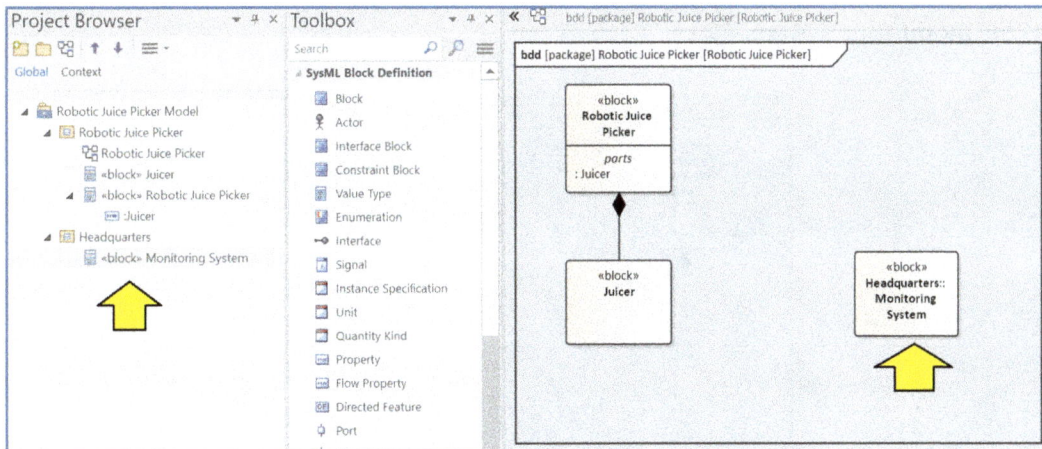

Figure 5-54 – Add headquarters monitoring system

Create a new package called "Headquarters". Right-click on the package in the project browser and add a block to the package called "Monitoring System". Drag the block to the diagram. Since the block is owned by a different package than the diagram, the block will be displayed as "Headquarters::Monitoring System". Notice that the monitoring system is not part of the robotic juice picker and does not (yet) have any relationship with it.

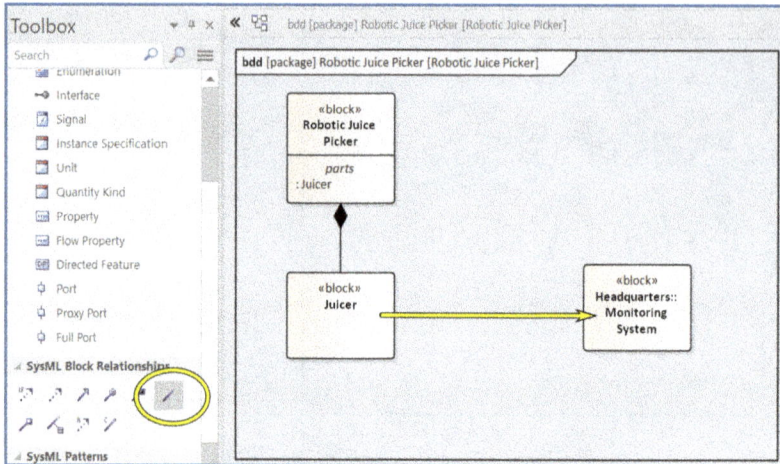

Figure 5-55 – Drag a reference association

Drag a reference association from the juicer (which is a part of the robotic juice picker) to the monitoring system.

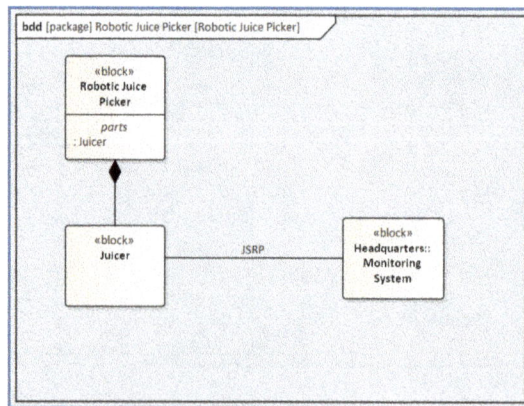

Figure 5-56 – Name the association JSRP

Double-click on the reference association and name it "JSRP". [27]

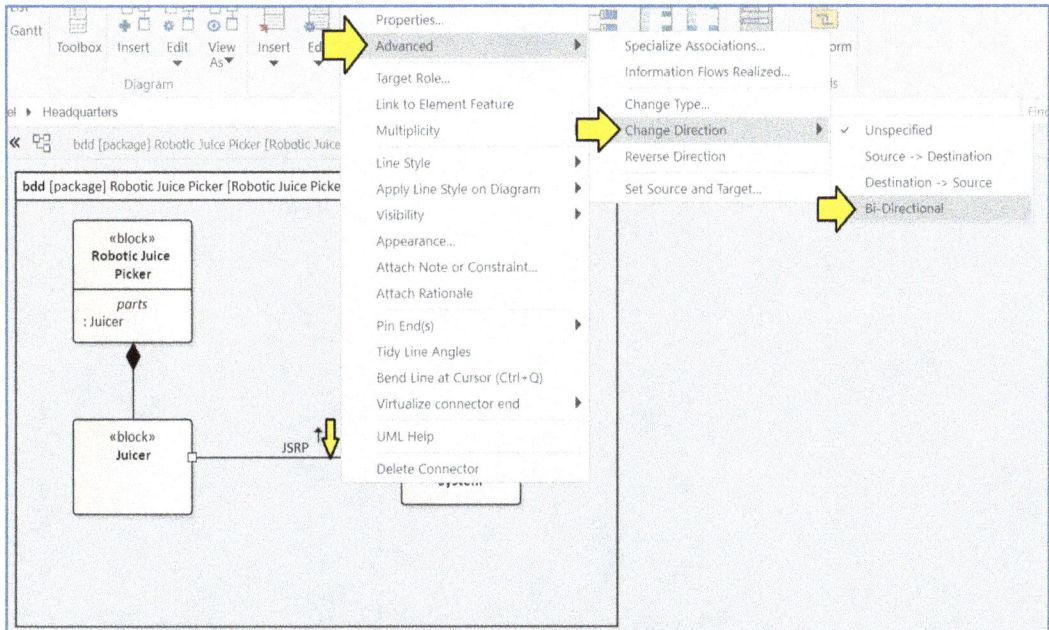

Figure 5-57 – Make the link bi-directional

Next you will need to make the link bi-directional. [28] Right-click on the link, select "Advanced", select "Change Direction", and select "Bi-Directional".

---

[27] "JSRP" stands for "Juicer Status Reporting Protocol". Someday you are going to build up a large international standards organization to discuss revisions to this important protocol.

[28] The need to make the link bi-directional is not mentioned in the SysML standard. This seems to be an internal requirement of *Enterprise Architect*.

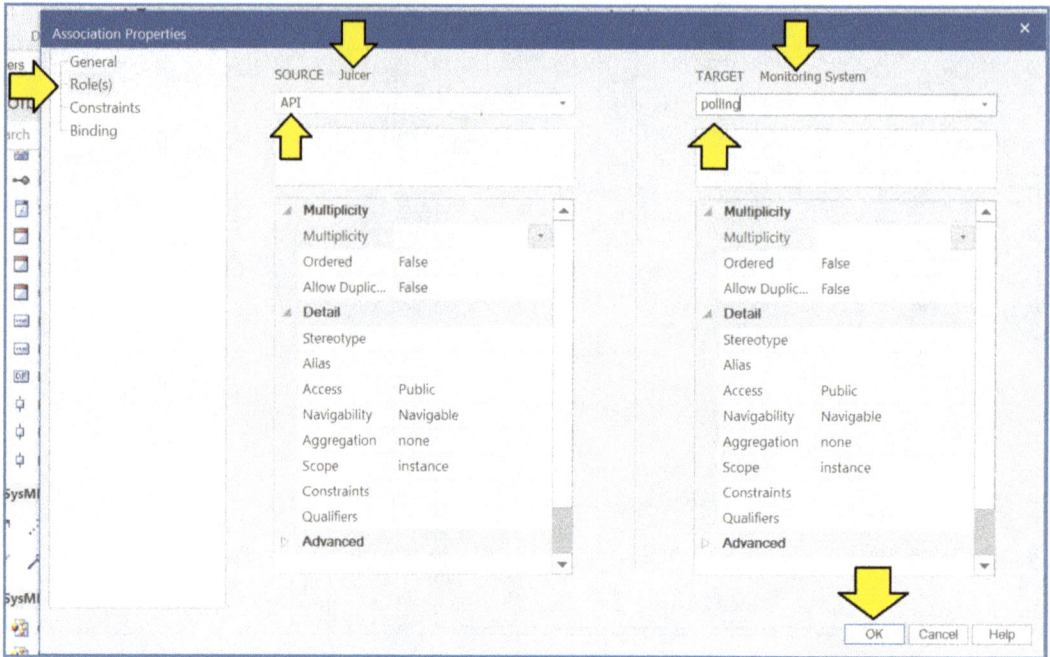

Figure 5-58 – Assign roles

Next we will name the roles of the ends of the association. Double-click the link to open the association properties dialog box. Select the "Role(s)" tab. Name the juicer end "API" for "Application Programming Interface". Name the monitoring system end "polling".

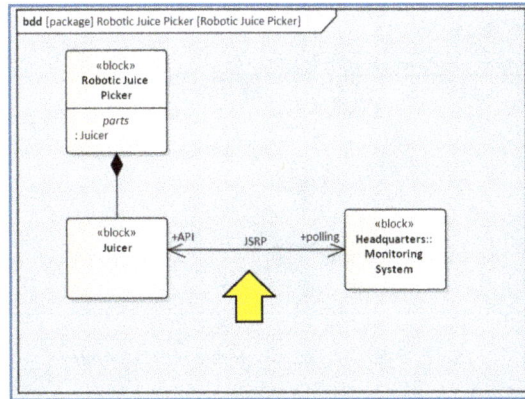

Figure 5-59 – Reference association defined

The completed reference association is shown in Figure 5-59. Before continuing, I need to point out two things:

- We are working on a block definition diagram which is intended for defining types, not instances. As such, the "JSRP" reference association represents a type of association between the juicer and the monitoring system, not an actual instance of a connection.

- One of the charming ideas in UML that SysML has inherited is the idea that the named roles actually end up belonging to the opposite ends of the association. We will soon see that the "polling" role is owned by the juicer and the "API" role is owned by the monitoring system.

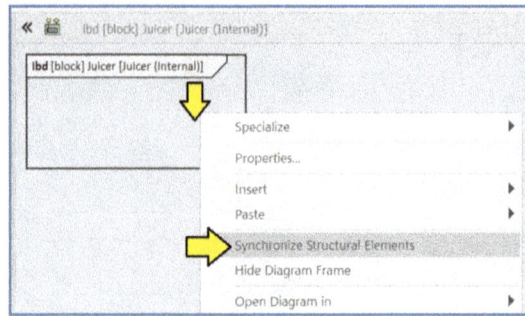

Figure 5-60 – Synchronize structural elements

Now we have to do a few steps to get the model updated. As a first step, create an internal block diagram for the juicer. Right-click in the body of that internal block diagram and select "Synchronize Structural Elements".

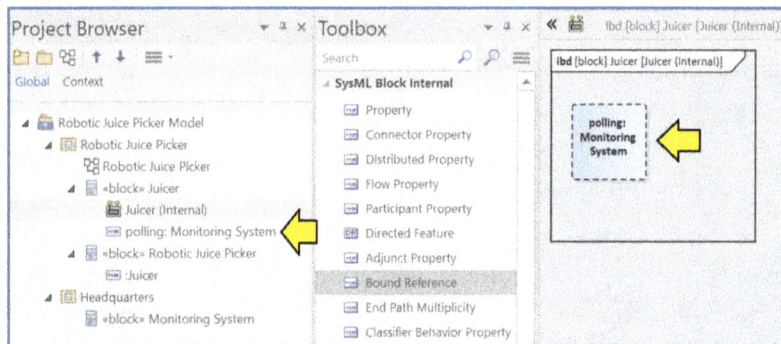

Figure 5-61 – Elements have been added

After updating structural elements, we now see that the juicer has an association with the "polling" end attached to the monitoring system.

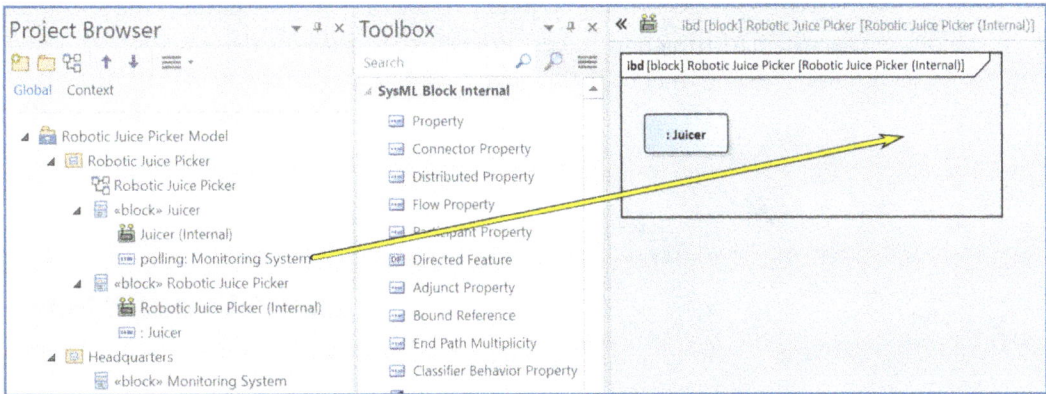

Figure 5-62 – Drag polling property to internal block diagram

Now we are ready to make the internal block diagram for the robotic juice picker. Right-click on the robotic juice picker in the project browser and create an internal block diagram. The internal block diagram will not initially show the juicer. However, if you use the "Synchronize Structural Elements" feature as shown in Figure 5-62 it will appear. After you have done that, drag the "polling:Monitoring System" property from the project browser to the diagram.

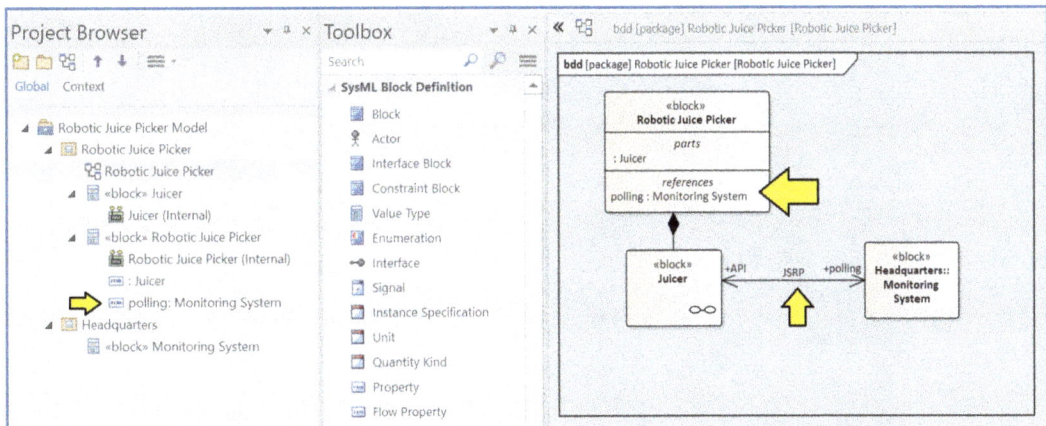

Figure 5-63 – Model consistency problem

The dragging operation will produce the dashed-line-border box in the internal block diagram called for by the SysML standard. However, the dragging operation will also introduce a consistency problem in the model. As shown, in Figure 5-63 the "polling:Monitoring System" property now appears to belong to the parent robotic juice picker block rather than to the child juicer block – even though the association arrow still correctly connects to the juicer block.

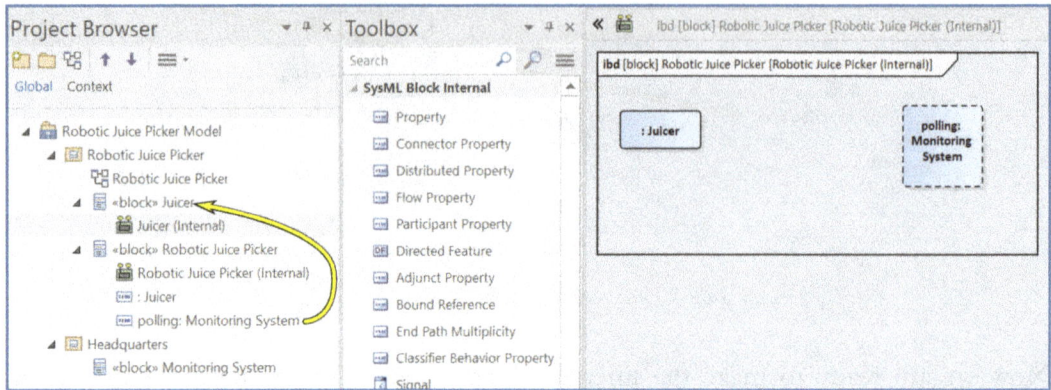

Figure 5-64 – Drag property back to juicer

Fortunately, the inconsistency problem is easy to fix: just drag the property back to the juicer block as shown in Figure 5-64.

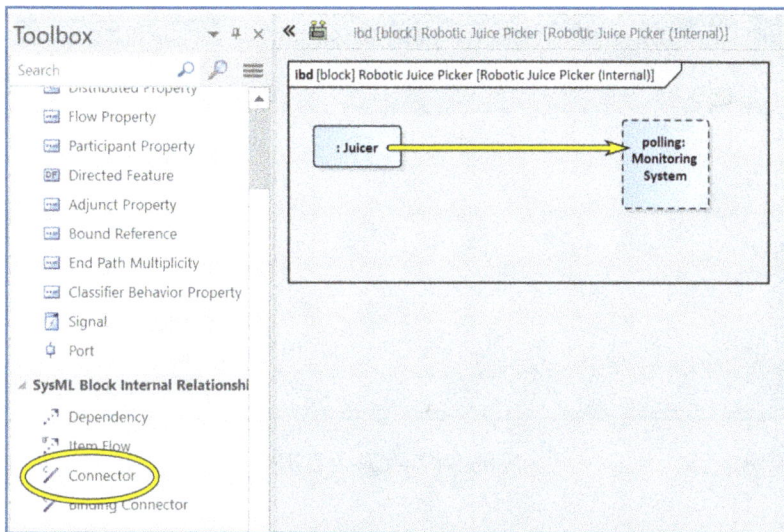

Figure 5-65 – Drag connector

Now we are ready to create an instance of the previously modeled "JSRP" association type. Select the connector icon in the toolbox and drag the connector from the juicer to the monitoring system.

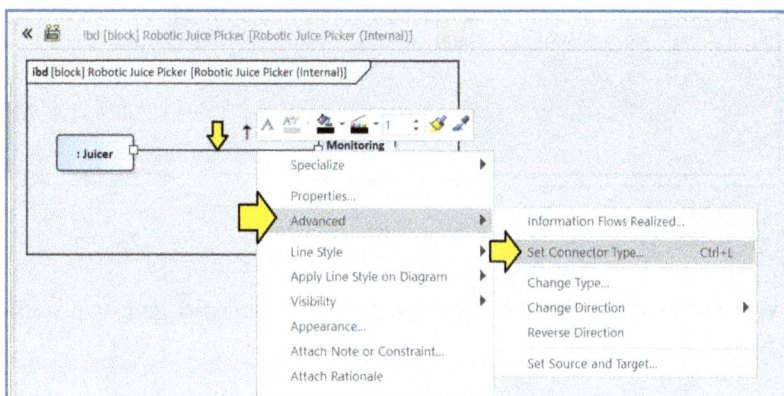

Figure 5-66 – Right-click to set connector type

Right-click on the connector, select "Advanced", and select "Set Connector Type...".

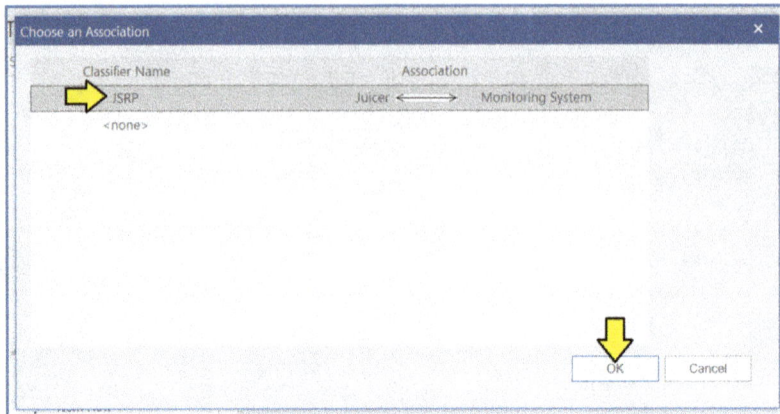

Figure 5-67 – Choose JSRP

In "Choose an Association" dialog box, select "JSRP" and click "OK".

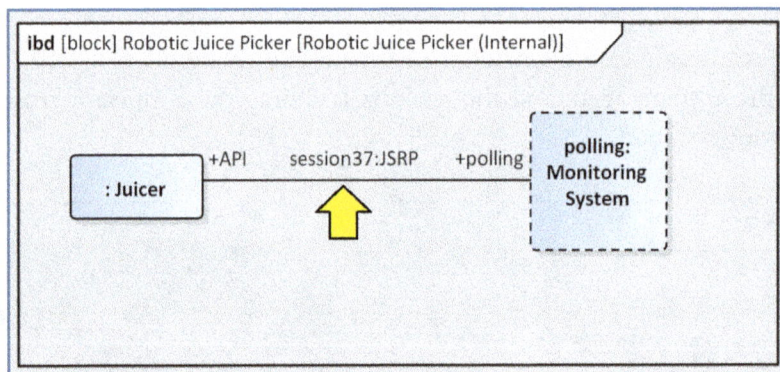

Figure 5-68 – Name the connector

Optionally, you can double-click on the connector again and give it a name like "session37".

Further Study

Here is a list of further topics you will want to study to hone your expertise.

- **association blocks** – typed connectors can also be typed by association blocks. Association blocks can (should) have an internal block diagram. Association blocks have special "participant" property.
    - [Friedenthal] – page 130

- **conjugation notation** – There is a small notation which we did not show that adds a tilde in front of a port to indicate that the direction of flow in or out of the port is reversed. Conjugation becomes important when you start using **flow properties** to indicate the direction of flow through a point. Note that in SysML version 1.6, the conjugation notation has been moved from the port to the interface block that types the port.
    - [Delligatti] – page 69
    - [Friedenthal] – page 126
    - [SysML1.5] – section 9.3.1.6 on page 82
    - [SysML1.6] – section C.7 on page 237

- **dot notation** – for deeply nested parts
    - [Delligatti] – page 72
    - [Friedenthal] – page 125

- **encapsulation** – allows the hiding of the contents of a block, a useful design strategy.
    - [Delligatti] – page 74
    - [Friedenthal] – page 125

- **flow properties** – are useful for showing the direction of flow through a port. Flow properties can also be typed to identify what kinds of blocks can flow through a port. **Flow Properties** specify what "can" flow through a port. **Item Flows** show what "does" flow through a port.

    - [Friedenthal] – page 139
    - [SysML1.5] – section 9.1.4 on page 76

- **item flows** – show the transmission of a certain type of content, typically a block. **Flow Properties** specify what "can" flow through a port. **Item Flows** show what "does" flow through a port.

    - [Delligatti] – page 69
    - [Friedenthal] – page 139
    - [SysML1.5] – section 9.1.4 on page 76

- **multiplicity** – There are two different notations for showing multiplicity on an internal block diagram.

    - [Delligatti] – page 67

Chapter 6 – Package Diagrams

Package diagrams help you show your stakeholders how your model is organized.

Visualizing Model Organization

One thing I have personally used package diagrams for is to make diagrams that show stakeholders the hierarchical relationship between certain model elements that live in different parts of the model. It is also possible to use a package diagram as a tool for visually creating the package hierarchy of your model. We will illustrate both techniques by recreating a version of the "Robotic Juice Picker" from the section *Connecting Things Outside the Block* on page 152.

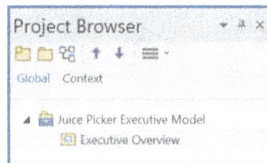

Figure 6-1 – Create model and base package

This will be an "Executive Model". [29] Create the basic model as shown in Figure 6-1.

---

[29] An "Executive Model" would be a model scrubbed of annoying, messy detail.

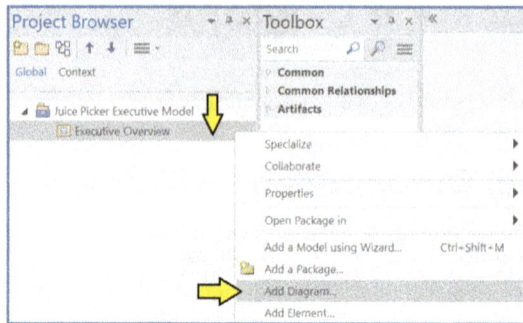

Figure 6-2 – Add a diagram

Right-click on the main package and select "Add Diagram...".

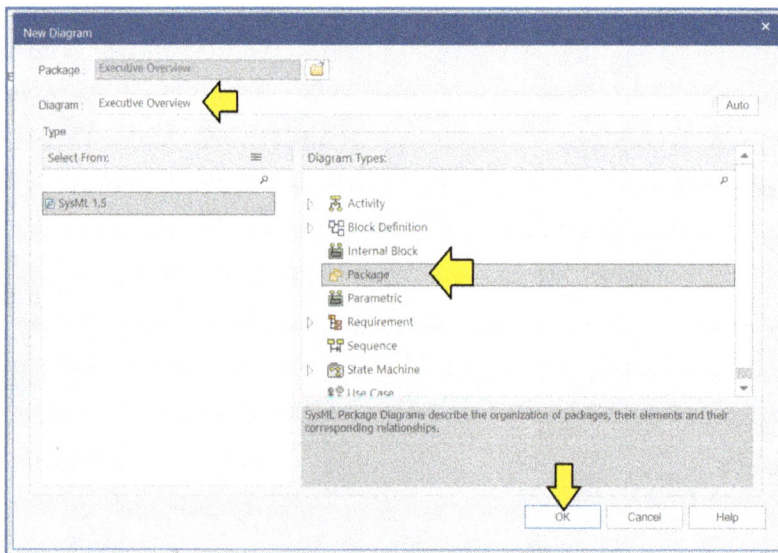

Figure 6-3 – Add a package diagram

Accept the default name of "Executive Overview". Select "Package". Click "OK".

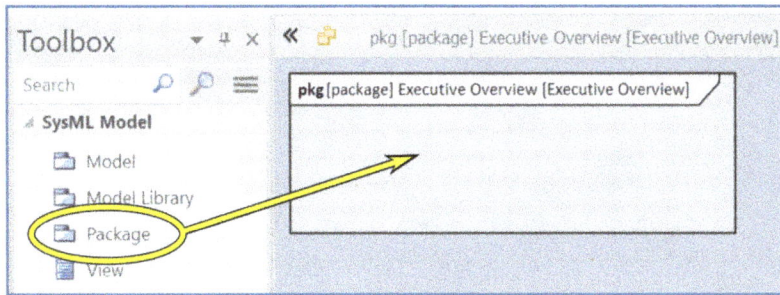

Figure 6-4 – Drag package to diagram

From the toolbox drag the package icon to the diagram.

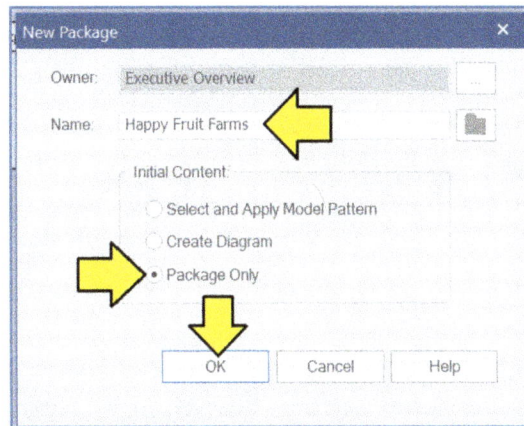

Figure 6-5 – Name the package

Name the package "Happy Fruit Farms". Select "Package Only". Click "OK".

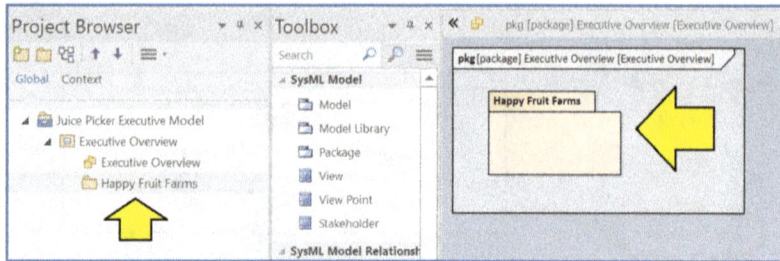

Figure 6-6 – Package created

Figure 6-6 shows that a package "Happy Fruit Farms" has been created nested within the "Executive Overview" package.

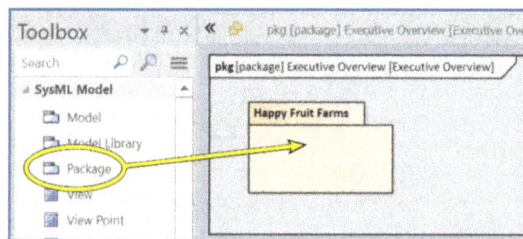

Figure 6-7 – Drag a package to within the first package

From the toolbox, drag another package to within the "Happy Fruit Farms" package. Note that you will find it easier to perform this step if you first drag the first package to make it larger.

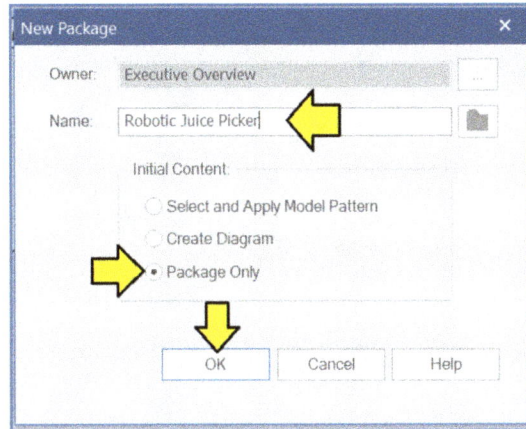

Figure 6-8 – Name the package

Name the package "Robotic Juice Picker".

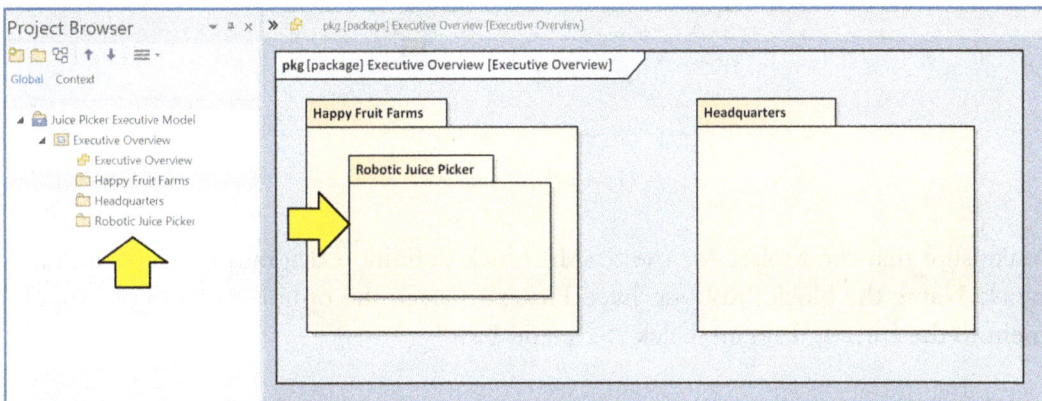

Figure 6-9 – Add another package

Rearrange the sizes and add another package called "Headquarters" as shown in Figure 6-9. Notice that the package "Robotic Juice Picker" appears to be nested within the "Happy Fruit Farms" package in the diagram but not in the project browser. We will go into this curious behavior in more detail in *Containment Relationship* on page 174. In the meantime, trust that the package is in fact nested.

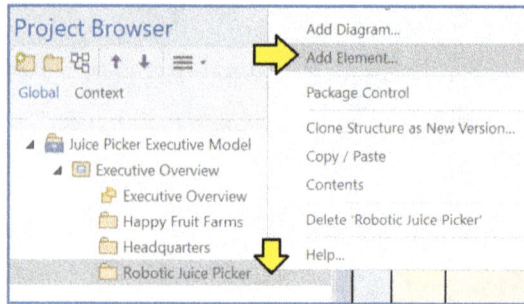

Figure 6-10 – Add element

Right-click on the "Robotic Juice Picker" package in the project browser and select "Add Element...".

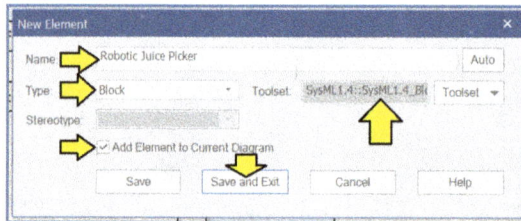

Figure 6-11 – Add block

Make sure that the toolset for the SysML block definition diagram is selected. Add a block. Name the block "Robotic Juice Picker". Check the option to add the new element to the current diagram. Click "Save and Exit".

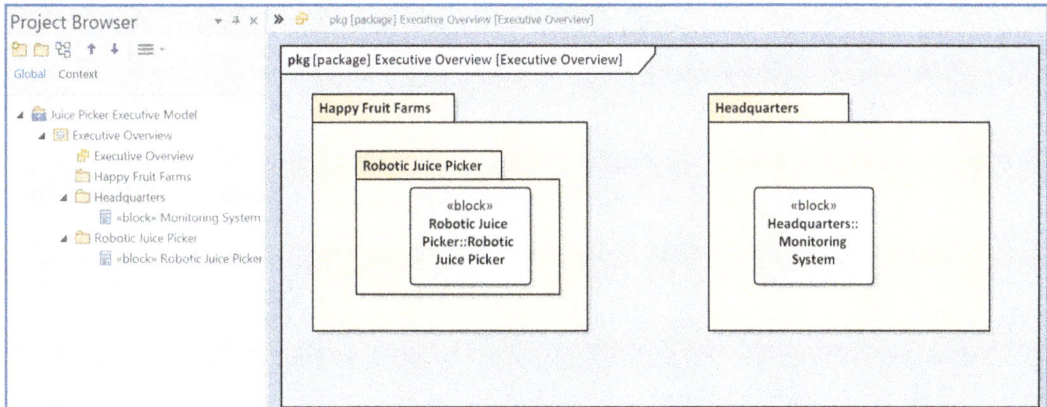

Figure 6-12 – Add another block

Adjust sizes and add a block called "Monitoring System" to the headquarters package as shown in Figure 6-12.

Make Toolbox Visible Again

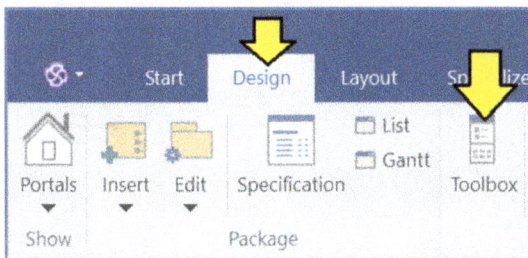

Oops! I hid the toolbox. You can always make the toolbox visible again by selecting the "Design" tab in the ribbon and then clicking on "Toolbox".

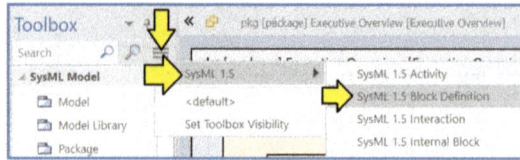

Figure 6-13 – Select block definition diagram toolbox

Next we are going to add a reference association. However, the reference association icon is not part of the package diagram toolbox. We will need the block definition diagram toolbox. Click on the three-bar logo in the toolbox header. Select *SysML 1.5*. Select "SysML 1.5 Block Definition".

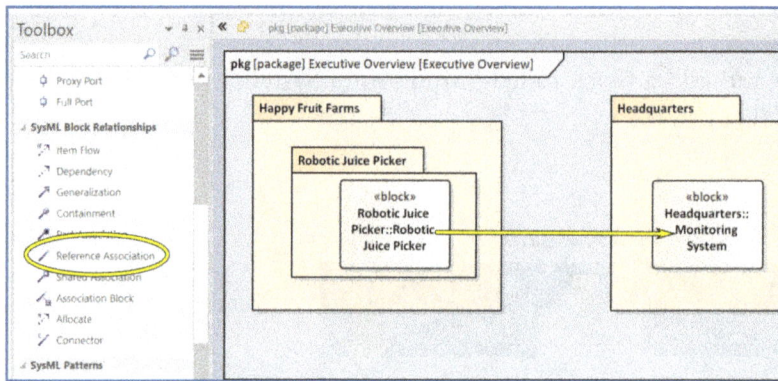

Figure 6-14 – Drag reference association

Drag a reference association between the two blocks.

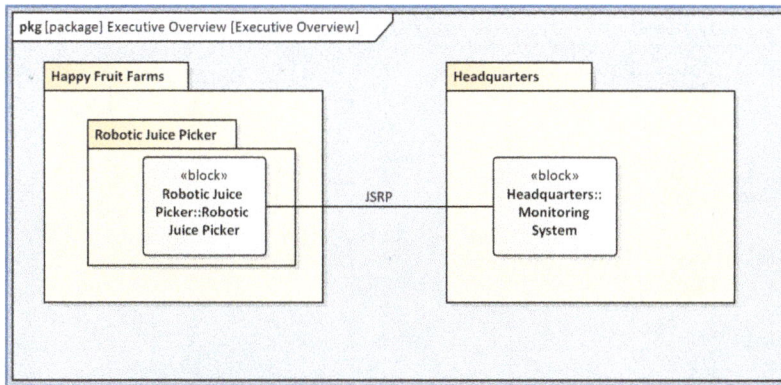

Figure 6-15 – Name the reference association

Name the reference association "JSRP" for "Juicer Status Reporting Protocol". Now we have a diagram suitable for explaining something to an executive.

The Proper Way to Name and Organize Packages

There isn't one. "What!? You aren't going to give us the perfect, universal, canonical structure for naming and organizing packages?!" Well, there certainly isn't any one answer that fits every system and every project. The famous Kung Fu master Bruce Lee is said to have once remarked that "Good form is what works". In a similar vein, my opinion on naming and organizing packages can be described as follows:

> *The proper way to organize and name your packages is the way that makes it as easy and intuitive as possible for your particular stakeholders to find what they are looking for.*

Import Relationship

SysML defines a relationship for importing one package into another.

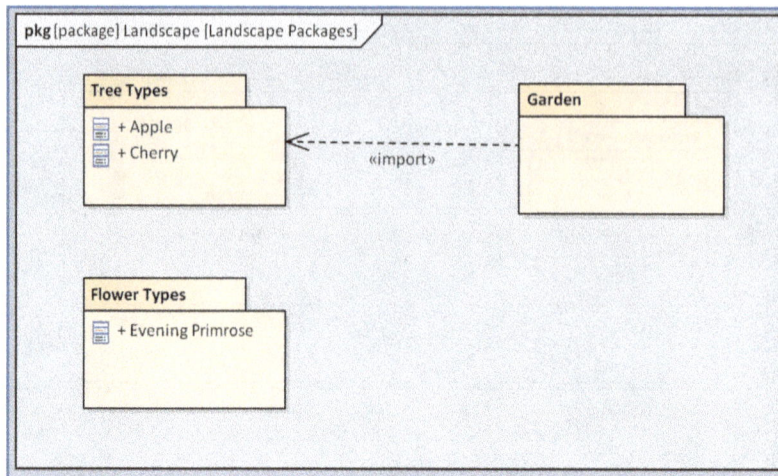

Figure 6-16 – The garden package imports the tree types package

The relationship shown in Figure 6-16 implies that the garden package can access contents of the tree types package as though they were local. [30]

Containment Relationship

SysML provides two methods of diagramming package containment:

1)   Nesting one package within another in a package diagram.

2)   Using the containment relationship arrow: a line with a circle containing a cross at the parent end of the relationship.

The *Enterprise Architect* implementation of these two diagramming features is somewhat different from that of other tools and also different from the presentations in the main SysML textbooks. The difference has to do with the focus on the diagram context rather than the relationship between the packages. In this section, we will work through some examples in order to understand the *Enterprise Architect* approach to containment.

---

[30] The behavior of this relationship in *Enterprise Architect* was not quite what I expected. A block definition diagram created in the garden package still shows tree types as external blocks.

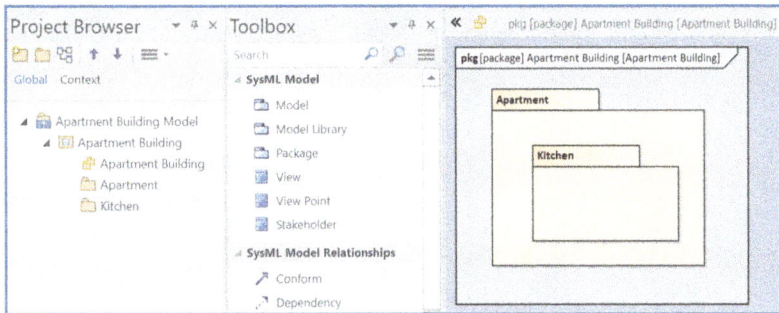

Figure 6-17 – Apartment building model

Using the SysML package diagram techniques described earlier in this chapter, construct the model shown in Figure 6-17.

1) The root package of the model is called "Apartment Building".

2) This root package owns the package diagram. This point is important.

3) As you drag the first package to the diagram and name it "Apartment", *Enterprise Architect* is placing the new package in the package that owns the diagram: "Apartment Building".

4) Practically speaking, you will want to enlarge the "Apartment" package in the diagram to get it ready for you to drag another package to the diagram and nest it inside of "Apartment".

5) As you drag the second package to the diagram, drop it inside of "Apartment", and name it "Kitchen". *Enterprise Architect* will again place the new package in the package that owns the diagram: "Apartment Building", **NOT** inside the immediate parent "Apartment Building".

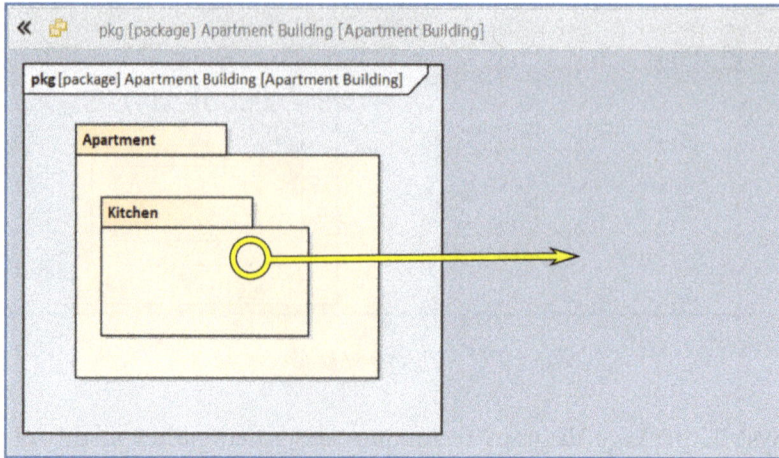

Figure 6-18 – Drag Kitchen right

Click on the kitchen folder in the diagram and drag it right until it is well outside of the apartment package.

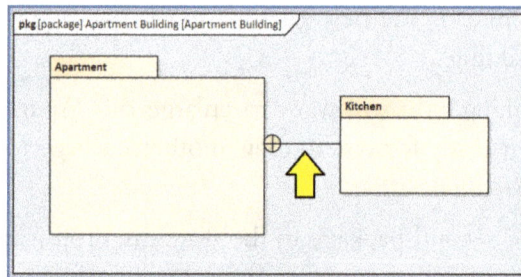

Figure 6-19 – Containment relationship appears

As you drag the kitchen package clear of the apartment package, *Enterprise Architect* automatically draws a containment relationship between the two packages.

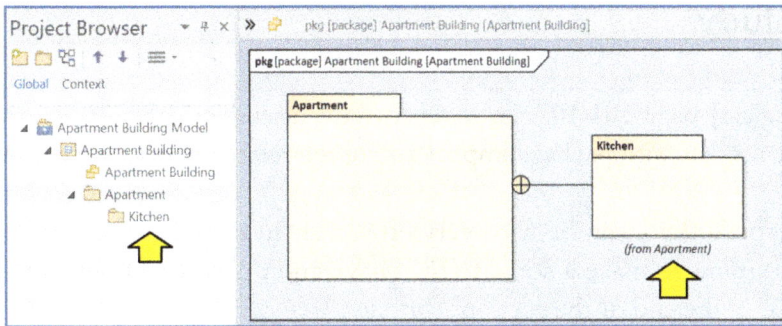

Figure 6-20 – Drag to nest in browser

If you select the kitchen package in the project browser and drag it into the apartment package, *Enterprise Architect* will add a notation in the diagram: "*(from Apartment)*" because the kitchen package is no longer a direct member of the package that owns the diagram.

Further Study

See [Douglass] page 101-107 for a very useful discussion of how to structure very large models with package import and usage relationships. Beyond that:

- **hyperlinks** – can be used very effectively in combination with package diagrams to make a sort of visual navigation diagram. Refer to the sidebar at the end of the section: *Parts and Multiplicities* on page 119.

- **models** – are specialized packages that are the root of a model. That is, it is possible to have multiple models in a single project and show them on a package diagram.
  - [Delligatti] – page 195
  - [Friedenthal] – page 102

- **model libraries** – are for creating libraries of reusable model elements.
  - [Delligatti] – page 195
  - [Friedenthal] – page 103

- **profiles** – are used to create a set of specialized model elements that apply to some specific domain. For example, I have a personal profile of special elements for modeling functional safety for automotive systems.
  - [Delligatti] – page 195
  - [Friedenthal] – page 369

- **qualified name string notation** – is a more compact method of showing nesting on a diagram.
    - [Delligatti] – page 192
    - [Friedenthal] – page 107
- **views and viewpoints** – are used to show a subset of the model that is relevant to a particular set of stakeholders.
    - [Delligatti] – page 196
    - [Friedenthal] – page 98

Chapter 7 – Activity Diagrams

Activity diagrams are a more powerful version of the traditional flowchart that most engineers have encountered somewhere in their education or careers. Activity diagrams are often the first kind of behavior diagram created. They lend themselves to turning oral stories into something more defined. Activity diagrams can display two kinds of flows:

- **Control Flows** – are really the traditional flowcharts, albeit in a more powerful form.
- **Object Flows** – document the flow of "stuff" through the activity and hence the system.

Control Flow

Control flows model different possible paths of execution in a system.

Basic Control Flow

As an introductory exercise, we are going to model my actions after waking up on a Sunday morning.

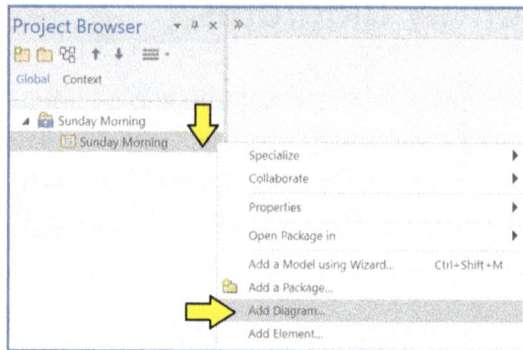

Figure 7-1 – Add activity diagram to a basic model

Create a SysML model and a main package. Right-click on the package and select "Add Diagram...".

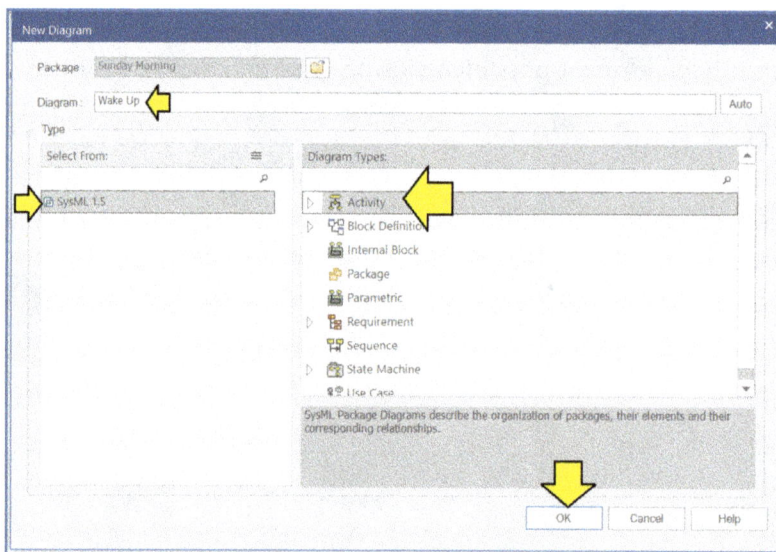

Figure 7-2 – Name the diagram

From the SysML 1.5 diagram types select the activity diagram. Name the diagram "Wake Up" and click "OK".

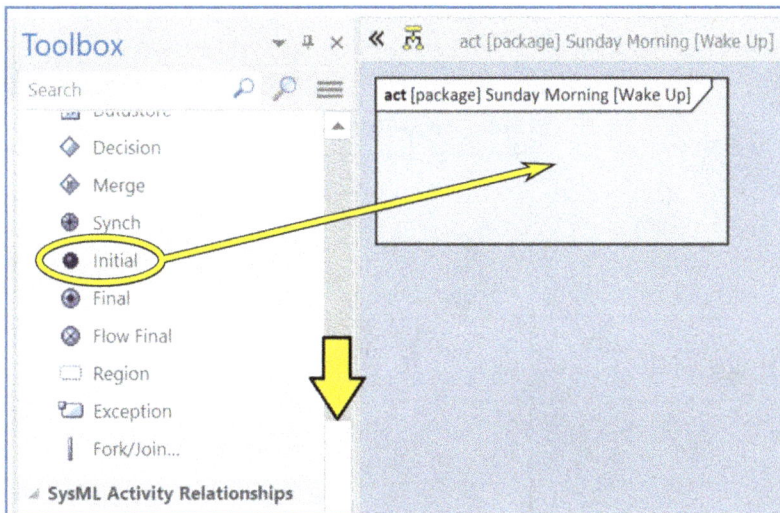

Figure 7-3 – Drag the Initial icon to the diagram

In the toolbox, scroll down and select the "Initial" icon. Drag the icon to the diagram.

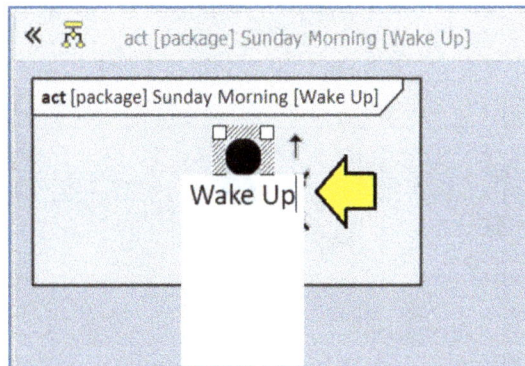

Figure 7-4 – Name the initial node

Name the initial node "Wake Up".

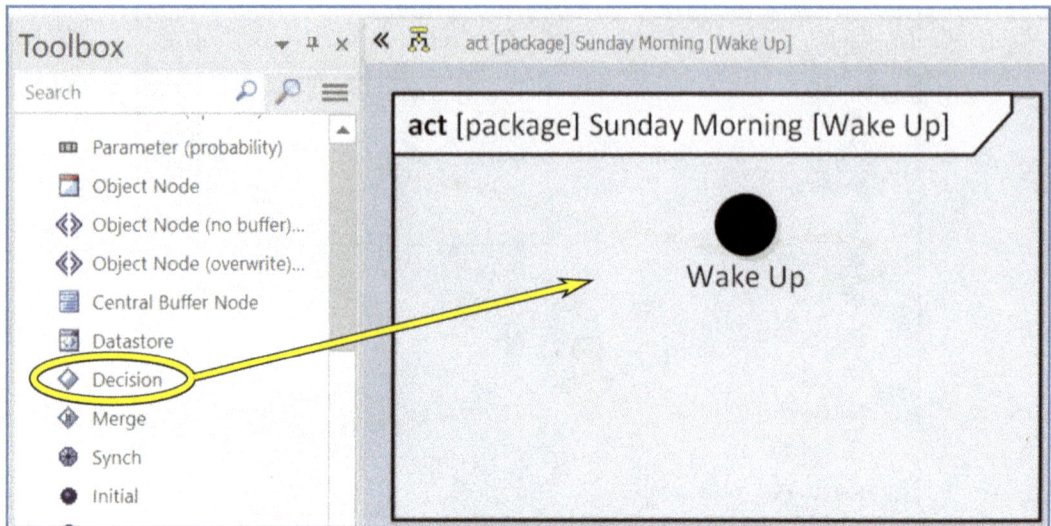

Figure 7-5 – Drag the Decision icon to the diagram

Find the "Decision" icon in the toolbox and drag it to the diagram.

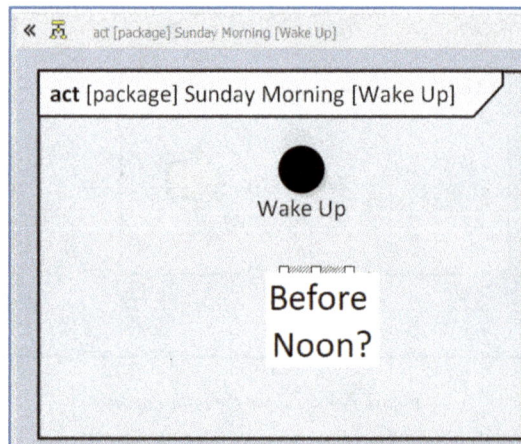

Figure 7-6 – Name the decision node

Name the decision node "Before Noon?"

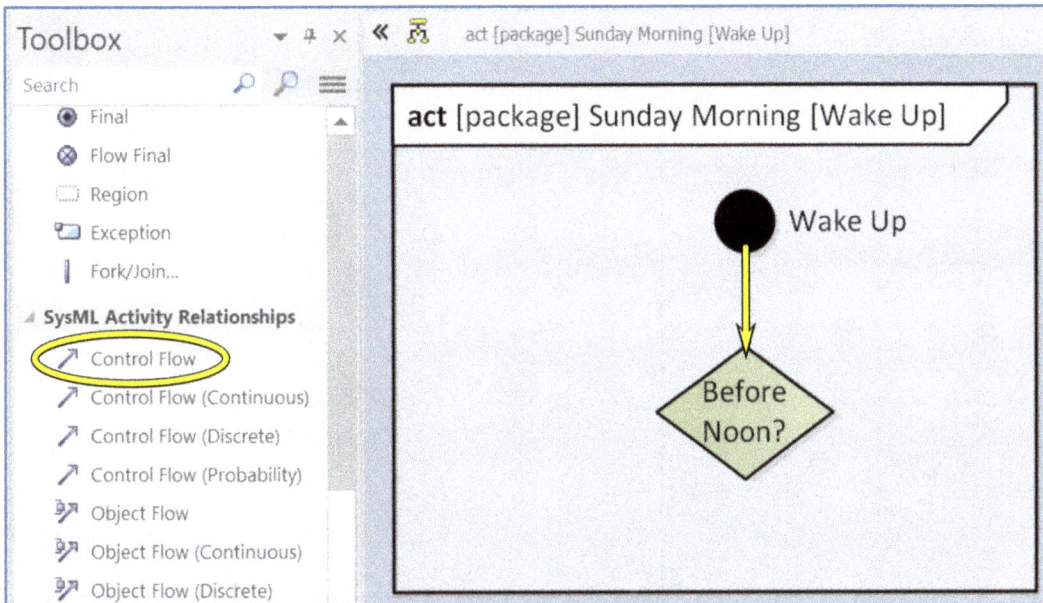

Figure 7-7 – Drag a Control Flow relationship

In the toolbox find and select the "Control Flow" icon. Drag a control flow relationship from the initial node to the decision node. [31]

---

[31] The standard suggests that control flow should be represented with a dashed arrow. *Enterprise Architect* does not show a dashed line by default. However, if you select "Configure" from the top menu bar, select "Options" from the ribbon, and then select the "General" tab, you will find an option to show a dashed line for control flow in a SysML model.

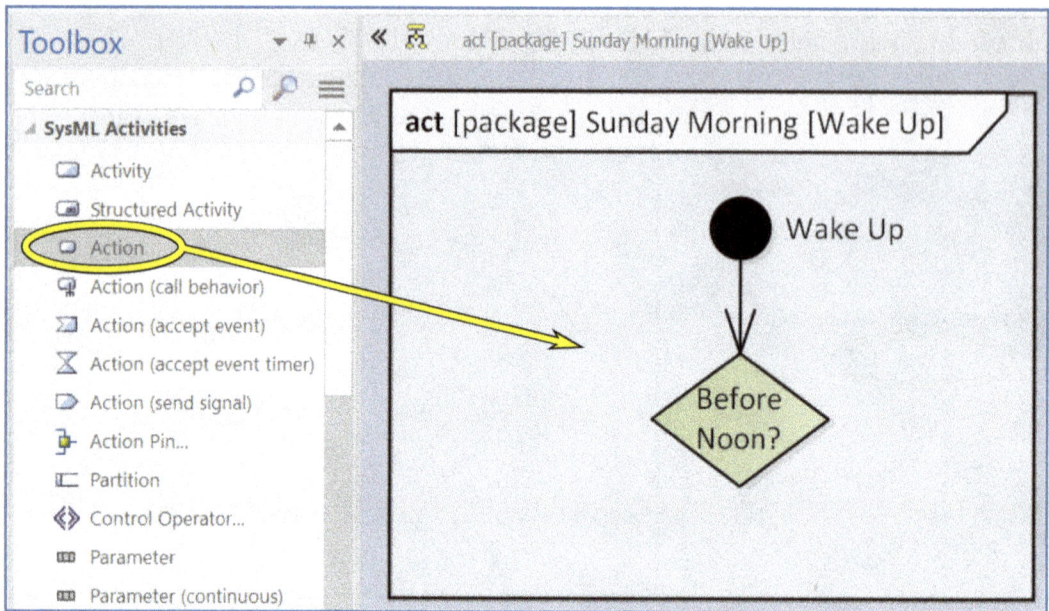

Figure 7-8 – Drag the Action icon to the diagram

In the toolbox, find the "Action" icon and drag it to the diagram.

Actions versus Activities

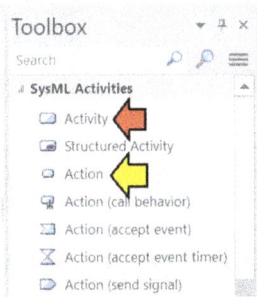

In the toolbox for the activity diagram, you will find icons for both **Activity** and **Action**. *Enterprise Architect* provides a lot more flexibility in terms of decomposing activities than the SysML standard actually envisions. For the moment, the "straight and narrow" approach is to use only the **Action** icon to represent an atomic unit of flow within an activity diagram.

We will discuss approaches to decomposing activities and the features of *Enterprise Architect* in more detail in *Decomposing Activities* on page 215.

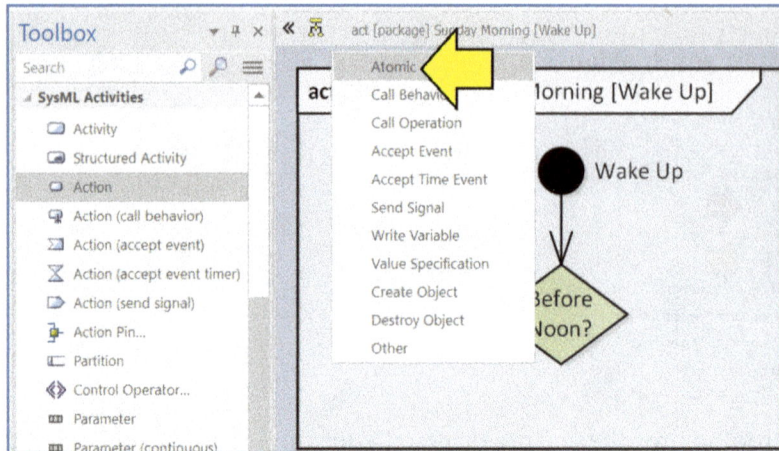

Figure 7-9 – Select Atomic

A menu will appear showing several possible types of actions. Select "Atomic". Name the action "Eat Breakfast".

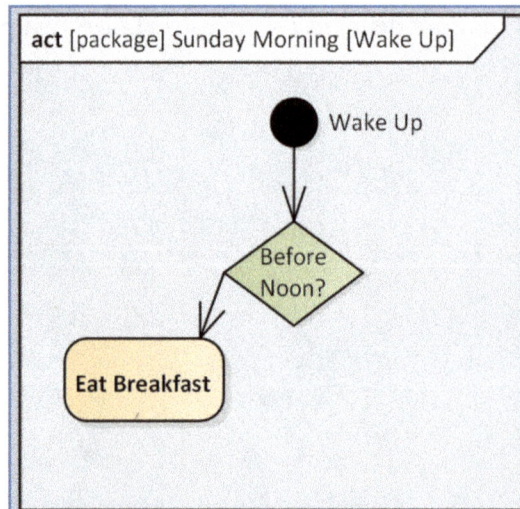

Figure 7-10 – Drag control flow to action

Select the control flow icon again and drag a flow from the decision node to the action. The result will be a short, stubby arrow.

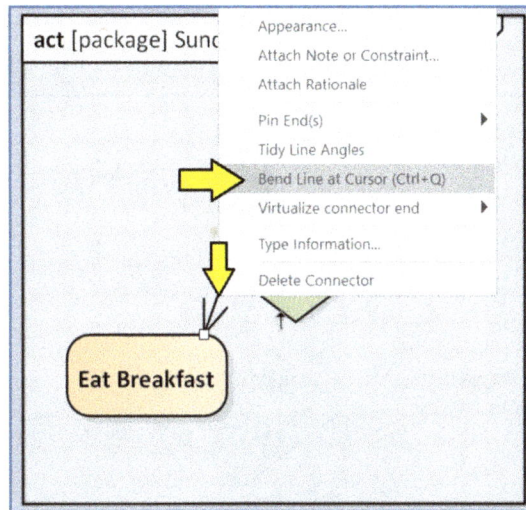

Figure 7-11 – Right-Click to Bend Line

In order to improve the appearance of the line, right-click on the control flow and select "Bend Line at Cursor (Ctrl+Q)".

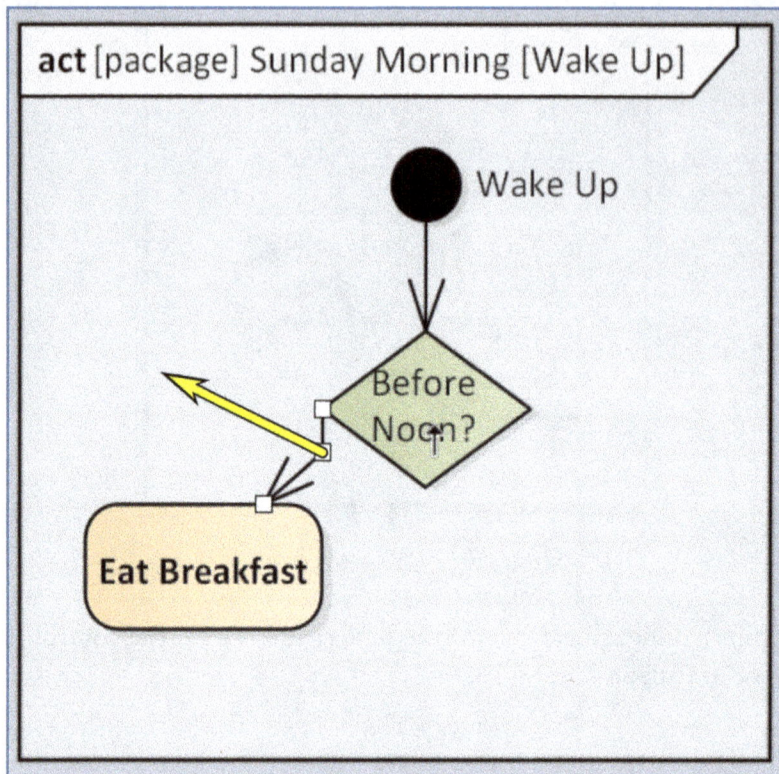

Figure 7-12 – Drag new node to make squared line

A new node will be created in the middle of the line. Click on the node and drag it to make a squared line.

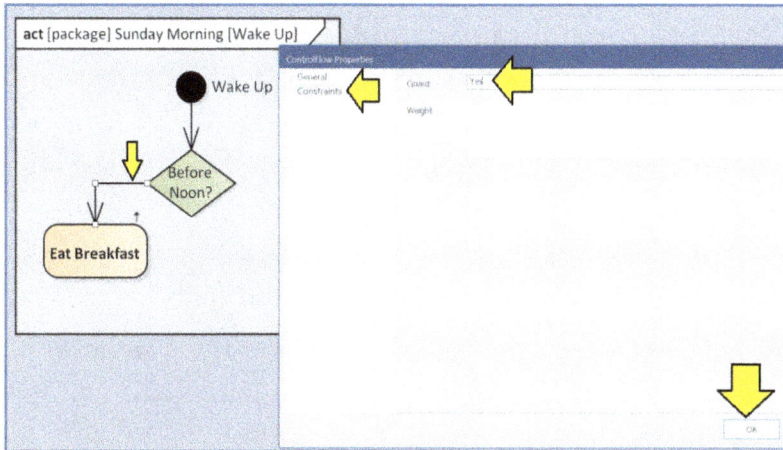

Figure 7-13 – Set the control flow guard

Double-click on the control flow, select "Constraints", enter "Yes" in the "Guard" field, and click "OK".

Guard versus Name

In Figure 7-13, we have chosen to set the guard condition rather than the name for the flow out of the decision node. Control flows can also be named. In fact, when you first double-click on the control flow, *Enterprise Architect* will open to the tab to allow you to set the name, rather than the tab to allow you to set the guard. However, strictly speaking, SysML requires that a guard be used here rather than a name.

You will see that in the resulting diagram, the guard condition is contained in square brackets. If you set the name rather than the guard, no square brackets will be shown. This difference will not matter much if you are only producing diagrams for other humans to read. However, if you are planning to use simulation on your model, or to generate source code, the difference will be important.

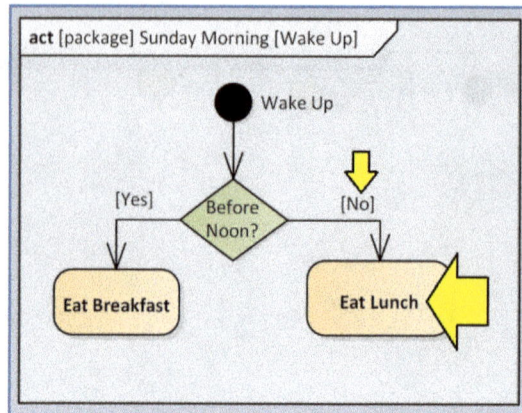

Figure 7-14 – Create second action

Create a second action called "Eat Lunch". Add a control flow with the guard: "No" from the other side of the decision node to the new action.

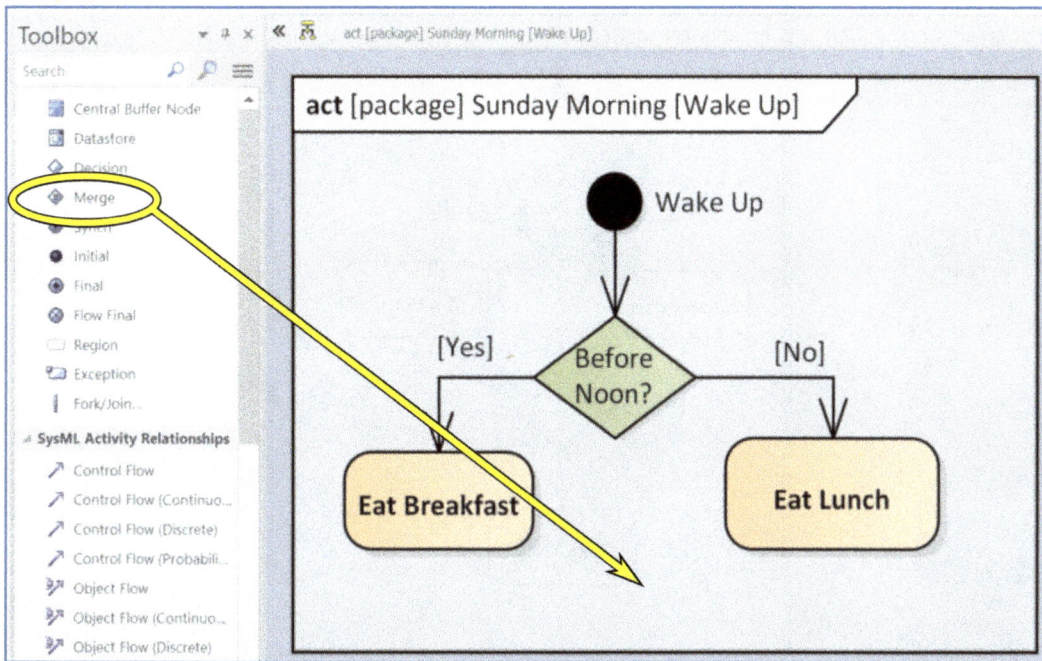

Figure 7-15 – Add Merge node

In the toolbox find the "Merge" icon and drag it to the diagram.

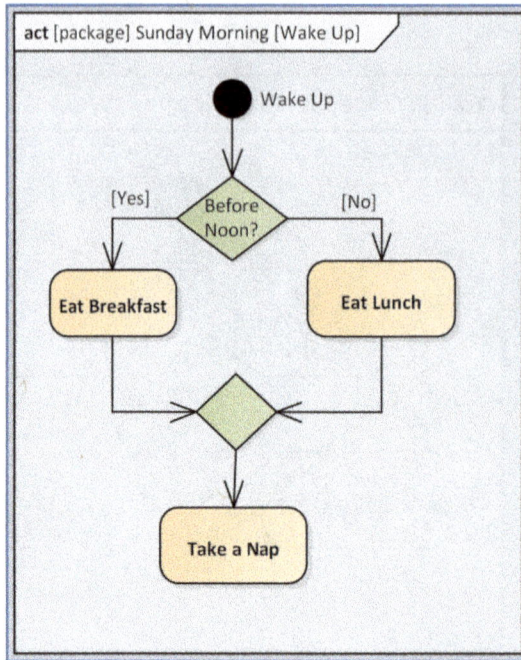

Figure 7-16 – Add another action and control flows

Add another action called: "Take a Nap". Drag control flows from the first two actions to the merge node. Drag an action from the merge node to the nap action.

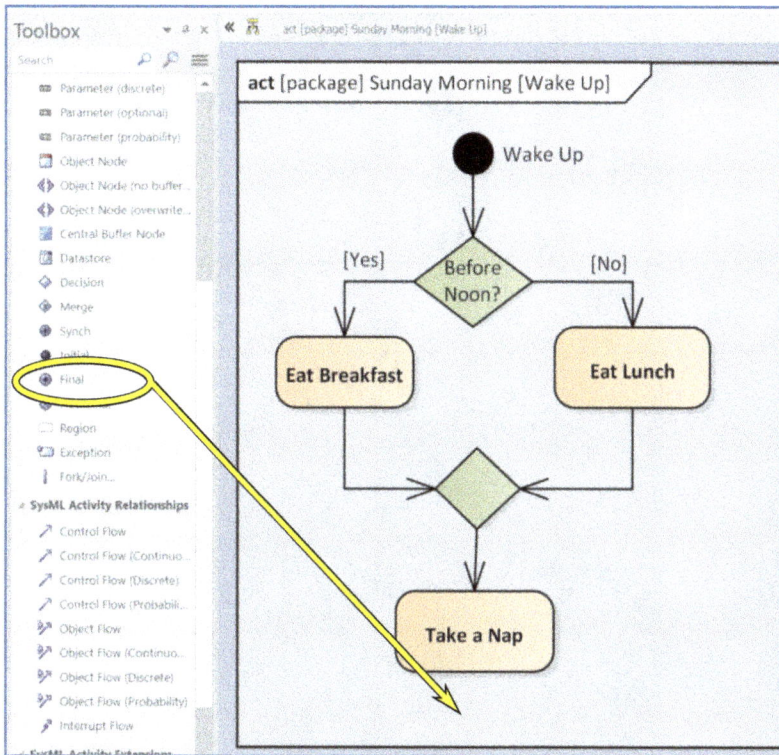

Figure 7-17 – Drag Final to the diagram

In the toolbox find the "Final" icon and drag it to the diagram. Name the final node "Done".

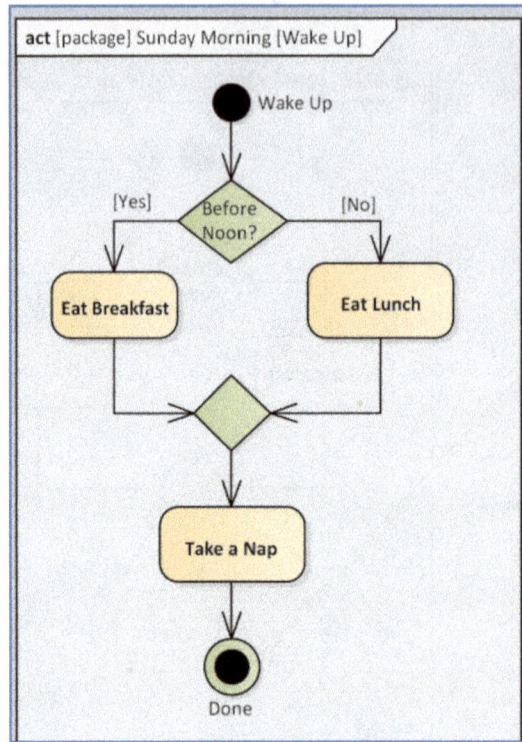

Figure 7-18 – Add control flow to complete

Drag a control flow from the nap action to the final node to complete the diagram.

Parallel Processing

The previous model was easy to understand. A single person (that would be me) wakes up on Sunday morning, eats either breakfast or lunch, and then takes a nap. The diagram elements were also quite straightforward – easily recognizable by anyone who has ever seen any sort of flowchart.

What if we want to several things to happen in parallel? This is the point at which SysML parts ways with traditional simple flowcharts. SysML supports the **Fork** and **Join** diagramming elements for modeling of parallel execution paths. These elements look a little funny at first. However, as we will see, they are quite expressive and powerful.

In order to demonstrate these elements, we are going to alter my Sunday morning model to give it a rather more gluttonous approach.

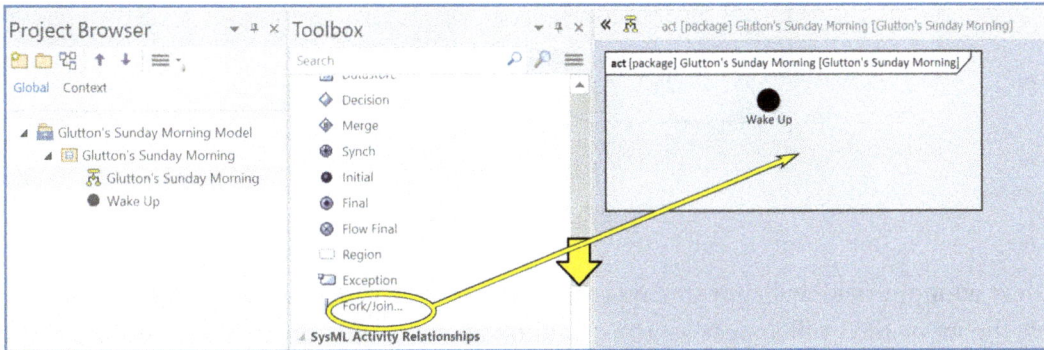

Figure 7-19 – Create Glutton model and add Fork

Create the "Glutton's Sunday Morning" model, create an activity diagram, and give it an initial node called "Wake Up" as before. In the toolbox find the "Fork/Join..." and drag it to the diagram.

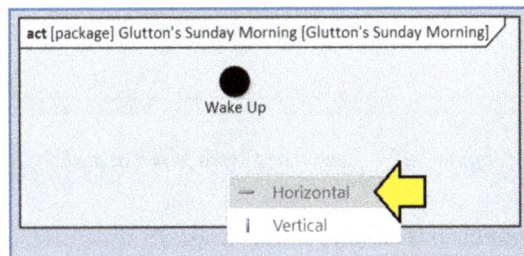

Figure 7-20 – Select Horizontal

A small window will pop up to select a horizontal or vertical fork symbol. Select "Horizontal".

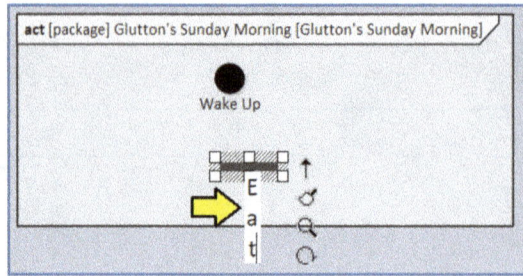

Figure 7-21 – Name the fork

Next an input field will appear. Enter the name for the fork: "Eat a Lot". In some cases, the input field will appear as a vertical box allowing only one letter on each line. In this case, you may find it more convenient to skip the name input field and double-click on the symbol to set its name afterwards.

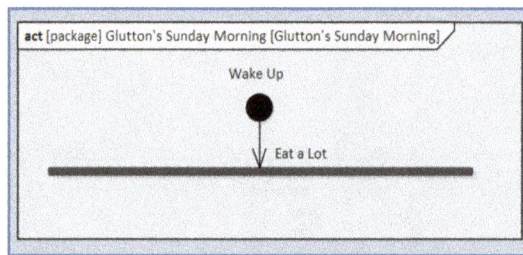

Figure 7-22 – Connect and adjust format as needed

Add a control flow connector from the initial node to the fork. Drag the text boxes to arrange nicely as needed.

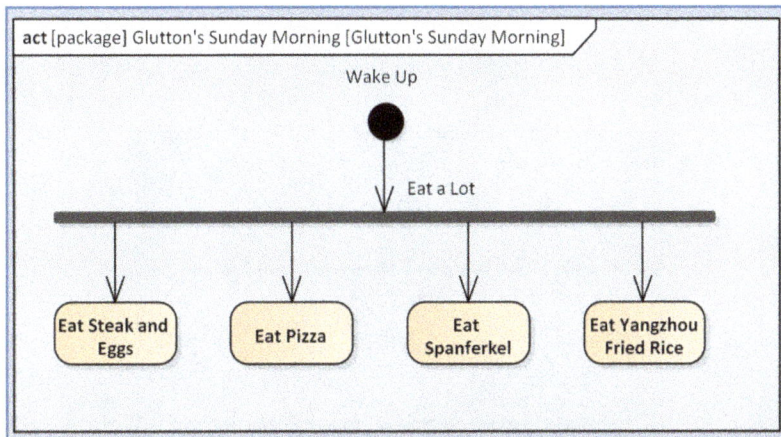

Figure 7-23 – Add four actions

Add four actions to the diagram:

1)   "Eat Steak and Eggs" – a favorite here in Texas.

2)   "Eat Pizza" – a favorite anywhere where one's spouse is not supervising carefully.

3)   "Eat Spanferkel" – Roasted piglet, a Bavarian/Austrian specialty.

4)   "Eat Yangzhou Fried Rice" – a popular Chinese wok fried rice dish originally from the city of Yangzhou, Jiangsu province, in China.

Add control flow arrows from the fork symbol to each of the actions.

The diagram (fragment – it isn't complete yet) shown in Figure 7-23 can be interpreted as meaning:

1)   Someone wakes up on Sunday morning which starts the activity.

2)   That person arrives immediately at the "Eat a Lot" fork node.

3)   Immediately upon arrival at the fork node, three more clones of the original person are created.

4)   The original person and the three clones proceed down the four outgoing control flow paths from the fork node...

5)   ...where they each begin gorging themselves on one "Not-a-Diet-Food" culinary delight.

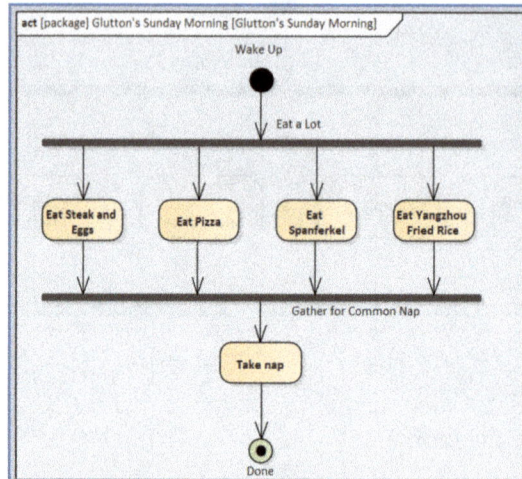

Figure 7-24 – Common Nap

How do we wrap this thing up?

1)   Drag a join node to the diagram. The join node is the same icon as the fork node. The difference in meaning comes purely from the diagram context.

2)   Name the join node: "Gather for Common Nap".

3)   Add control flows from the four eating activities to the join node.

4)   Add another action below the join node called: "Take nap".

5)   Add an activity final node called: "Done".

6)   Add control flows from the join node to the nap and from the nap to the final node.

The rest of the diagram (now complete) shown in Figure 7-24 can be interpreted as meaning:

1)   The four clones gather at the join node, waiting patiently until all four of them have finished eating.

2) Once all four clones are present and accounted for, they fuse back into a single person.

3) The reconsolidated single person takes a massive nap.

4) Upon completion of the nap, the activity terminates.

Independent Completion

The parallel eating system we designed in the previous section works well initially and the consolidated single person gains weight steadily. In ongoing usage, however, some issues become apparent. Notably, the clone assigned to eat pizza tends to order the "Football Team Monster Deluxe" pizza: a gigantic creation, more than a meter in diameter with extra-thick wheat crust, five kinds of cheese, every topping on the menu, with extra jalapeños and anchovies on the side. Needless to say, Pizza Guy takes quite a while to finish which leaves the other three clones stuck at the join node, impatiently waiting for their nap.

In order to resolve this problem, we redesign the activity to allow each clone to exit the activity (and cease to exist) independently. We will introduce this flexibility by using a **flow final** node for each branch of the activity.

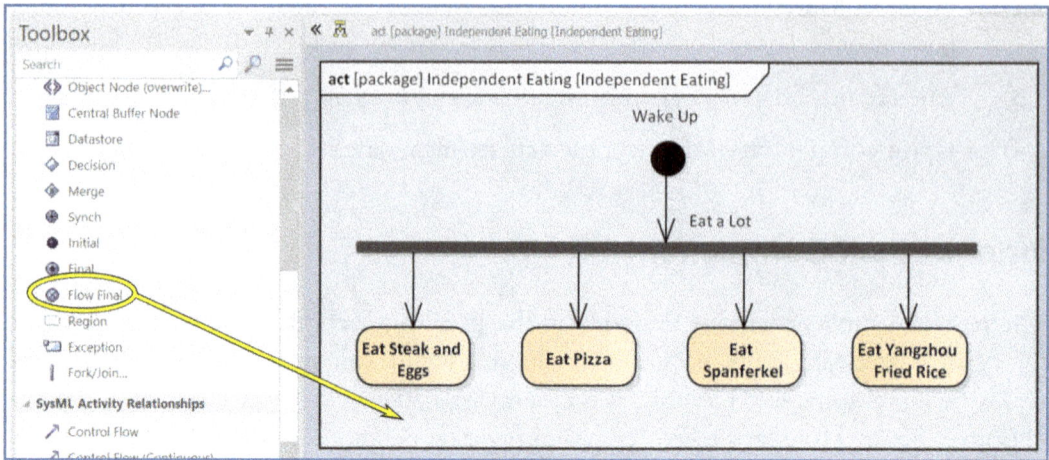

Figure 7-25 – Add Flow Final nodes

The first step is to remove the join, the nap, and the "Done" activity final node. Find the "Flow Final" node in the toolbox and add four of these to the diagram.

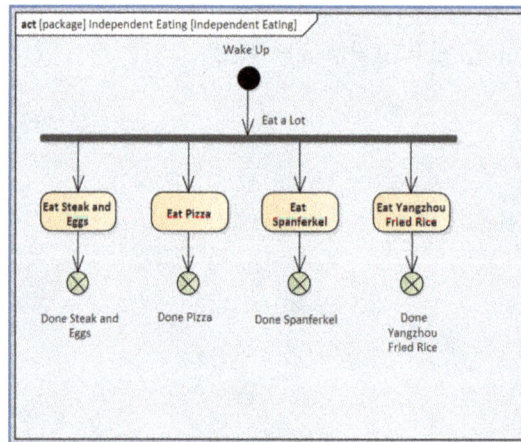

Figure 7-26 – Independent completion

Name the four flow final nodes to match the actions and add control flows. The completed diagram is shown in Figure 7-26.

This diagram can be understood as allowing each of the four clones to complete his eating task as rapidly or slowly as desired. Each one exits the activity independently. [32]

Race to the Finish

What if we want to limit the clone's calorie intake slightly? We can put a bit of a lid on the process by replacing the **flow final** nodes with **activity final** nodes.

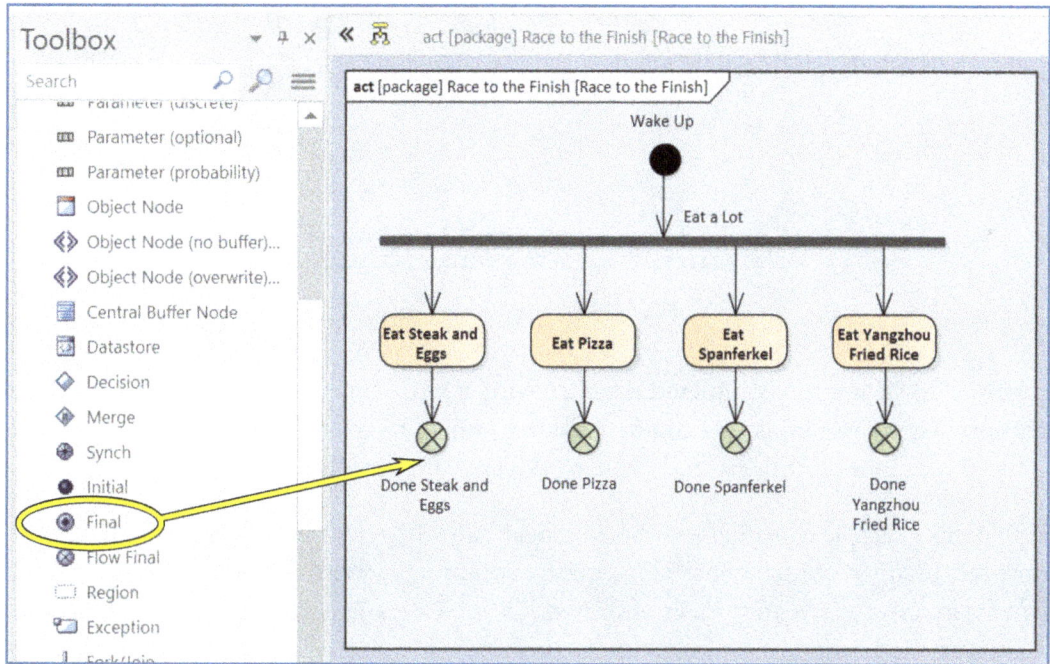

Figure 7-27 – Replace flow final with final nodes

Select the "Final" icon in the toolbox and drag four copies to the diagram. You will have to rename them manually, delete the flow final nodes, and reconnect the control flows. Note that deleting the flow final nodes from the diagram will not delete them

---

[32] Since there is no flow that leads to an activity final node, the activity remains alive as a "ghost", even though there are no longer any flows in it – probably not a good design for a real product. However, in the early stages of modeling a real system, you would probably just add a note to the diagram about this concern and come back later to add more detail to take care of that problem.

from the model. You will also need to delete them from the model in the project browser as well.

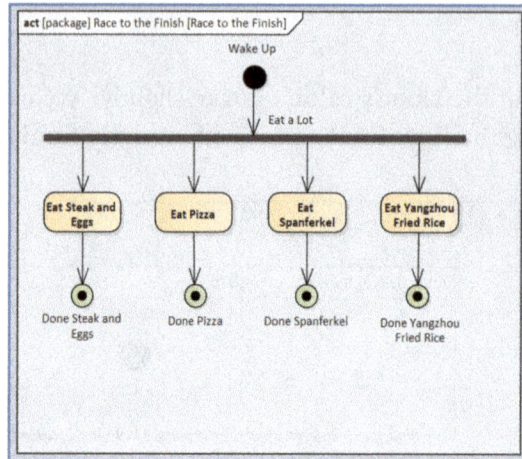

Figure 7-28 – Activity final nodes

Figure 7-28 shows the completed diagram with activity final nodes. The nuance of this version of the diagram is that the first clone to finish terminates the entire activity. The other three clones terminate and cease to exist in mid-mouthful.

While this example of eating may seem a little silly, the real-life use case is quite easy to imagine. In any resource-constrained system, you might want to initiate several threads of activity on a speculative basis and then kill the losers as soon as a winner emerged. That way, the losing threads would not consume any more resource (power, fuel, compute power) than needed once it became clear that they would not become the winner.

Object Flow

In the previous sections we looked at control flow. Activity diagrams can also be used to model the flow of "stuff" through a system. When used to model the flow of data, activity diagrams can be quite powerful. It is easy to make activity diagrams that clearly show how the data is transformed as it moves through the system.

In order to illustrate the principle, we are going to model a system similar to the Google Library Project: [33]

1) Books will be scanned by a scanner.

2) The scanned images will be processed by an optical character recognition (OCR) system.

3) The raw character data file will be processed by an artificially intelligent semantic processor to recognize structure and possibly correct errors from the scanning and OCR operations.

4) The resulting structured text will be stored in a schema-less "NoSQL" database. [34]

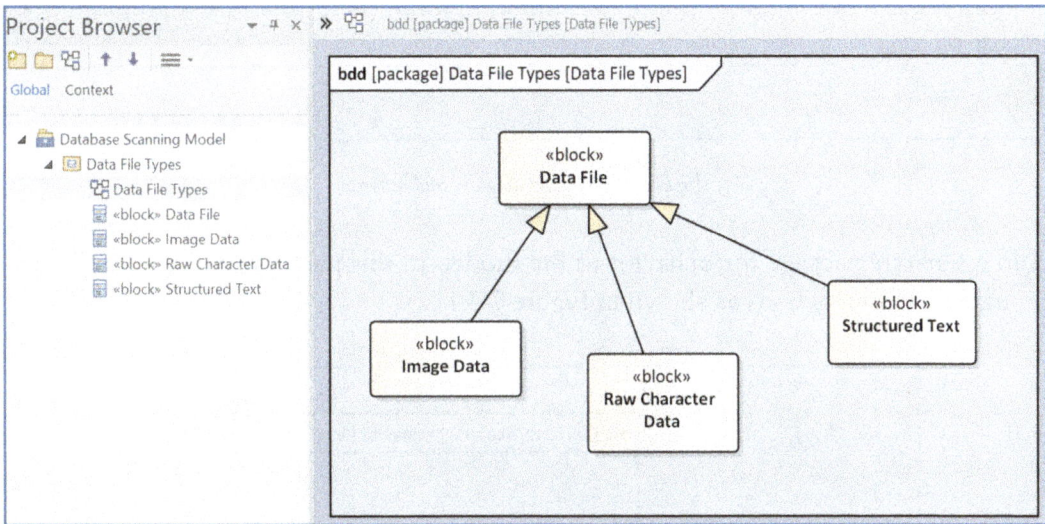

Figure 7-29 – Data file types

We will assume that the data is passed around the system in data files, which might have some common characteristics. Create a simple model, create a block "Data File" and create three more files that generalize from it:

- Image File – would be a file of pixels, typically TIFF, but possibly also PNG or JPEG data.

---

[33] https://en.wikipedia.org/wiki/Google_Books

[34] I happen to be partial to MongoDB. https://www.mongodb.com/

- Raw Character Data – would be UTF-8 encoded character data.

- Structured Text – would be the same UTF-8 encoded character data but re-structured with additional text to identify structural hierarchy. The format would likely by XML but could also be JSON.

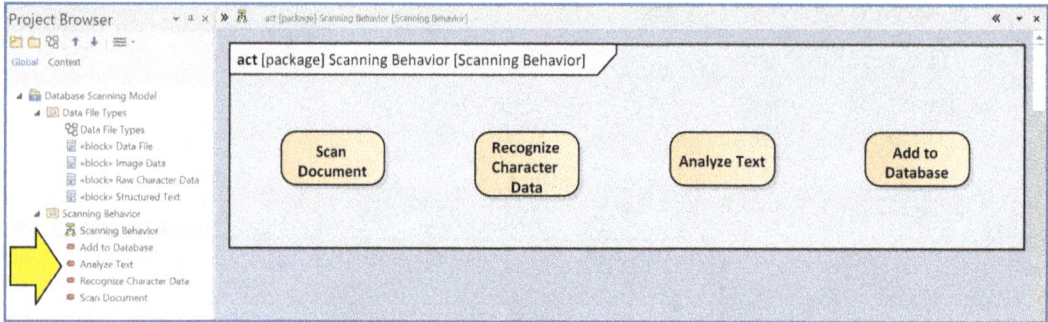

Figure 7-30 – Add diagram and actions

Add a separate package for behavior to the model. In this package, add an activity diagram. Create four actions as shown in Figure 7-30.

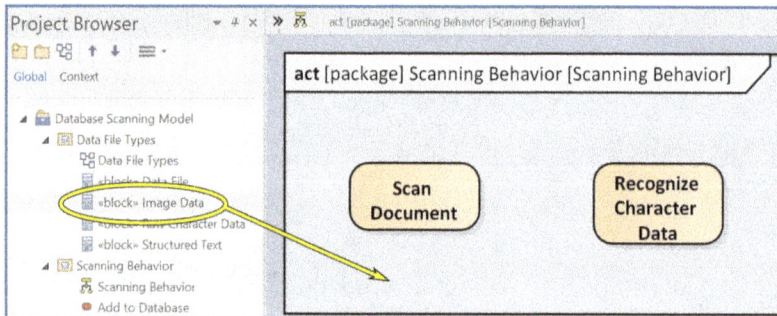

Figure 7-31 – Drag the Image Data block to the diagram

Drag the "Image Data" block from the project browser to the diagram

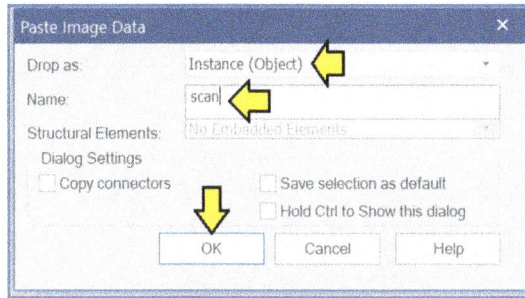

Figure 7-32 – Name the object

A dialog box will open. In the "Drop as:" field accept the default of "Instance (Object)". The "Name:" field will default to a string containing the block name. Using the same name for the instance and the block can be confusing. Name the instance: "scan". Click "OK".

Typed vs Untyped Objects in Activity Diagrams

Do we need to create a type hierarchy for objects in activity diagrams? No. You can use untyped objects if you like and many people do. However, using typed objects as I am showing here is not difficult and it makes your model much more expressive.

If you would prefer to use untyped objects in your diagrams, you can drag them directly from the toolbox to your diagram.

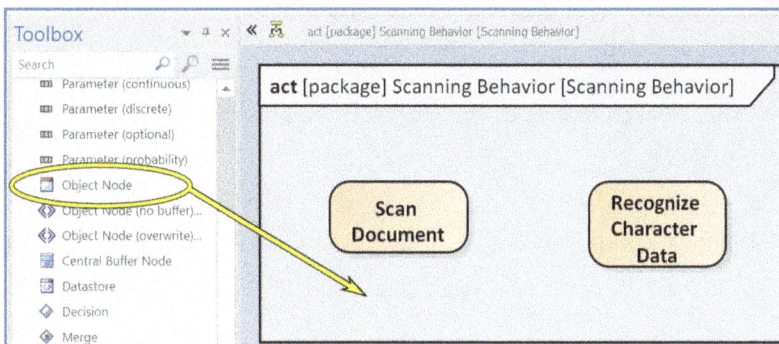

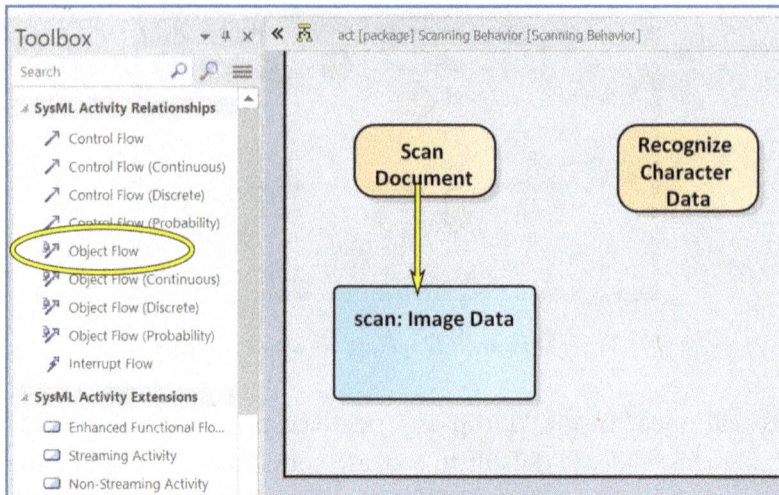

Figure 7-33 – Drag an object flow

Select the "Object Flow" icon in the toolbox and drag a flow from the action to the object.

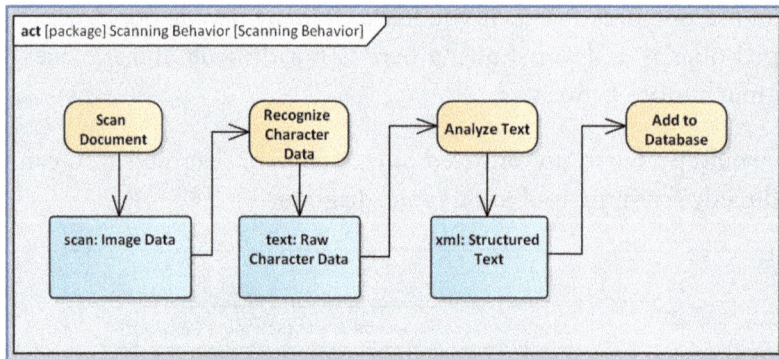

Figure 7-34 – Object flow complete

Create two more objects and link them with object flows as shown in Figure 7-34.

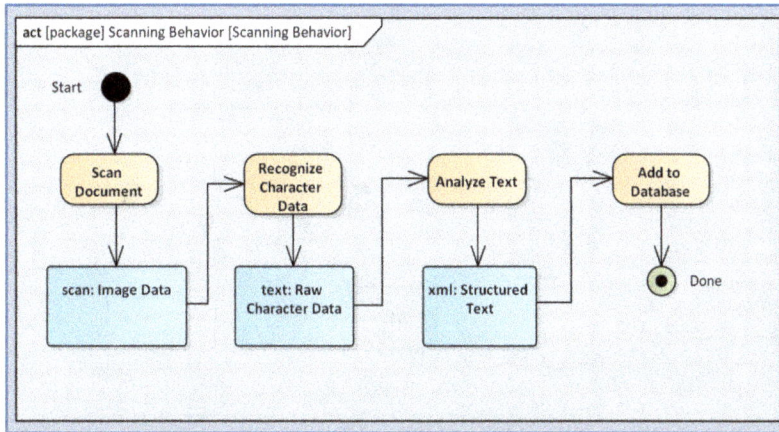

Figure 7-35 – Adding initial and final nodes

You can also add initial and final nodes as shown in Figure 7-35. Note, however, that no objects flow between the initial node and the first action. As such, the arrow is a control flow arrow, not an object flow arrow. The arrow from the final action and the final node is likewise a control flow for the same reason.

It is also possible to pass objects into and out of activity diagrams using **Activity Parameters**. See *Further Study* on page 225.

Allocating to Partitions

In the previous section, we modeled the behavior of the database scanner system, but we did not model any actual hardware. Let's extend the model to include some hardware and show how the actions get allocated to the hardware.

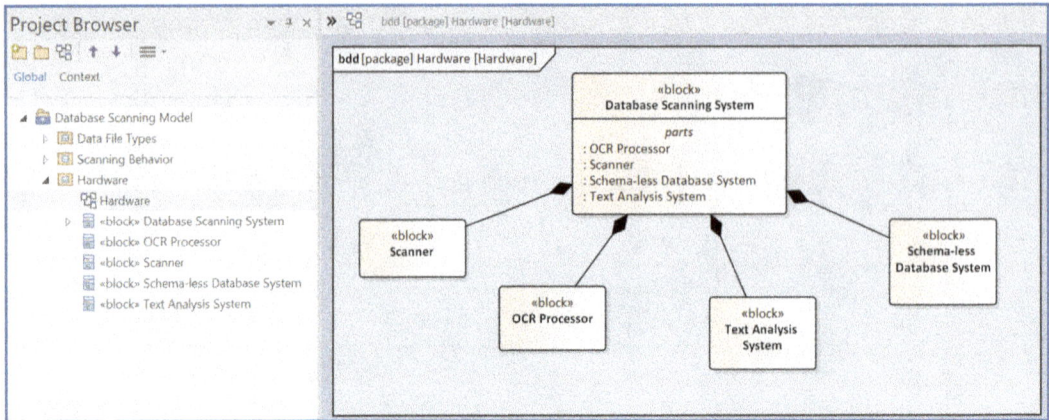

Figure 7-36 – Add hardware

Add a new package to the model called "Hardware". Add a block for the overall system. Add blocks for the four hardware components. Add composition relationships between the four hardware components and the overall system.

In order to show how the actions in the diagram are allocated to different system elements, we will use the **Partition** feature of the SysML activity diagram.

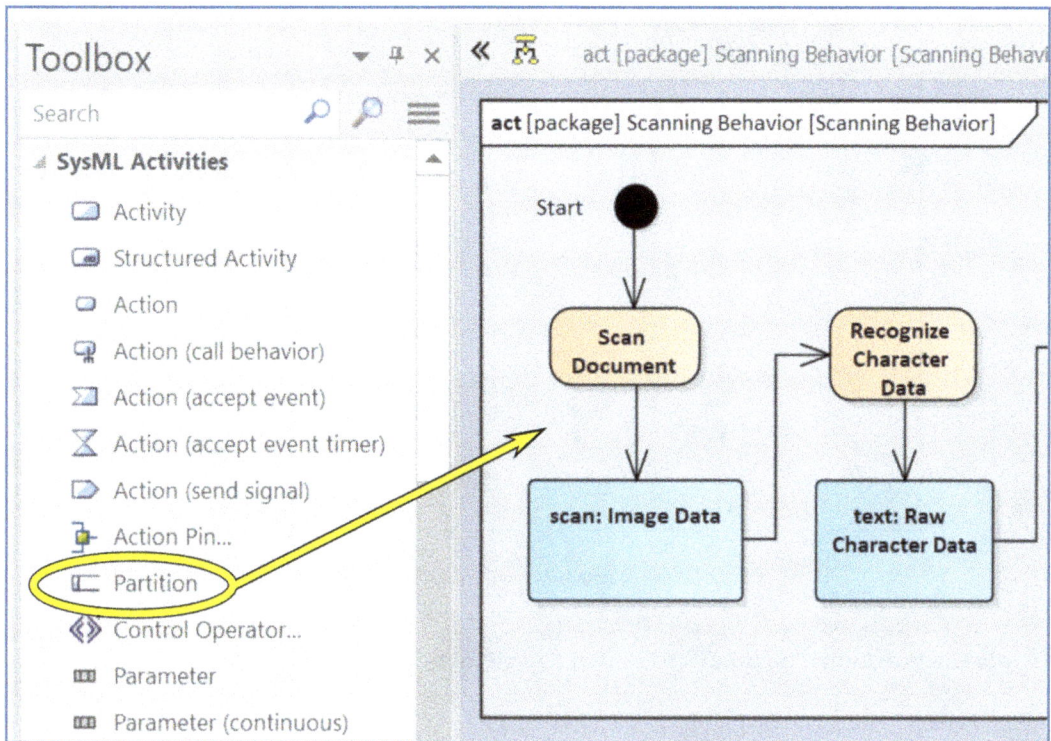

Figure 7-37 – Drag the Partition icon to the activity diagram

Reopen the activity diagram in the model. Find the "Partition" icon in the toolbox and drag it to the diagram.

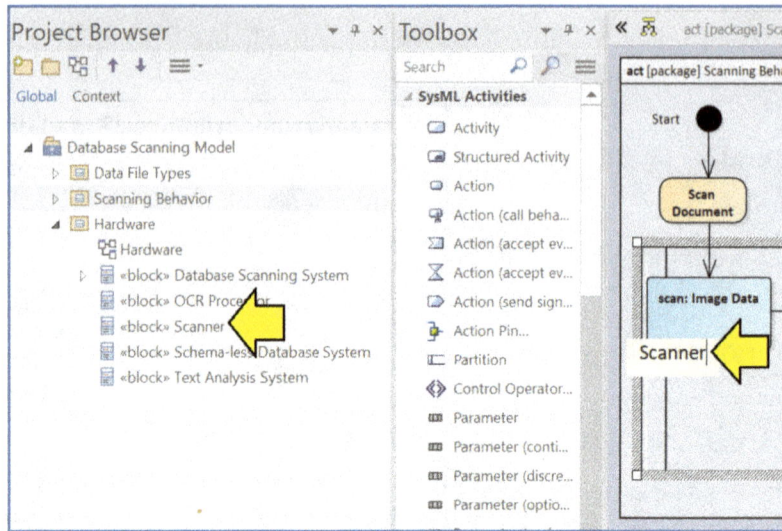

Figure 7-38 – Name partition to match system element

Name the partition: "Scanner" to match the element in the project browser. [35]

---

[35] The exact implementation of this step varies from tool-to-tool. With *Enterprise Architect*, you have to match the name manually.

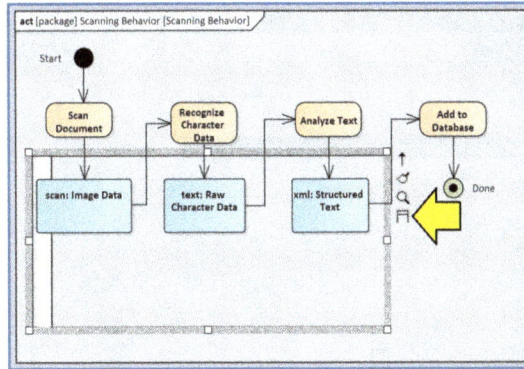

Figure 7-39 – Click vertical icon to flip partition

Partitions can be either horizontal or vertical. *Enterprise Architect* creates horizontal partitions by default. Click on the vertical control icon to flip the partition to be a vertical partition.

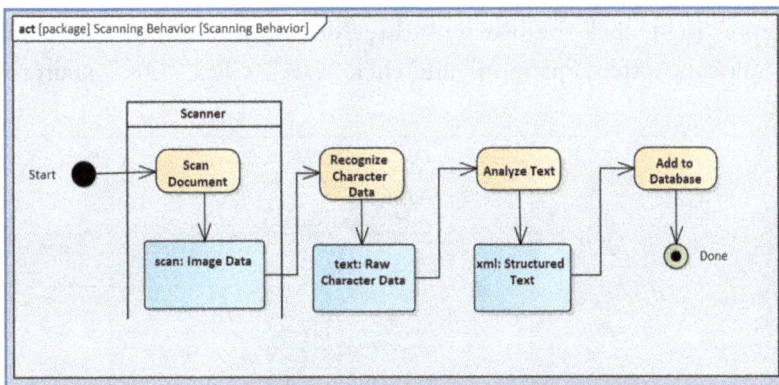

Figure 7-40 – Rearranged diagram

After the partition flips to vertical, use the drag controls to size it and drag elements around a little bit until the layout looks like Figure 7-40.

Next we want to clarify that the name "Scanner" indicates an allocation relationship.

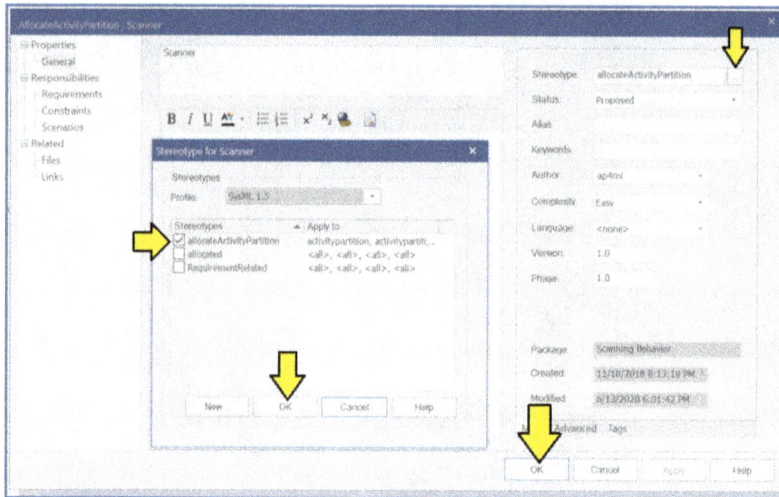

Figure 7-41 – Set to allocateActivityPartition

Double-click on the partition in the diagram. A dialog box will appear. To the right of the "Stereotype:" field, click the box with three dots in it. Another child dialog will appear. Select "allocateActivityPartition" and click "OK". Click "OK" again to apply.

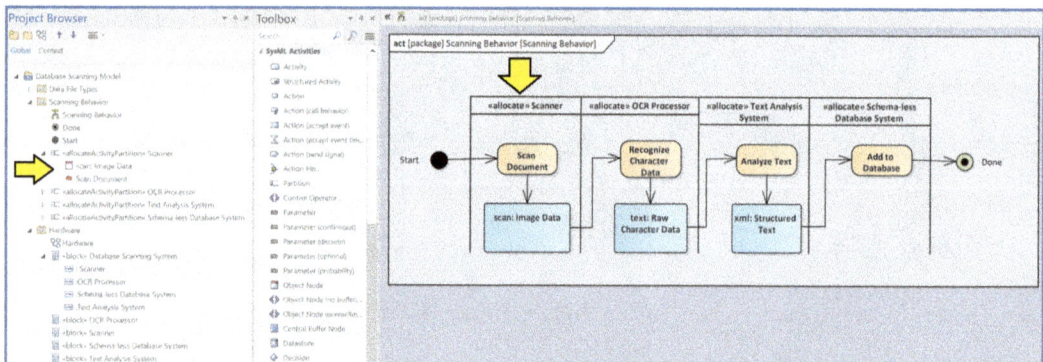

Figure 7-42 – Allocation complete

Add three more partitions and drag things around until the diagram looks like Figure 7-42. Notice that *Enterprise Architect* has nested the actions and the objects under each partition in the project browser.

Decomposing Activities

What if we have a complicated activity that we want to decompose into a series of smaller activities? There are several possible different approaches here, some envisioned by the standard, and some unique to *Enterprise Architect*.

Activities on a Block Diagram

One way to decompose activities is to put them in a block diagram and use composition relationships between the master activity and the subactivities. [36] In order to explore the subject of activities in a block definition diagram, we will model a complex activity: the preparation of breakfast.

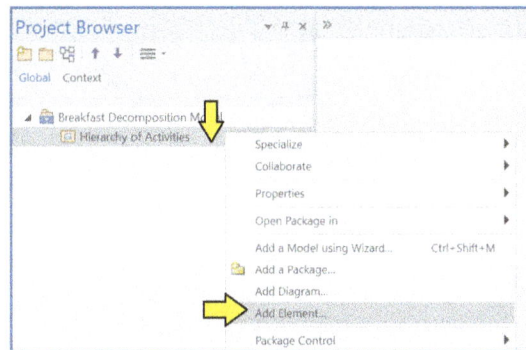

Figure 7-43 – Add Element

Create a basic model and a package. Right-click on the package and select "Add Element..."

---

[36] See [SysML1.5] section 11.3.1.1 on page 118.

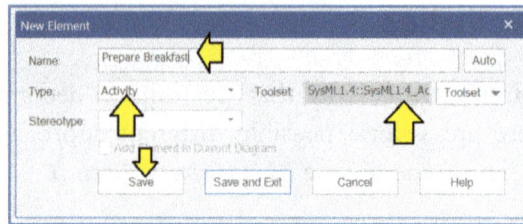

Figure 7-44 – Select and name activity

In order to add an activity to the model:

1) Pull down the "Toolset" menu and select the activity diagram toolset.

2) In the "Type:" box select "Activity".

3) Name the activity: "Prepare Breakfast".

4) If you click: "Save" rather than "Save and Exit" the dialog box will remain open to define additional activities.

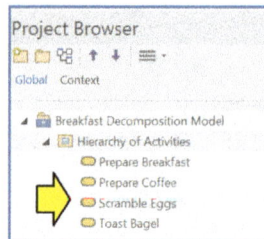

Figure 7-45 – Add three more subactivities

Add three more activities for preparation of coffee, toasting of a bagel, and scrambling of some eggs.

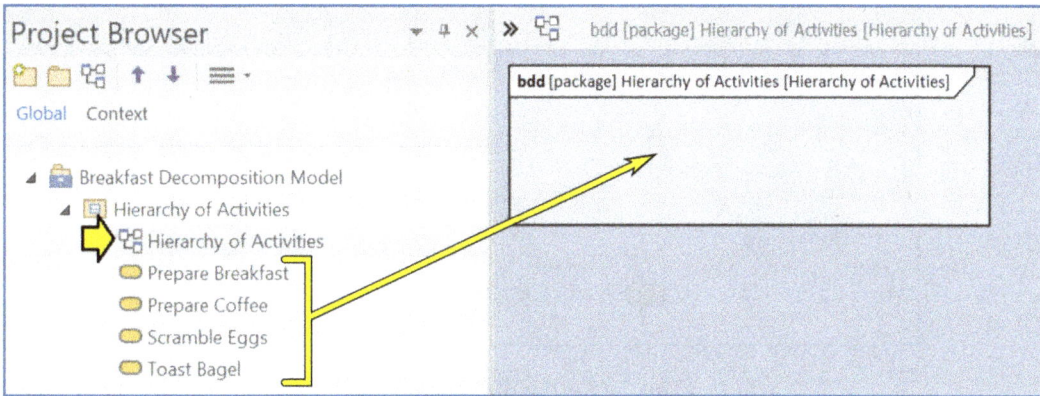

Figure 7-46 – Add block definition diagram

Add a block definition diagram to the model and drag the activities to it. In the dialog box that pops up, select the default value of "Link" for "Drop as:".

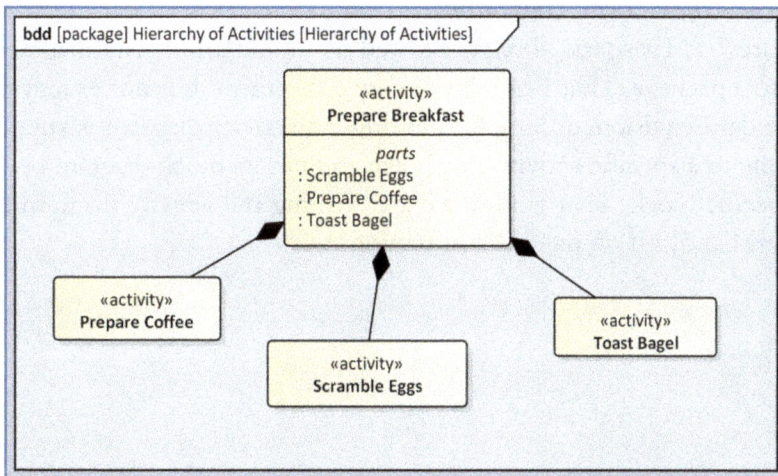

Figure 7-47 – Decomposed activity

Add composition relationships between parent activity of preparing breakfast and the three subactivities. The decomposed activity is shown in Figure 7-47.

Call Actions

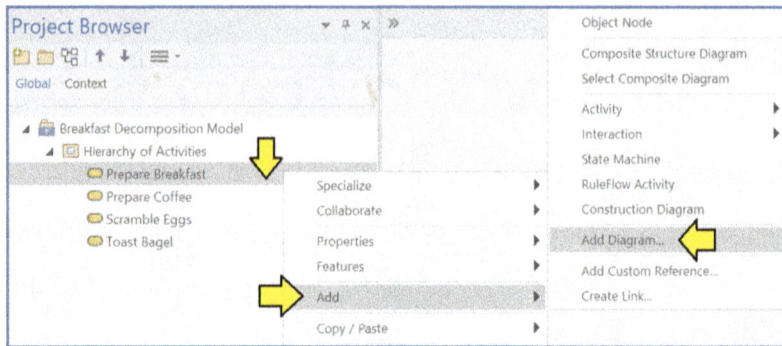

Figure 7-48 – Add diagram to activity

Create the model and four activities as before. Right-click on the main breakfast preparation activity and select "Add" and then "Add Diagram".

Who Owns the Activity Diagram?

In Figure 7-1, *Enterprise Architect* allowed us to add an activity diagram directly to a package. That flexibility is very convenient, but not exactly what the standard envisioned. Strictly speaking, an activity diagram is supposed to belong to a specific activity, much like an internal block diagram belongs to a specific block. That is how we are creating the activity diagram here. See [SysML1.5] list on page 194 in section A.1.

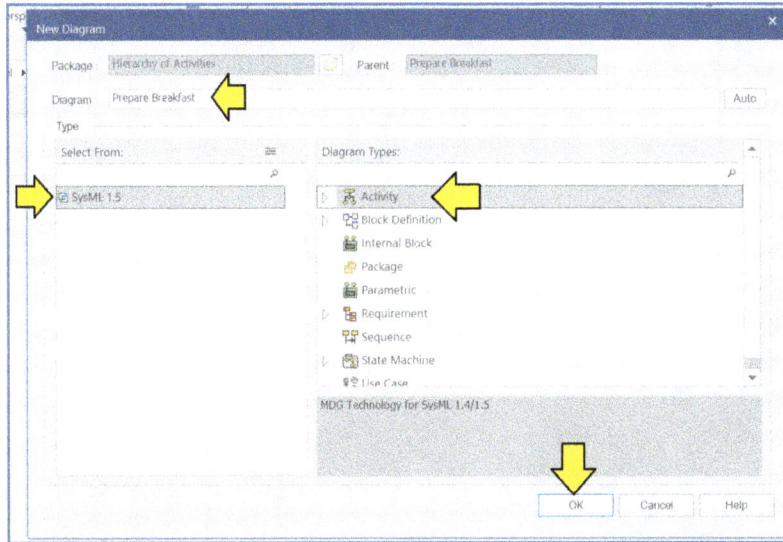

Figure 7-49 – Name the diagram

Name the diagram: "Prepare Breakfast". In the "Select From:" column, click to select: "SysML 1.5". In the "Diagram Types:" column, select "Activity". Click "OK".

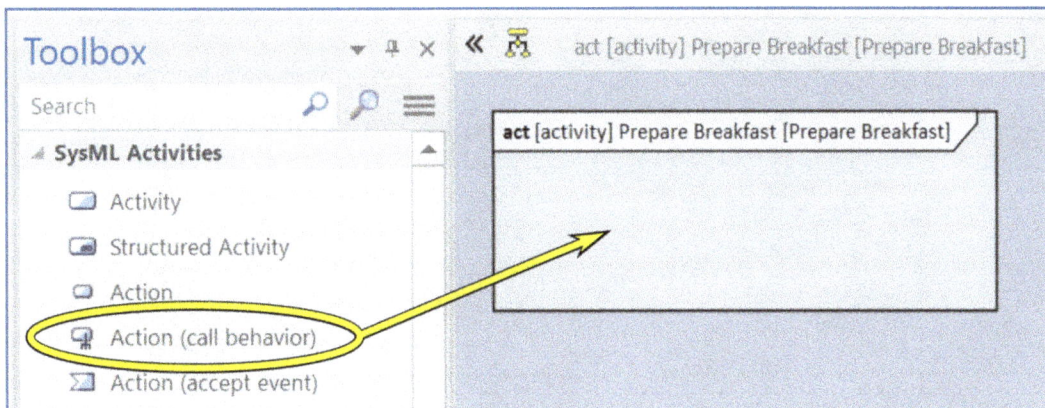

Figure 7-50 – Drag call behavior to the diagram

In the toolbox find the "Action (call behavior)" icon and drag it to the diagram.

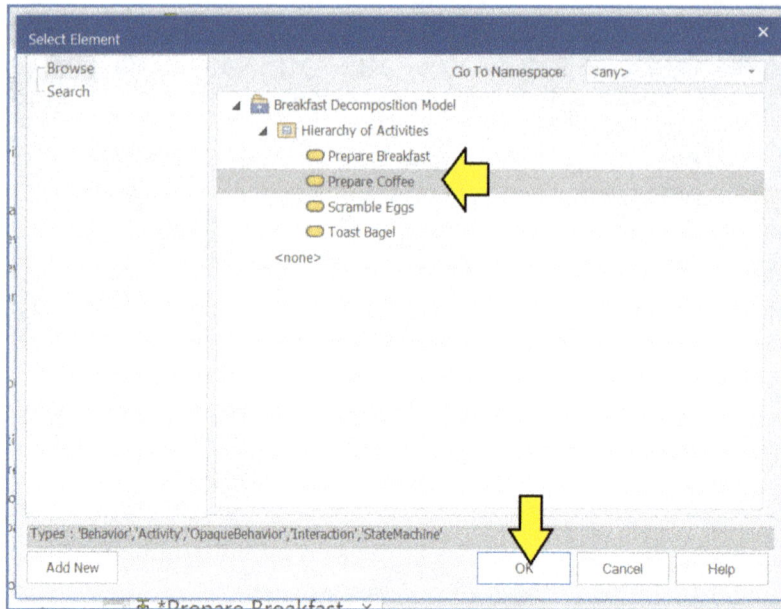

Figure 7-51 – Select prepare coffee

The "Select Element" dialog box will appear. Browse to the "Prepare Coffee" activity and select it. Click "OK".

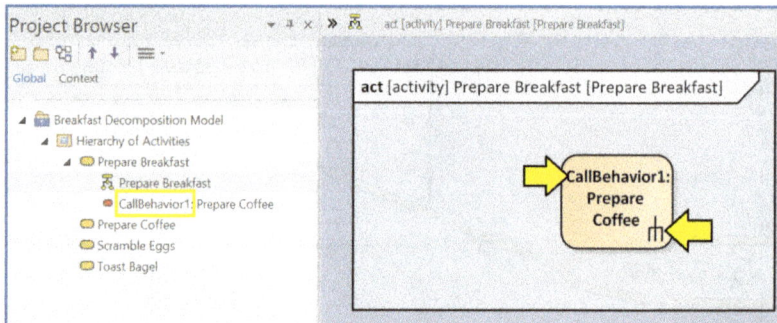

Figure 7-52 – Notice rake symbol and default name

After clicking "OK" we can observe two interesting points about the updated diagram.

1) *Enterprise Architect* has inserted the rake symbol into the "Action (call behavior)" box in the diagram. Since the action "Prepare Coffee" does not (yet) have

its own activity diagram, the rake symbol does not mean much. However, if we were to add an activity diagram to "Prepare Coffee", we would be able to click through to that diagram.

2) *Enterprise Architect* has given the "Action (call behavior)" element a (not very meaningful) default name. Double-click on the element and change the default name of "CallBehavior1" to "coffee".

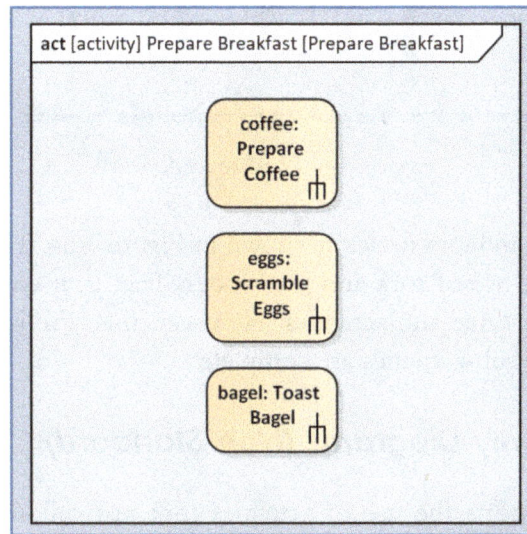

Figure 7-53 – Notice rake symbol and default name

Add "Action (call behavior)" elements for the other two behaviors.

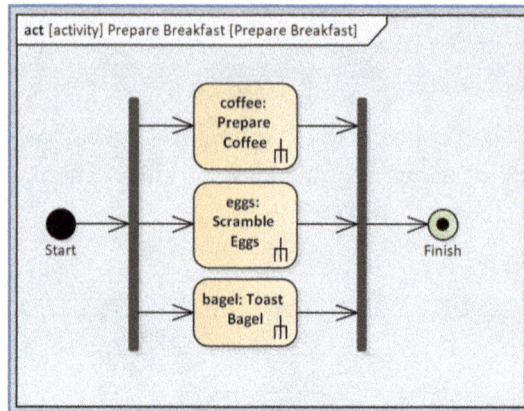

Figure 7-54 – Finish up the diagram

Add initial, final, fork, and join nodes as shown in Figure 7-54. This diagram is actually a good example of the use of fork and join nodes. That is, if you are like me, you are going to multitask the three sub-activities. However, the "Prepare Breakfast" activity can't exit until all three sub-activities are complete.

Activities on Activity Diagrams (Non-Standard)

Enterprise Architect supports the use of activities (not just call actions) in activity diagrams. While this feature is not strictly speaking part of the SysML standard, you may find it useful.

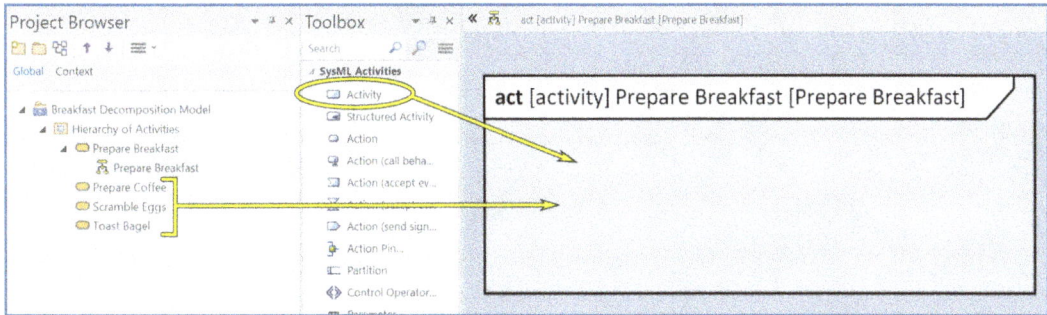

Figure 7-55 – Drag activities

Returning to our breakfast model, we once again create an activity diagram for the activity "Prepare Breakfast". We now have two options for using activities directly in this diagram:

1) We can drag the activity icon from the toolbox to the diagram.

2) We can drag the subactivities from the project browser to the diagram.

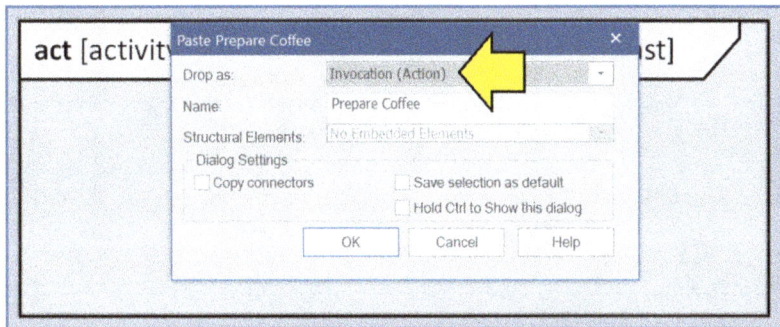

Figure 7-56 – The tool prompts for an invocation

Go ahead and drag "Prepare Coffee" from the project browser to the diagram. A dialog box will appear with the default to create the invocation of a call behavior. In other words, *Enterprise Architect* is gently herding you back towards the standard approach. For the moment be stubborn: override the default and create a link to the activity.

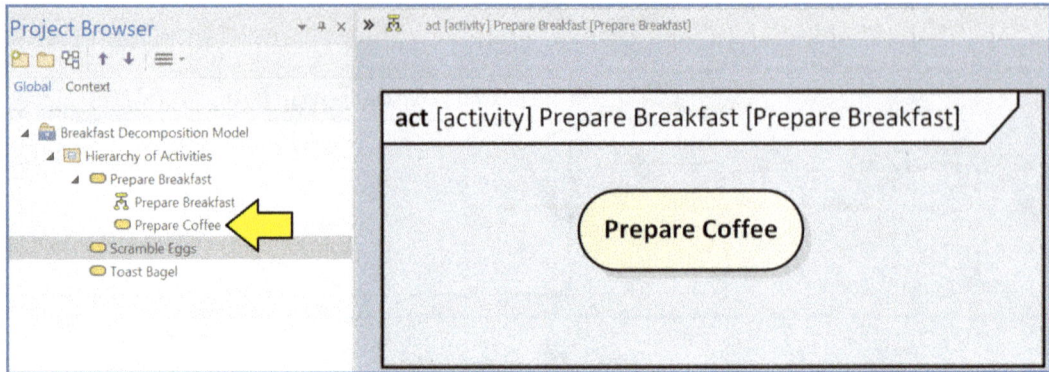

Figure 7-57 – The activity is now nested

Done. We have an activity on an activity diagram. However, something else interesting has happened. The activities are now nested in the project browser.

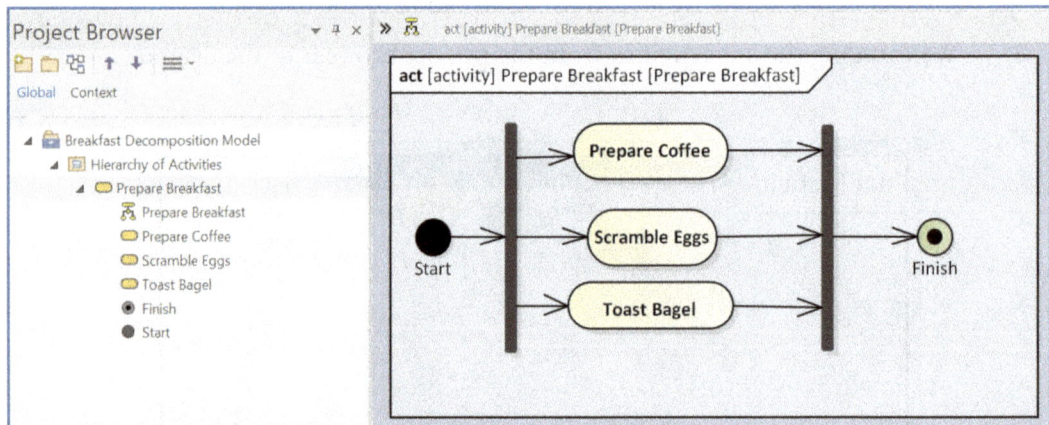

Figure 7-58 – Finished nesting

We can finish up the diagram by dragging in the other two activities and adding initial, final, fork, and join nodes.

Strictly speaking, this is not a standard diagram. However, it is simpler, easier to read, and has less distracting notation than the "standard" diagram shown in Figure 7-54 on page 222.

Further Study

Here is a list of further topics you will want to study to hone your expertise.

- **Activity parameters** – can be attached to the frame of an activity diagram to model input to an activity:
    - [Delligatti] – page 97
    - [Douglass] – page 126
    - [Friedenthal] – page 210

- **Opaque notation** – is the SysML method of putting actual statements for a specific programming language in a diagram:
    - [Delligatti] – page 94
    - [Friedenthal] – page 240

- **Pin notation** – is a more compact notation for object flows which allows you to put more things on a diagram:
    - [Delligatti] – page 96
    - [Douglass] – page 125
    - [Friedenthal] – page 208

- **Signals** – allow you to model the transmission of messages to other blocks as well as the reception of messages from other blocks:
    - [Delligatti] – page 107
    - [Friedenthal] – page 221

- **Streaming** – allows you to model the simultaneous processing of multiple tokens:
    - [Delligatti] – page 98
    - [Friedenthal] – page 210
- **Token flow** – was introduced above. For more detail, take a look at:
    - [Delligatti] – page 92
    - [Douglass] – page 128
    - [Friedenthal] – page 208
- **Wait time actions** – allow you to model the passage of time as part of a control flow:
    - [Delligatti] – page 110
    - [Friedenthal] – page 229

Chapter 8 – Sequence Diagrams

Sequence diagrams are one of the most powerful tools for forging a common understanding among stakeholders about how a system is supposed to work. That having been said, sequence diagrams can be more intricate than they first appear. In this chapter, we will take a closer look at sequence diagrams and some of their detailed features.

Basic Sequences - Revisiting the Doorbell System

In *Adding a Sequence Diagram* on page 43, we created a simple sequence diagram. Frankly speaking, however, we were playing fast and loose with the rules for properly constructing sequence diagrams. In this section, we will go back and recreate the sequence diagram for the doorbell system paying closer attention to all the details.

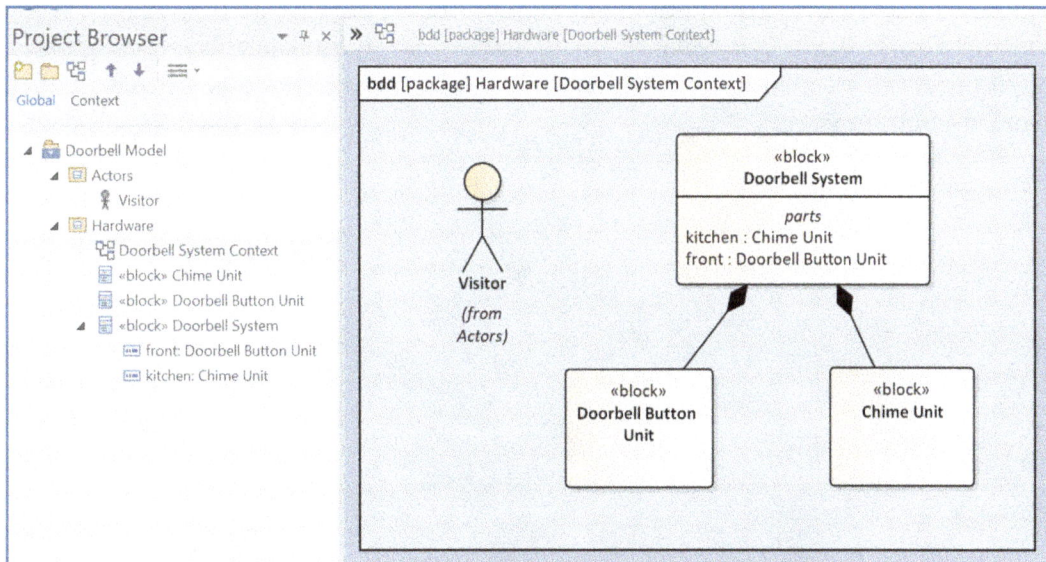

Figure 8-1 – The basic doorbell system

First, we will strip our previous doorbell system back to the visitor, the button unit, and the chime unit. [37]

Looking at our original sequence diagram in Figure 2-55 on page 50, the first problem we are going to correct is the context for the sequence diagram. In our original quick start model, we simply added the sequence diagram to a package. Strictly speaking, a package cannot own a sequence diagram in SysML. A sequence diagram needs to be owned by an **interaction** which is a model element owned by a block.

Since this SysML restriction is often confusing and arcane for beginners, *Enterprise Architect* flexibly allows sequence diagrams to be added to packages. However, a sequence diagram owned by a package is not correct SysML and we are going to correct our doorbell model to come into line with the standard.

Looking again at the original sequence diagram, the second problem is that we put the visitor and the blocks directly on the diagram as owners of their lifelines. The general practice in SysML and UML is for lifelines to represent "roles". Used in SysML, "role" generally means a part relationship.

Our game plan is going to be to add a "Visitor Arrival" interaction to the "Doorbell System" block of which the button unit and the chime units are parts. What about the visitor? This visitor is not really a part of the system. Fortunately, *Enterprise Architect* allows us to create a "property" within a block which is another type of role and will work for our purposes.

---

[37] *Sparx Systems* significantly altered the behavior of actors between versions 14 and version 15.2 of the tool, no longer allowing actors to be part of reference associations, but still allowing them as properties on a block. The procedure in this section was updated to work with version 15.2 of the tool.

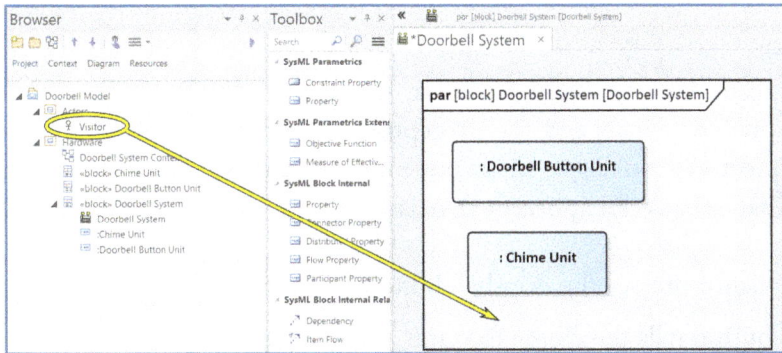

Figure 8-2 – Drag the actor to the internal block definition diagram

Add an internal block diagram to the doorbell system block. Drag the chime and button part properties to the diagram. Drag the actor to the diagram.

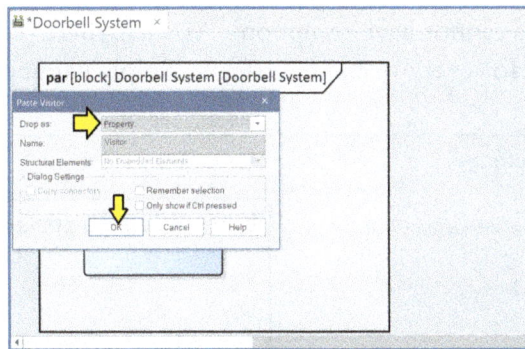

Figure 8-3 – Drop as property

After releasing the mouse button, be sure "Drop as:" is set to "Property" and click "OK". The tool will give the property a default name. Delete the default property name.

The doorbell system is now ready to accommodate an interaction and its sequence diagram. That is, we have three crisp roles for the lifelines:

- :Doorbell Button Unit
- :Chime Unit

- :Visitor

Before we create the interaction, however, we need to do one more preparation step: we need to prepare signals and their receptions for the messages in the sequence diagram to connect to. Looking again at our original sequence diagram in Figure 2-55 on page 50, we can see several apparent signals:

1) The visitor presses the doorbell button.

2) The button tells the chime to start.

3) The chime tells the button to start flashing.

4) The chime tells the button to stop flashing.

Observant readers will notice that the flashing button and the return to a dull glow are also signals of a sort that are perceived by the visitor. However, here we run into a limitation of SysML: actors cannot have receptions. As such, there really is not a way to link a signal to the visitor. However, we can fall back to simply naming the message.

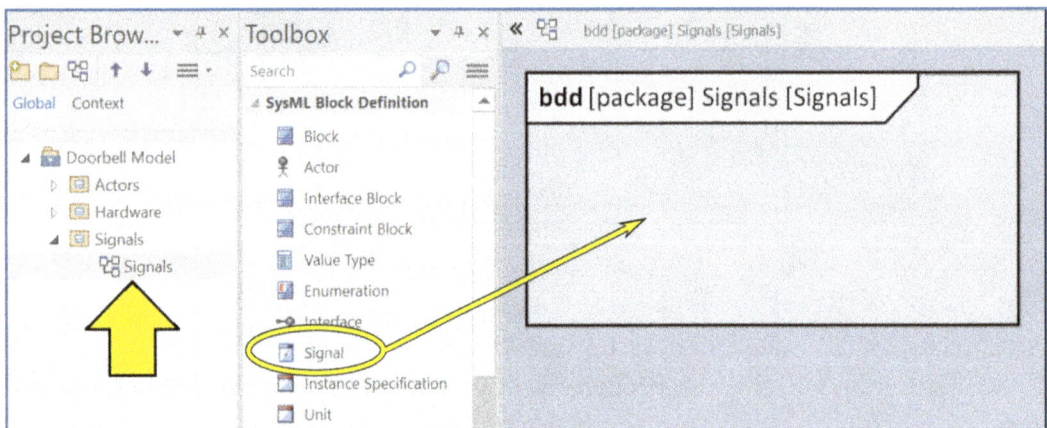

Figure 8-4 – Drag the signal to the diagram

1) Create a new package for signals.

2) Create a new block definition diagram within the new package.

3) In the toolbox, select the signal icon and drag it to the diagram.

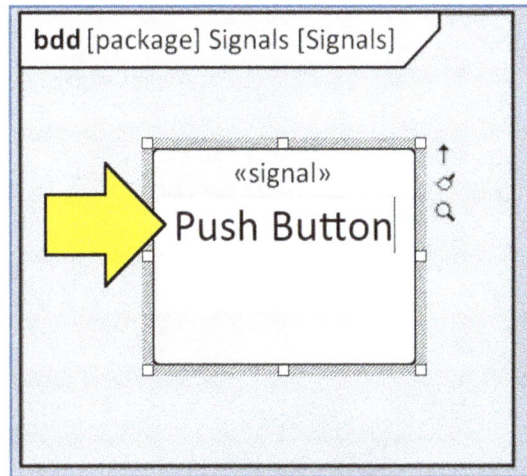

Figure 8-5 – Name the Signal

Name the signal "Push Button". Create three more signals called:

- "Start Chime"
- "Start Flashing"
- "Stop Flashing"

Now we are ready to add the receptions to the blocks.

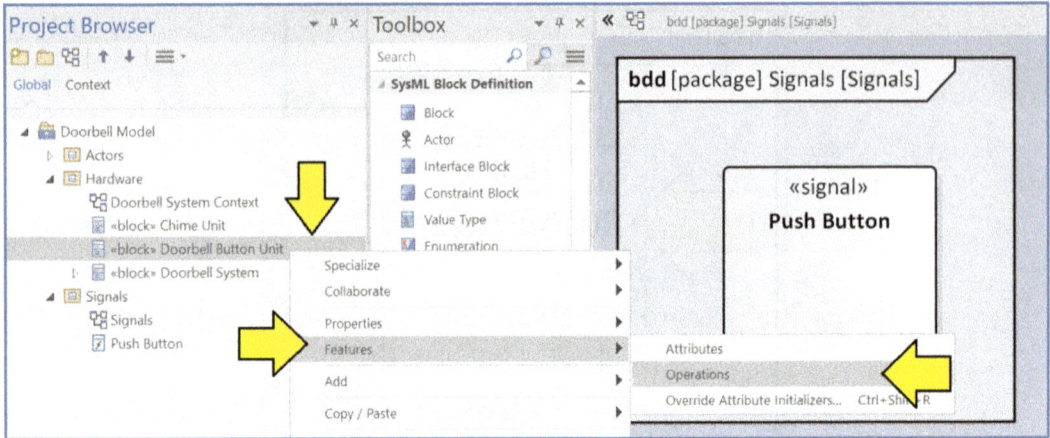

Figure 8-6 – Right-click and open operations panel

Right-click on the doorbell button unit, select "Features" and then "Operations".

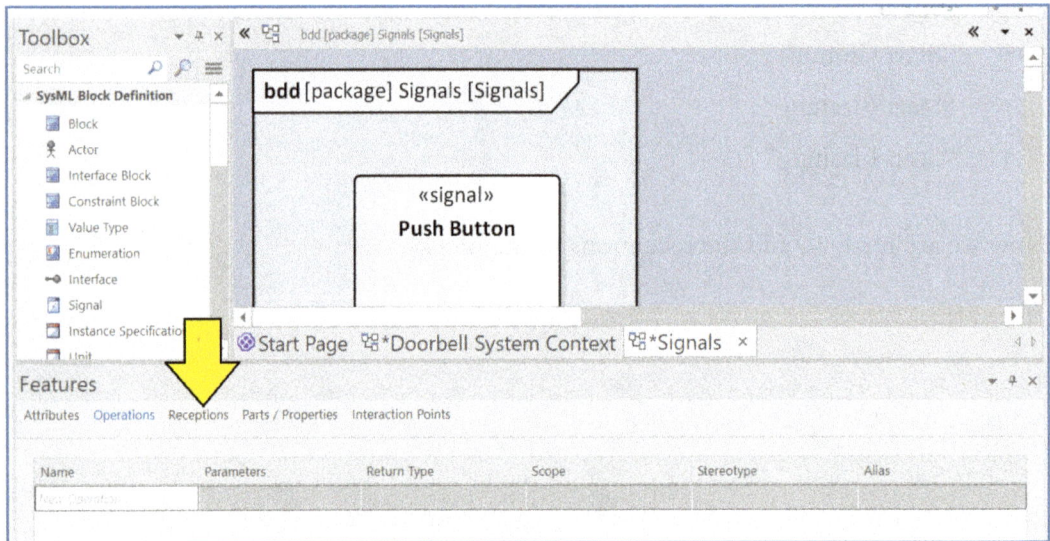

Figure 8-7 – Click on receptions

A multipurpose panel will open. Click on "Receptions".

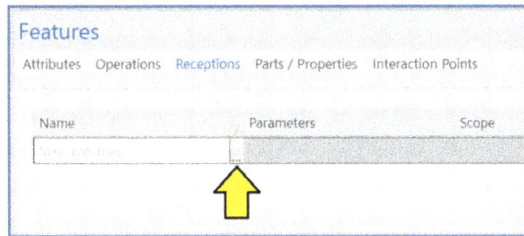

Figure 8-8 – Click on three dots

Click on the three dots field to create a new reception.

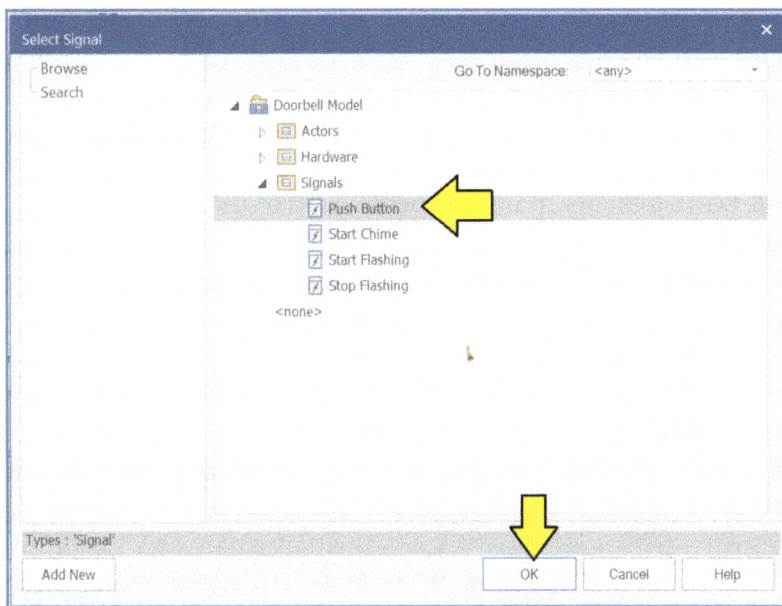

Figure 8-9 – Select push button

Navigate to "Push Button". Select it. Click "OK".

Let's stop for a second and catch our breath. What have we actually done here? What we have done is put the future subsystem designers of the doorbell button unit on notice that there will be an incoming signal called: "Push Button" and the subsystem designers need to provide appropriate functionality (the reception) to handle that signal.

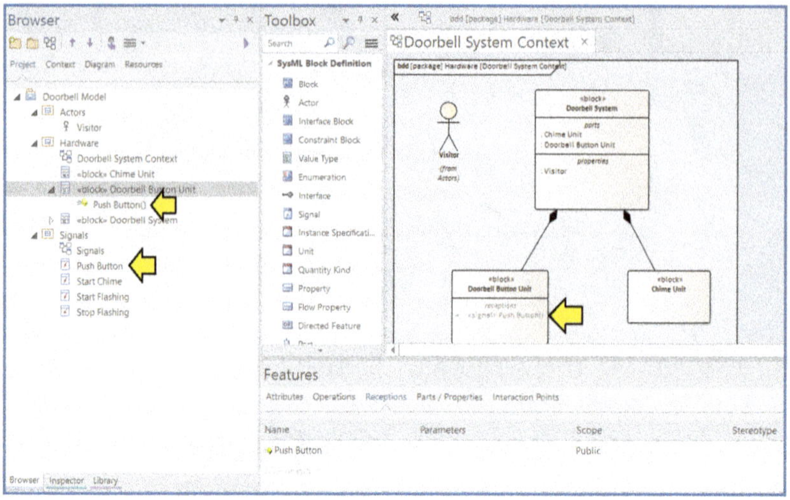

Figure 8-10 – Reception has been added to the model

Figure 8-10 shows that the reception has been added to the model.

1) Add a reception to the chime unit block for "Start Chime".

2) Add a reception to the doorbell button unit block for "Start Flashing".

3) Add a reception to the doorbell button unit block for "Stop Flashing".

Now we are ready to add the interaction and its sequence diagram to the doorbell system block.

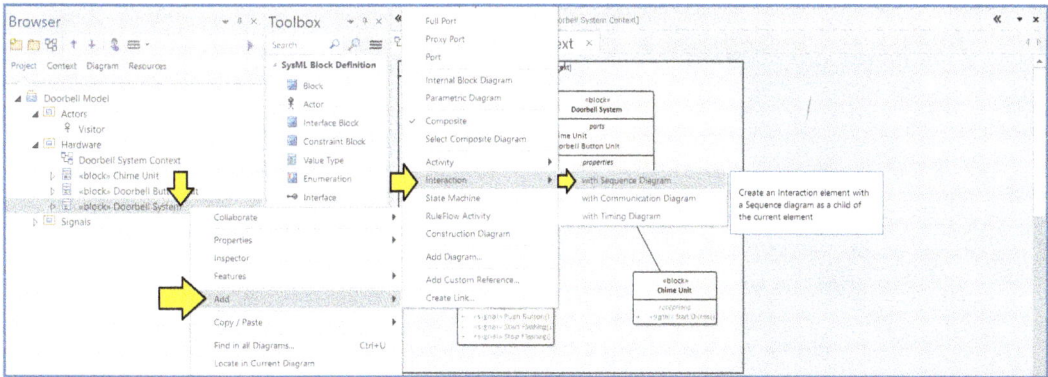

Figure 8-11 – Add interaction and sequence diagram

Right-click on the doorbell system block in the project browser. Select "Add" and "Interaction" and "with Sequence Diagram".

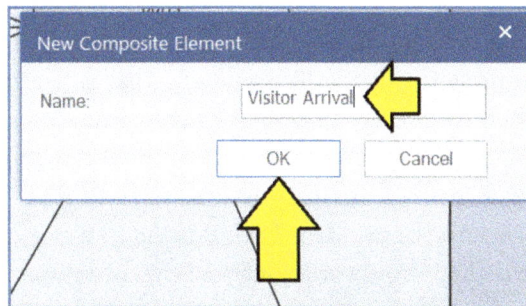

Figure 8-12 – Name the interaction

Name the interaction "Visitor Arrival" and click "OK".

Interaction and Diagram are Not the Same Thing

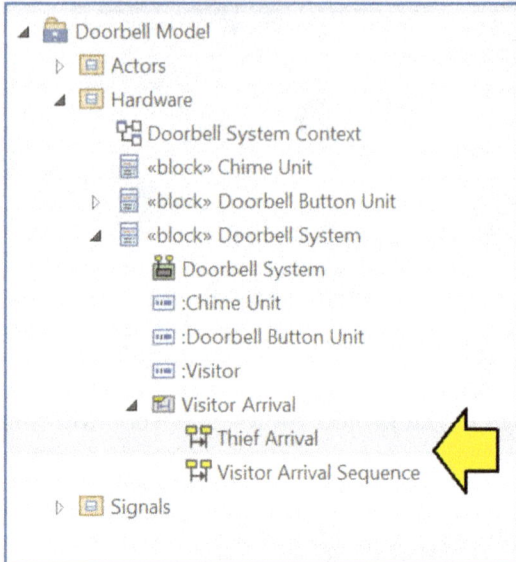

- ▲ 🔒 Doorbell Model
  - ▷ 🔲 Actors
  - ▲ 🔲 Hardware
    - 🔲 Doorbell System Context
    - 🔳 «block» Chime Unit
    - ▷ 🔳 «block» Doorbell Button Unit
    - ▲ 🔳 «block» Doorbell System
      - 📷 Doorbell System
      - 🔲 :Chime Unit
      - 🔲 :Doorbell Button Unit
      - 🔲 :Visitor
      - ▲ 🔲 Visitor Arrival
        - 🔲 Thief Arrival
        - 🔲 Visitor Arrival Sequence
  - ▷ 🔲 Signals

Notice that the interaction and the sequence diagram are not the same thing. By using the F2 rename function, we can rename the sequence diagram to something different than the name of the interaction. We can also add multiple sequence diagrams to one interaction to show different aspects of the interaction. I am a fan. I would much rather have ten simple sequence diagrams that show variations in how an interaction could play out, than have one sequence diagram with lots of intricate notation to show all the options.

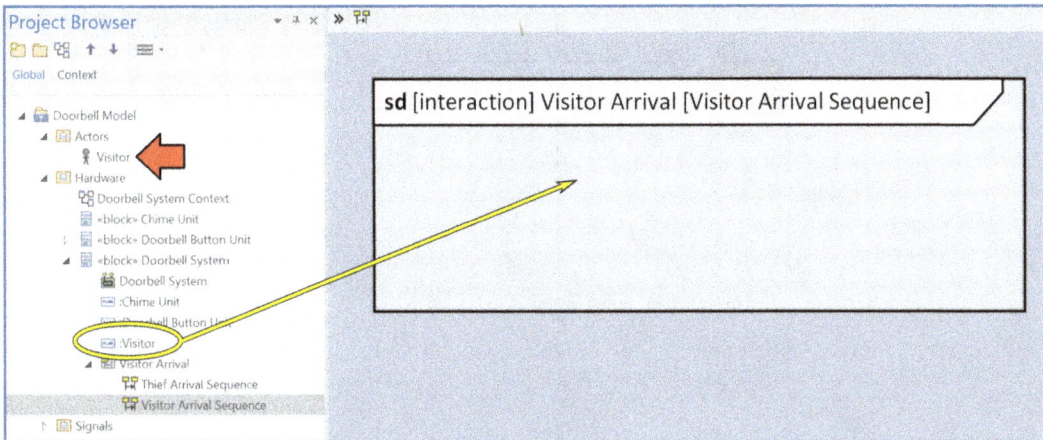

Figure 8-13 – Drag :Visitor role to diagram

Drag the ":Visitor" role to the diagram. Be careful not to drag the primary definition of the visitor actor. Drag the visitor role within the doorbell system.

Drag the ":Doorbell Button Unit" and the ":Chime Unit" roles the diagram as well.

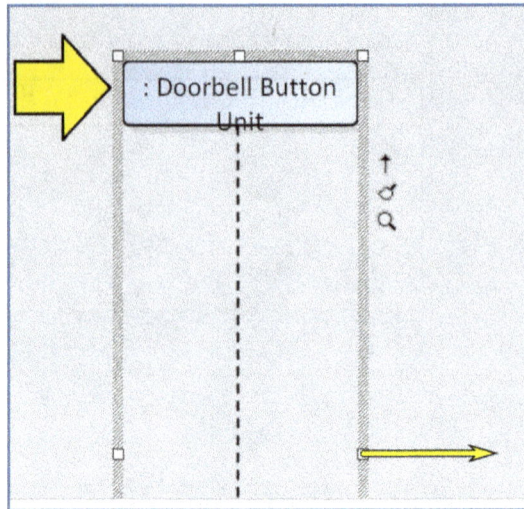

Figure 8-14 – Drag to fix lifeline width

If the name of the doorbell button unit does not fit nicely within the box at the top of the lifeline, you can select the lifeline and use the dragging icon to make the lifeline wider.

Now we are ready to create our first message.

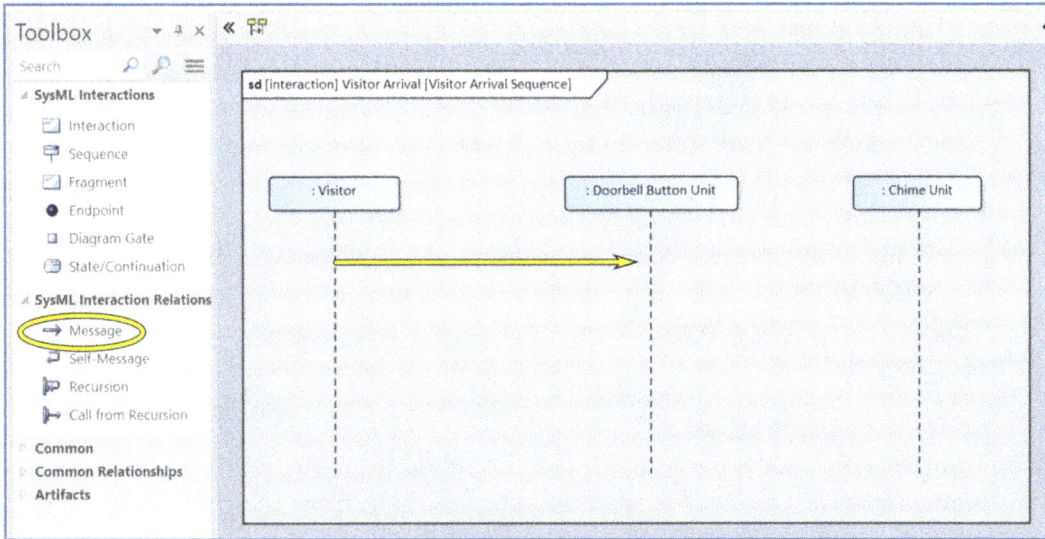

Figure 8-15 – Drag to create message

Select the message icon in the toolbox and drag from the visitor lifeline to the doorbell button unit lifeline.

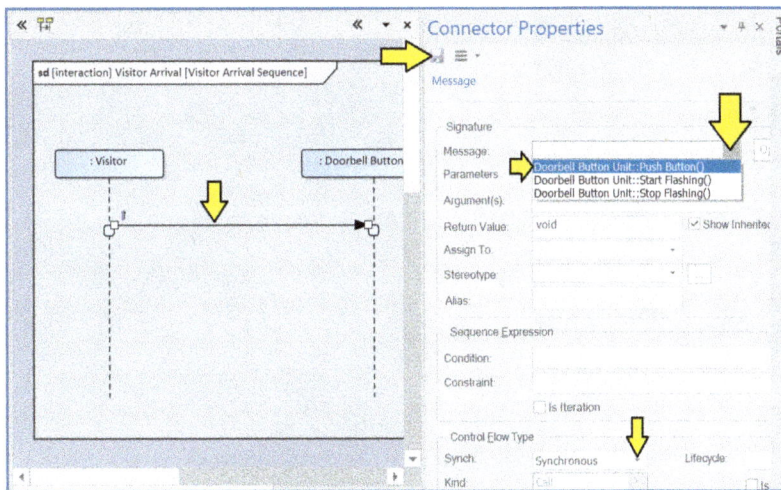

Figure 8-16 – Select the push button reception

1)   Double-click on the message arrow.

2)   The "Connector Properties" panel will appear.

3)   Pull down the selection list for the field "Message:".

4)   Since the arrow ends at the doorbell button lifeline, the three receptions previously defined for the corresponding block will appear.

5)   Select the "Push_Button()" reception.

6)   Under "Control Flow Type" pull down the selector for "Synch:" and select "Asynchronous".

7)   In the "Connector Properties" panel, click on the diskette icon to save your changes.

When you are done, add a message to start the chime from the doorbell button unit to the chime unit. Add messages to start and stop flashing from the chime unit back to the doorbell button unit.

We are finally ready to add the flashing button visible message for the visitor. As mentioned above, from a SysML point of view, the visitor cannot own a reception for a signal. However, we can still add a message to the sequence diagram.

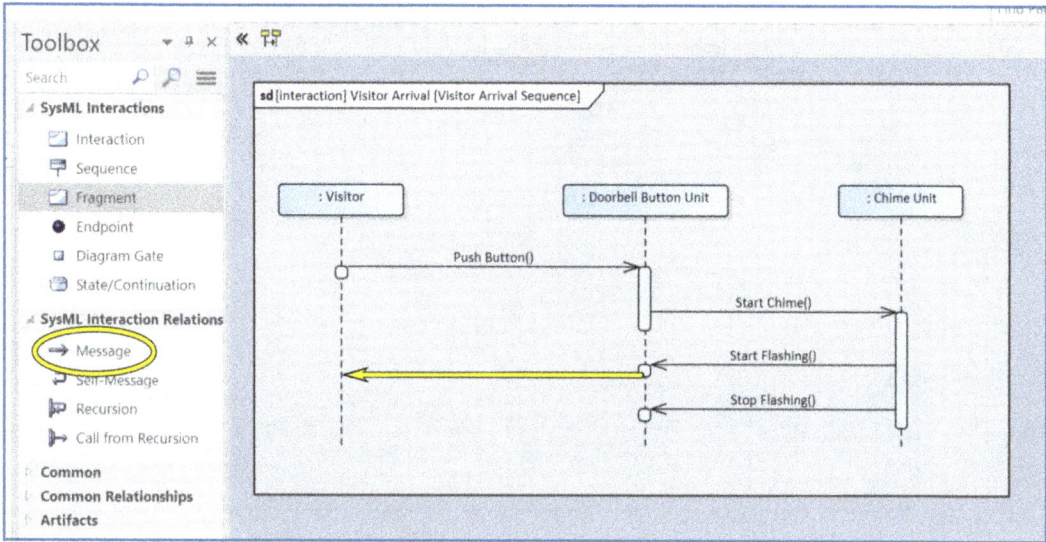

Figure 8-17 – Drag a message back to the visitor

Drag a message from the doorbell button unit back to the visitor.

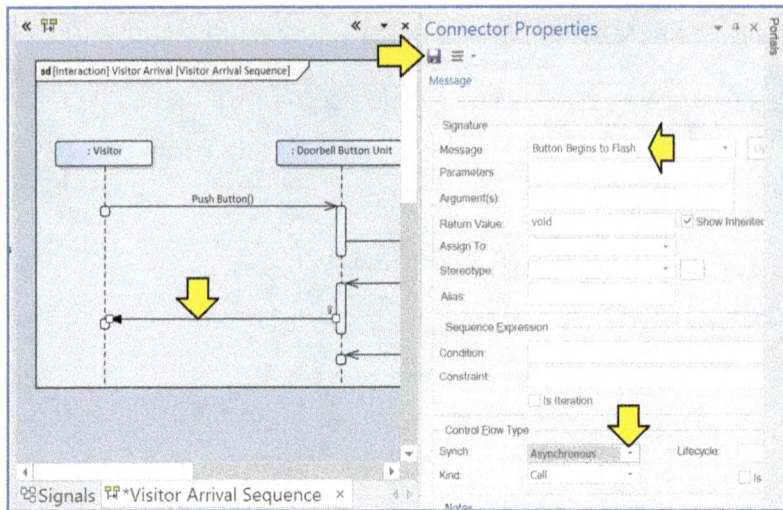

Figure 8-18 – Name the message

Double-click on the new message. Name it: "Button Begins to Flash". Select asynchronous under "Control Flow Type". Click on the diskette icon to save your changes.

Add a second message for: "Button Returns to Dull Glow".

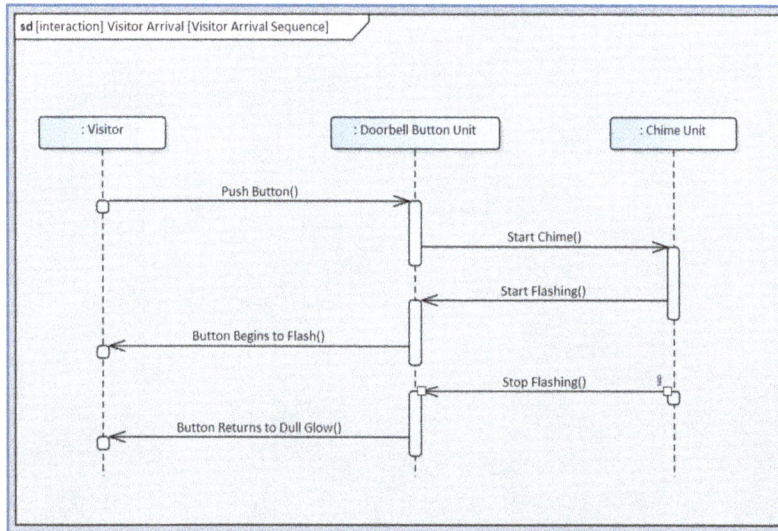

Figure 8-19 – Completed sequence diagram

Synchronous Messages

So far, we have been using asynchronous messages in all of our sequence diagrams. In this section, we are going to take a closer look at synchronous messages and in the process explore some other detailed features of sequence diagrams.

First, we will construct a very simple file storage system in order to explore the following features of sequence diagrams:

- Reply messages
- Self-messages
- Using self-messages to kick off block operations

Our sample system will be a highly intelligent "No Excuses" file storage system. You give it a file and it stores it. If there is not enough space, it automatically compacts the existing data in storage to make space.

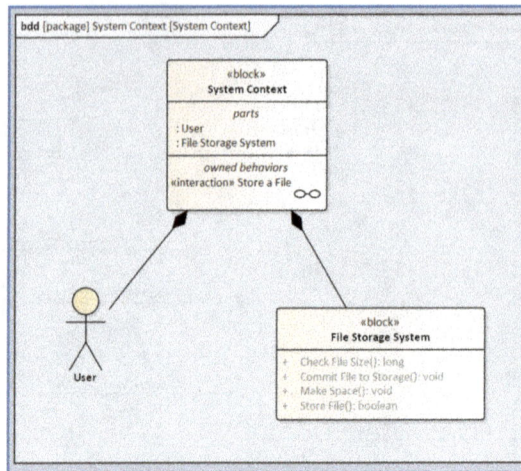

Figure 8-20 – Set up basic system

Set up the basic system as shown in Figure 8-20.

1) Create a block for the file storage system.

2) Add an actor called "User"

3) Create a block for the system context.

4) Add composition relationships as shown.

5) Add an internal block diagram for the system context, right-click on the diagram, and run "Update Structural Elements" to make the user show up in the project browser as a property of the system context – as shown in Figure 5-60 on page 158.

6) Add four operations to the file storage system block using the procedure shown in *Operations and Receptions* on page 108.

   1) **Store File –** This is the main operation invoked by the user. It takes an untyped parameter "file" as input and returns a Boolean.

   2) **Check File Size –** This operation is used to check the size of the file submitted by the user. It takes an untyped parameter "file" as input and returns a long.

3) **Make Space** – The operation is the no excuses operation that makes space as needed. It takes a long as input for the amount of space needed. It returns a void.

4) **Commit File to Storage** – This is the local operation to actually store the file once enough space has been created. It takes an untyped parameter "file" as input and returns a void.

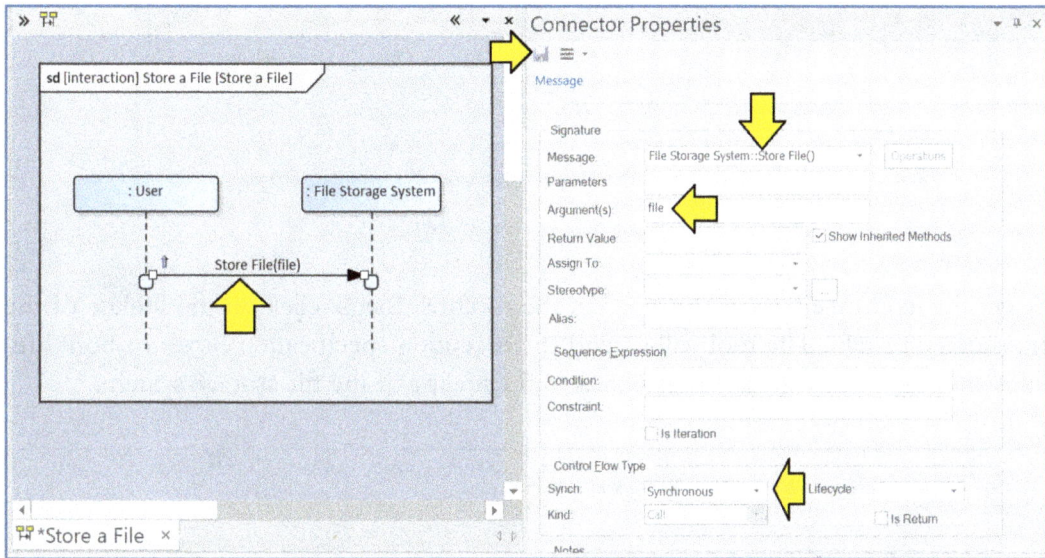

Figure 8-21 – Create interaction, add lifelines, add first message

Add an interaction called "Store a File" to the system context block as shown in the previous section. Add lifelines for the user and the file storage system. Create the first message:

1) Assign it to the (main) "Store File" operation.

2) Enter "file" in the arguments field.

3) Accept the default of synchronous message.

4) Click the diskette icon to save your changes.

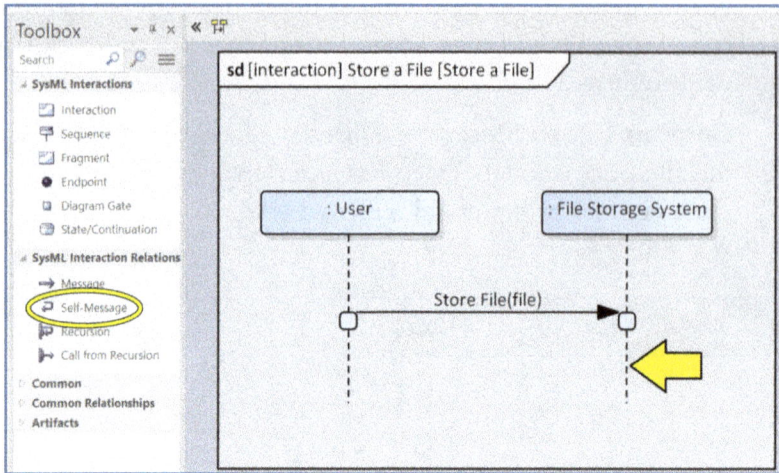

Figure 8-22 – Add self-message

Select the icon called "Self-Message" in the toolbox. Single-click on the lifeline of the file storage system. The tool will extend the execution specification boxes of both lifelines and add a message that loops back to the lifeline of the file storage system.

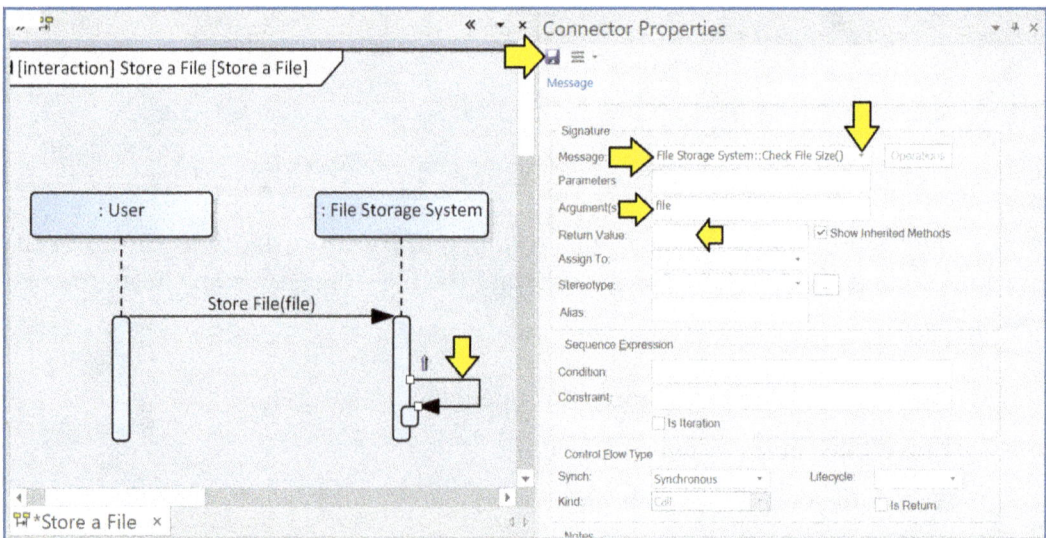

Figure 8-23 – Set properties of self-message

1)   Click once on the self-message to select it.

2) Small white rectangles will appear on both ends of the self-message.

3) Once the message is selected, double-click the self-message to open the connector properties dialog box. [38]

4) Pull down the "Message:" selection control and select the operation "Check File Size".

5) Add "file" in the "Argument(s):" field.

6) Remove "long" from the "Return Value:" field.

7) Click the diskette icon to save your changes.

Add two more self-messages, one for "Make Space" with an argument of "FileSize" and one for "Commit File to Storage" with an argument of "file".

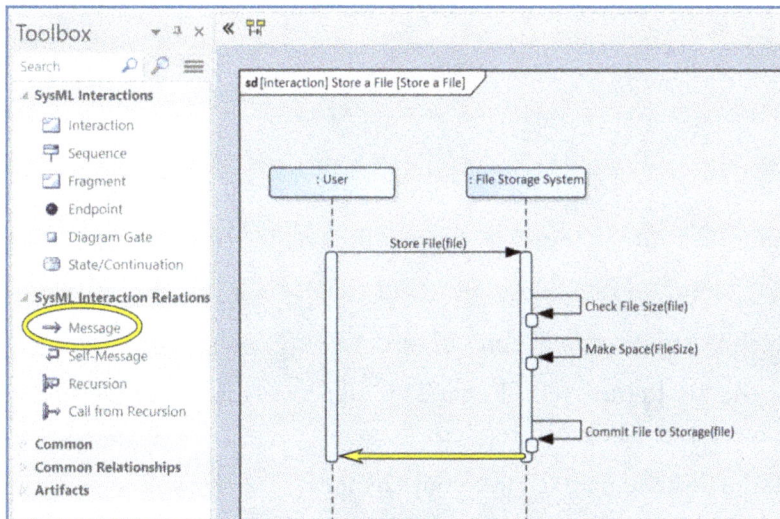

Figure 8-24 – Add final reply message

Now we are ready to draw the final reply message. Drag a message from the file storage system to the user. Notice that *Enterprise Architect* does not have a specific icon for

---

[38] If you double-click the self-message without first selecting it you will open the properties dialog box for the diagram rather than for the self-message.

a reply message. We will change the normal message to a reply message in the connector properties.

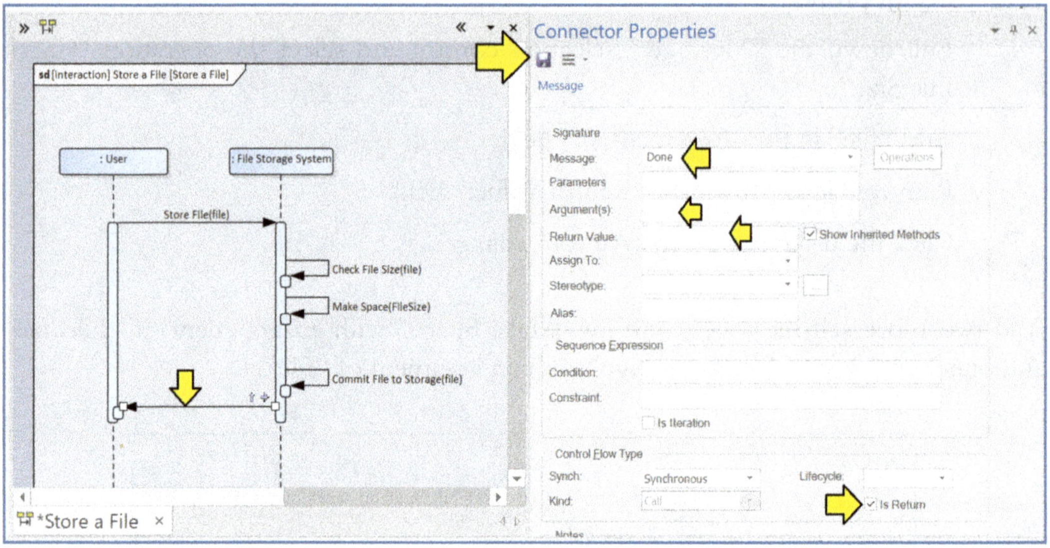

Figure 8-25 – Set Is Return to create reply message

1) Double-click on the message to open the connector properties dialog box.

2) Enter "Done" in the "Message:" field.

3) Clear the "Argument(s):" and "Return Value:" fields.

4) Click the "Is Return" checkbox. This step converts the message from an ordinary message to a SysML reply message.

5) Click the diskette icon to save your changes.

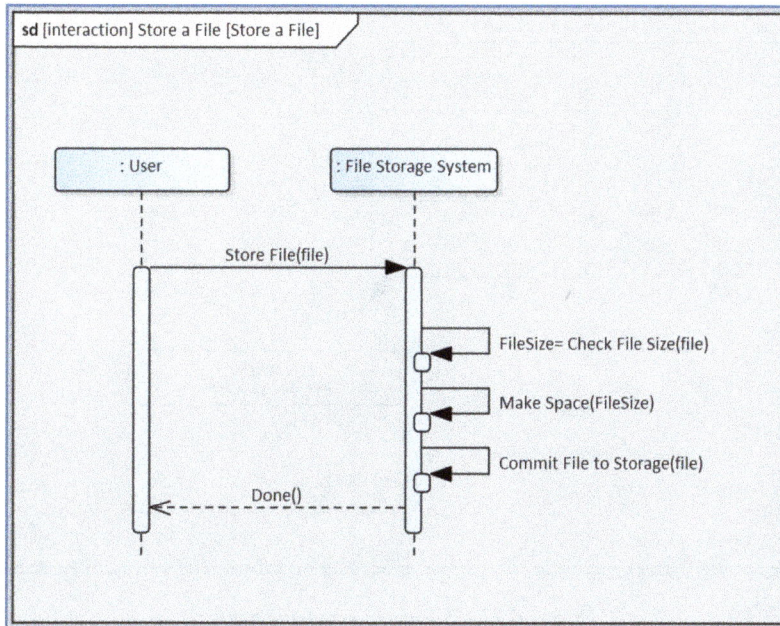

Figure 8-26 – Completed sequence diagram

The completed sequence diagram is shown in Figure 8-26. Notice that the final message is now a dashed line, the notation defined for reply messages in SysML.

Next, we are going to extend the system slightly to demonstrate two more SysML notations:

- Creation and termination of lifelines
- Nested execution specifications

In order to demonstrate these two notations, we are going to extend our file storage system to have an explicit garbage collection task. When the system needs to make space, it will create the garbage collector task. The garbage collector task will run until it has recovered enough space and then terminate.

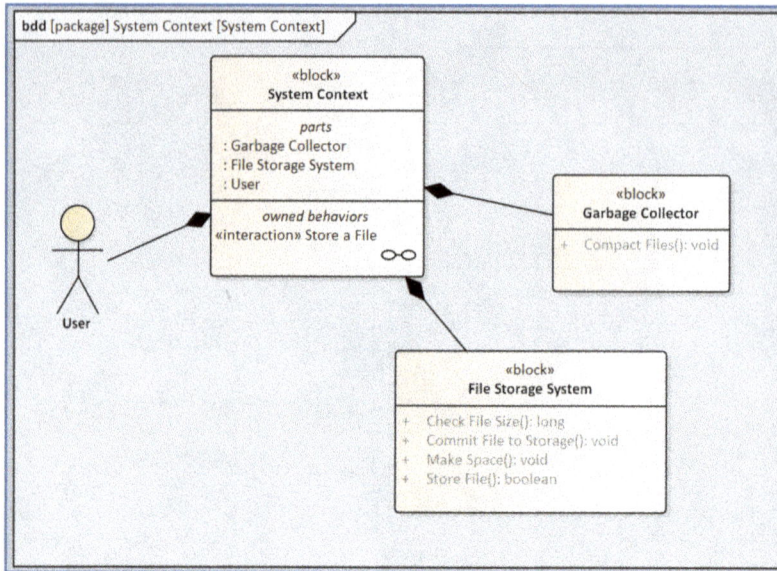

Figure 8-27 – Set up extended basic system

Extend the system by adding the "Garbage Collector" block as shown. Add an operation "Compact Files" to the garbage collector block. Add a lifeline for the garbage collector block to the sequence diagram.

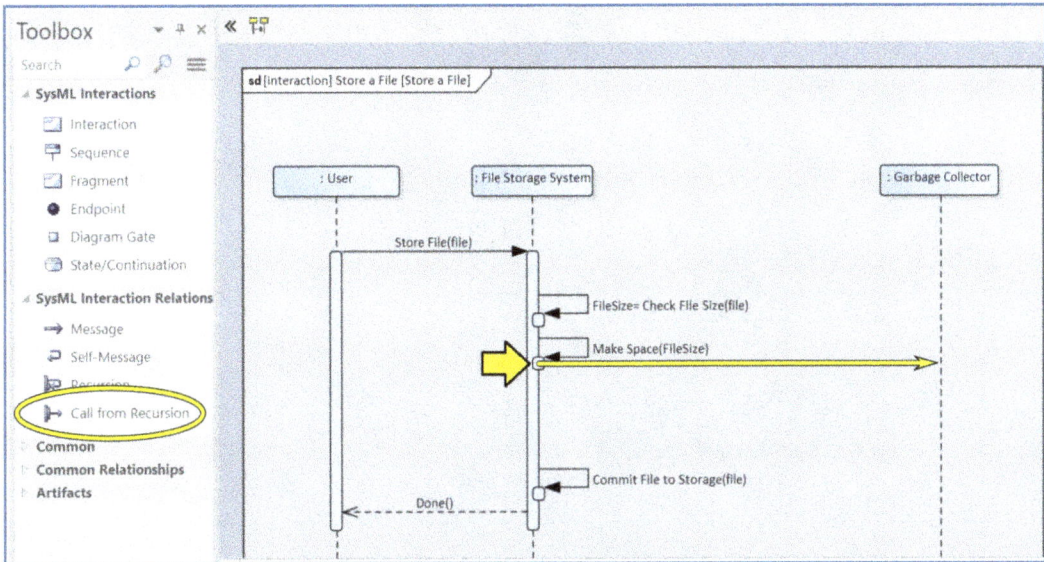

Figure 8-28 – Add a call from recursion

In the toolbox select the "Call from Recursion" icon. Drag a message from the small rectangle at the end of the "Make File Space" self-message to the garbage collector lifeline.

Notice that in addition to drawing the message, *Enterprise Architect* extends that small rectangle into a longer rectangle. This is the notation for a nested execution specification.

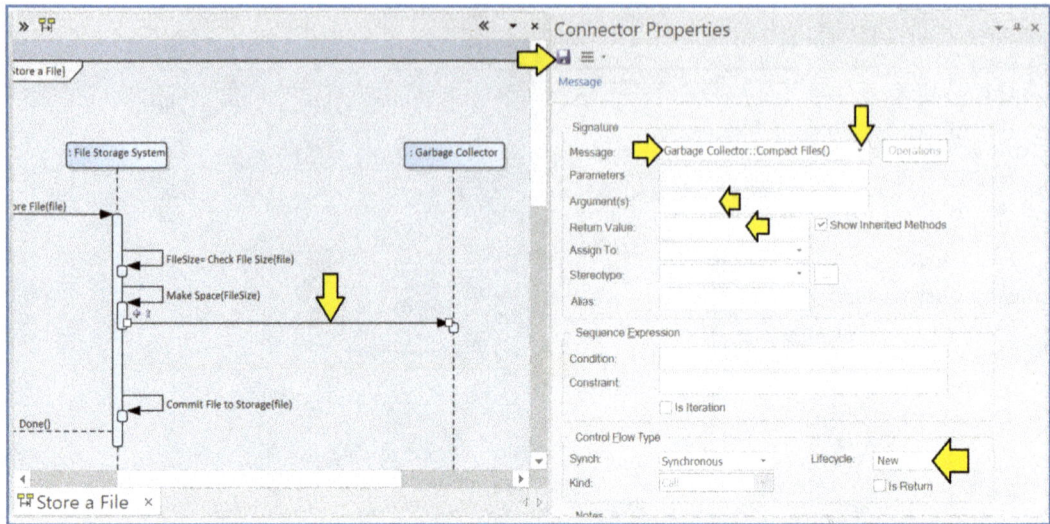

Figure 8-29 – Add a call from recursion

1) Double-click on the message to open the connector properties dialog box.

2) Select "Compact Files" in the "Message:" field.

3) Clear the "Argument(s):" and "Return Value:" fields.

4) In the "Lifecycle:" field select "New". This step converts the message from an ordinary message to a SysML create message.

5) Click the diskette icon to save your changes.

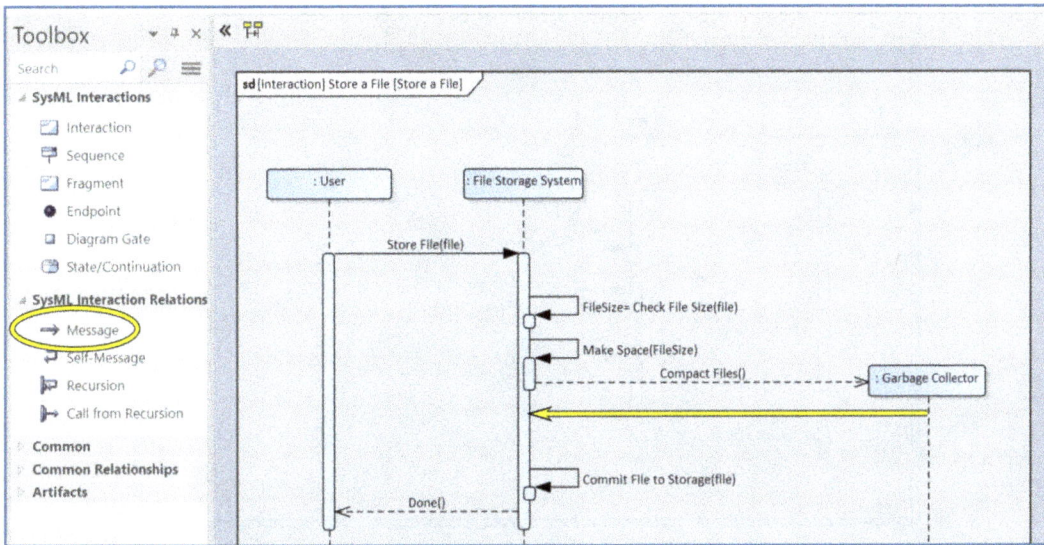

Figure 8-30 – Draw reply message

Draw a reply message from the garbage collector lifeline back to the file storage system lifeline. Use the connector properties dialog properties to check the "Is Return" as before.

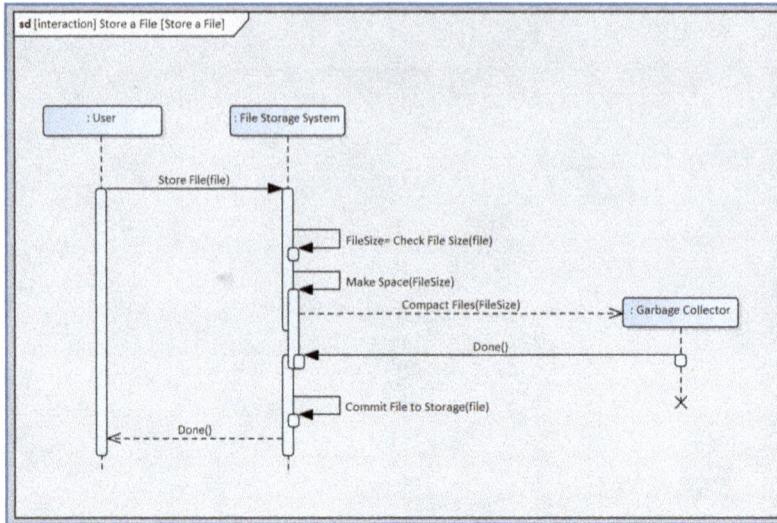

Figure 8-31 – Completed sequence diagram

The completed sequence diagram is shown in Figure 8-31. Notice that the lifeline for the garbage collector now shows as terminated. Since the lifeline was created with a synchronous message, the reply message terminates the lifeline.

Finally, we are going to take a closer look at parameters in sequence diagrams. In order to demonstrate the technique, we will use a model of a device that calculates the volume of a block. The device has a user interface that accepts length, height, and width from the user and calls a back-end volume calculator to calculate the volume.

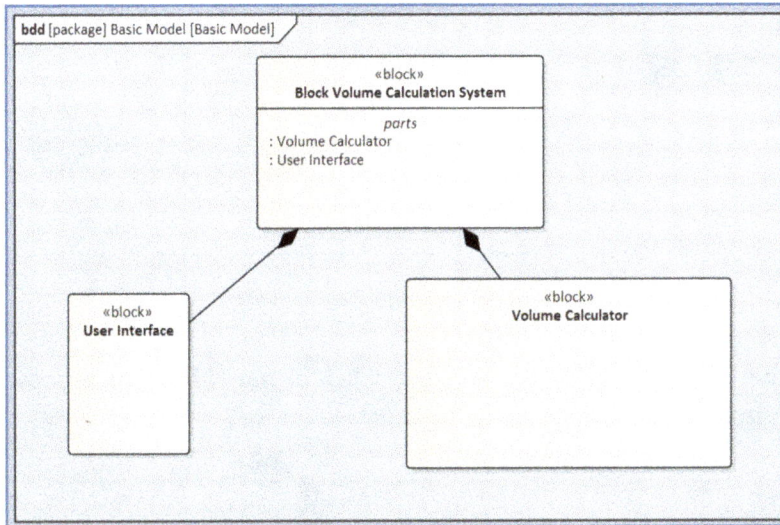

Figure 8-32 – Set up the basic model

Set up the basic model as shown in Figure 8-32.

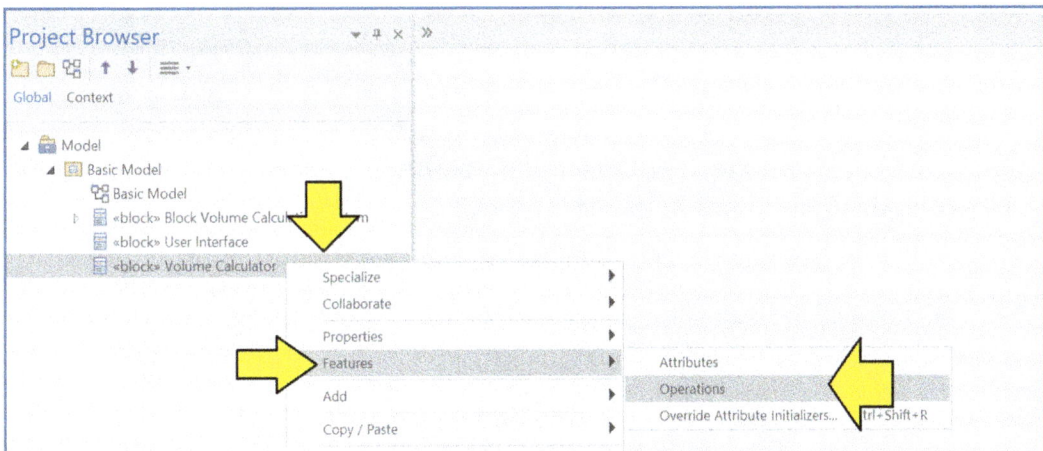

Figure 8-33 – Add an operation to the volume calculator block

Next, we will want to add an operation to the volume calculator block to perform the actual calculation. Right-click on the volume calculator block. Select "Features" and then "Operations".

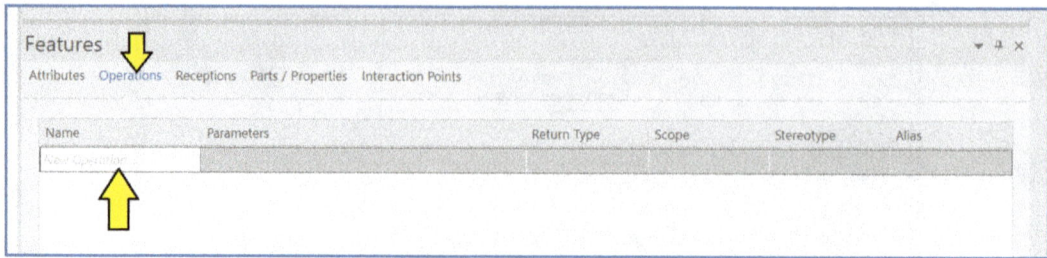

Figure 8-34 – Create a new operation

Make sure the "Operations" tab is selected. Click in the "New Operation..." field and enter the name of the new operation: "CalculateVolume".

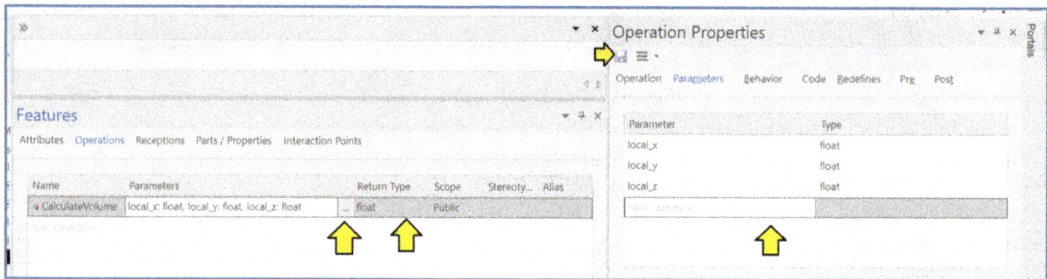

Figure 8-35 – Set the parameters for the operation

1)   Double-click on the three dots in the parameters field of the features panel to open the "Operations Properties" panel.

2)   Add three new parameters: "local_x, local_y, local_z".

3)   Set them all to float. [39]

4)   Click the diskette icon to save your changes.

5)   Back in the features panel, set the return type to float.

---

[39] "float" = "real"

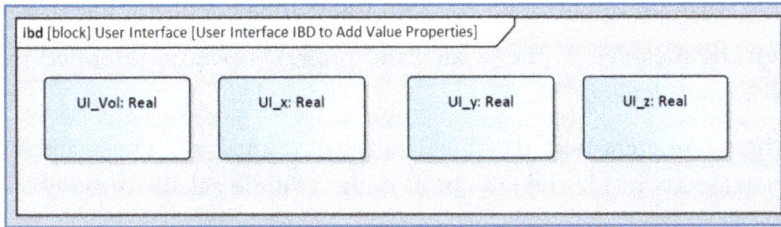

Figure 8-36 – Use internal block diagram to add properties

Next, we will need to add some value properties to the user interface block. Use the procedure shown in *Value Properties* on page 93 to bring in the *Enterprise Architect* standard type library. Create an internal block diagram for the user interface block. Drag the ValueType "Real" from the standard type library to the internal block diagram four times to create properties as shown in Figure 8-36.

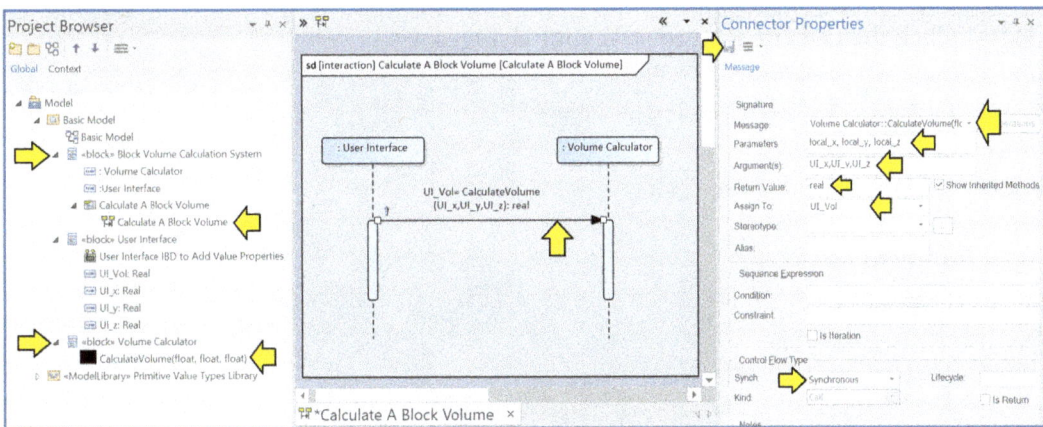

Figure 8-37 – Create sequence diagram and first message

Now we are ready to create a sequence diagram message with detailed passing of parameters:

1) Add an interaction called "Calculate a Block Volume" to the block volume calculation system.

2) Add lifelines for the user interface and the volume calculator.

3) Add a message from the user interface to the volume calculator.

4)   Double-click on the message to open the connector properties dialog box.

5)   Assign the message to the "CalculateVolume" operation defined previously in the volume calculator block.

6)   Set the parameters field to: "local_x, local_y, local_z". These are the names of the parameters inside the operation in the volume calculator block.

7)   Set the arguments field to: "UI_x, UI_y, UI_z". These are the names of the properties inside the user interface block.

8)   Set the return value to: "real". This setting means that the operation inside the volume calculator block will return its result as a real number (rather than as a Boolean or an integer).

9)   Set the assign to field to: "UI_Vol". This is the name of the property inside the user interface block that will receive the result.

10)   Accept the default control flow type of synchronous.

11)   Click the diskette icon to save your changes.

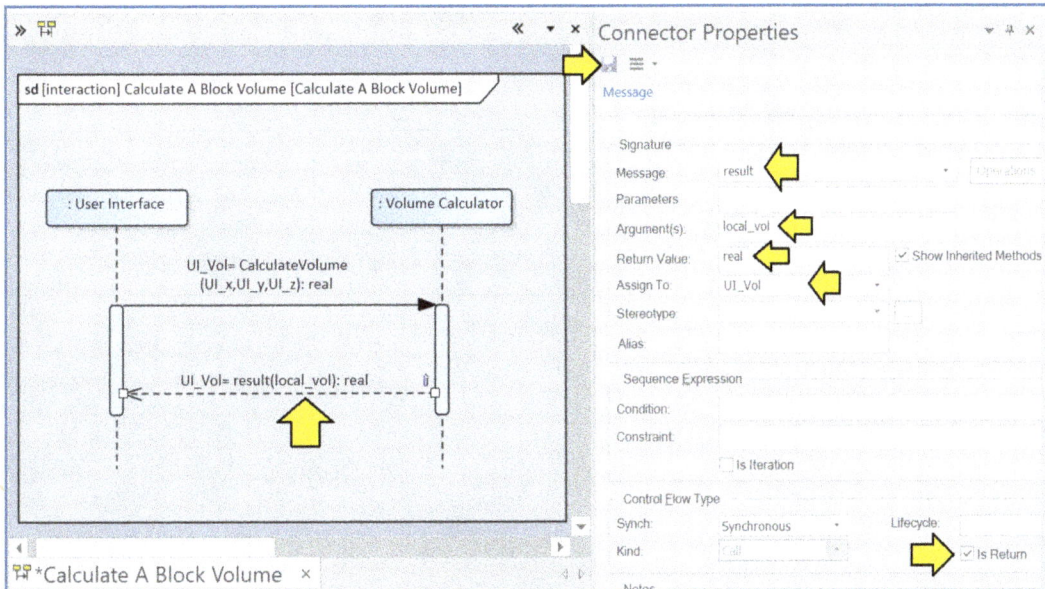

Figure 8-38 – Add reply message

Add a reply message:

1) Add a message from the volume calculator back to the user interface.

2) Double-click on the message to open the connector properties dialog box.

3) Select "IsReturn" in the lower right corner of the connector properties dialog box.

4) Name the message "result". This name is just for clarity and does not have any particular model significance.

5) Leave the parameters field blank.

6) Set the arguments field to: "local_vol". This is the internal variable that the operation inside the volume calculator will use to store the result.

7) Set the return value to: "real". This setting means that the operation inside the volume calculator block will return its result as a real number (rather than as a Boolean or an integer).

8) Set the assign to field to: "UI_Vol". This is the name of the property inside the user interface block that will receive the result.

9)   Click the diskette icon to save your changes.

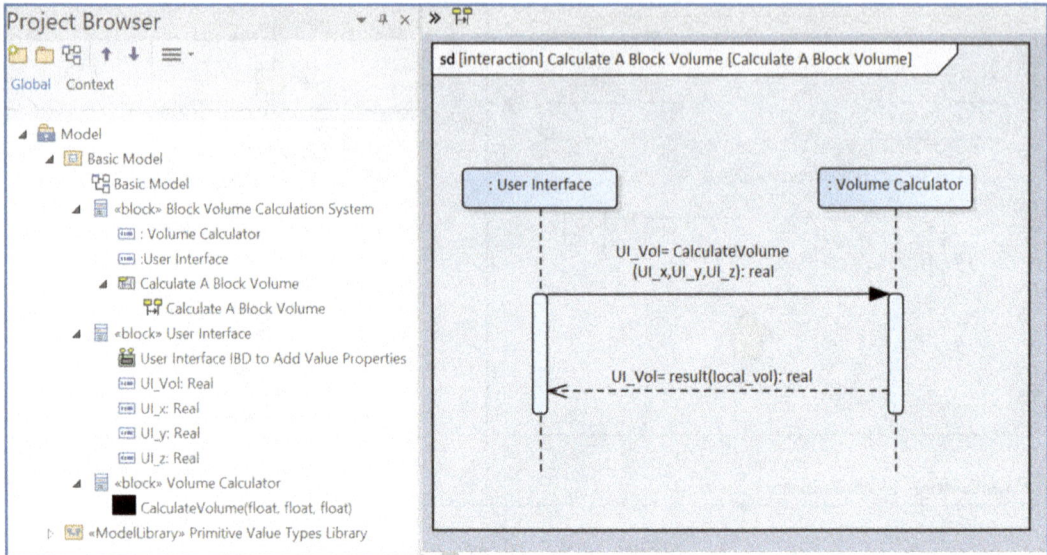

Figure 8-39 – Completed sequence diagram

The completed sequence diagram is shown in Figure 8-39. The detail of how the parameters are passed back and forth is clear. Which is to say, those details are not as clear as they would be in a real programming language like C, C++, or Java. However, there is enough detail present to guess more-or-less what the underlying embedded software calls would look like.

Parameters on Sequence Diagram Messages

SysML allows you to define parameters for messages in sequence diagrams. Use this feature carefully. First, they can make your diagram quite cryptic. Imagine a sequence diagram with 20 messages, all showing the level of parameter detail shown in Figure 8-39! Second, this level of detail is likely to change frequently during the course of your project. Specifying parameter-level detail in your sequence diagrams is setting yourself up for a diagram maintenance headache. The issue of having to constantly work to keep parameter lists embedded in sequence diagrams current is a variation of the complexity problem described in *Over Modeling* on page 350.

Combined Fragments

What if your interaction is more complicated than a simple sequence of messages? SysML provides a type of diagramming feature known as a **combined fragment** for showing many types of complicated interaction. [SysML1.5] defines 12 types of combined fragments. Let's make a simple model of the interaction of a customer with an automated bank teller (ATM) to illustrate the **alt** combined fragment.

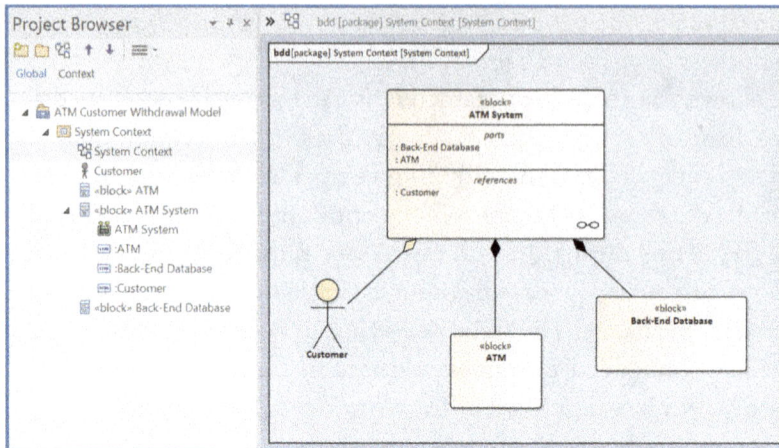

Figure 8-40 – Set up a basic model

Set up a basic model with a customer, an ATM, and a back-end database as shown in Figure 8-40. [40]

---

[40] In order to get the ":Customer" reference to show up in the *references* compartment of the ATM system block and in the project browser, you may need to make an internal block diagram of the ATM system, right-click on the internal block diagram, and select "Synchronize Structural Elements".

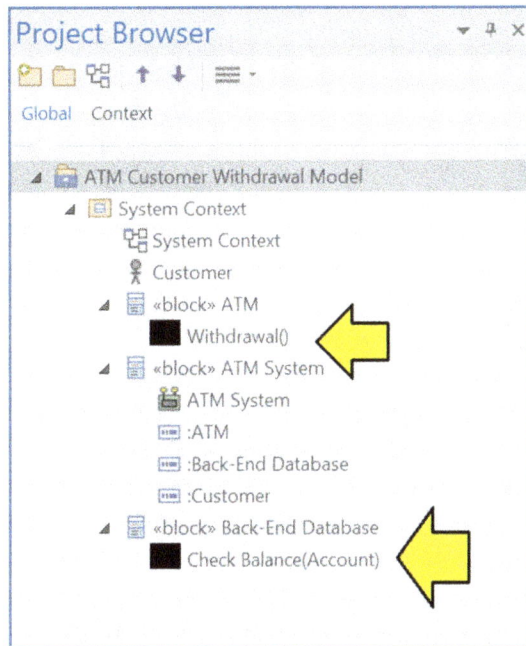

Figure 8-41 – Add operations to blocks

Add an operation called "Withdrawal" to the ATM block. Add an operation called "Check Balance" to the back-end database block. [41]

---

[41] Refer to *Operations and Receptions* on page 108 for instructions on adding an operation to a block.

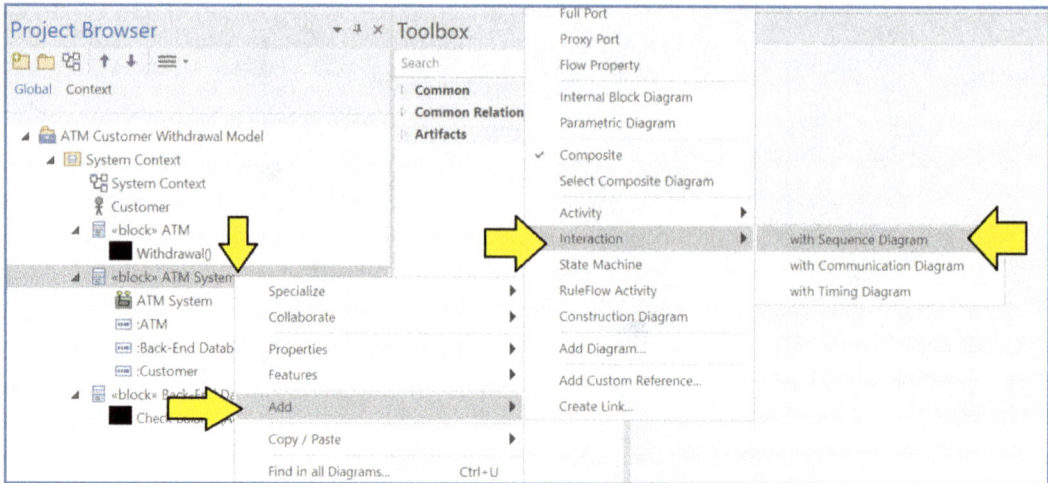

Figure 8-42 – Add an interaction to the ATM system block

Right-click on the ATM system block in the project browser and add an interaction. Name the interaction "Customer Withdrawal Request".

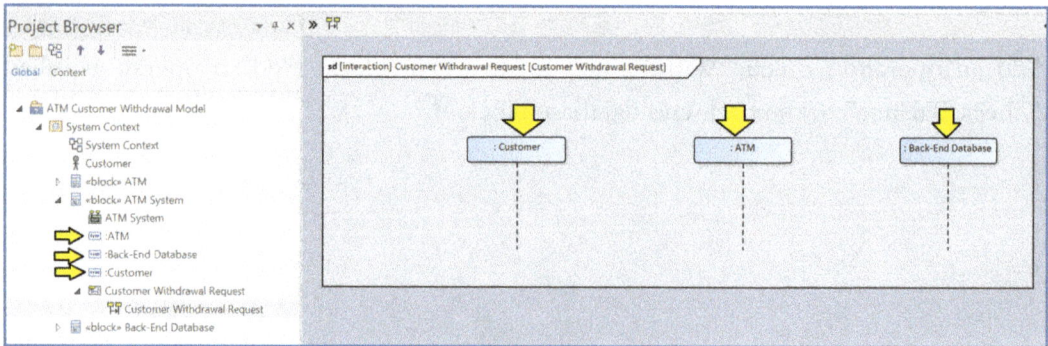

Figure 8-43 – Create the lifelines

Drag the roles (references/parts) for the customer, the ATM, and the back-end database to the sequence diagram to create the lifelines.

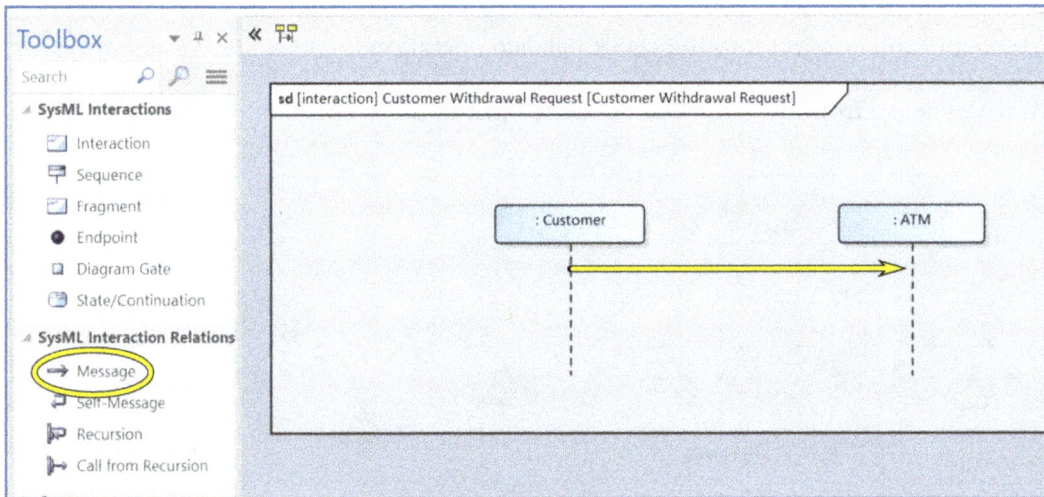

Figure 8-44 – Create the first message

Select the message icon in the toolbox and drag a message from the customer lifeline to the ATM lifeline.

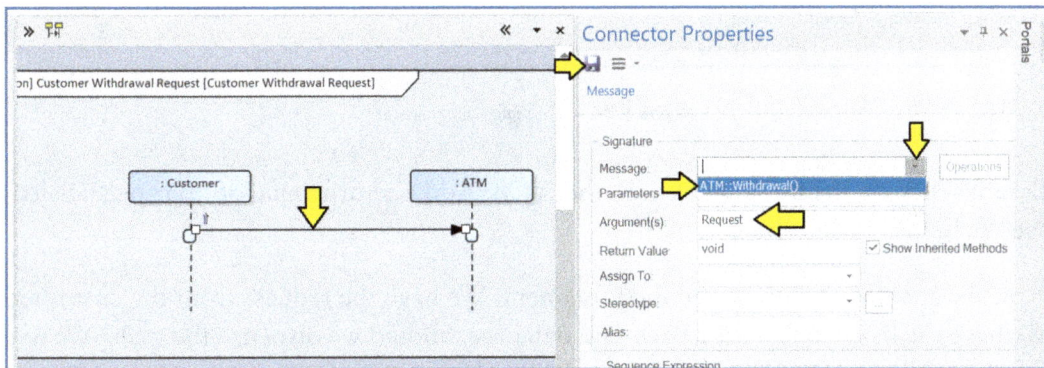

Figure 8-45 – Connect message to operation

Double-click on the message. Pull down the message selector and select the withdrawal operation. Add the string: "Request" in the argument field. Click the diskette icon to save your changes.

Add a second message from the ATM to the back-end database with the argument "Account" and connect it to the check balance operation.

Add a message from the back-end database back to the ATM.

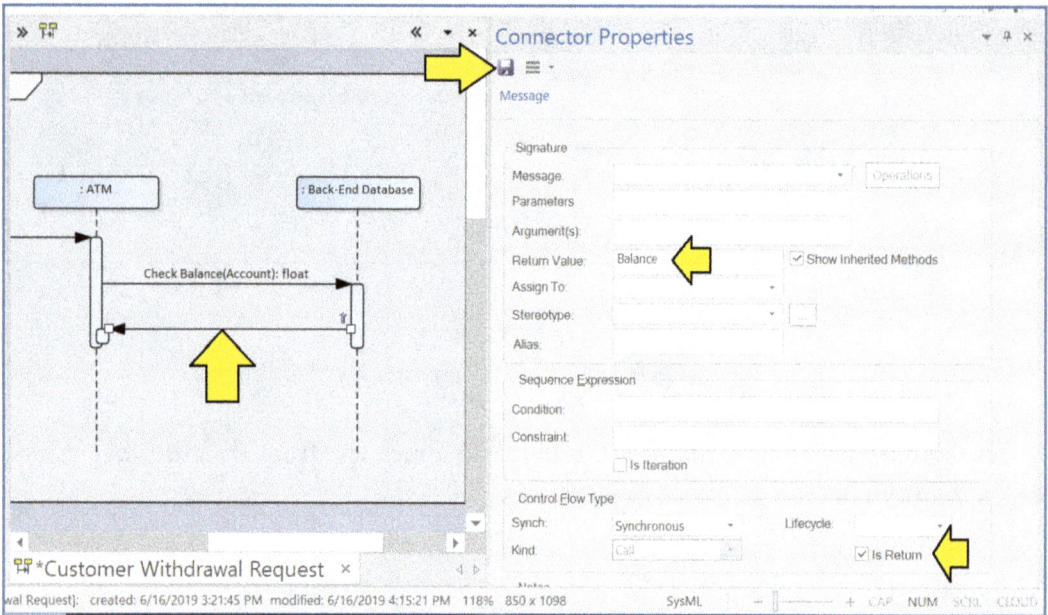

Figure 8-46 – Configure reply message

Double-click on the message back to the ATM. Add a return value of "Balance". Select the "Is Return" check box.

Now we are ready for the combined fragment. We have the request from the customer. We have the balance from the back-end database. Should we dispense the cash? We will use the "alt" combined fragment to model the decision.

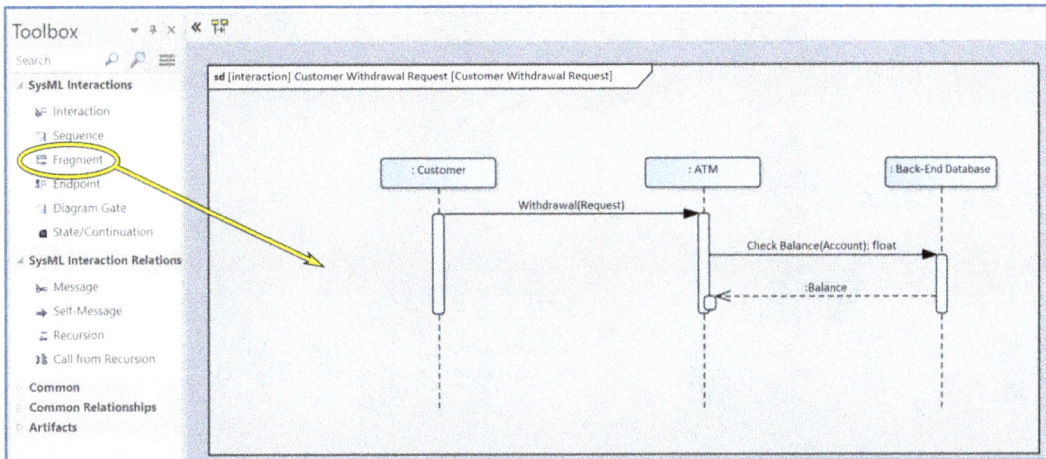

Figure 8-47 – Drag a fragment to the diagram

In the toolbox select the "Fragment" icon and drag it to the diagram.

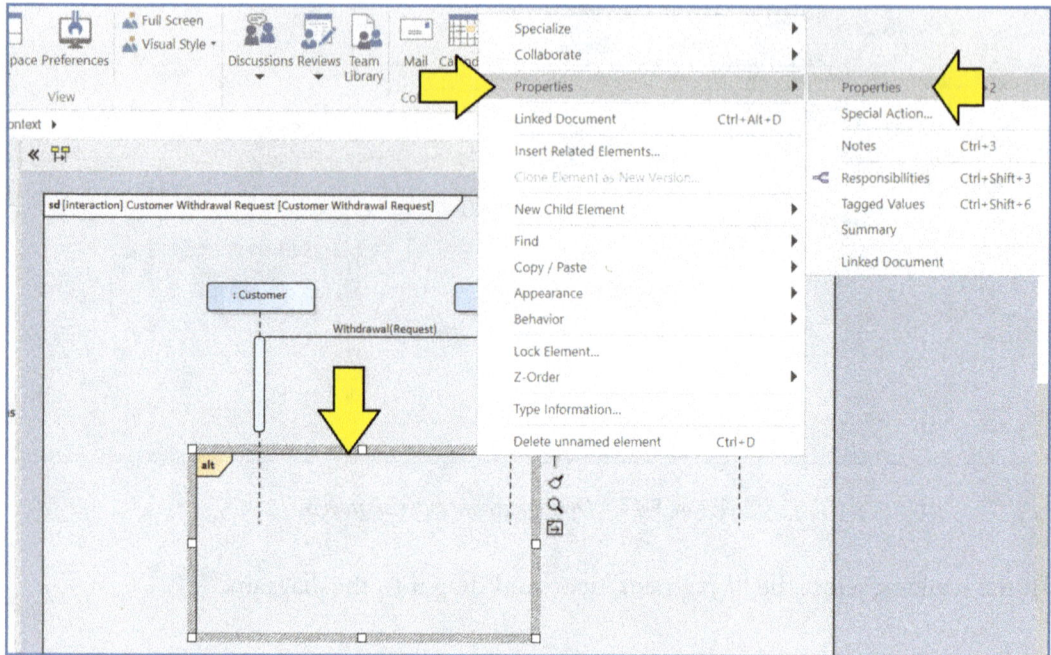

Figure 8-48 – Size the fragment, open the properties dialog

Use the box controls on the fragment to move it around and resize it until it covers the bottom of the lifelines for the customer and the ATM. Be sure the fragment box is selected. Right-click on the fragment box, click "Properties" and click "Properties" again.

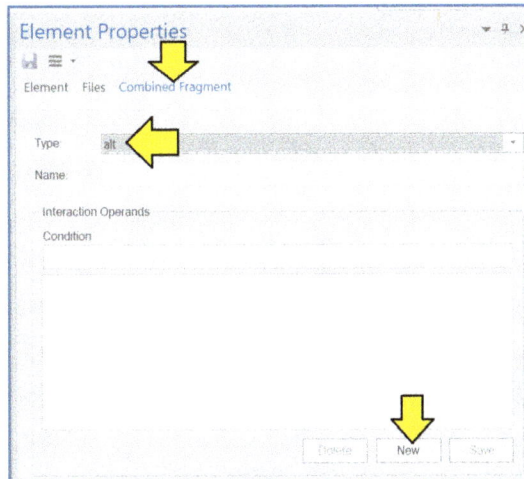

Figure 8-49 – Create a new condition

Once the "Element Properties" dialog opens, click on "Combined Fragment". The subpanel for combined properties will appear. SysML supports 12 types of combined fragments. We are interested in "alt" which happens to be the default. If you like, you can name the fragment. Click "New" to create a new condition.

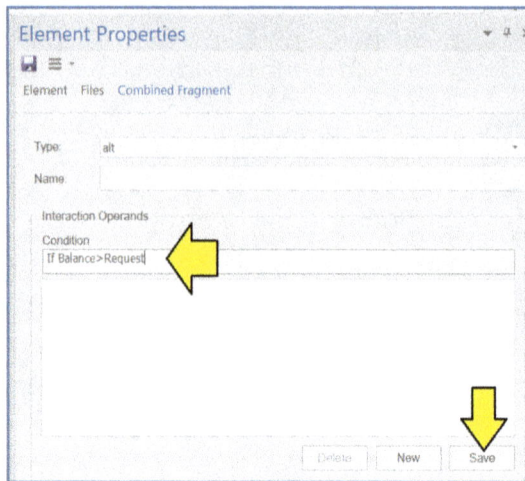

Figure 8-50 – Set the main condition

Enter the main decision condition "If Balance>Request" and click "Save". This is, if the customer has more in his account than he has requested as a withdrawal, we will grant the request.

Click "New" again and add another condition for "Else". Close the dialog box.

Adjust the size and position of the fragment until it looks nice with the conditions not overlapping the lifelines.

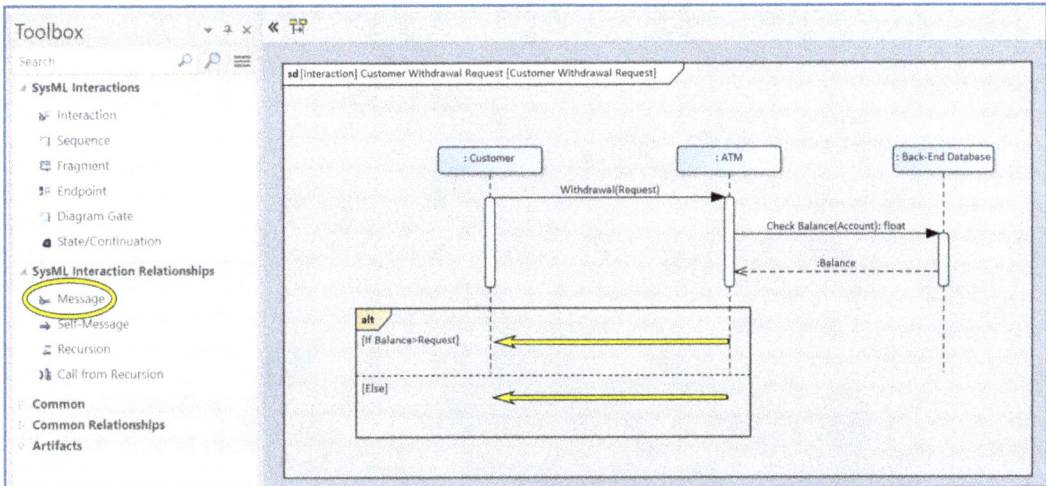

Figure 8-51 – Draw two reply messages

In the toolbox select the message icon again. Draw two messages from the ATM to the customer as shown in Figure 8-51. Name the first message: "Dispense Cash". Name the second message: "Display Error Message". Set both messages to be "Is Return" in the same properties panel where you assign the name.

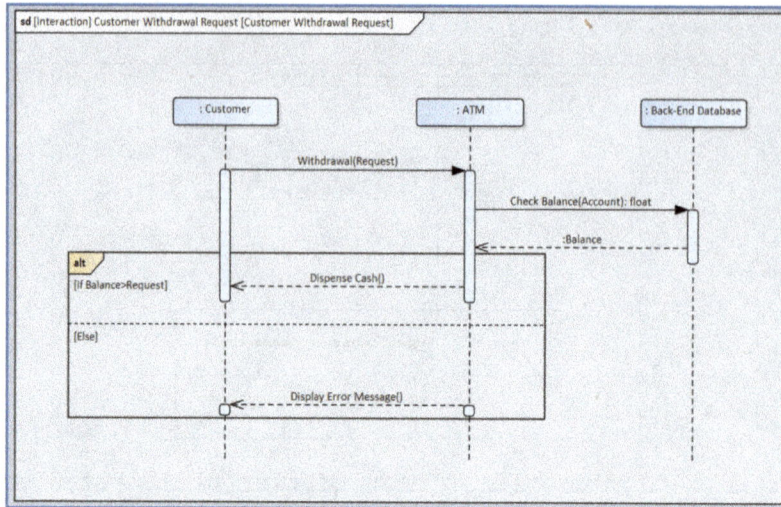

Figure 8-52 – Completed sequence diagram with alt combined fragment

The completed sequence diagram is shown in Figure 8-52. We have modeled an interaction with two alternate outcomes, one if the customer has a balance sufficient to cover the withdrawal, a second if he does not.

SysML defines the following types of combined fragments:

- **seq** – Weak Sequencing
- **alt** – Alternatives
- **opt** – Option
- **break** – Break
- **par** – Parallel
- **strict** – Strict Sequencing
- **loop** – Loop
- **critical** – Critical Region
- **neg** – Negative
- **assert** – Assertion
- **ignore** – Ignore

- **consider** – Consider

A full discussion of all twelve types is beyond the scope of this book.

Should you use combined fragments?

Frankly speaking, I am not a fan of combined fragments. I have two main concerns about combined fragments:

1) They make your sequence diagrams difficult to understand for any-one except a UML or SysML expert.

2) The urge to use a combined fragment is an indicator that you may have passed the point of diminishing returns in terms of modeling rather than coding. For more on this problem see *Over Modeling* on page 350.

Rather than using combined fragments, I tend to do one of the following:

- Use several simpler sequence diagrams – as noted above, one inter-action can have multiple sequence diagrams.

- Raise the level of abstraction in the diagram so that the messy de-tail shown in the combined fragment is not needed.

- Augment the diagram with a text requirement that explains the messy detail.

Further Study

SysML supports a rich set of advanced notations for sequence diagrams. These advanced notations should be used sparingly as they tend to make the sequence diagrams difficult to understand for stakeholders who are not SysML experts.

- **combined fragment types** – SysML supports 12 different types of combined fragments.
    - [Delligatti] – page 144
    - [Friedenthal] – page 260
- **coregion** – Coregions are an alternate more compact notation for the parallel combined fragment.
    - [Friedenthal] – page 260
    - [SysML1.5] – page 134 Table 12.1
- **interaction use** – The interaction use is a mechanism that allows a complex interaction to be decomposed into a set of smaller sequence diagrams.
    - [Delligatti] – page 151
    - [Friedenthal] – page 265
- **message from diagram frame** – In a sequence diagram, it should be possible to draw a message from the diagram frame to a lifeline. See [SysML1.5] Figure D.10 on page 226. Such a message indicates input arriving from outside the context of the interaction. Formally, SysML considers these to be "gates to an interaction". *Enterprise Architect* does support the notation of having a message from the diagram frame. However, the tool provides an icon in the toolbox called "Diagram Gate" which can be dragged to just inside the diagram frame and used as an anchor for an incoming message arriving from outside the context of the interaction.
    - [SysML1.5] – page 196 ("gates on interactions" can be included in the diagram frame.)
    - [Delligatti] – page 152, Figure 7.18 and page 153
    - [Friedenthal] – pages 265-266

- **message types** – Beyond the asynchronous and synchronous call messages, there are a number of other message types available. For example, some message types create or destroy other lifelines. Other notations allow the modeling of lost and found messages.

  - [Delligatti] – page 131
  - [Friedenthal] – pages 253, 256

- **selector expression** – SysML inherits its concept of multiplicity from UML. One of the quirks of the UML multiplicity concept is that there is no way to explicitly refer to one of the multiple parts. For example, if you define a block "airplane" that has a part "wing" with a multiplicity of two, you will find it impossible to create references to the "left" or "right" wing. As with UML, the one exception is in the sequence diagram. The selector expression allows you to differentiate the two wings instances.

  - [Delligatti] – page 128
  - [Friedenthal] – page 250

- **state invariants** – State invariants can be added to a sequence diagram to denote conditions that must be true at that point in the lifeline.

  - [Delligatti] – page 143
  - [Friedenthal] – page 264

- **time/duration constraints** – Time and duration constraints can be modeled in a sequence diagram.

  - [Delligatti] – page 141 and Figure 7.11 on page 142
  - [Friedenthal] – page 258

Chapter 9 – State Machine Diagrams

State machine diagrams show the behavior of an entity as it transitions between states. In the SysML case, the entity is usually a block.

Basic State Machine Diagrams

For our basic state machine, we will model a college dormitory at a very simple level. We will imagine that the students who occupy the dormitory are all doing the same thing at the same time. They have the following states:

- Studying
- In Class
- Cleaning
- Eating
- Party
- Sleeping

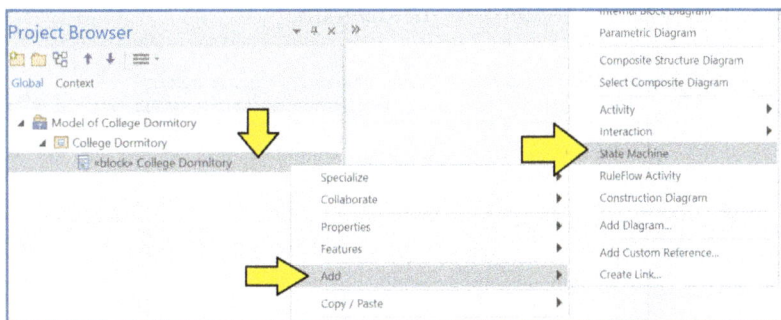

Figure 9-1 – Create a simple model and add a state machine

Create a simple model. Right-click on the block that represents the college dormitory and use the context menu to add a state machine to the block.

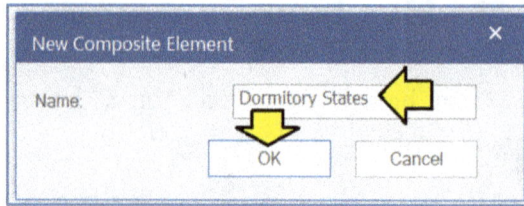

Figure 9-2 – Name the state machine

Give the state machine a name.

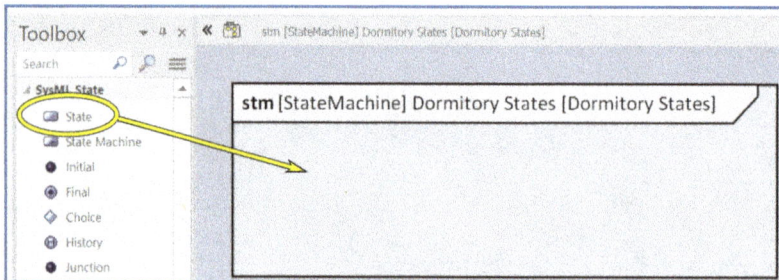

Figure 9-3 – Drag state icon to diagram

Drag the state icon from the toolbox to the diagram.

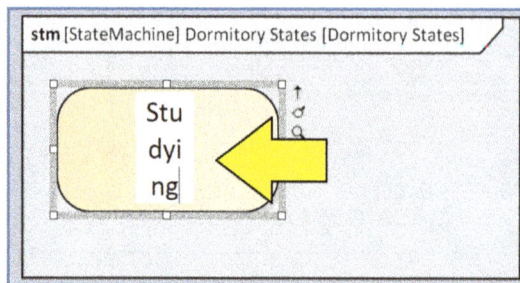

Figure 9-4 – Name the state

Name the state: "Studying".

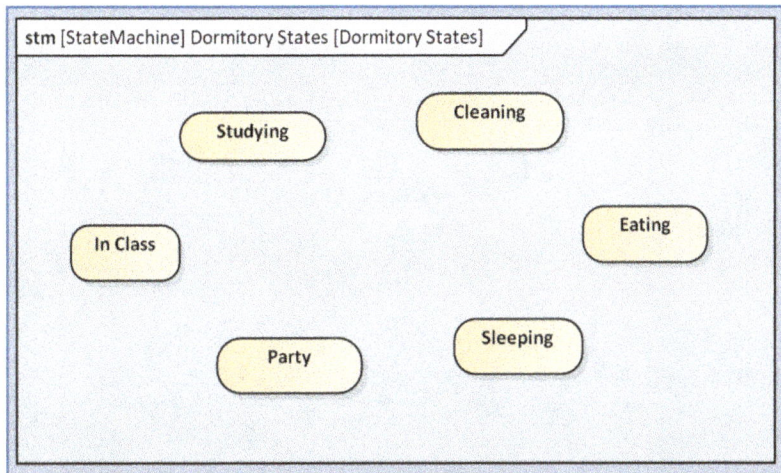

Figure 9-5 – Add the remaining states

Add the remaining states. This diagram is a great start but does not yet show the legal transitions between states.

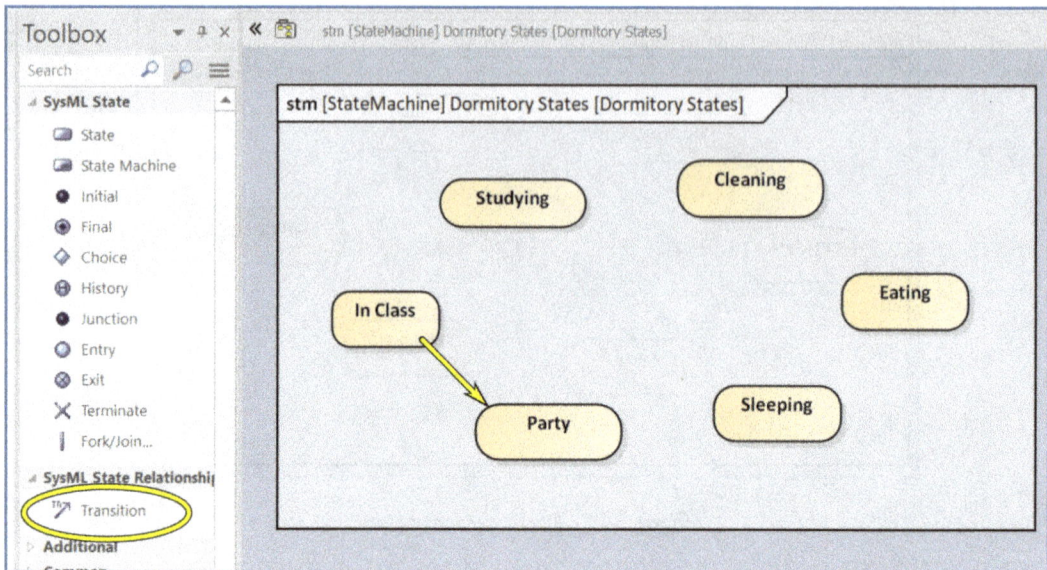

Figure 9-6 – Select transition icon and drag

Select the transition icon in the toolbox. Drag a transition from "In Class" to "Party". Notice that this transition makes sense in the context of college student behavior. A transition in the opposite direction makes less sense and we will not model such a transition.

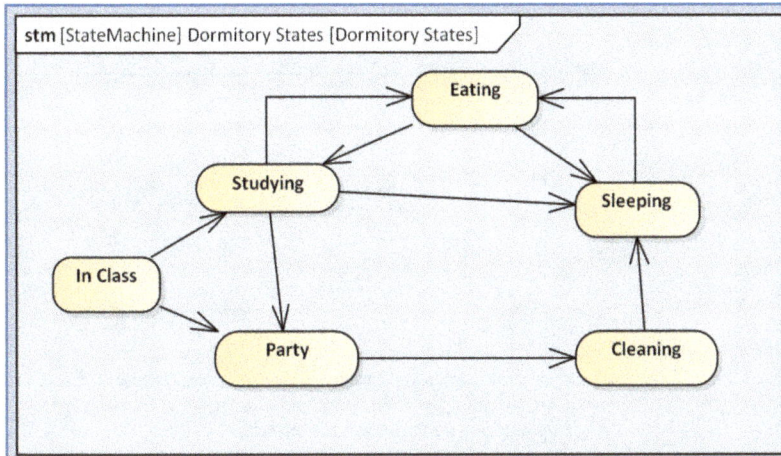

Figure 9-7 – Add other transitions

Add other transitions to the diagram. Now we have the states described as well as the legal transitions between states. However, we have not modeled the creation of the college dormitory.

SysML provides a concept called a **pseudostate** for modeling more complex transition points between states. The state machine cannot sit in a pseudostate. Rather, control must pass through the pseudostate immediately. In particular, SysML provides the **initial** and **final** pseudostates for modeling the start and end of the existence of the state machine.

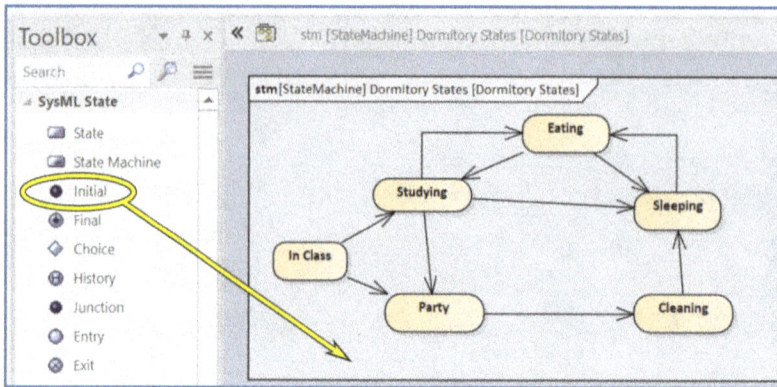

Figure 9-8 – Add an initial pseudostate

Drag the icon for the initial pseudostate from the toolbox to the diagram.

Drag a transition from the initial pseudostate to the party state. The modeling implication is that instant a college dormitory is created, its initial state is that of a party in progress.

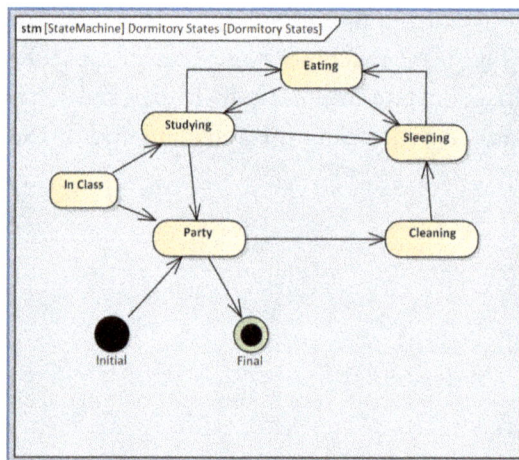

Figure 9-9 – Add the final pseudostate

Those who pay attention to the news in the United States will be familiar with the phenomenon of a college dormitory being shut down (that is, ceasing to exist) because of an untoward event during an out-of-control party. We will want to model that transition with a final pseudostate. You will find an icon for final pseudostate in the toolbox just below the icon for initial pseudostate. Drag the final pseudostate icon to the diagram and add a transition from the party state to the final pseudostate.

SubStates

States can have several forms of composite structure. The simplest of these forms is a state that contains substates. In this section, we will extend our previous model so that the "Eating" state becomes a **composite state** with several substates.

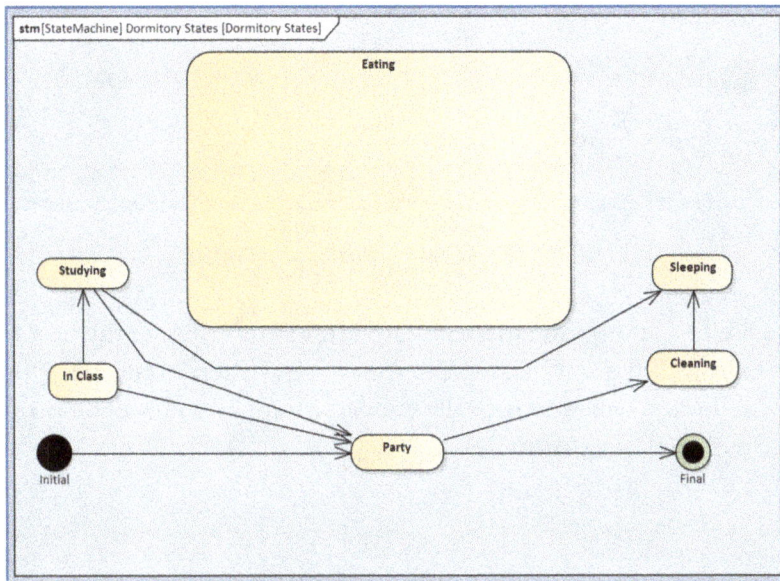

Figure 9-10 – Rearrange to make eating state larger

First rearrange the diagram so that the eating state is a lot larger.

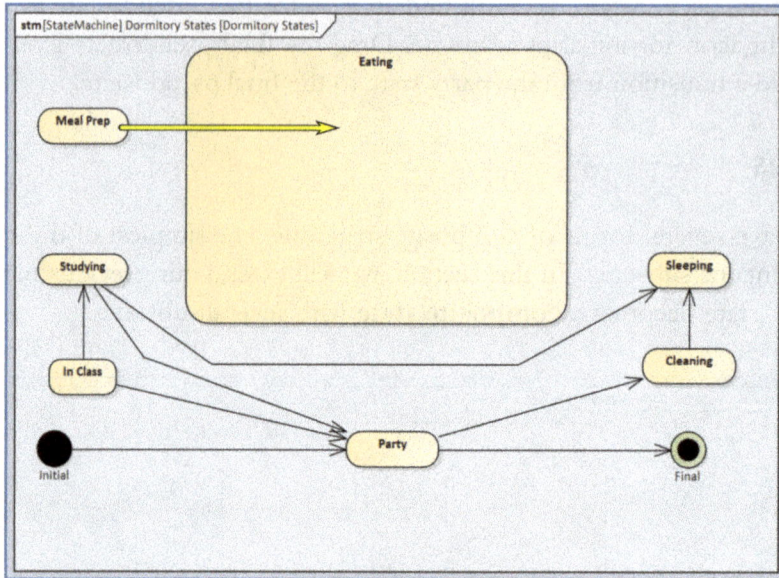

Figure 9-11 – Create substate for Meal Prep

Drag a new state to the diagram and name it "Meal Prep". Resize the new state so that it is smaller than the "Eating" state. Drag the "Meal Prep" state onto the "Eating" state. *Enterprise Architect* will automatically convert "Eating" to be a composite state and make "Meal Prep" one of its substates.

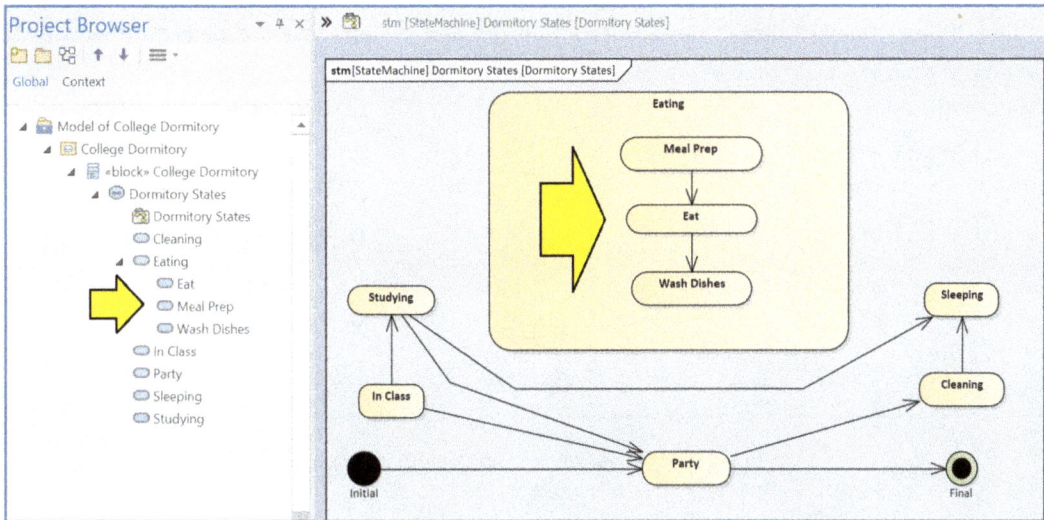

Figure 9-12 – Add two more substates

Add two more substates for "Eat" and "Wash Dishes". Drag transitions between the substates. Now we have modeled the substates of "Eating". Implicitly we could assume that "Meal Prep" must be the first substate since there is no transition for entering that substate. However, we can model the entry and exit points more explicitly.

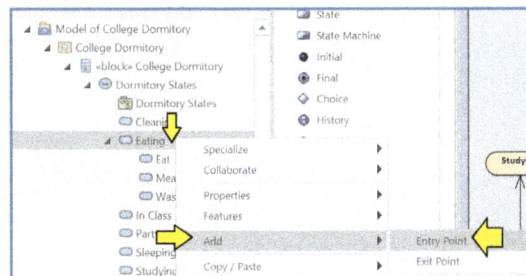

Figure 9-13 – Right-click on Eating and add entry point

In the project browser, right-click on "Eating", select "Add", and then select "Entry Point". This action will add an **entry point** pseudostate to the "Eating" state. The same menu can be used to add an **exit point** to a state.

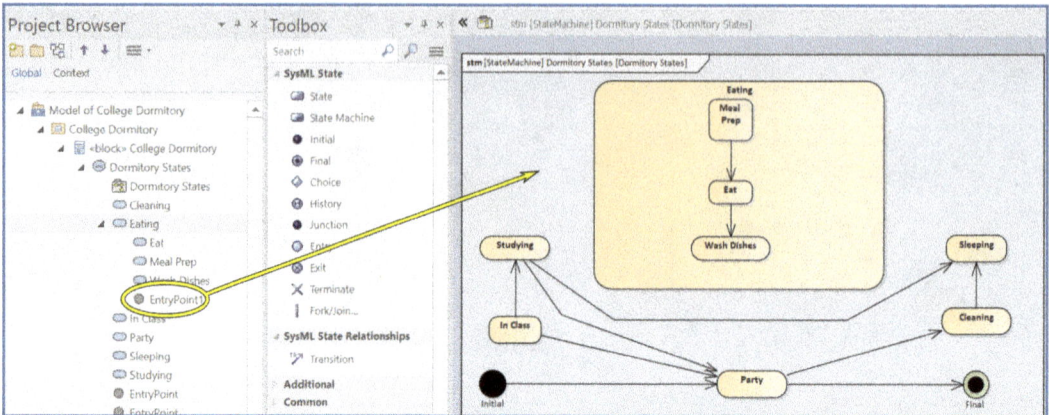

Figure 9-14 – Drag the new entry point to the diagram

Drag the new entry point to the diagram. The entry point will automatically snap onto the edge of the "Eating" state.

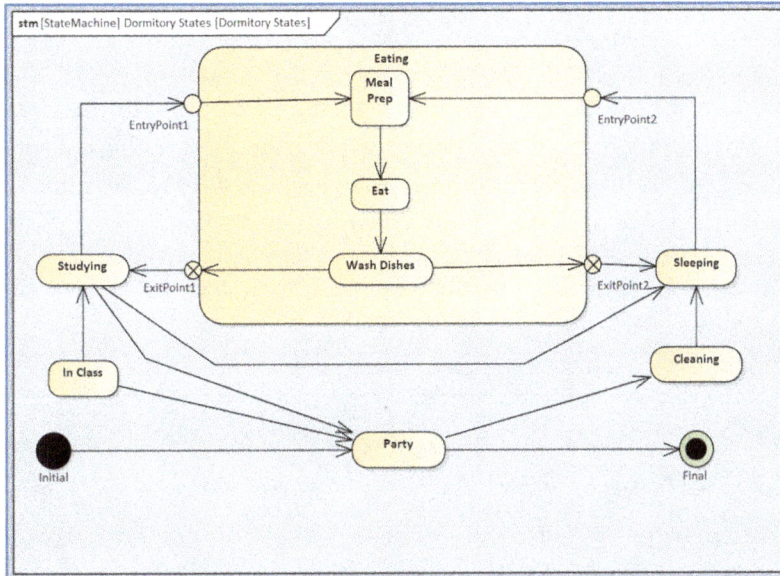

Figure 9-15 – Completed diagram showing substates

Add another entry point and two exit points to the "Eating" state. Drag them onto the diagram and add transitions as shown in Figure 9-15.

There are a number of other options for modeling composite states as well as transitions to and from substates to other (regular) states. See *Further Study* on page 300.

Triggers and Transitions

So far, we have shown a lot of transitions between states, but we have not covered anything about the conditions under which those transitions occur. In this section we will look at control of the transition. SysML defines two controlling attributes for a transition:

- **trigger** – The trigger is the cause of the transition.

- **guard** – The guard is a logical condition that controls whether the transition will complete or not.

In our model of the college dormitory, we will add a trigger and a guard to the transition from "In Class" to "Party".

Use the procedure shown in *Value Properties* on page 93 to bring in the *Enterprise Architect* standard type library. Create an internal block diagram for the college dormitory. Drag the ValueType "Boolean" from the standard type library to the internal block diagram and create the value property "PartyScheduled".

Right-click on the college dormitory block and add a signal called "Class_Bell".

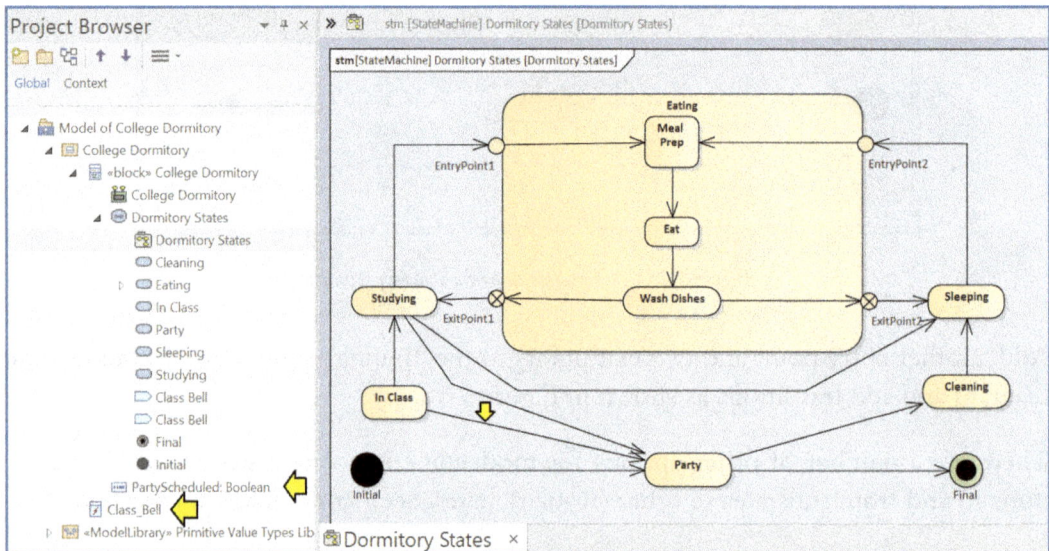

Figure 9-16 – Double-click on the transition

Double-click on the transition from "In Class" to "Party".

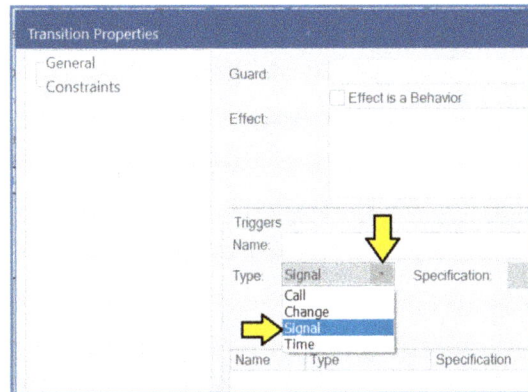

Figure 9-17 – Select signal

The "Transition Properties" panel will appear. Pull down the selector for "Type:" and select "Signal".

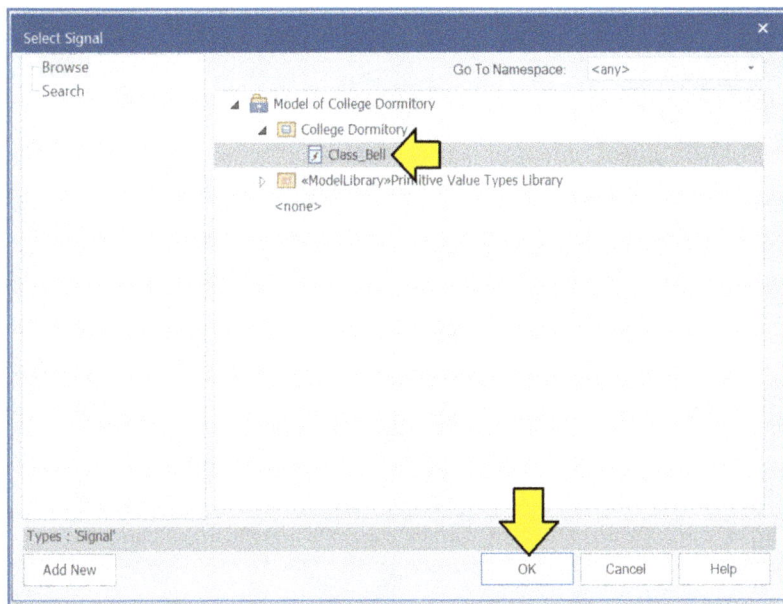

Figure 9-18 – Select Class_Bell and click OK

The "Select Signal" panel will appear. Select "Class_Bell" and click "OK".

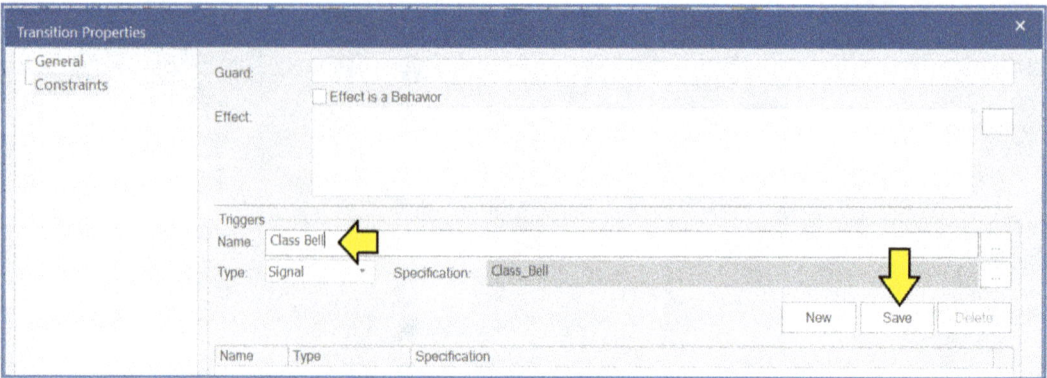

Figure 9-19 – Name the trigger

Back in the transition properties panel, name the trigger "Class Bell" and click "Save". Notice that it is possible to define more than one trigger for a transition.

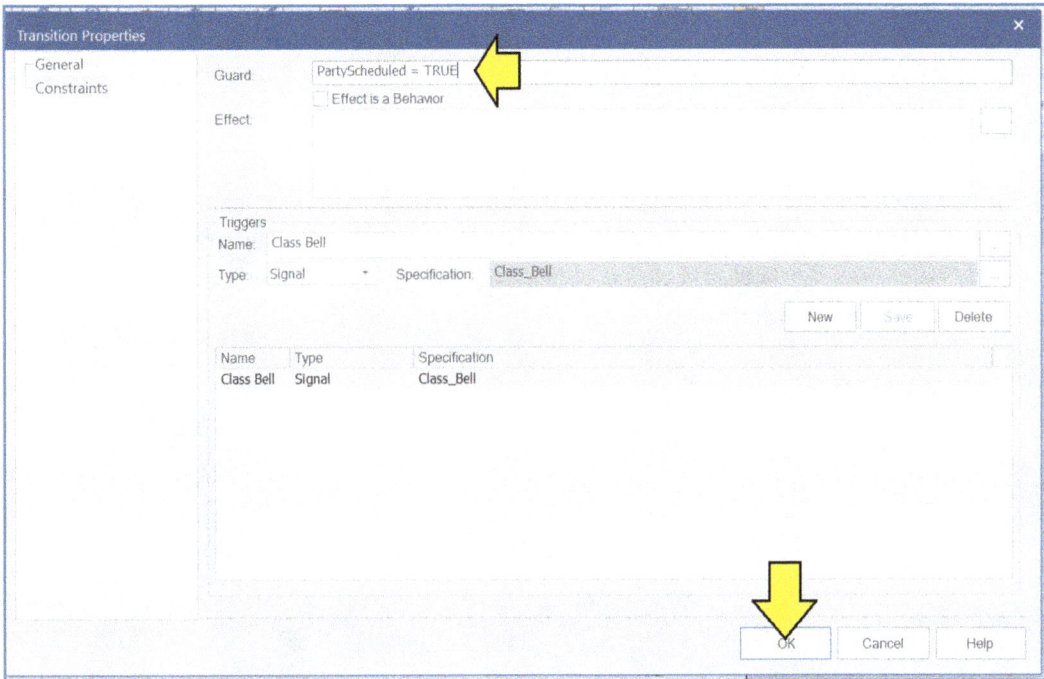

Figure 9-20 – Add Guard

In the "Guard:" field, enter: "PartyScheduled = TRUE" and click "OK".

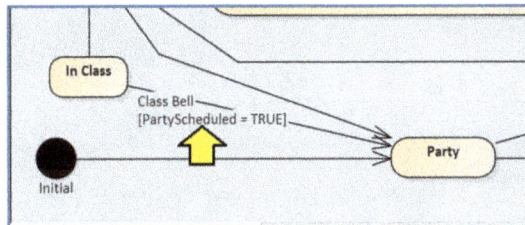

Figure 9-21 – Adjust position of trigger and guard notation

Adjust the position of the trigger and guard notation as needed.

Observant readers will notice that there wasn't a panel to select the "PartyScheduled" value property. In fact, the syntax of the guard statement is undefined. The guard statement is more of an informal notation for the next engineer who will have to design something – probably software – to produce the intended effect. [42]

Adding Behaviors

State machine diagrams allow the specification of behaviors that can occur at several different points in the life of a state or a transition. In order to illustrate the modeling of such behaviors, we will add some more detail to the "In Class" and "Party" states and the transition between them.

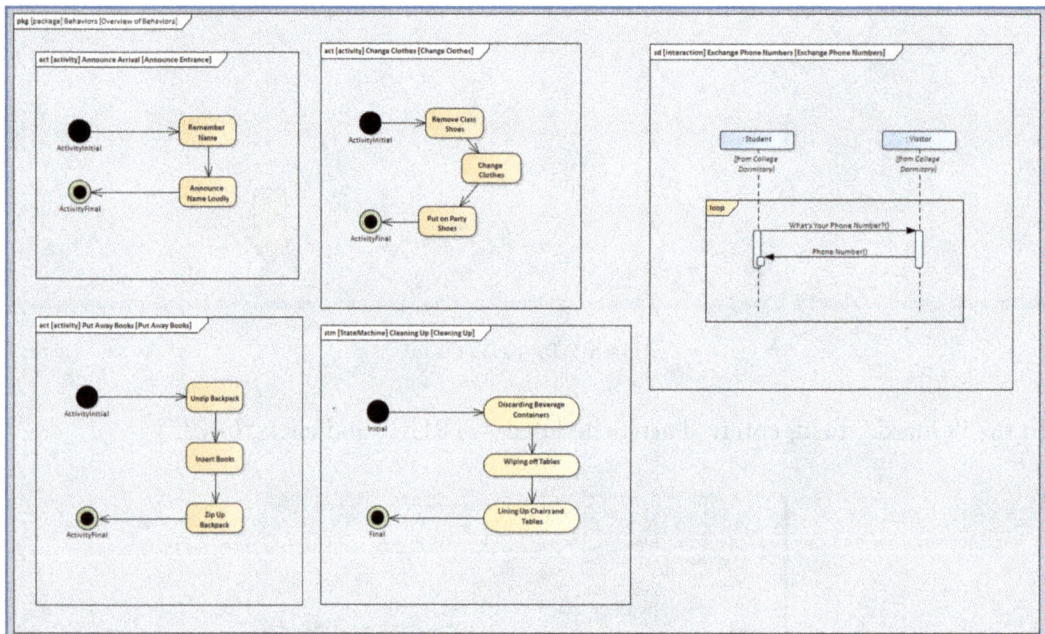

Figure 9-22 – Define several behaviors

For this purpose, we will define five behaviors:

- "Put Away Books" *(Activity)* – This activity behavior will occur as the system is exiting the "In Class" state.

---

[42] If the informal notation is a problem for your project, one alternative is to use opaque notation to insert statements from an actual formal programming language. See *Further Study* on page 300.

- "Change Clothes" *(Activity)* – This activity behavior will occur during the transition from "In Class" to "Party".

- "Announce Arrival" *(Activity)* – This activity behavior will occur as the system is entering the "Party" state.

- "Exchange Phone Numbers" *(Interaction)* – This interaction behavior will run continuously while the system is in the "Party" state.

- "Cleaning Up" *(State Machine)* – This state machine behavior will run while the system is exiting the "Party" state.

Using a Package Diagram as a Frame for Multiple Diagrams

One handy little feature of *Enterprise Architect* is the ability to use a package diagram as a sort of frame to line up multiple smaller diagrams as seen in Figure 9-22 on page 292. This usage is not really part of SysML, but it can be helpful to show the context of several diagrams side-by-side. Just drag the smaller diagrams onto the package diagram and select option to drop as a diagram frame.

Each state in a state machine diagram can have three associated behaviors:

- **entry** – This behavior occurs when the state is entered, regardless of how it is entered. [43] The entry behavior is **atomic** and executes to completion, even if the system receives a new trigger before the entry behavior is complete.

- **do** – This behavior runs while system is in the state. This behavior might be something that executes once or something that runs continuously. In either case, the **do** behavior is not atomic and will be interrupted as soon as the state receives a valid trigger.

- **exit** – This behavior occurs when the state is exited, regardless of how it is exited. The exit behavior is **atomic** and executes to completion, even if the system receives a new trigger before the exit behavior is complete.

---

[43] One of the applications of a self-transition is to cause the entry behavior to be executed over again. See *Further Study* on page 300.

First, we will add an exit behavior to the "In Class" state.

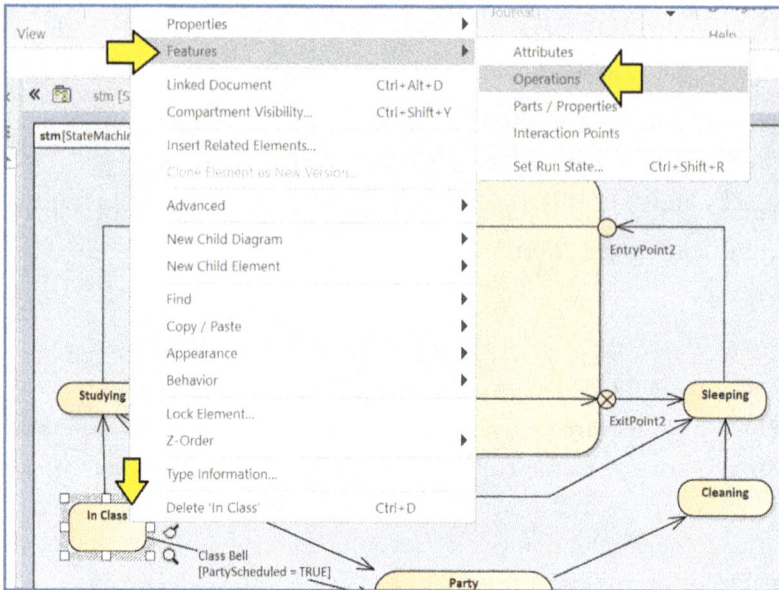

Figure 9-23 – Right-click and open features panel

In the state machine diagram, right-click on the "In Class" state, select "Features" and then "Operations".

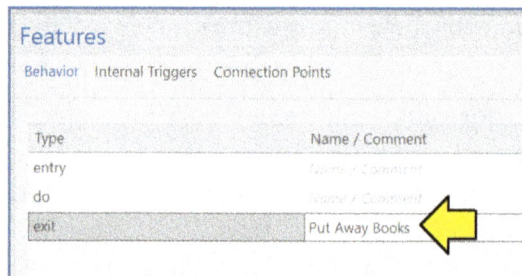

Figure 9-24 – Enter the exit behavior

In the exit field, enter "Put Away Books" and press enter.

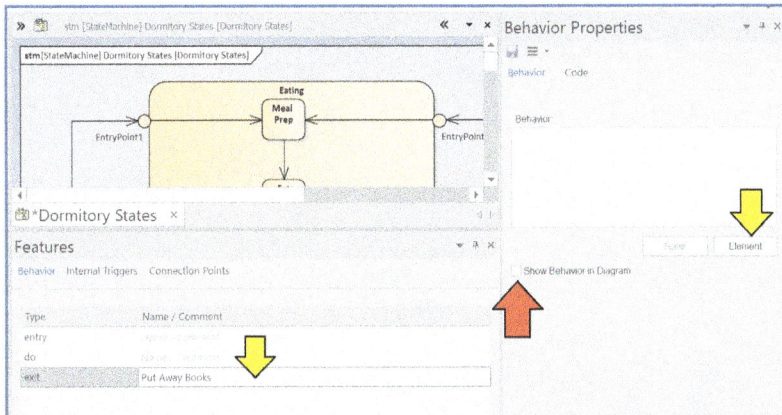

Figure 9-25 – Double-click to open behavior properties panel

Double-click next to "Put Away Books" to open the behavior properties panel. Do **not** click on "Show Behavior in Diagram". [44] Click on "Element".

---

[44] Frankly speaking, the function of *Enterprise Architect* is a bit awkward here.

1) If you do not enter a name in the features panel, nothing will be shown for the behavior in the project browser.

2) If you do enter a name in the features panel, and also select "Show Behavior in Diagram" the diagram will show both.

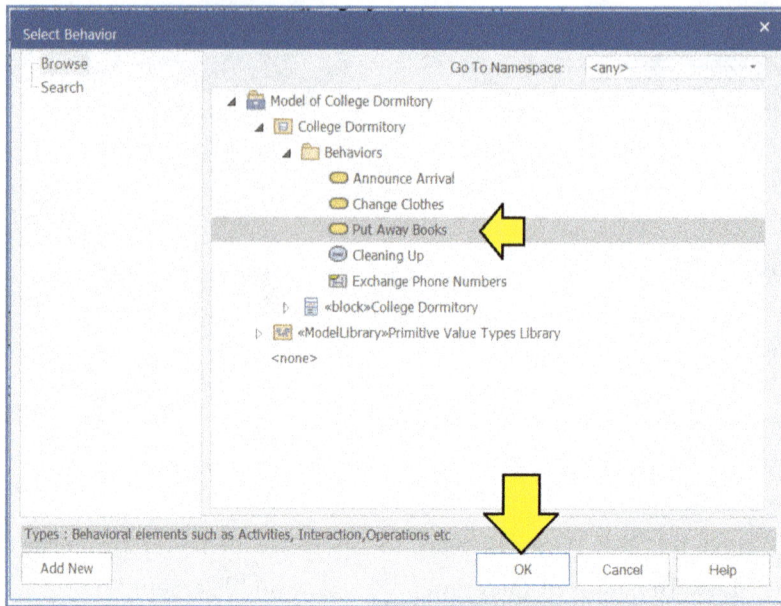

Figure 9-26 – Select exit behavior

The select behavior panel will open. Select "Put Away Books" and click "OK".

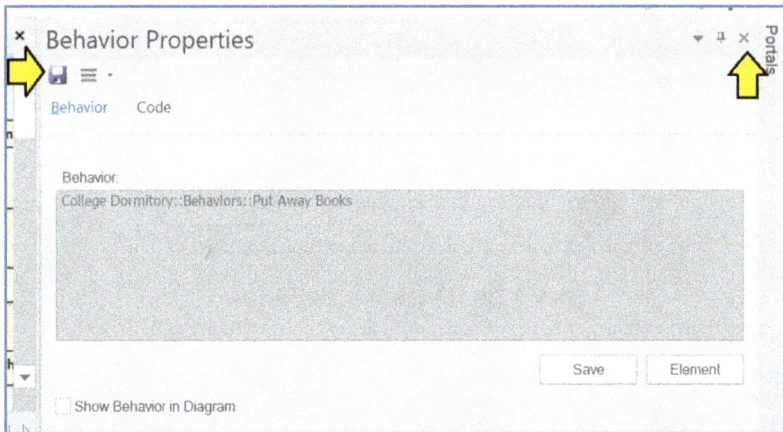

Figure 9-27 – Save changes and exit

Click on the diskette icon to save changes and on the "X" in the upper right corner to close the behavior properties panel. Click on the "X" in the upper right corner of the features panel to close the features panel.

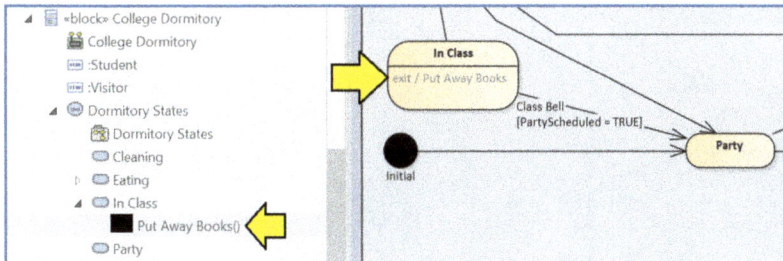

Figure 9-28 – Exit behavior visibile in project browser

The exit behavior has been added in the project browser. There is also a new notation inside the state for the exit behavior.

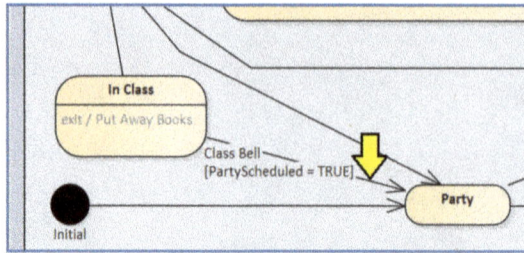

Figure 9-29 – Double-click transition again

Double-click the transition again.

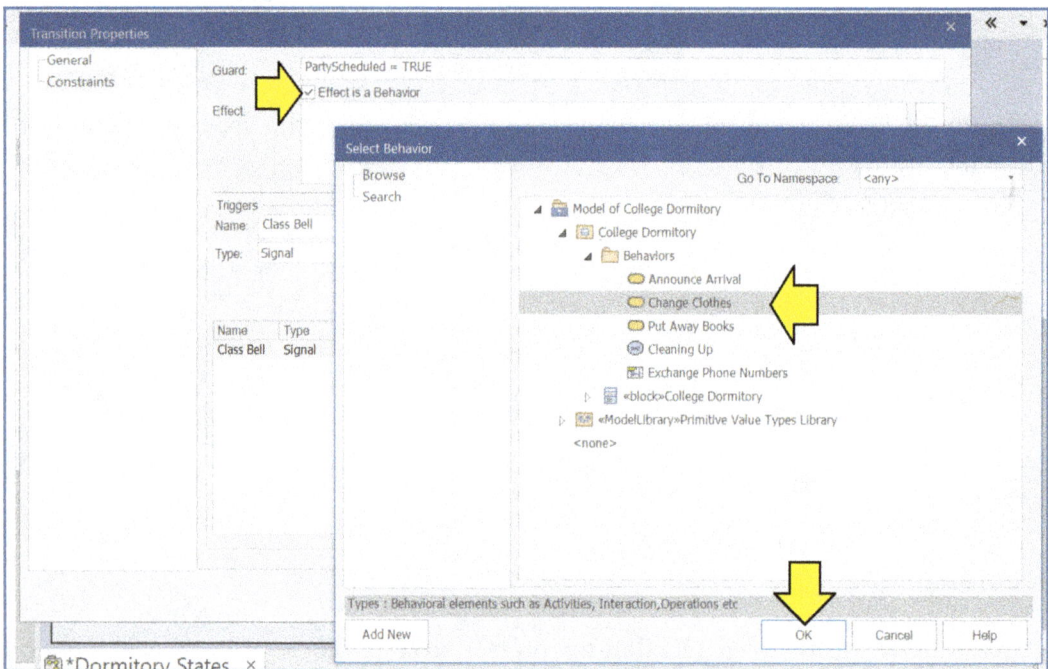

Figure 9-30 – Select the behavior

1) The transition properties panel will appear.

2) Click to select "Effect is a Behavior".

3) The select behavior panel will appear.

4) Select "Change Clothes".

5) Click "OK" to close select behavior panel.

6) Click "OK" to close select transition properties panel.

7) Adjust position of transition text legend showing trigger, guard, and effect.

Right-click on the "Party" state, select "Features" and then "Operations". Set the behaviors as follows:

- **entry –** Announce Arrival

- **do –** Exchange Phone Numbers

- **exit –** Cleaning Up

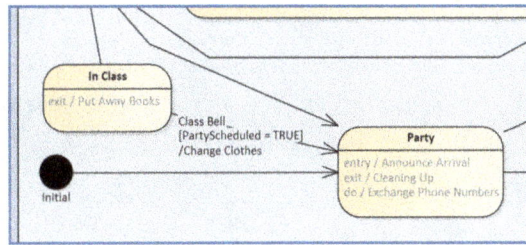

Figure 9-31 – Behaviors complete

The behaviors are now complete. Note that the sequence of behaviors:

1) Put Away Books – exit behavior of the "In Class" state

2) Change Clothes – effect of the transition

3) Announce Arrival – entry behavior of the "Party" state

form a **run-to-completion step** and are treated as atomic. That is, all three behaviors will run in sequence and cannot be interrupted, even if the system receives a new trigger.

Further Study

Here are is a list of further topics you will want to study to hone your expertise.

- **composite structure** – We covered substates in *SubStates* on page 283. However, there are more options for composite states and further reading is recommended it you want to make more detailed state machine diagrams.
  - [Delligatti] – page 160
  - [Douglass] – pages 136-140
  - [Friedenthal] – pages 283-291

- **event types** – In *Triggers and Transitions* on page 287, we briefly introduced signal events as triggers for a transition. Several other types of events are available such as time-based events.
  - [Delligatti] – page 166
  - [Douglass] – page 133
  - [Friedenthal] – page 275

- **opaque notation** – Opaque notation is the SysML method of putting actual statements for a specific programming language in a diagram:
  - [Delligatti] – page 159
  - [Friedenthal] – pages 239, 278

- **pseudostates** – Pseudostates are not real states but conditions that are transited before, after, or in between states. The initial and final states are examples of pseudostates.
  - [Delligatti] – page 171
  - [Douglass] – page 140
  - [Friedenthal] – page 279

- **regions** – State machine diagrams can be split into regions. The regions show two or more sets of states that exist in parallel.

  - [Delligatti] – page 173

  - [Douglass] – page 139 ("AND-states")

  - [Friedenthal] – pages 275, 285

- **self-transition** – A transition can start and end at the same state. Typically, a self-transition might be used to cause some operation to occur (without changing to a different state) when a certain signal arrives. The internal transition is closely related to the self-transition.

  - [Delligatti] – page 162

  - [Douglass] – page 132

  - [Friedenthal] – page 278

Chapter 10 – Use Case Diagrams

The development of high-quality use cases is a complex endeavor which is beyond the scope of this book. (See *Further Study* on page 309.)

The SysML diagrams for use cases, on the other hand, are extremely simple. In fact, they are so simple that this chapter is going to be a bit brief. There are basically no hidden property settings or other mysterious functions. There are just a few icons and connectors in the toolbox, and these behave exactly as expected. As such, I am going to dispense with most of the explicit explanation of dragging and dropping and just show finished diagrams with a bit of commentary. [45]

---

[45] If you have somehow jumped directly to this chapter without reading anything else in the book and do not yet understand how to drag icons to diagrams, you may want to review *Quick Start* on page 9.

Basic Use Case Diagrams

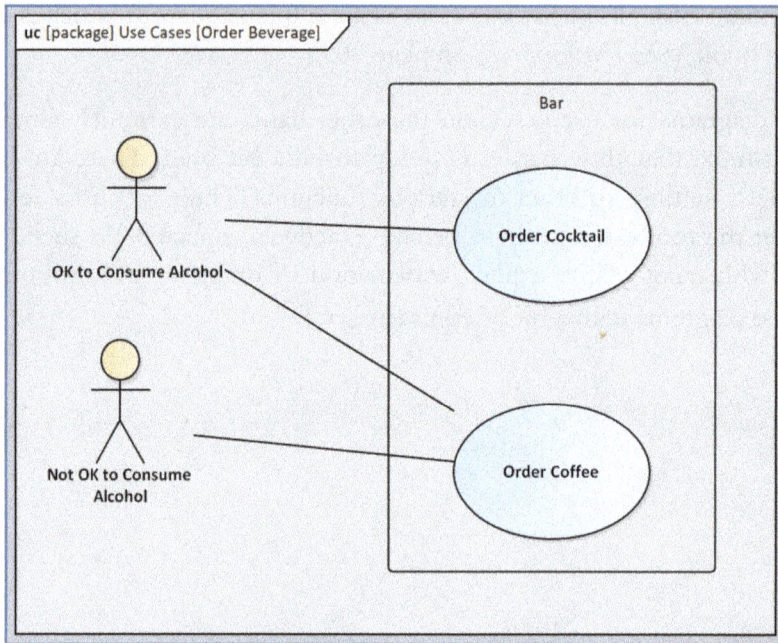

Figure 10-1 – Basic use cases

Figure 10-1 shows two use cases for customers at a bar that serves coffee and cocktails. We have two actors: one can drink alcohol; the other cannot. The use case for ordering cocktails applies only to the actor that can drink alcohol. The use case for ordering coffee applies to both actors.

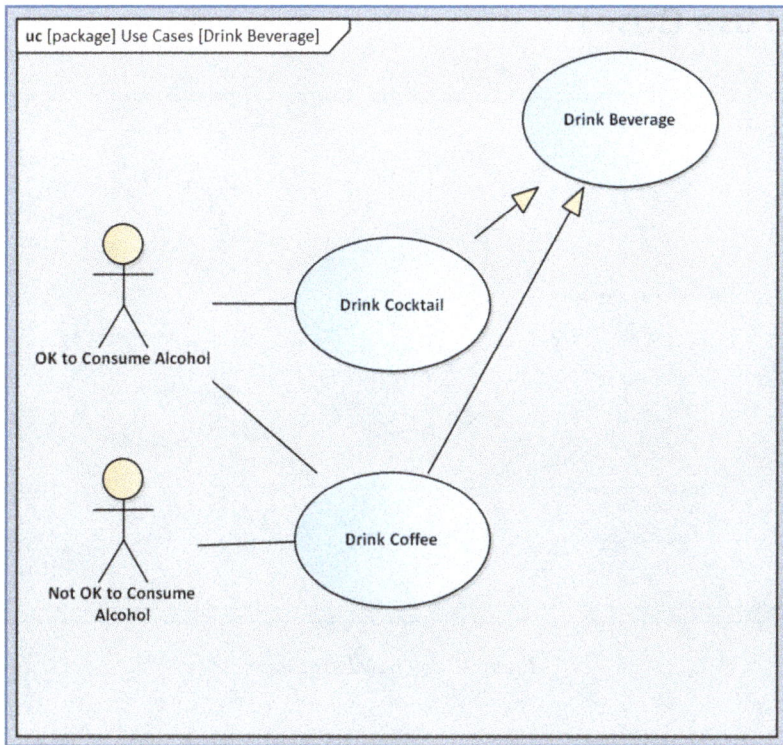

Figure 10-2 – Use cases can be generalized

Use cases can be generalized and specialized just like blocks. The use cases for drinking a cocktail and drinking a cup of coffee are specializations of the more general use case for drinking a beverage.

Included Use Cases

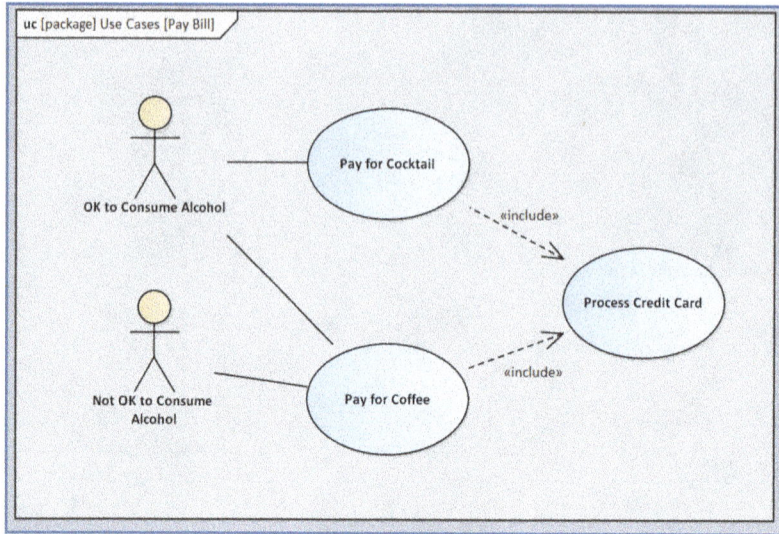

Figure 10-3 – Included use case

The use cases for paying for a cocktail or a cup of coffee both include the common use case of processing a credit card payment.

Extension Points

SysML offers a mechanism for modeling extensions of use cases. Extensions are often special cases for handling problems. We will add an extension use case to "Drink Coffee" to handle the rare but annoying problem of the cream curdling in the coffee.

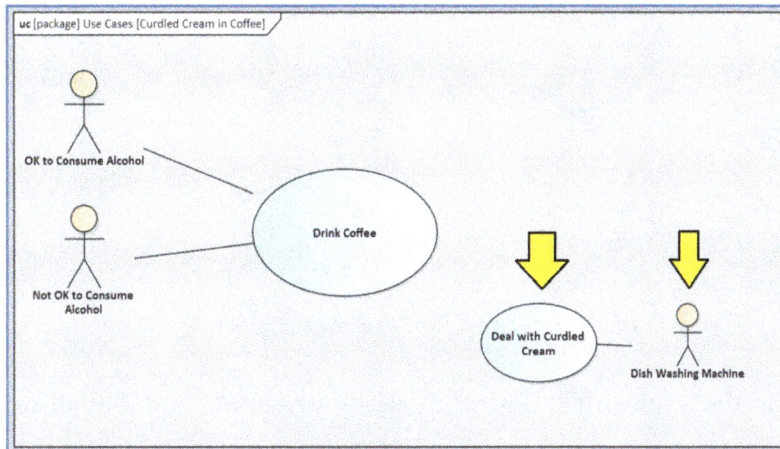

Figure 10-4 – Reuse drink coffee

Reuse the drink coffee use case and two customer actors. Add a use case for dealing with the curdled cream and a new actor called: "Dish Washing Machine".

Notice that the stick figure looks a little odd when the actor is not actually a human. Fortunately, SysML provides an alternate notation for a nonhuman actor.

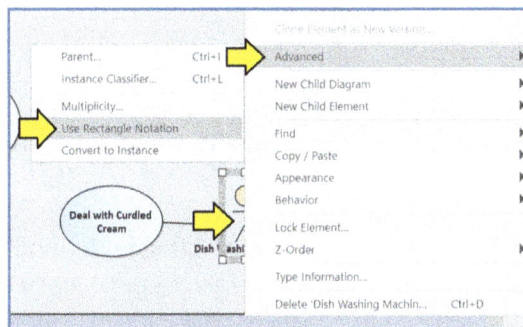

Figure 10-5 – Use rectangle notation

Right-click on the actor. Select "Advanced" and then "Use Rectangle Notation".

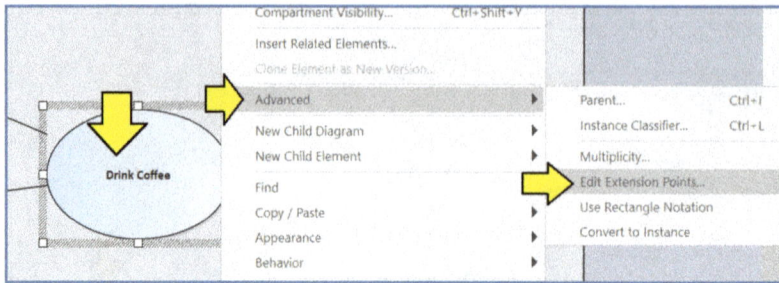

Figure 10-6 – Open extension point panel

Right-click on the drink coffee use case. Select "Advanced" and then "Edit Extension Points...".

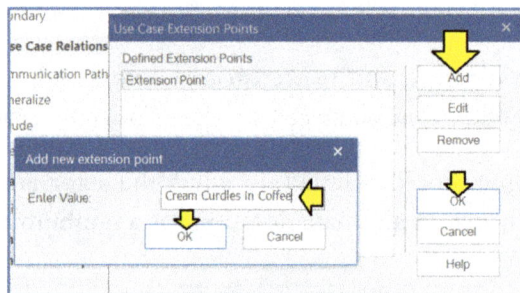

Figure 10-7 – Add extension point

Click "Add". Enter the name for the extension point: "Cream Curdles in Coffee". Click "OK" twice.

Select the "Extend" relationship in the toolbox. Drag an extend relationship from the use case to deal with curdled cream to the use case to drink coffee.

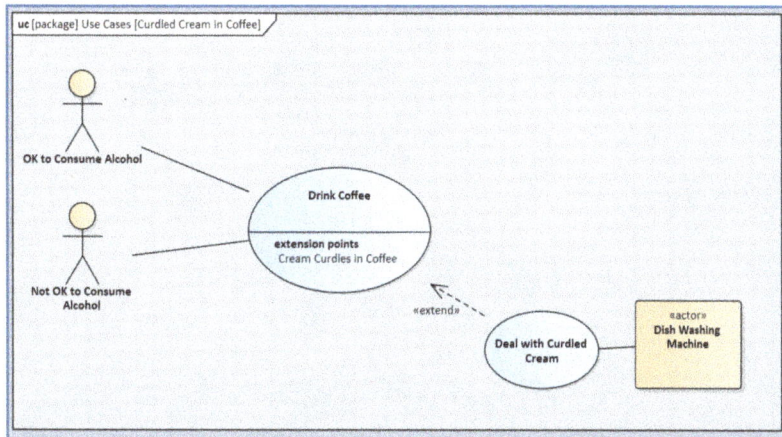

Figure 10-8 – Extended use case

Further Study

As mentioned above, the SysML diagrams for use cases are quite simple. As such, for this chapter I am going to direct you to books rather than topics.

- **[Cockburn]** – Read this book for an extensive treatment of techniques for organizing and writing use cases.

- **[Delligatti]** – Read the entire chapter (pages 77-88) on use case diagrams. Pay particular attention to the remarks about things you should *not* do with use cases and use case diagrams.

- **[Douglass]** – One could argue that this entire book is about use cases. This is a systems engineering methodology flow book and the author discusses use cases in quite a bit of detail showing how they fit in at each stage in the development of a system.

Chapter 11 – Requirements Diagrams

Creating and managing large sets of requirements is a science of its own. Some European universities even offer full degree programs just in requirements engineering. In *Requirements Engineering Books* on page 372 you will find a list of books on this subject. A full discussion of requirements engineering is far beyond the scope of this book.

That having been said, SysML requirements diagrams are quite simple. The toolbox for the requirements diagram contains just two icons and six relationships. We have already covered the basics of how to create and manipulate requirements diagrams in *Adding a Requirements Diagram* on page 28. In this chapter, we will just take a look at a few key aspects of the diagrams and their usage in *Enterprise Architect*.

Single Version of the Truth

One of my favorite use of the SysML requirements diagram is to create "Single Version of the Truth" diagrams. [46]

---

[46] **Note:** Here we are talking about creating a limited scope "Single Version of the Truth" within the "Shared Vision for the System". The goal is to create just enough clarity so that a specific set of stakeholders can do their jobs without making mistakes. We are **not** attempting to turn the SysML model into the universal repository of all data for the system.

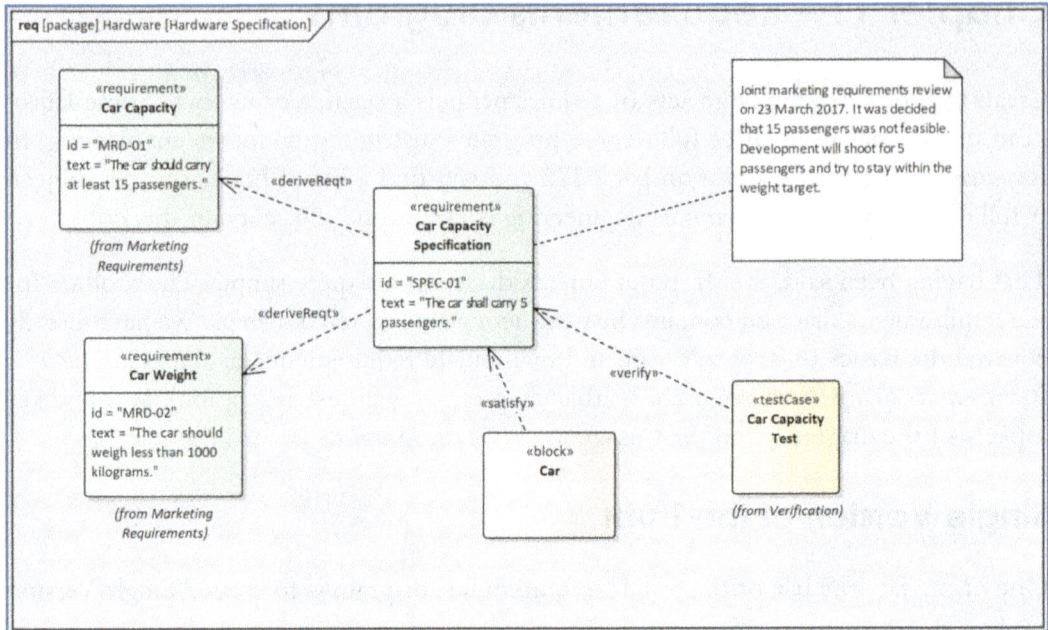

Figure 11-1 – Resolving conflicting requirements

1) Marketing presented us with conflicting requirements (actually goals) for the product: "MRD-01" and "MRD-02".

2) A meeting was held on 27 March 2017 to decide what to do. The note explains the consensus from the meeting.

3) "SPEC-01" is the agreed upon specification of what development will attempt to build.

4) The car is the system element that has to satisfy "SPEC-01".

5) A testcase has been defined to verify that the car complies with "SPEC-01".

A diagram like Figure 11-1 ties together the entire discussion for all the stakeholders. It shows what marketing wanted. It shows what development agreed to build. It documents the history of the discussion. It shows which element needs to meet the requirement and it identifies a testcase for that element. In my experience, this sort of diagram is extremely helpful for documenting the "Why" which is often much more important over time than the "What".

Names versus Text

Some organizations have a history of managing requirements in the form of specification documents. Such organizations may not be used to separating the name of a requirement and the text of the requirement. These organizations may be reluctant to start creating separate names for each requirement. However, as such organizations transition to using graphical approaches like SysML to manage requirements relationships, they will soon find that not separating the name and the text of the requirement produces unwieldly results.

In order to illustrate the problem, we will take a look at a set of typically convoluted requirements with very long, tangled requirement sentences.

ID	Name	Text
ATBSQ-1	Closure Angle	The automatic teabag squeezer's cantilevered arm assembly shall have a closure angle not to exceed the angle of the polarization between the major political parties in Washington divided by the rate of martini consumption per patron at a bar frequented by at least 5% of all lobbyists within a 10 kilometer radius of K street in Washington DC.
ATBSQ-2	Throughput	The throughput of the automatic teabag squeezer shall be sufficient to squeeze within 5 minutes the required number of teabags of a regional meeting of the Bagged Tea Lovers of America meeting held in one of the 37 most populous cities in North America.
ATBSQ-3	ANSI, CEN, JIS Compliance	The automatic teabag squeezer shall comply with ANSI/AHAM ATBSQ-7-2019 Left-handed teabag squeezing, CEN/TC 572ATBSQ Uniform teabag squeezing apparatus, and JIS ATBSQ 9722:19 Harmonious Squeezing of Teabags.

Figure 11-2 – Long requirement sentences

What happens in our SysML model if we do not distinguish between name and text?

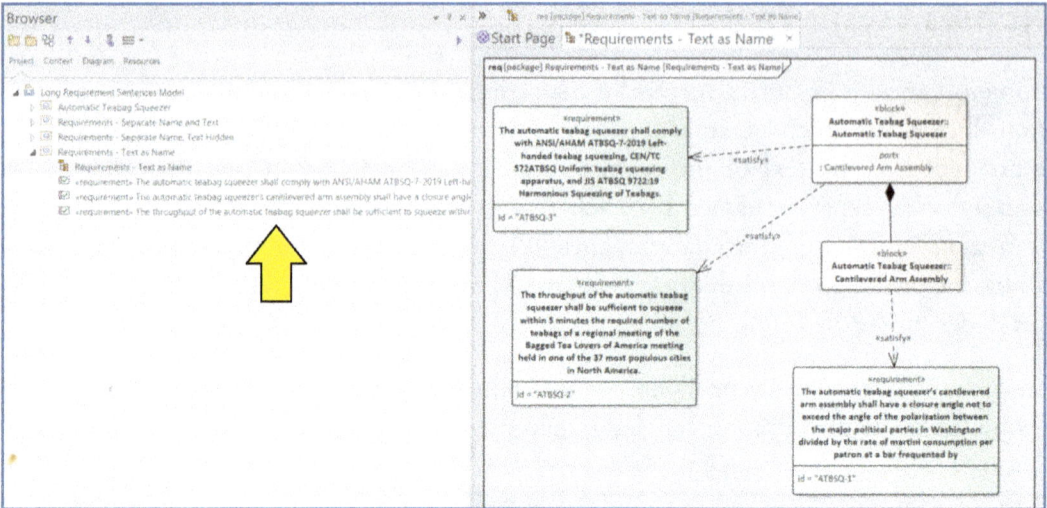

Figure 11-3 – Long names are cumbersome

In SysML, element names are not optional. In other words, if we don't have separate names and text, we have no choice but to use the text that we have as the SysML "requirement name" and leave the "requirement text" blank.

As we can see, this approach leads to a cumbersome structure in the project browser. Also, *Enterprise Architect* will not swallow an arbitrary amount of text for an element name. Looking carefully, the reader will notice that requirement ATBSQ-1 has been truncated by *Enterprise Architect*.

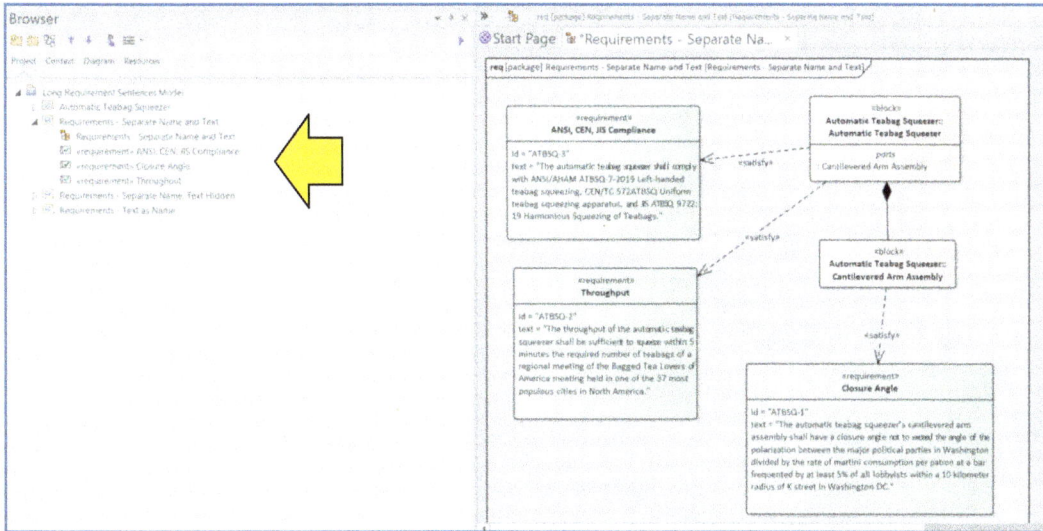

Figure 11-4 – Separate names are better

After we rework the model to use separate names, we can see significant improvements:

- The project browser is much easier to work with.

- The requirements diagram is a little easier to read with small bold summaries of each requirement.

- Requirement ATBSQ-1's full text is no longer truncated. The element name has a lot of other semantic functions in SysML and really should not be a long string. The requirement text, however, is just a text block and can be much longer.

What if our diagram is getting crowded?

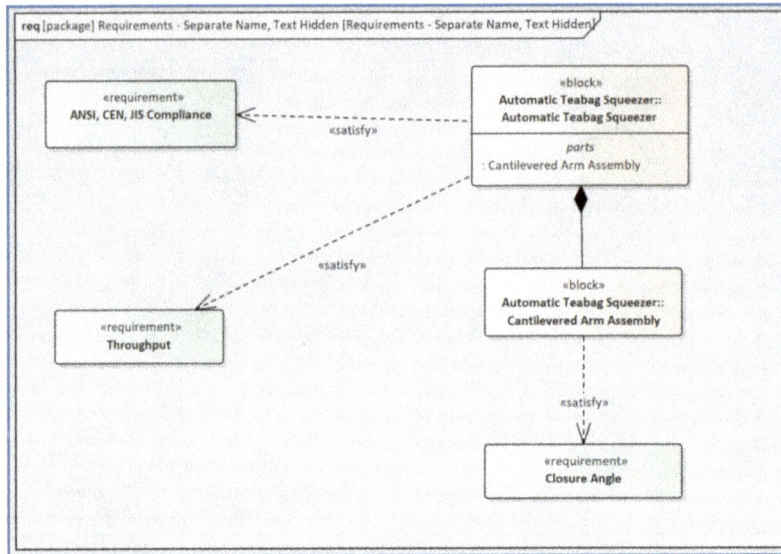

req [package] Requirements - Separate Name, Text Hidden [Requirements - Separate Name, Text Hidden]

«requirement»
ANSI, CEN, JIS Compliance

«block»
Automatic Teabag Squeezer::
Automatic Teabag Squeezer

parts
: Cantilevered Arm Assembly

«satisfy»

«satisfy»

«requirement»
Throughput

«block»
Automatic Teabag Squeezer::
Cantilevered Arm Assembly

«satisfy»

«requirement»
Closure Angle

Figure 11-5 – Text can be hidden

Using the "Compartment Visibility..." context menu, it is possible to turn off the display of "Tags" which makes the requirements symbols much more compact. [47]

Configuring Requirement Tools to Separate Name from Text
Some requirements management tools come configured by default to manage requirements as whole sentences or even paragraphs within word-processed documents. The good news is that most tools can be configured to separate the name from the requirement text. You just need to have the discussion with your requirements administrator and the supplier's technical support staff.

---

[47] *Enterprise Architect* does not provide a function to select which tags get displayed. Turning off tags turns off both ID and text.

Requirement IDs

The ID field of the SysML requirement is quite important. Although it does not have a specific semantic function in SysML, these IDs are critical for **requirements traceability** which is beyond the scope of this book but is critical for any sort of safety-critical system.

In a system that needs to demonstrate requirements traceability, there will be thousands of requirements, components, and testcases by the time the system is designed. I recommend that you tinker out a requirement numbering system that allows the user to easily spot related and similar artifacts. That is, if:

- a market requirement
- an architecture requirement
- a system component
- a design requirement for that component
- a testcase for the design requirement

...are all related, it is handy if they all have visibly similar ID numbers. [48] I usually use an alphanumeric pattern like this:

TTT-MAJ-MIN-NNN

Where the fields have the following meanings:

- *TTT* – Type of requirement. Is this a marketing requirement? A government regulation? A system architecture requirement? A detailed design requirement?
- *MAJ* – Major. Major subsystem.
- *MIN* – Minor. Might be a component, or a topic of interest.
- *NNN* – Number. I usually start out with three digits here.

---

[48] In fact, when I design this sort of system, I often end up making a UML profile of specialized stereotypes of the «block» and the «requirement» elements. I add the ID tag to all of these elements so that I can make a consistent end-to-end numbering scheme.

Can you run into problems with this sort of system? Absolutely, but here are a few tricks to minimize the pain:

1) Leave ranges of numbers open. I number the first requirement "001", the second "005", the third "010", and so on. Just making a habit of this sort of skipping makes it easier to go back later and insert things you forgot on the first pass.

2) Don't worry about perfect alignment. For any given topic there will be different numbers of requirements at different levels. Shoot for "Good Enough" similarity and don't bother struggling to achieve perfect alignment.

3) Keep it simple. Don't go overboard setting up 97-character ID strings. Fuzzy and short is better than precise and unreadable.

Random ID Numbers and Name Versus Text in Requirements

At your company, you may be using a formal requirements management software tool. Some of these tools – even some rather expensive tools made by famous companies – come configured by default to assign random six-digit numbers to requirements. The sales personnel for the companies that sell these sorts of tools will often argue that managing requirements numbering schemes is difficult and that it is much more convenient to have random six-digit numbers as requirements IDs. While I do understand the tricks and problems associated with managing a requirement numbering scheme, I don't agree with the random number approach. It is usually worth the effort to create and maintain a rational requirements numbering scheme.

The good news is that most requirements tools (even those expensive tools made by famous companies) can be configured to allow for the assignment of meaningful ID strings. You just need to have the discussion with your requirements administrator and the supplier's technical support staff.

Tables, Matrices, and Reports

SysML defines the existence of matrices and tables for requirements but provides no further information about what they should look like or how they should work.

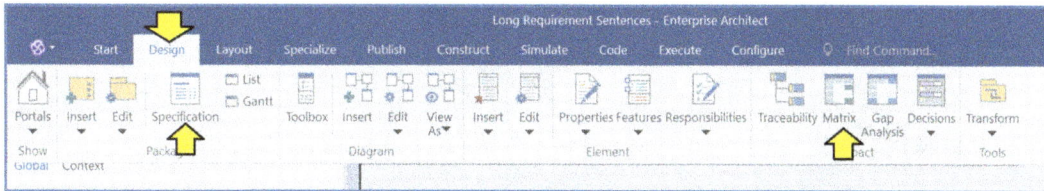

Figure 11-6 – Reporting tools

Click on the design ribbon to expose icons for the specification manager and the relationship matrix wizard.

Further Study

Requirements engineering is a complex subject. If you are going to be doing anything beyond the simplest requirements for your system, I encourage you to look through the list of books in *Requirements Engineering Books* on page 372 and select one or more for detailed study.

As for SysML requirements diagrams themselves, here are some topics for further study:

- **rationale** – Although not part of the SysML requirements diagram definition, SysML defines a modeling element for rationale that can be used in a requirements diagram.
    - [Delligatti] – page 213
    - [Friedenthal] – page 317

- **requirements notation** – In addition to the normal notation presented in this chapter, there are some other alternatives for the notation of requirements and relationships.
    - [Delligatti] – page 209
    - [Friedenthal] – page 316

- **requirement relationships** – SysML defines six kinds of requirement relationship. Our main reference books contain detailed descriptions for each type of relationship.
    - [Delligatti] – page 205
    - [Douglass] – page 96
    - [Friedenthal] – page 314

- **subclassing requirements** – Since SysML 1.5 is built on top of UML, it is possible to create a UML profile and subclass the SysML requirement model element into more specialized requirement types.
    - [Friedenthal] – page 312

Chapter 12 – Parametric Diagrams

This chapter will be about the use of parametric diagrams to model mathematical relationships. Most books separate the discussion of constraints from the discussion of parametric diagrams. I think that parametric diagrams are easier to understand if we start with a simple constraint statement on a single block and build up from there.

Single Constraint

The simplest case is a single block with a single constraint. We will make a simple model of a cylinder and use a constraint to specify its volume.

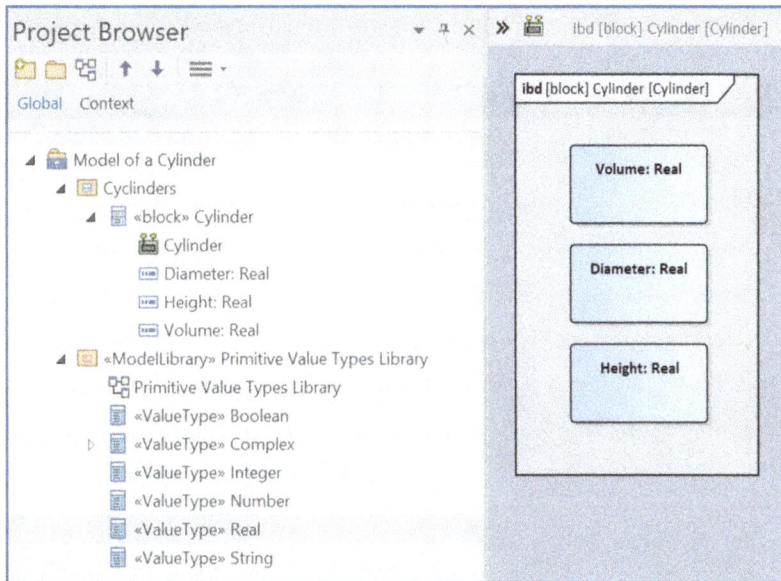

Figure 12-1 – Create basic model of a cylinder

Create a basic model of a cylinder. Use the procedure shown in *Value Properties* on page 93 to bring in the *Enterprise Architect* standard type library. Create an internal block diagram for the cylinder. Drag the ValueType "Real" from the standard type library to the internal block diagram three times to create value properties for volume, diameter, and height.

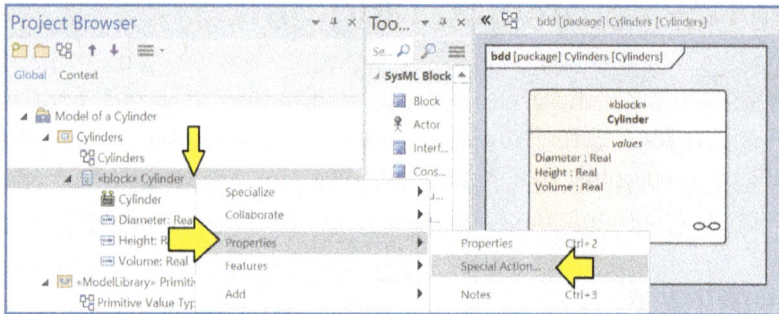

Figure 12-2 – Open special action

In the project browser, right-click on the cylinder block, select "Properties" and then "Special Action...".

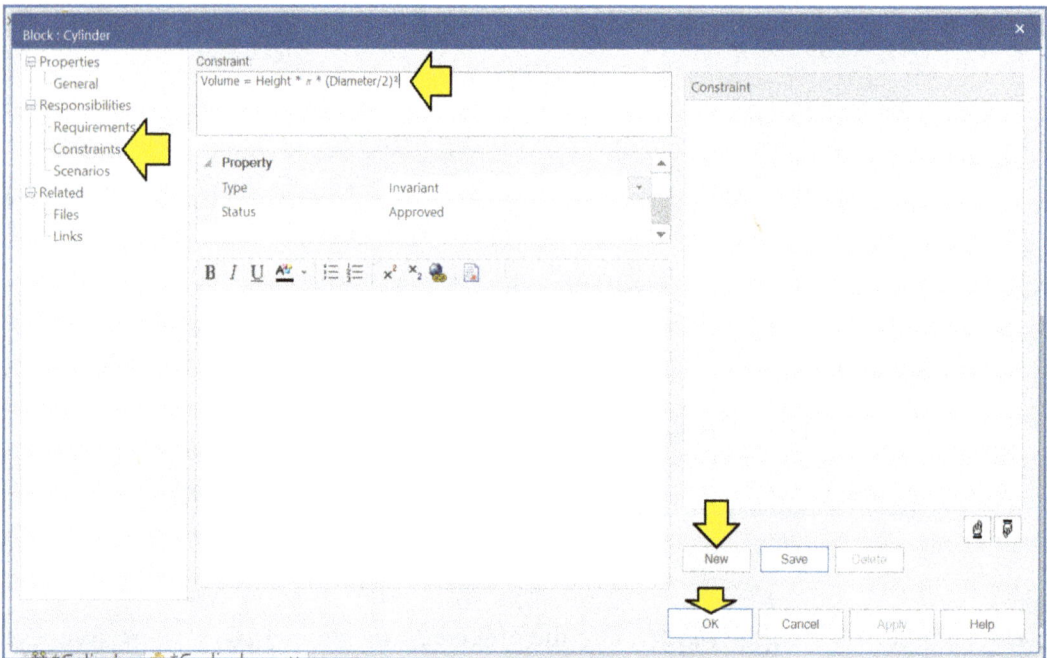

Figure 12-3 – Enter constraint formula

Select the "Constraints" panel. Enter "Volume = Height $* \pi *$ (Diameter/2)^2" in the "Constraint:" field. [49] Click "New" and then click "OK".

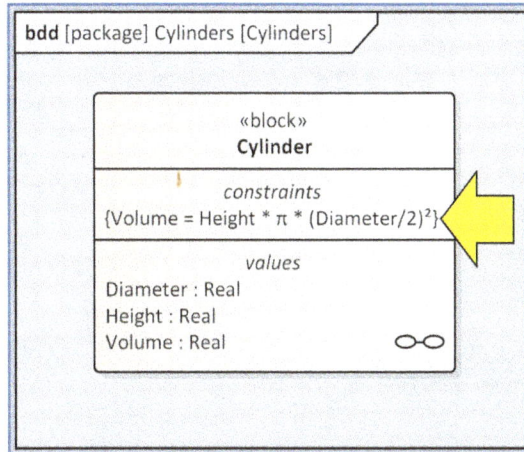

Figure 12-4 – Constraint added

Constraint Blocks

In the previous section, we added a constraint to a block. This operation was fairly straightforward, but has two obvious weaknesses:

- **Reuse of Equations** – Obviously if an equation is buried inside of block A, there is no easy way to reuse the same equation in block B.

- **Complex Equations** – The equation-inside-the-block approach is acceptable for simple equations but does not provide any method of breaking down complex equations into smaller pieces.

SysML addresses both of these challenges by introducing a modeling element called the **constraint block**. However, before diving into either of these two complicated scenarios, we are going to introduce the constraint block (and the parametric diagram) by simply reworking the previous section's model to use an external constraint block instead of a constraint inside the block.

---

[49] I have used an internet search for "Unicode pi" to find, copy, and paste the " π " character and a similar search for "Unicode squared" to find, copy, and paste the " ² " character into the tool. See Figure 4-37 on page 101.

First, use the properties, special actions menu to find and remove the constraint from cylinder block. Before removing the constraint, be sure to copy and paste the equation "Volume = Height * π * (Diameter/2)²" to a temporary file somewhere. We will need it again in a moment.

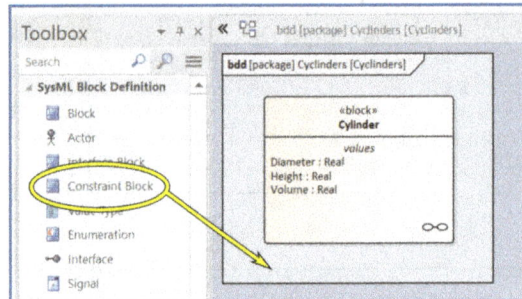

Figure 12-5 – Drag constraint block to diagram

From the toolbox, drag the constraint block icon to the block definition diagram containing the cylinder block. *Enterprise Architect* has a very elegant wizard for creating constraint blocks that will appear next.

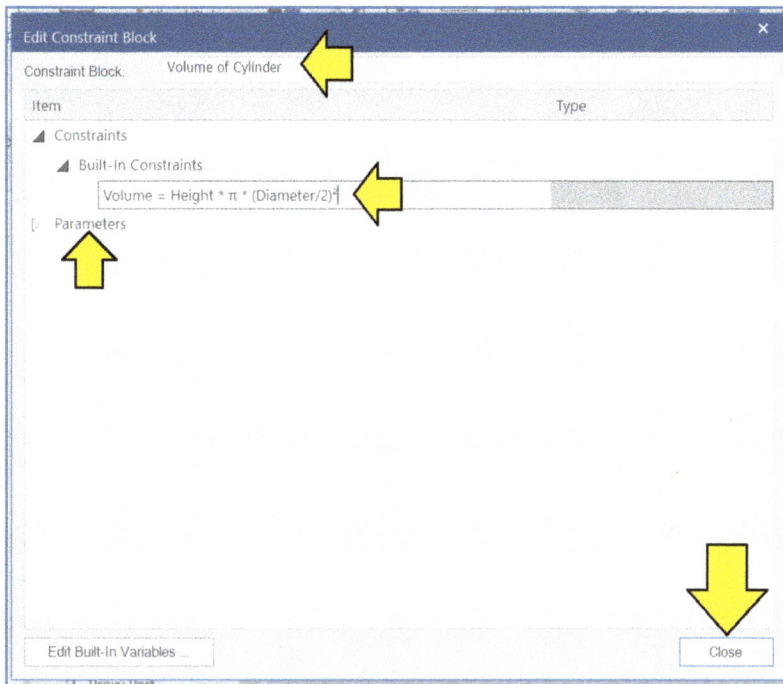

Figure 12-6 – Name the constraint and add equation

1) In the field "Constraint Block:" enter the name for the constraint block: "Cylinder Volume".

2) Copy and paste the equation "Volume = Height * π * (Diameter/2)²" into the "Built-In Constraints" field.

3) Click the word "Parameters". The wizard will parse the equation you entered and define **constraint parameters** for volume, height, and diameter.

4) Click "Close".

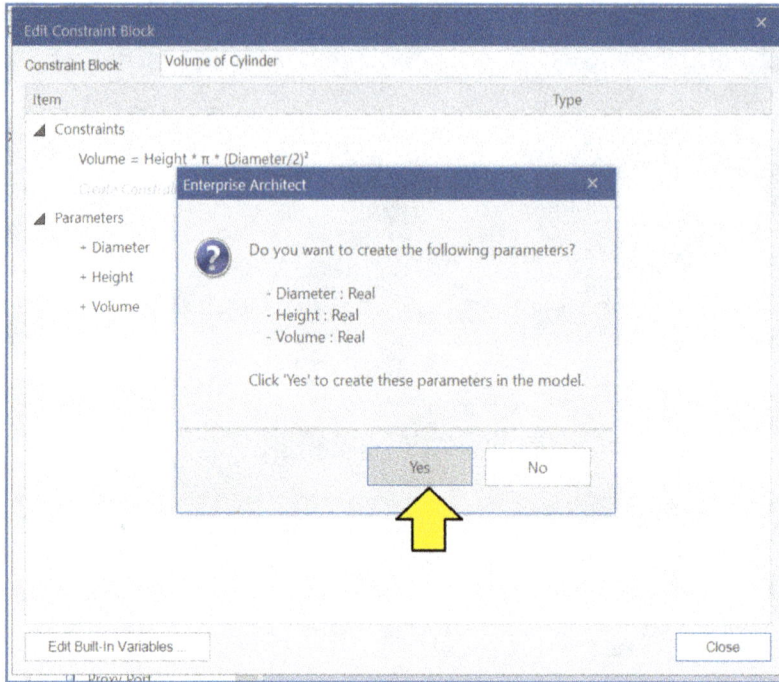

Figure 12-7 – Click Yes to accept

Click "Yes" to accept the definition of constraint parameters that the wizard extracted from the equation.

Right-click on the cylinder block again and select properties and special action to open the panel to define constraints.

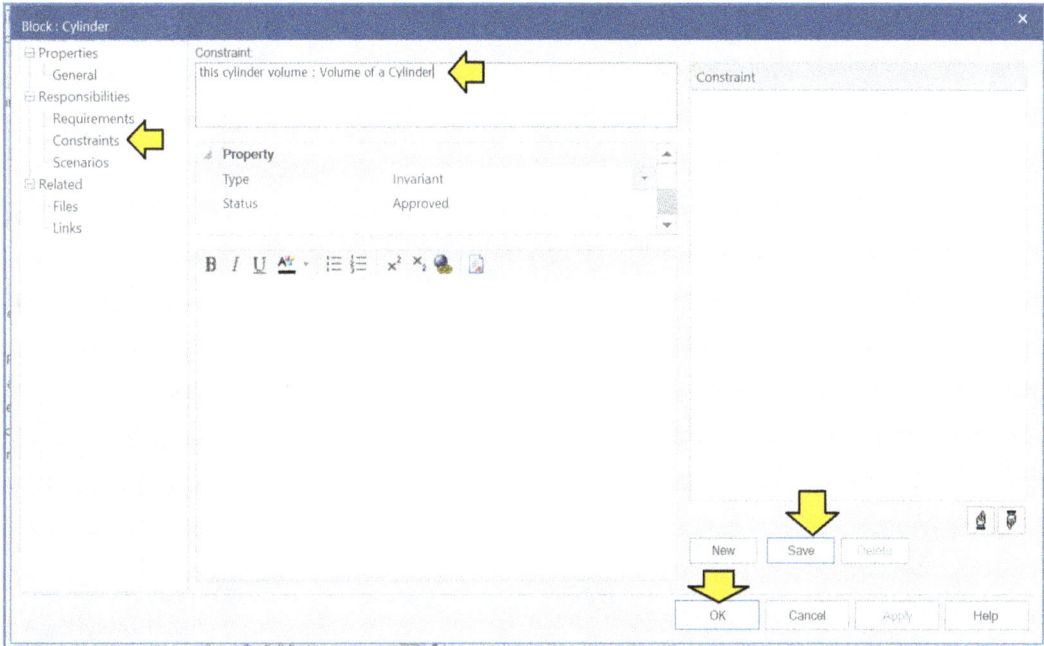

Figure 12-8 – Define constraint in block

Select the constraints subpanel. In the "Constraint:" field, enter "this cylinder volume : Volume of a Cylinder". This string has the meaning:

- A constraint named: "this cylinder volume"
- which is of type: "Volume of a Cylinder" (which points to the constraint block that we just defined.)

Click "Save" and then "OK".

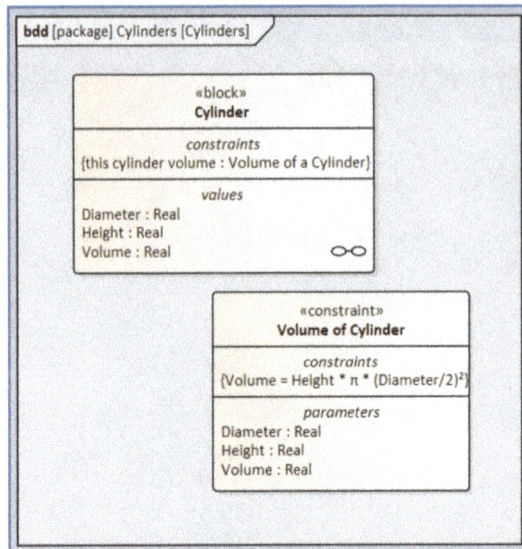

Figure 12-9 – So far, so good

So far, so good. Everything looks very neat and pretty. The problem is that looks can be deceiving. The parameter names in the constraint block neatly match the value type names in the cylinder block. This symmetry might lead one to assume that SysML would spot the obvious similarity – and the hint in the block's constraint declaration – and figure out how to put it all together.

One would be wrong. We could just as well have declared the equation in the constraint block to be: "Bananas = Apples * π * (Oranges/2)²" and let the *Enterprise Architect* wizard declare matching constraint parameters. SysML can't guess what is what simply by name similarity. We have to show it what is connected explicitly, and this is where the parametric diagram comes in.

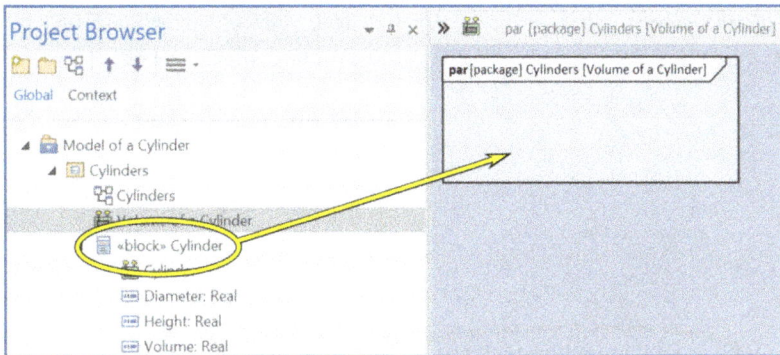

Figure 12-10 – Drag block to parametric diagram

Right-click on the cylinders package and add a parametric diagram. Drag the cylinder block to the diagram.

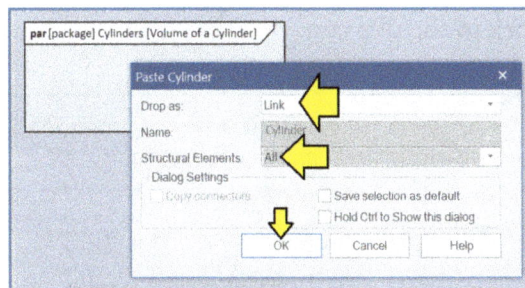

Figure 12-11 – Drop as link

After you release the mouse, a panel will appear that controls the drag-and-drop operation. Change the "Drop as:" type to "Link". Under "Structural Elements:" select "All". Click "OK".

Right-click on the block, select "Compartment Visibility...", and turn off the display of the *constraints* and *values* compartments. Resize the block as needed.

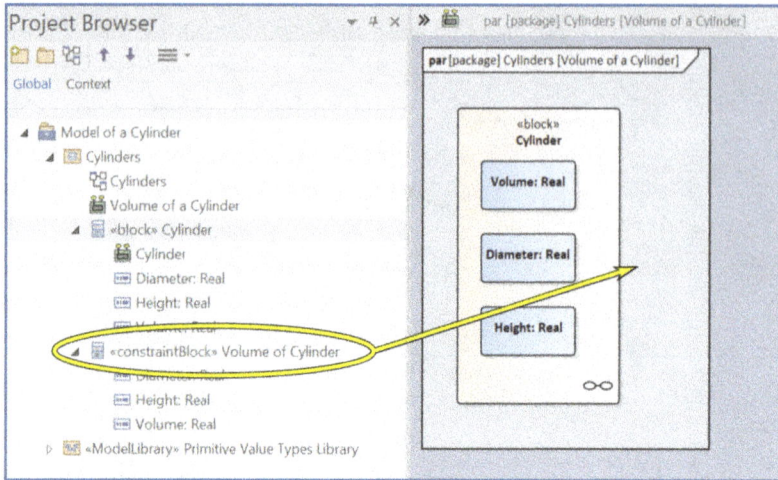

Figure 12-12 – Drag constraint block to diagram

Drag the constraint block to the diagram.

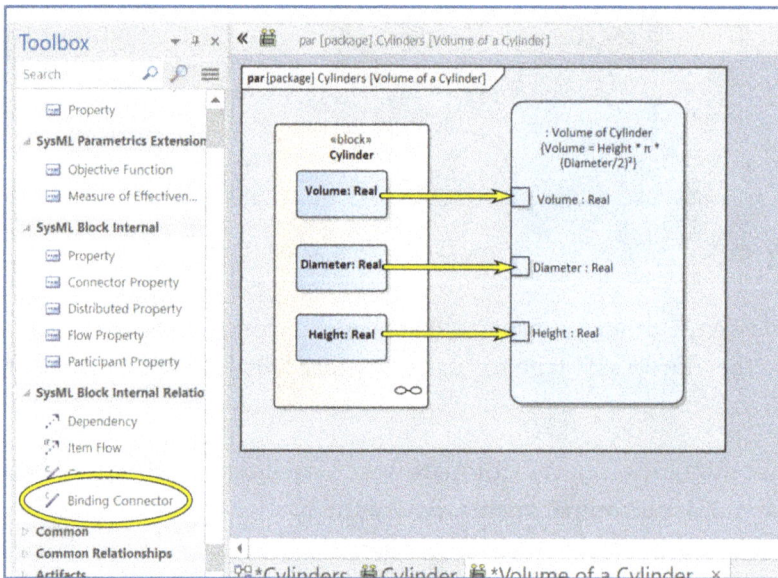

Figure 12-13 – Drag binding connections

Next, we will use a **binding connector** to connect value properties to parameters. Re-size and reposition the constraint block as needed. Drag the constraint parameter boxes up and down along the border of the constraint block until they align nicely with the value properties in the block. Select the "Binding Connector" icon in the toolbox. Drag binding connections between the value properties in the block and the matching constraint parameters on the border of the constraint block.

A **binding connector** is used to specify that two values must be equal at all times.

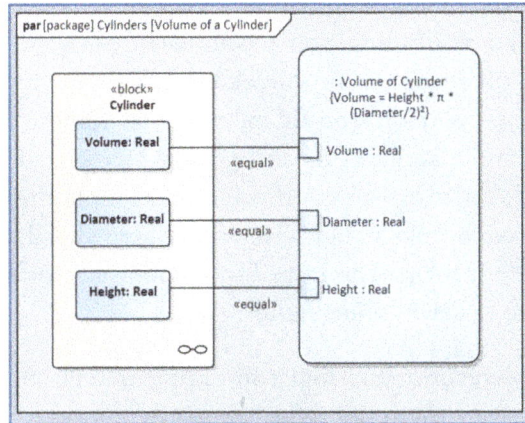

Figure 12-14 – Completed parametric diagram

The completed parametric diagram binds value properties in the block with their corresponding constraint parameters in the constraint block.

Organizing Inputs and Outputs

Examining Figure 12-14 there is no directionality in the binding connectors. It is hard (impossible actually) to see what depends on what or which way the information flows. All that SysML specifies is that the ends of each binding connector be equal at all times.

This directionless modeling is apparently very helpful for advanced academic studies of linear optimization techniques. It is somewhat less wonderful for making practical, easy-to-understand diagrams for day-to-day engineering problems. Near the top of my wish list for the planned SysML version 2 is the simple addition of an optional arrowhead on the binding connector to make it more obvious which direction the information is flowing. The academic folks could turn off the arrowhead and use the diagrams in their current form. The rest of us could use arrowheads and make diagrams that were easier to understand.

In the meantime, I recommend that you draw parametric diagrams with a consistent direction to them. I prefer left-to-right and try to organize my diagrams so that the sources of data are on the left of the diagram and the calculated results on the right wherever possible.

Reuse of Constraint Blocks

What if we want to use the same constraint block in multiple places? We won't be able to directly use the constraint block in a parametric diagram this way because connecting one constraint parameter (in the constraint block) to two different value properties in two different blocks would not be valid. Instead, we will need to work with instances of the constraint block.

While it might be possible to create instances for everything, my preferred approach is to create an "Equation Context" block and make everything a property of that block.

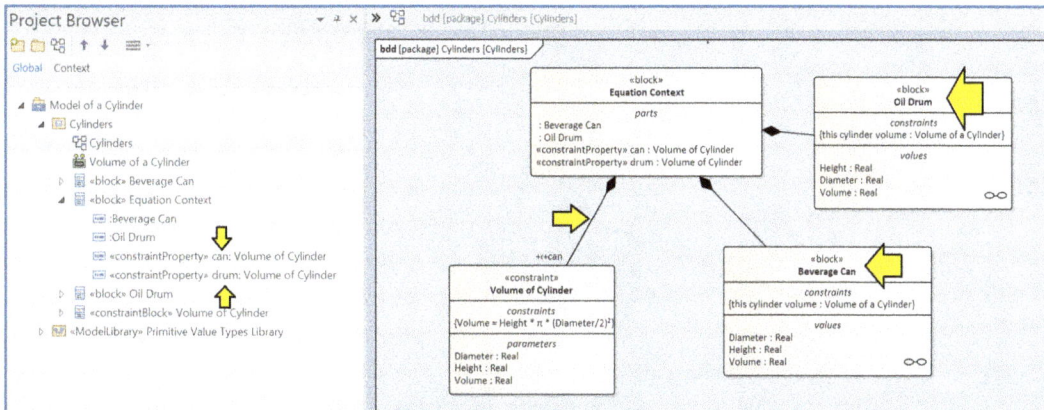

Figure 12-15 – Create equation context

1) Create a block definition diagram and a block for the equation context.

2) Create two kinds of cylinder block, one for beverage cans and one for oil drums.

3) Drag composition relationships from the cylinder blocks to the equation context block.

4) Drag the constraint block onto the diagram.

5) Drag the composition relationship from the constraint block to the equation context block twice. Only one arrow will show in the diagram, but two constraint properties will be created in the project browser.

6) Use F2 in the project browser to give the constraint properties names. Name one "can" and the other "drum".

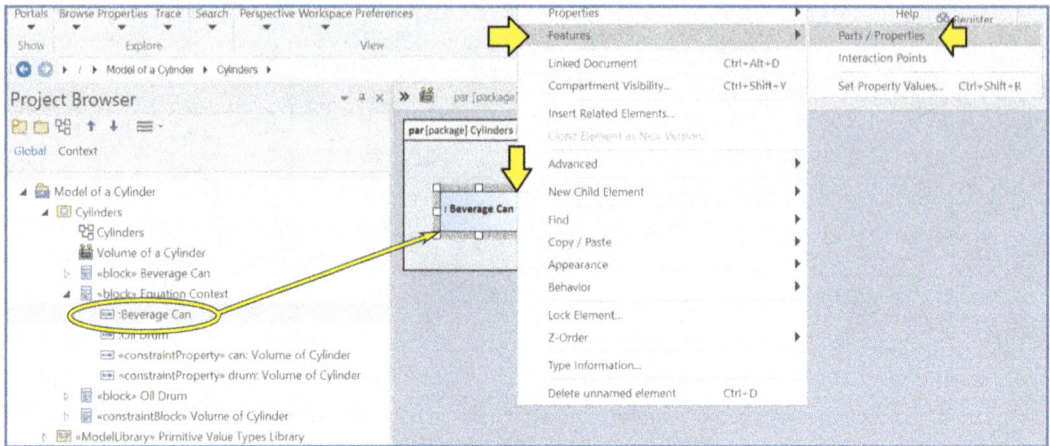

Figure 12-16 – Drag can to diagram

Drag the beverage can part to the parametric diagram. The first time you drop it on the diagram, no value properties will be displayed. Right-click on the block on the diagram and select "Features" and then "Parts/Properties".

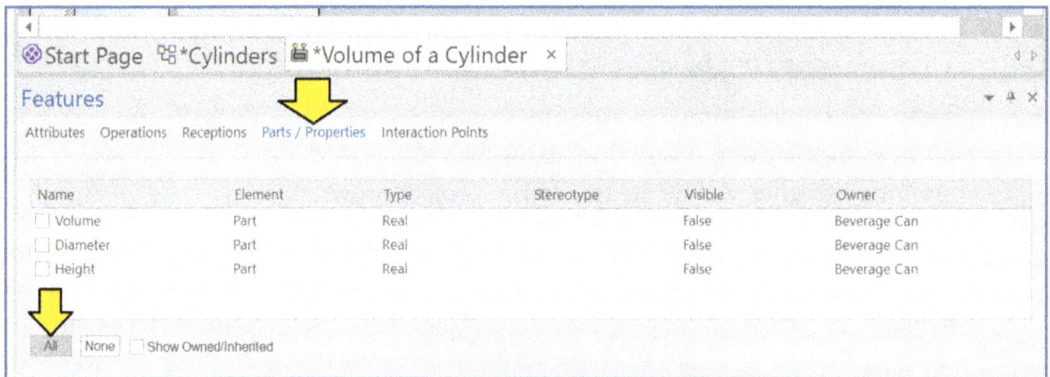

Figure 12-17 – Click All in the Features panel

The features panel should open with the "Parts/Properties" subpanel will appear. The three value properties should be visible. Click "All". Drag to adjust the size of the beverage can symbol until the three value properties are nicely displayed inside of it. [50] Do the same thing to the oil drum to add its symbol and properties to the diagram. Do the same thing with the two constraint properties. Drag and resize until the two constraint properties and their parameters are nicely aligned with the two part properties and their value parameters. As before, use binding connectors to connect them.

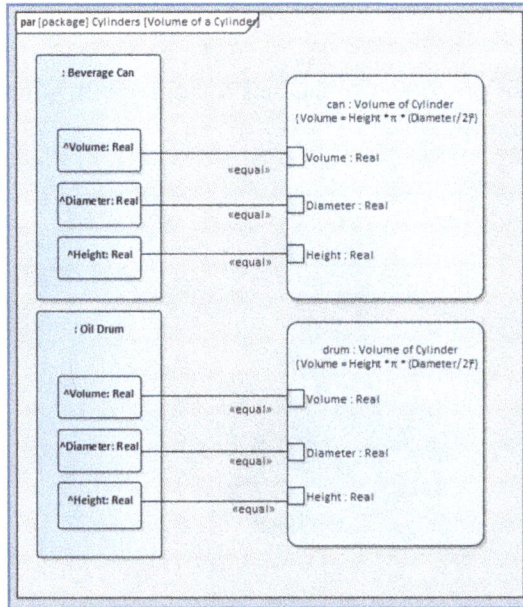

Figure 12-18 – Completed parametric diagram with reused constraint block

Now we have the completed parametric diagram with reused constraint block. That is, we have two instances (actually constraint properties) of the "Volume of a Cylinder" constraint block connected to instances (actually part properties) of two different blocks. However, if we edit the formula in the original constraint block, it will change in both instances of the constraint block. [51]

---

[50] You may find it easier to expand the size of the symbol in the diagram before adding the value properties to it.

[51] You might need to close and reopen the model to make the parametric diagram display the updated formula.

Breaking Down a Complicated Formula

Constraint blocks can be cascaded to break a complicated formula down into more understandable pieces.

To demonstrate the composition of a complicated formula from simpler elements, we will calculate the mass of a statue.

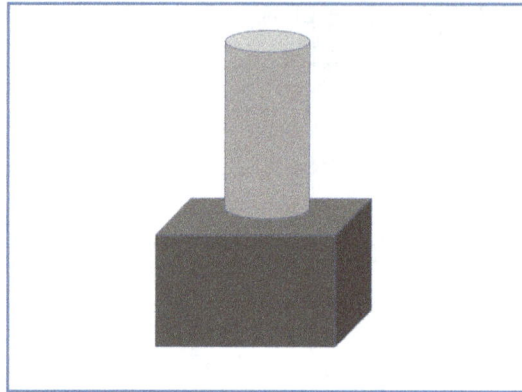

Figure 12-19 – The statue

Thanks to a large donation from a prominent citizen, a world-famous abstract artist has been commissioned to create a new statue for the recently renovated plaza in front of city hall. The artist's concept is called: *"The Sublime Pathos of the Onward March of Time"* and in keeping with the artist's famous minimalist style, it is a round pillar standing upright on a rectangular base. The material will be concrete. There will be no distracting adornments or patterns on the statue. The city planning department needs to know the mass of the statue so that they can properly prepare the foundation to sit it on.

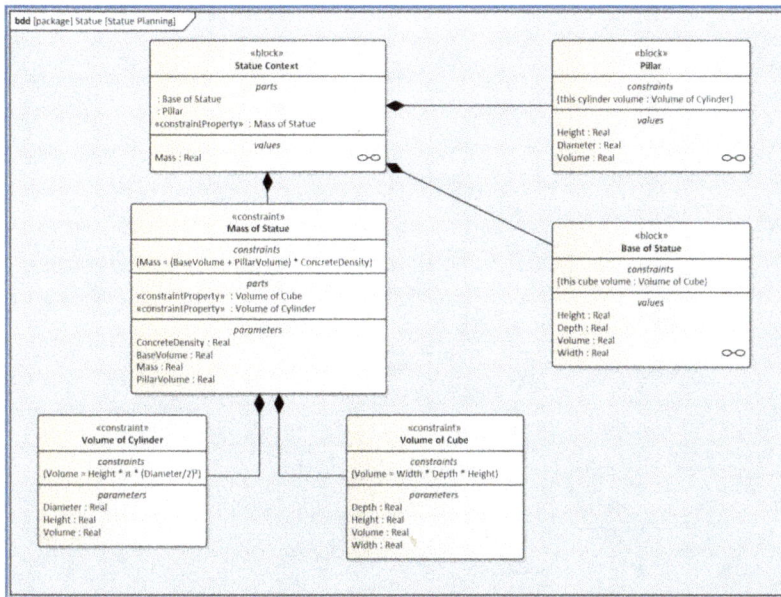

Figure 12-20 – Set up the context

Using the techniques from the previous sections, we can set this model up as shown in Figure 12-20.

Notice that we have used composition to break down the slightly more complicated "Mass of a Statue" calculation into three pieces:

1) A volume calculation for the base.

2) A volume calculation for the cylindrical pillar.

3) A mass calculation that combines the two volumes and multiplies them by a factor for the density of concrete.

Next, we will use a parametric diagram to wire everything together.

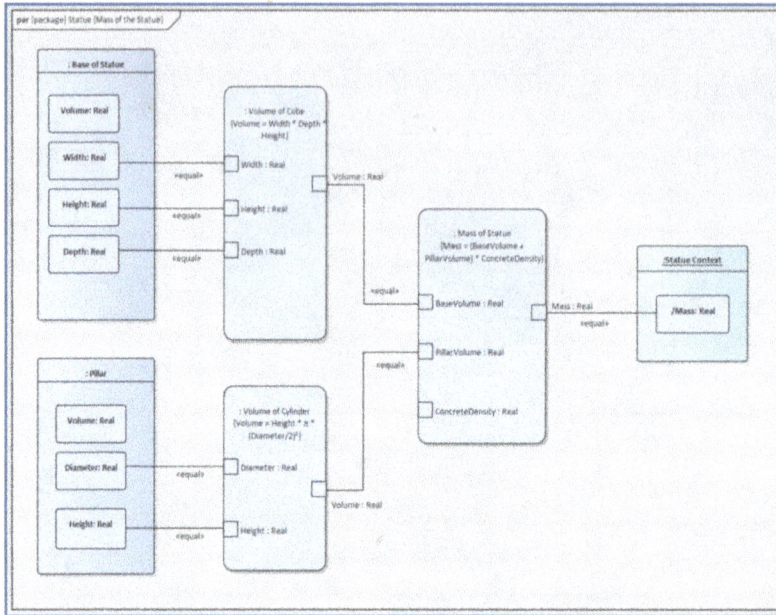

Figure 12-21 – Completed diagram

Once again, binding connectors can be used to connect everything together as shown in Figure 12-21.

1) We haven't decided which handbook to use for the density of a concrete number, so it is not connected to anything yet.

2) Notice that we have not connected the volume value parameters in the base and pillar to the output of their respective calculations. Actually, we could do so, leaving two binding connections from each of the volume calculation outputs. However, adding these extra binding connectors would make the diagram harder to understand and we don't actually need those two volume value properties to be set.

3) As mentioned above, this diagram is set up to flow from left to right. However, SysML parametric diagrams are directionless. In principle, we could define the desired volume for the statue, define a few of the other values/dimensions, and work backwards to calculate the missing inputs.

Further Study

The Georgia Tech Parametrics Primer [Peak] is quite helpful. Beyond that, [Friedenthal] contains more information about different ways to apply SysML parametric diagrams. In particular:

- **parameter characteristics** – There are some additional parameter characteristics such as "{unique}" that can be used to specify the nature of the constraint parameters in more detail.

    - [Friedenthal] – page 188

- **time-based analysis** – Additional information about using parametric diagrams for time-based analysis

    - [Friedenthal] – page 195

Chapter 13 – Challenges Ahead

Congratulations! If you have made it this far, you are now able to make all of the basic SysML diagrams using *Enterprise Architect*. You should be well-positioned to practice and continue to extend and deepen your modeling skill.

So far, so good. However, unless you are a millionaire recluse with some very complicated hobbies, your SysML diagrams will not be useful unless you can use them to interact with other humans. Usually those other humans will be coworkers in a large and complicated organization – an organization working on projects of sufficient complexity to warrant the use of SysML. This is the point at which things get tricky. You are going to encounter some surprising objections and misconceptions. As you go deeper, you will also encounter some surprises in your own use of the technology. The manner in which you end up using SysML may end up being rather different from what you imagined when you started.

A fully exhaustive discussion of these factors is far beyond the scope of this book. In fact, an exhaustive treatment of the subject would not end up being a book about engineering, but rather a book about cognitive psychology, sociology, or political science. However, at least I can give you a brief introduction to a few of the things you are likely to encounter early in your journey. The following sections cover some of the more common challenges.

Common Objections

As you get excited about the potential of SysML to help your organization and start trying to spread the vision, you are going to run into some objections. Actually, you are going to run into a *lot* of objections. In the next few sections, we will cover a few of the most common objections and give you some ideas about how to consider and discuss them in a nuanced manner.

First – Is MBSE Right for Your Project?

Before we delve into the most common objections for introducing SysML and/or MBSE, we have to consider the fact that the people objecting may be right: SysML and

MBSE might not be a good fit for your project. In fact, the percentage of projects that will benefit from a determined deployment of MBSE techniques is actually fairly small.

Figure 13-1 – The cat-eating-cheeseburger application

For example, consider a team that is working on the cutting-edge mobile social media application shown in Figure 13-1. Would this team benefit from a careful MBSE work-up of their application? Probably not. This team would face several challenges that would make SysML or MBSE adoption difficult:

1) **Requirements –** The team has no idea what the end user requirements are. In fact, the end users have no idea what the end-user requirements are either.

2) **Concept –** They don't really have one. Their goal is simply to get the cat-eating-cheeseburger application on the market as fast as possible and see if anyone is interested.

3) **Quality –** No one cares if the cat fails to eat a cheeseburger every now and then. In fact, the failure to eat a cheeseburger might end up being entertaining in its own right. [52]

---

[52] In the 1980s when I was developing software for IBM, these sorts of behaviors were often referred to as "Feechurs", as in: "That's not a bug, it's a *Feechur*".

4) **Schedule –** The application needs to ship yesterday and to be updated every few hours after that until customers lose interest in it.

Introducing a very slow and meticulous architectural planning process to the cat-eating-cheeseburger team isn't likely to be helpful. In fact, it is likely to contribute to the failure of the team if it slows down their application deployment and they get beaten to market by the competing *Shiba-Inu-with-Inscrutable-Expression* application.

So, what kinds of projects might benefit? Generally, the two ingredients that a project needs to be a good candidate for SysML and MBSE are:

1) **Overwhelming Complexity –** The project needs to be so complicated that it is impossible for the team members to keep track of all the requirements in their heads or even with spreadsheets.

2) **Severe Consequences for Mistakes –** Mistakes generally need to have the potential to instantly end executive careers, cause unimaginable financial losses, or cause horrific injuries.

However, even when a project has plenty of both of these ingredients and painful failures are already happening regularly, many project leaders can be amazingly resistant to any sort of behavior change that might help get the problems under control. Don't be surprised if you meet a lot of resistance, even if the failures are already starting to happen.

Needless to say, if your project resembles the cat-eating-cheeseburger application, you should consider learning SysML purely as a personal hobby. You can save yourself a lot of frustration and disappointment by not even trying to convince the cat-eating-cheeseburger team to change their development approach and start modeling things carefully before implementing them.

Objection – Why Can't We Just Use PowerPoint?

Figure 13-2 – PowerPoint is excellent for compelling presentation of high-level concepts

PowerPoint is an outstanding presentation tool with some strong drawing features. However, PowerPoint is not really an engineering tool and has a number of limitations in terms of Systems Engineering:

- **No Standard Syntax** – Everyone's diagrams look different. PowerPoint's drawing features are great for high-level concept presentations, but PowerPoint struggles as you try to draw with any level of consistency and precision.

- **No Underlying Data Model** – If you make a 100 page presentation full of something called "fluid" and you find later that you need to change that to read "liquid" you will need to go back and manually find all the "fluid" boxes in the presentation and change them one-by-one.

- **No Tool Integration** – Although it is out of the scope for this book, SysML tools like *Enterprise Architect* are easy to integrate with other engineering management tools such as requirements database systems. PowerPoint does not really integrate with anything.

Make no mistake: PowerPoint is an excellent tool and I use it regularly. However, it is not a substitute for a SysML modeling tool like *Enterprise Architect*.

Objection – Why Can't We Just Use Visio?

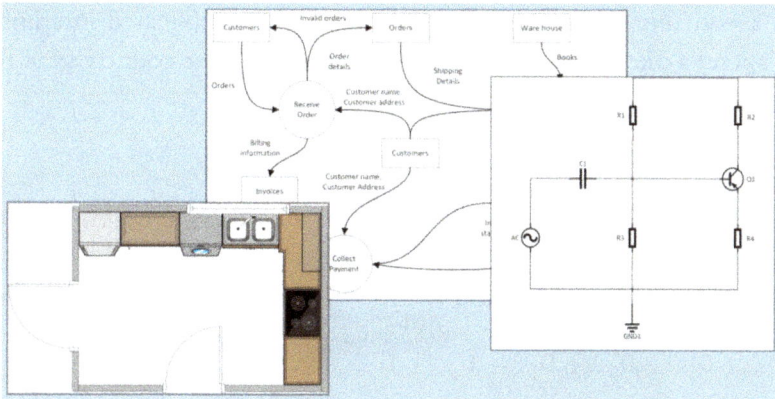

Figure 13-3 – Visio sample diagrams

Visio is a powerful diagram drawing tool produced by Microsoft. Visio can produce a wide variety of technical and business drawings including organization charts, flow charts, floor plans, and circuit diagrams. There is even a SysML 1.0 stencil for Visio [53]. That having been said, Visio has no underlying model or tool integration.

Objection – Why Can't We Just Use Spreadsheets?

Spreadsheets are also very powerful tools. I use spreadsheets daily. In fact, SysML itself provides table structures for requirements. That having been said, SysML is about relationships between the elements of your model. Spreadsheets are excellent for managing row/column style relationships, but SysML relationships are more of a web or a network and are difficult to represent in a spreadsheet.

Objection – Why Can't We Just Use Text Documents?

Just writing things out in text is an intuitive approach that does not scale well. Again, text is a sort-of two-dimensional medium. As you start adding lots of links and cross-

---

[53] See [Visio-SysML] on page 380.

references to the text to make it represent the more graph/node interlinked nature of complex requirements, the text gets harder and harder to understand.

If you need a concrete example of the problem with complicated interlinked text requirements, spend a pleasant afternoon reading through your country's tax regulations.

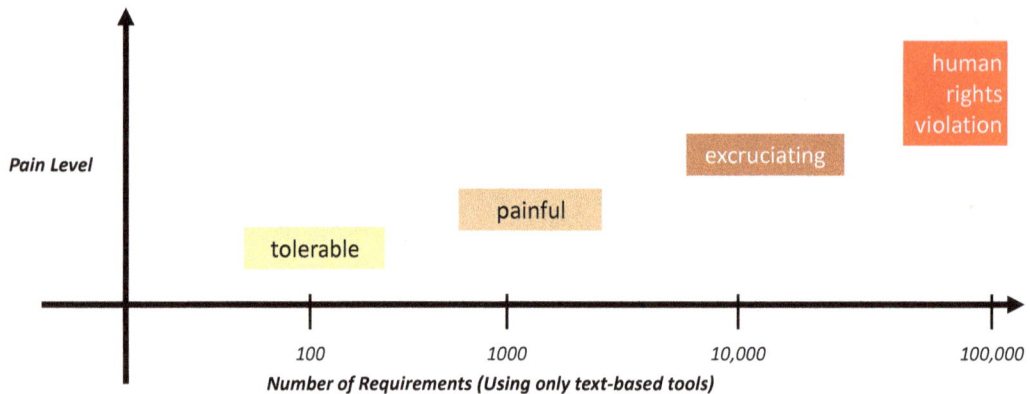

Figure 13-4 – The increasing level of pain in text-only requirement systems

As shown in Figure 13-4, managing requirements (and hence specifications) purely and only with text is only manageable when the number of requirements is small.

- **~100 Requirements** – The situation is manageable. You can write the text-based requirements in a document or perhaps put them in a spreadsheet.

- **~1,000 Requirements** – The problem has become painful. Very likely by this point you have given up on the spreadsheet and switched over to a purpose-built requirements management tool like IBM's DOORS NG or one of its competitors such as Visure Requirements or Jama.

- **~10,000 Requirements** – The problem has become excruciating, even with the purpose-built requirements tool.

- **~100,000 Requirements** – You start to get visits from human rights protection organizations.

Common Misconceptions

In this section we introduce some common misconceptions about SysML that you will encounter as you start introducing SysML to your organization. These are not really objections, as much as assumptions commonly made by people who do not yet have enough information about the subject.

Misconception – The PowerPoint Compiler

Neither *Enterprise Architect* nor SysML itself are "PowerPoint Compiler" technologies. SysML and MBSE exist to enable a common understanding between a diverse set of stakeholders. These stakeholders each have specialized tools for their domain and these tools do the compiling of the final product.

One thing that confuses this point somewhat is that *Enterprise Architect* is originally a UML tool and is much older than SysML itself. As such, *Enterprise Architect* has features designed to partially generate code from UML diagrams. These features are still advertised and can lead to some level of misplaced expectations.

Misconception – Project Speedup

One more subtle misconception is that all of the improved clarity provided by SysML and MBSE techniques will lead to a dramatic project speedup.

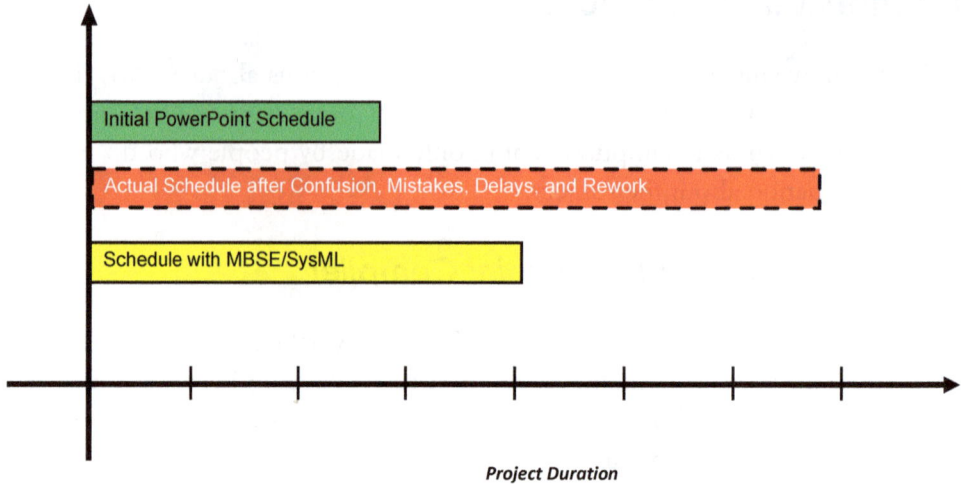

Figure 13-5 – Do MBSE and SysML speed up the project?

Adding SysML (or any MBSE technique) to a project, does not create the impression of a dramatic project speedup. Quite the opposite, creating high-quality SysML diagrams takes a significant amount of time, especially when the team is still just learning to use the tools.

What about the overall project schedule? Disciplined use of SysML by a team will probably bring in the **actual project schedule** considerably, especially if SysML is used in a disciplined manner, project-after-project. The challenge, however, is that using SysML carefully in a project will tend to create the impression of a "bureaucratic slowdown". The team will tend to compare the progress of the project using SysML to the imagined *PowerPoint project schedule* and grumble that things are moving painfully slowly.

Misconception – Drill-Down Hierarchy

SysML is not a magic sauce that you can just pour over a complex systems project to instantly transform it into a simple, executive-friendly, easy-to-understand, drill-down hierarchy.

Part of the problem lies in the manner in which SysML models hierarchy. See *SysML versus UML* on page 353.

The more subtle problem is that any project worth applying SysML to will invariably have multiple layers of abstraction that don't actually completely map to each other. Systems engineers use the concept of "allocation" to connect such not-entirely-coherent layers and SysML does include an *«allocate»* relationship for this purpose. However, these sorts of layer-to-layer allocation are never as neat and tidy as one would like. Perfect, simple drill-down rarely exists in real systems and not surprisingly it is difficult to portray simply in SysML models of those systems.

Misconception – Modeling Equals Simulation

When you mention modeling to executives, many will assume that you are talking about simulation. Simulation certainly involves mathematical modeling. Systems modeling, however, is a different topic. In fact, one of the main applications of SysML is to model systems in which the information available about the system is too imperfect to allow for any sort of mathematical description.

That having been said, model-based systems engineering techniques and SysML can be very helpful in managing sets of interacting mathematical simulations. At the INCOSE International Symposium 2018, Dr. Tina Morrison of the FDA gave a very interesting presentation on this sort of combined use of modeling and simulation in the evaluation of medical devices. [54]

Subtle Problems

Overly Intricate Diagrams

Which brings us to an important point:

Hetherington's Rule: *Avoid creating diagrams that confuse your stakeholders.*

This rule may seem obvious, but it is easy to go astray on this point. SysML comes with dozens of intricate notation options. You can quickly lose track of what you are

---

[54] See: [InSilicoMedicine]

doing and diagram yourself into oblivion. One day you will find yourself at the front of the room explaining your marvelous diagrams and suddenly notice that the entire room is staring at you as though you were a mumbling space alien stepping out of a flying saucer. [55]

If you find that you absolutely must use the super-intricate features, I recommend that you try to confine them to narrow sections of the model that only your most technical stakeholders will need to interact with.

Over Modeling

In *Overly Intricate Diagrams*, I mentioned the danger of getting carried away with obscure SysML notation. There is a second, more subtle danger: modeling too much.

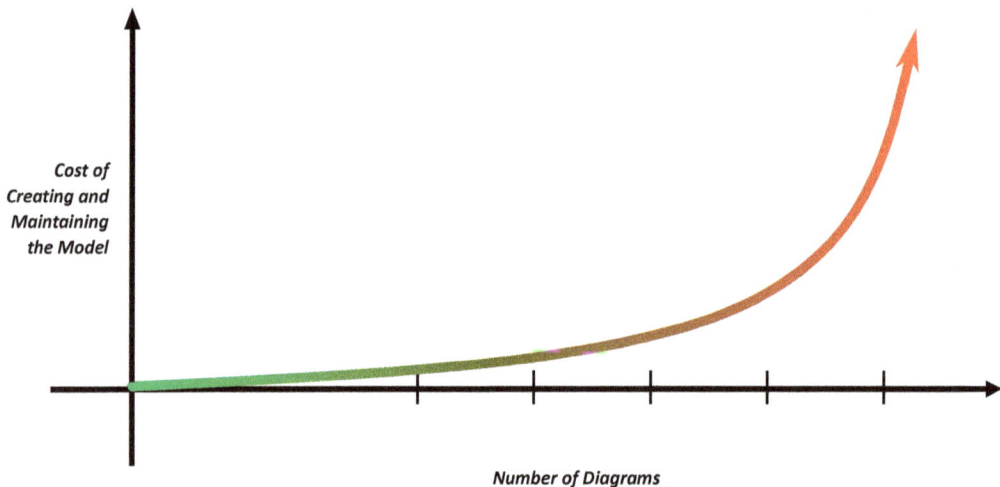

Figure 13-6 – The more detailed the model, the more expensive

The problem is that model development has its own costs. As the scope of your model expands, these costs start to multiply with each other. You have to think carefully about the lifecycle of the model. If stakeholders are going to continue to reference the model, then the model must be maintained. If the stakeholders start encountering inac-

---

[55] Yes. I have had exactly this experience.

curacies in the model or portions of the model that no longer reflect realty, the model's value as the *Single Version of the Truth* will deteriorate rapidly. On the other hand, the more you model, the more costly it becomes to maintain the model. As you start using the modeling power to link all sorts of different aspects of the system concept together, you also create a maintenance burden in keeping all those links up-to-date and accurate. [56]

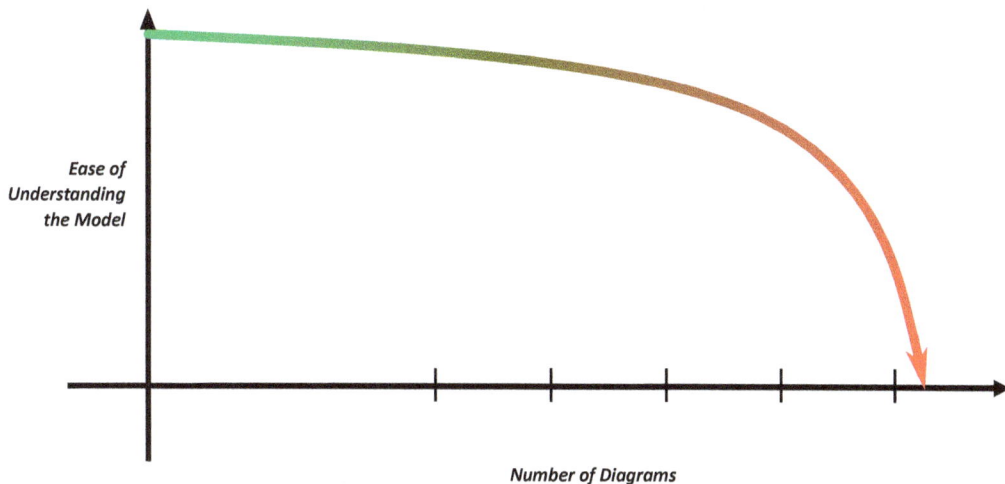

Figure 13-7 – Complex models are hard to understand

The second aspect of this problem is the ease of finding things for anyone other than the person who first entered the model in the tool. As the model increases in complexity, it quickly becomes difficult for anyone other than the person who did the initial modeling to find anything. In fact, if the person who did the initial modeling goes away and works on another project for a year, even that original modeler can find it surprisingly difficult to find things in a complicated model.

---

[56] One of the early leaders in the UML arena is said to have taken the position that models should be produced on whiteboards and that the whiteboards should be erased at the end of each discussion.

Executable Models

SysML 1.5 is a profile built on top of UML. UML in turn has its origins in the Computer Aided Software Engineering movement of the 1980s. At that time, there was a strong belief that in the future, all software would be developed graphically.

Since the 1980s, the graphical vision has become entrenched in the mechanical engineering world. Walk around the design floor of a shipyard or an automobile maker's research and development center and you will see row after row of mechanical engineers working on 3D graphical representations of mechanical parts.

In other areas, the graphical approach has not ultimately taken hold. Graphical development of software is a tiny percentage of the overall development of software. More surprisingly, graphical approaches have largely disappeared in the logic portion of chip development as well. When you walk around the design floor of a major international semiconductor giant, mostly you see engineers staring at screens of code – Verilog, VHDL, System C, C, and TCL scripts. If you ask one to bring up a graphical schematic diagram, it might take several minutes of head-scratching, if they can bring one up at all.

At a European software quality conference in 2014 I talked with a young, Dutch verification engineer and she had a very succinct description of the problem:

> *"We found that sequence diagrams were very useful for forging a common understanding with the stakeholders about what the system was supposed to do. However, we found that those sequence diagrams resulting from the stakeholder discussions would not compile. There was not enough information in the diagrams for the compiler to make unambiguous decisions. Unfortunately, once we added enough information to the sequence diagrams so that they would compile, we found that the detailed sequence diagrams had become incomprehensible to the stakeholders."*

That tends to be the rub: SysML is wonderful in the early stages of clearing up misunderstandings between stakeholders. However, when you move past that point and try to make it actually compile into a product, you quickly pass a point at which it is faster and more effective to code the detail directly.

That having been said, all of our existing SysML tools are actually UML tools with modifications. They all have code generators built in. Furthermore, there is still a community of believers. If you are interested in pursuing automatic code generation, I recommend that you use your favorite internet search engine to look for "Executable UML".

SysML versus UML

SysML "1.x" is defined as a profile on top of UML. Back in the early 2000's when the first SysML team assembling the standard, there were obvious and compelling reasons to approach the creation of SysML in this manner:

- A robust UML tool ecosystem was already in place.

- UML itself was designed to be extended in this manner.

- Many of the diagram types that the team wanted to implement were already in existence in UML. SysML would be able to adopt these diagram types with few if any changes.

While the approach of leveraging the existing UML tool ecosystem has been an effective approach to bootstrapping the development of SysML, there are some things about building SysML on top of UML that make the resulting modeling environment a bit confusing to use. Some of the key problems include:

1) **Parts and Composition** – SysML blocks are built on top of UML classifiers which are a construct created for object-oriented programming. That "everything is an object" philosophy from the 1990s included a doctrine that all objects must be dynamically initialized the first time they are used. Students of object-oriented programming languages like Java and C++ spend a lot of time learning about constructor routines. While this approach was interesting at the time as a potential new programming paradigm in the 1990s and early 2000s, [57] making SysML parts work in this manner makes nested block structures a bit confusing to work with.

2) **Multiplicity** – Even in UML the multiplicity concept was not very well developed. If you define a block "airplane" with 2 "wing" blocks, you will be sur-

---

[57] The level of enthusiasm in the programming language community for object-orientation seems to have dropped off considerably in recent years.

prised to find later that there is no way to explicitly reference the two wing blocks as "left" and "right". This peculiarity is inherited directly from UML.

3) **Multiple Layers** – SysML blocks can have "properties" which are actually built on top of UML "attributes" and the tools in many cases let you see the information both ways.

4) **Other UML Extensions** – That extension-by-profile feature of UML was attractive to a lot of different people and all of the major SysML modeling tools also include a dozen or more other specialized UML extensions. Those other modeling applications and all of the little quirks and features that were added to the tools to support them make the tools more complicated for SysML beginners.

I do not recommend that beginners spend a lot of time digging into the UML aspect of the modeling environment. However, it is worth being aware of the underlying UML. In many cases when you run into a confusing tool behavior, that behavior will be related to this layer-on-top-of-UML structure.

SysML Version 2

The SysML community is currently working on a "Version 2" for SysML. SysML V2 is not a minor update. It is a substantial re-engineering of SysML to overcome some of the problems encountered in the first version. This re-engineering and the subsequent re-engineering of tools to support the new approach is expected to take until the early 2020's. Here are a few of the key goals for the effort as of press time for this book:

1) Cut the connection between SysML and UML

2) Airtight compatibility suite

3) API to allow 3rd party apps to manipulate models in tools

4) Enable intuitive drill-down behavior for nested block structures

5) Named roles for multiple parts

6) Object enhancements, make it easier to track serial-numbered instances

Appendix A – Ordering and Installing

Sparx Enterprise Architect is easy to order and to install. The following sections provide tips on specific things to consider.

What to Buy

Sparx offers a number of different editions of *Enterprise Architect*. The most recent pricing levels are available at: http://www.sparxsystems.com/products/ea/editions/?source=ea14

The current pricing tiers have changed from those of a few years ago. In fact, the product pricing has been reduced and the feature content increased – a very customer-friendly move. Within the current tiers as listed on the website [58]:

- **Corporate** – should be able to handle almost everything in this book except parametrics, which are an advanced feature of SysML.

- **Unified** – should be able to handle everything in this book and includes simulation capabilities.

- **Ultimate** – will be most interesting for deployment to larger teams.

Once you have purchased the license, Sparx will send you an email with your license key number as well as instructions for downloading and installing the product.

If you are part of a larger organization with license key management infrastructure, a floating key license version is available as well.

Maintenance

Like most similar commercial tools, the product comes with one year of free support and upgrades. After the first year has finished, in order to continue to get support and upgrades, you will need to pay an annual maintenance fee.

---

[58] Website edition information as of 8 October 2018

Node Locking

Unlike many similar tools, *Enterprise Architect* is not node locked. However, as of version 14, the tool now has an activation code. The end user license agreement for version 14 allows for the use on a single computer and one personal backup computer. Here is the text from the end user license agreement:

> *As the primary user of the computer or device on which the Software Product is installed, You may make a second copy for your exclusive use on either a home or portable computer.* (59)

Note that Sparx also offers very reasonably priced floating licenses. If your team is large enough to support a license key server, floating licenses could be an attractive alternative for your team.

Windows Environment

Generally, I have found *Enterprise Architect* to be very simple and robust and not sensitive to the particular configuration of my machine. However, just for the record, I am writing this book using a Lenovo X1 Carbon 6th generation notebook.

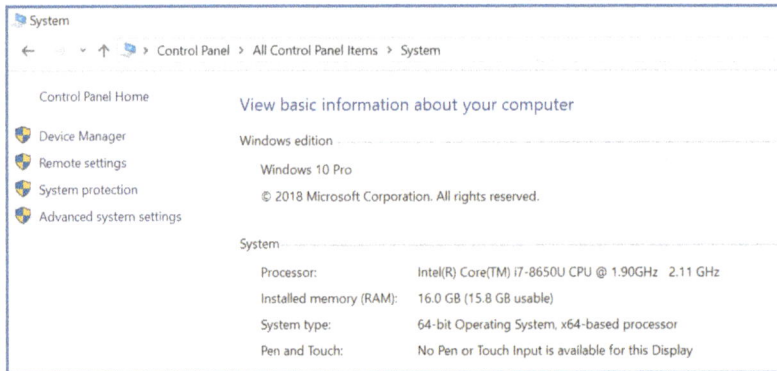

Figure A-1 – The author's machine

---

(59) Text from end user license agreement for version 14 as of 13 May 2018

Installing the Tool

Installation of *Enterprise Architect* is generally quite straightforward. If you encounter problems, you can simply send an email to support@sparxsystems.com. I have found Sparx support to be quite helpful, generally responding by the next business day and sometimes responding within a few hours.

Downloading the Installation File and User Guide

After you purchase the tool, you will receive an email with logon credentials to a secure website.

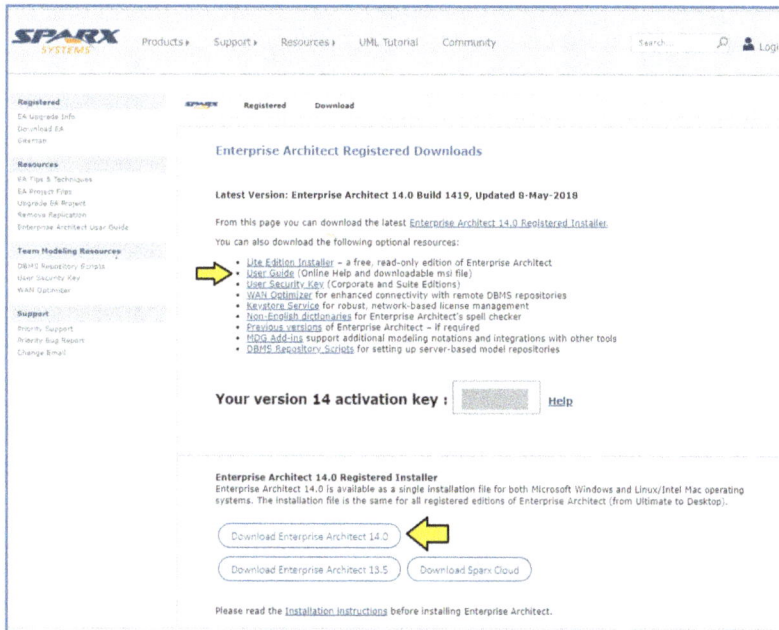

Figure A-2 – Sparx download website

From this website, you can download the installation file. You can also download the user manual which can be handy if you do a lot of work on airplanes or in other locations with limited internet connectivity. Be sure to note your activation code (My code is grayed out in Figure A-2.)

Figure A-3 – Move installation file to a convenient temporary directory

After downloading the installation file, move it to a convenient temporary directory. Double-click on the installation file to start the installation process.

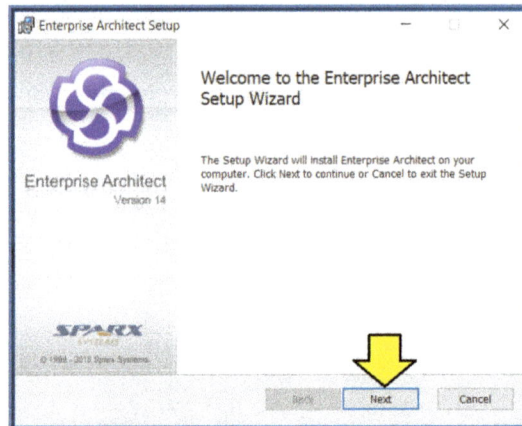

Figure A-4 – Click Next to continue

After a few seconds of preparation, a confirmation screen will appear. Click "Next" to continue.

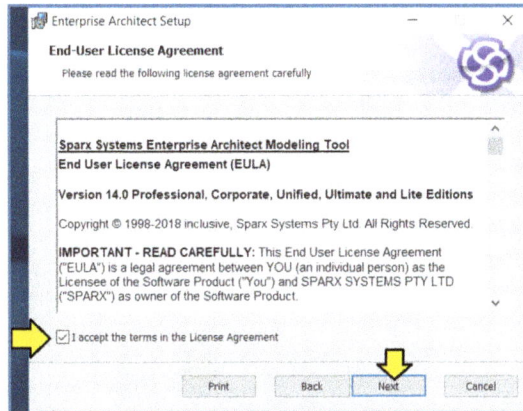

Figure A-5 – Accept terms and click Next to continue

Next, the end user license agreement (EULA) appears. The Sparx EULA is a very reasonable five pages in length, is written in plain English, and contains no strange or unusual provisions. After reviewing the agreement, click the radio button to accept it and click "Next" to continue.

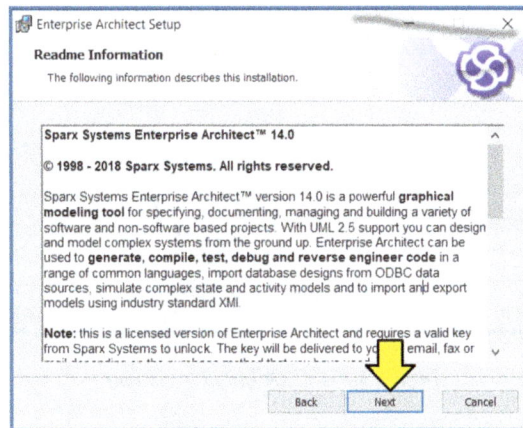

Figure A-6 – Review Readme and click Next to continue

Review the Readme text and click "Next" to continue.

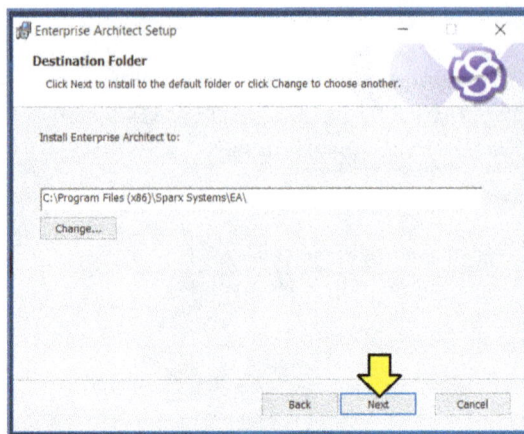

Figure A-7 – Accept installation directory and click Next to continue

Accept or change the installation directory and click "Next" to continue.

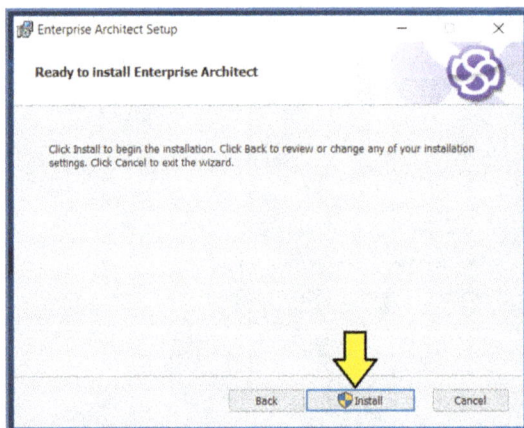

Figure A-8 – Click Install to continue

Click "Install" to start the installation. A Windows security pop-up will appear. Enter a valid administrator password to approve installation of the software.

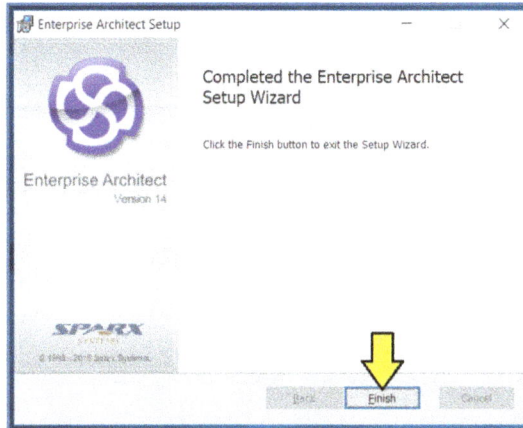

Figure A-9 – Click Finish

Click "Finish" to complete the installation.

Desktop Launch Icon

The Sparx installation will create an icon on your Windows desktop.

You can also start the tool from Windows 10 start by typing the first few letters of "Enterprise Architect" and selecting the tool when it pops up.

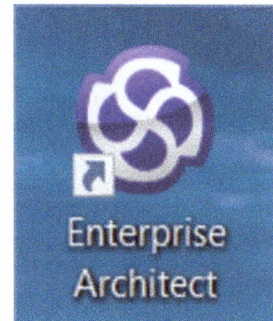

Figure A-10 – EA icon

Version Activation

When you start or update *Enterprise Architect* you may be presented with a version activation screen.

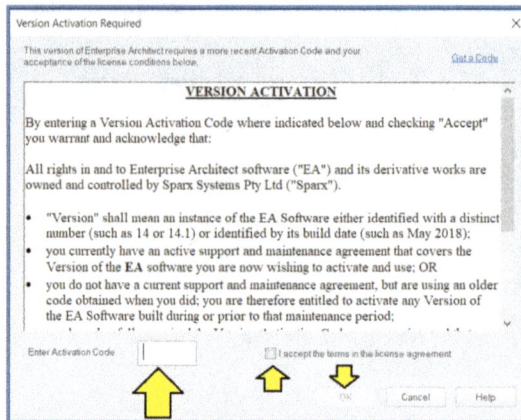

Figure A-11 – Version activation panel

Enter the activation code from Figure A-2 on page 359 as shown in Figure A-11.

Program Look and Feel

Enterprise Architect has a variety of "look and feel" options. The screenshots in this book are taken with the default Microsoft® Visual Studio 2016 look and the "Colorful" theme.

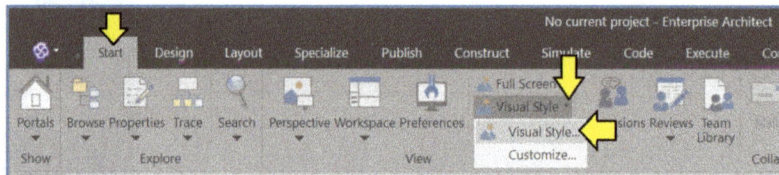

Figure A-12 – Select visual style

From the "Start" ribbon, pull down the "Visual Style" menu and select "Visual Style...".

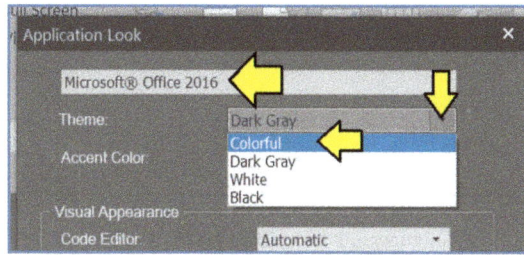

Figure A-13 – Select colorful theme

In the "Application Look" window pull down the "Theme:" menu and select "Colorful". Click "OK" to apply the setting and close the window.

Unicode Support

Enterprise Architect uses the Microsoft JET engine from Microsoft Access as its underlying database. *Enterprise Architect* ships with and is setup by default to use the JET3.5 engine, a rather old version. This version of JET uses the old Western European codepage and as such cannot support Unicode characters properly. [60]

Enterprise Architect has a setting to enable use of the JET4.0 engine which supports Unicode.

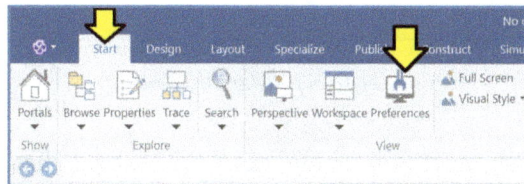

Figure A-14 – Select Preferences from the start ribbon

From the start ribbon select "Preferences".

---

[60] Feedback from Sparx Systems indicates that newer versions of *Enterprise Architect* default to JET4.0 support. Sparx also recommends using one of the DBMS options as all current databases support Unicode. Use of a DBMS is out of scope for this book, but Sparx support will be happy to help you set this up.

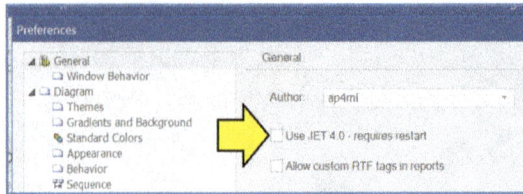

Figure A-15 – Click use JET4.0

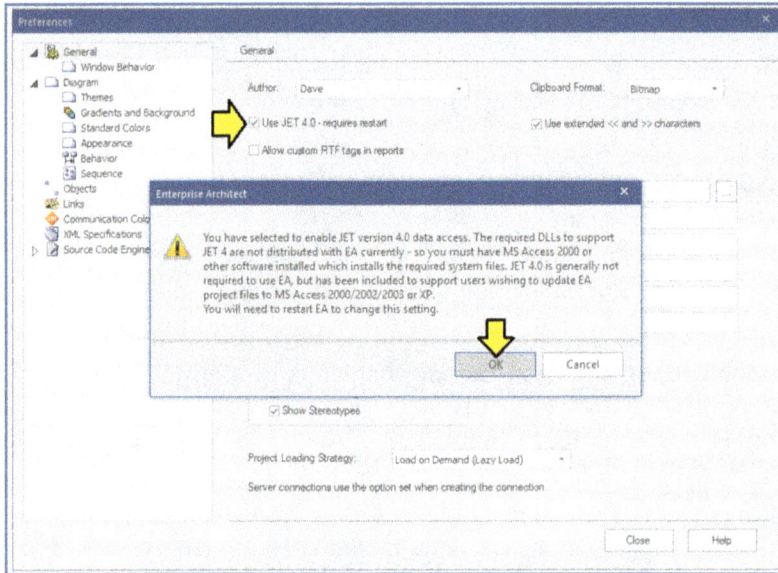

Figure A-16 – JET4.0 DLL warning

After enabling JET4.0 support, a warning panel will appear that explains the need for Access 2000 or greater in order to get access to JET4.0. At first this might be cause for concern if you don't have a license of Microsoft Access...

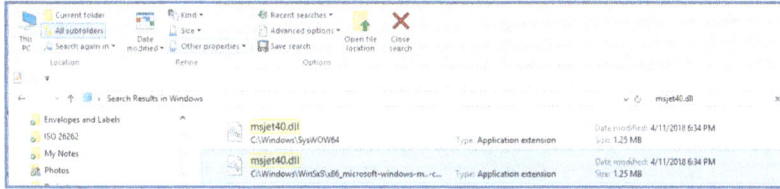

Figure A-17 – The JET4.0 engine seems to be standard in Windows 10

However, the observant reader will notice that "Access 2000" would be a product version that Microsoft prepared for release in the year 2000 AD and that this date was quite a while ago. As of Windows 10, the JET4.0 DLL seems to be shipped as part of the operating system.

Click "OK" to dismiss the warning and "Close" to update the setting. Exit *Enterprise Architect* and restart to fully enable JET4.0 support.

If you need to include East Asian text (Japanese, Chinese, or Korean) or bidirectional text (Hebrew, Arabic) in your model, you will obviously need to enable JET4.0 support. However, even if you think you only need English, you should enable JET4.0 support. Virtually all internet technology uses UTF-8 [61] encoding and many special punctuation marks, emoticons, and similar special symbols like "registered trademark" are now routinely encoded in Unicode rather than the old Western European codepage used by the JET3.5 engine.

Note: in addition to restarting *Enterprise Architect*, you will need to recreate any previously created models from scratch. Attempting to add Unicode text to a model previously created with the JET3.5 engine will not work well. [62]

Example Unicode Model

In the examples files directory *Examples\Apx01_Install\A1.6_Unicode* you will find a small example model using Unicode characters.

---

[61] UTF-8 is a method of encoding that preserves 7-bit ASCII compatibility for plain English and punctuation at the cost of using two bytes per special European character and three bytes per East Asian character.

[62] If you have a significant number of legacy JET3.5 models that need to be converted for use with Unicode text, contact Sparx support for assistance.

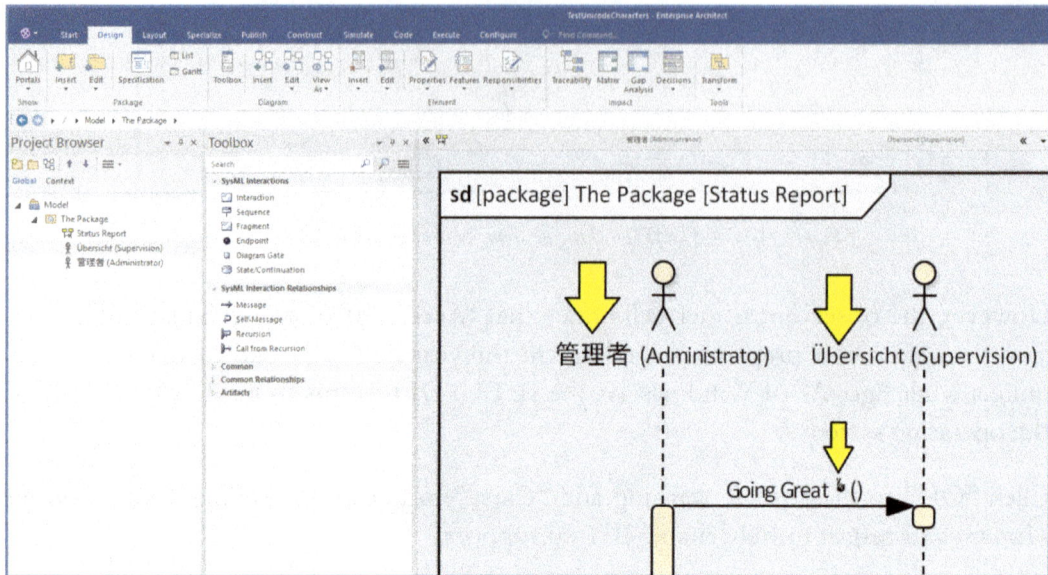

Figure A-18 – Example of model with Unicode characters

In the example model, we have:

- a Japanese administrator "管理者" ("kanrisha");

- who is sending a status message: "Going Great";

- to the somewhat nebulous "Übersicht" ("supervision") in Germany.

If we look carefully at the status message, however, we see that our administrator is less than entirely confident of the status and hence the message includes the emoji "fingers crossed". [63]

Figure A-19 – Emoji

---

[63] The emoji "fingers crossed" is Unicode Ü. See: https://emojipedia.org/hand-with-index-and-middle-fingers-crossed/

Setting XMI Export Default

If you are going to create XMI files from your models to share modeling information with other tools, it is important that you set the options to have Sparx create UTF-8 XMI files rather than using the obsolete "windows-1252" (Western European) code-page.

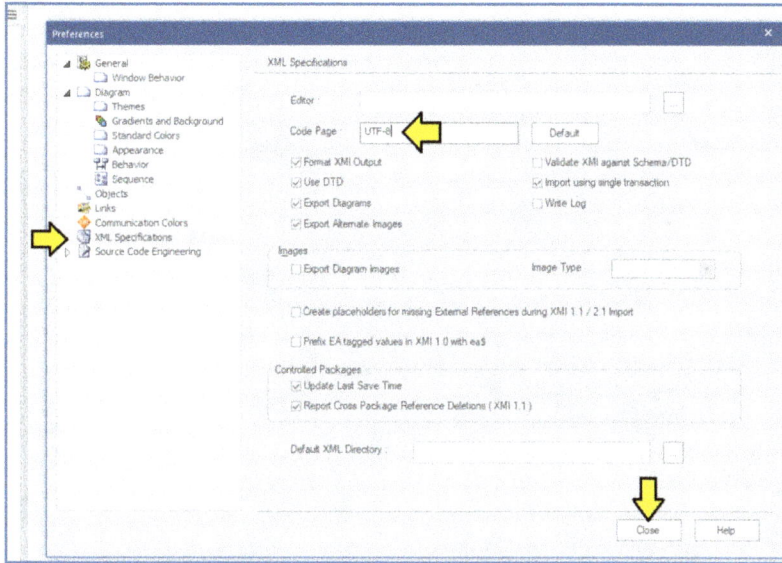

Figure A-20 – Setting Unicode for XMI export

In the "Preferences" window, select the "XML Specifications" tab. In the "Code Page:" field, replace "windows-1252" with "UTF-8". Click "Close" to apply the setting and dismiss the window.

Appendix B – Further Reading

As the author of this book, I hope you have found the material useful and easy to understand. However, this book is merely a beginning. In the following sections, I have listed a number of good books that you can read for more in-depth coverage of SysML and some related subjects.

SysML Books

- **Delligatti, Lenny** – *SysML Distilled: A Brief Guide to the Systems Modeling Language*. Addison-Wesley Professional, 2013

  SysML Distilled is an excellent, compact, all-around text for engineers who want to develop a more thorough understanding of SysML. In fact, this book is my primary "go to" reference when I have questions about the more subtle/advanced details of SysML. Prior to working as a systems engineer, Lenny Delligatti had experience both as a naval officer and as a high school mathematics teacher. This leadership and instructional background comes through in his well-organized, and straightforward textbook.

- **Douglass, Bruce Powel** – *Agile Systems Engineering 1st Edition*. Waltham, MA, USA:Morgan Kaufmann, 2015

  Bruce Powel Douglass was involved in the development of specifications for both UML and SysML and is a prolific author, having written extensively about the use of UML for realtime applications.

  The scope of this book is somewhat broader than the other two, including more guidance on methodology. The treatment of SysML is brief – one chapter, 80 pages. However, that 80 pages includes some important insights, such as his treatment of:

  - role versus type (page 88)
  - the relationship of block definition, internal block definition, and package diagrams (page 94)
  - model organization for a large project (page 104)

- value properties in blocks, parts, and instances (page 108)

  This book also goes into depth on the development and management of use cases and requirements.

- **Friedenthal, Sanford and Alan Moore, Rick Steiner** – *A Practical Guide to SysML, Third Edition: The Systems Modeling Language.* Morgan Kaufmann, 2014

  This book is the authoritative reference on SysML and its authors are key leaders in the ongoing development of the standard. Since the SysML standard itself includes limited explanatory content, this book is helpful as a sort of window into the intent of the leaders of the SysML standard development.

Books on Use Cases

- **Cockburn, Alistair** – *Writing Effective Use Cases.* Addison-Wesley, 2001

  Use cases are used in both software development and systems engineering. Writing effective use cases is not easy. Where do you start? What do you include? How much is too much? This book is regarded by many to be best book ever written on this difficult topic.

Requirements Engineering Books

- **Beatty, Joy and Anthony Chen** – *Visual Models for Software Requirements.* Microsoft Press, 2012

  Joy Beatty and Anthony Chen present an excellent step-by-step method for developing requirements for typical IT end-user applications. The authors present a method for using Microsoft Visio to produce diagrams for clarifying the structure and behavior of the IT application to be developed. Visio is chosen because it is more widely available, less expensive, and easier to learn to use than most SysML tools.

- **Hull, Elizabeth and Ken Jackson, Jeremy Dick** – *Requirements Engineering, 3rd Edition*. Springer, 2010

    This is a compact and concise textbook suitable for a university-level introductory course on requirements engineering. For readers with no background in systematic requirements management, this book does a good job of covering basics like requirements elaboration. [64]

- **van Lamsweerde, Axel** – *Requirements Engineering, From Systems Goals to UML Models to Software Specifications*. Wiley, 2009

    This is a thoroughly researched book with an emphasis on formal methods. Professor van Lamsweerde is a proponent of formally structured specification languages – a restricted form of English that reads a little bit like a programming language. He is also a recognized authority on goal-oriented requirements engineering. After thoroughly covering the basics of requirements engineering, this book uses structured specification languages and goal-orientation to teach a method for developing the UML models for a software application.

- **Leffingwell, Dean** – *Agile Software Requirements: Lean Requirements Practices for Teams, Programs, and the Enterprise*. Pearson Education, Inc., 2011

    Dean Leffingwell's book actually contains little about requirements. On the other hand, his book is a superb distillation and discussion of the various organizational techniques that fall under the umbrella of "Agile" As he points out, project scope/cost, project schedule, and project quality are an iron triangle. You can only control two of these at a time. Any enlightened executive team that is responsible for the purchase and development of a safety-critical system will do well to think carefully about requirements prioritization and the possible application of some modified Agile approaches to get the best possible scope coverage while not compromising on safety or schedule.

---

[64] Requirements elaboration is a very basic topic that gets surprisingly little treatment in some of the other larger books on requirements.

- **Pohl, Klaus** – *Requirements Engineering: Fundamentals, Principles, and Techniques.* Springer, 2010

  If you can only afford one formal reference text for requirements engineering, this is the one you should buy. Klaus Pohl's book is the most comprehensive requirements textbook that I have encountered so far. It is clear and well-structured. It very helpfully lays out the evolution of key ideas in the field of requirements engineering with meticulous attribution of the original sources.

  Klaus Pohl also addresses some of the messy reality that is glossed over in other more academic treatments of requirements engineering. I particularly like his treatment of the interaction between "What" and "How" in section 2.3.3 on page 27.

Other Related Books

- **INCOSE** – *INCOSE Systems Engineering Handbook: A Guide for System Life Cycle Processes and Activities, 4th Edition.* Wiley, 2015

  This is the handbook of the International Council on Systems Engineering. As such, it is a handy, compact compendium of standard systems engineering techniques – including, but not limited to model-based systems engineering.

- **Jenney, Joe with Mike Gangl, Rick Kwolek, David Melton, Nancy Ridenour, Martin Coe** – *Modern Methods of Systems Engineering: With an Introduction to Pattern and Model Based Methods, 4th Edition.* CreateSpace Independent Publishing Platform, 2011

  This book gives a solid overview of general systems engineering techniques with an overview of model-based and pattern methods as promised by the title. However, what I found most valuable was actually chapter 2 with its brief but fascinating accounts of:

  - The development of the highly innovative Cord 810 in 1935 by a 3-person design team in about six months – including the production of 100 prototype vehicles. This feat would be utterly unimaginable in today's automobile industry.

- The development of World War II aircraft in which the designers had offices on balconies overlooking the line that was producing the first aircraft. This close proximity allowed them to step out and look at the aircraft in seconds, as well as walk down a stairway and touch it within a minute.

This chapter does an excellent job of setting the correct frame of reference: the real problem is neither fancy tools nor abstract modeling grammars; the real problem is the complexity of the human communication. Even though chapter 2 is brief, for me this chapter alone is worth the purchase price of the book.

- **Brambilla, Marco and Jordi Cabot, Manuel Wimmer** – *Model-Driven Software Engineering in Practice.* Morgan & Claypool Publishers, 2012

    One challenge in looking into model-driven and model-based engineering methods is that most of the key textbooks were written ten or more years ago. This concise book is an excellent up-to-date review of activity in the field. The book is particularly useful for navigating the blizzard of acronyms and related standards.

    I particularly like Chapter 5 "Integration of MDSE in Your Development Process". Since the initial surge of enthusiasm in the early 2000's, model-driven approaches have suffered a number of setbacks and there are quite a few disillusioned veterans around. [65] Chapter 5 covers some of the different sociological problems that model-driven development can introduce into an organization such as fears about job security. Chapter 5 is a must-read for anyone considering introducing model-driven or model-based engineering techniques to a larger product development organization.

---

[65] Many of these disillusioned modeling experts were key early founders of the Agile movement and now resist documentation in any form, especially any sort of modeling.

- **Kelly, Steven and Juha-Pekka Tolvanen** – *Domain-Specific Modeling: Enabling Full Code Generation.* Wiley IEEE Computer Society Press, 2008

  One of the weaknesses of SysML is that its rich descriptive power comes with a significant learning curve. Certain aspects of SysML are inherited from UML and can be confusing to users without a background in computer science. The direction of arrows that show a relationship between two blocks can seem counterintuitive to a mechanical engineer. The ends of a relationship between an engine and a crankshaft may be marked as "target" and "client" by the tool. What does that mean!?

  Domain-Specific Modeling attacks this problem by deliberately sacrificing the idea of a universal, interoperable set of graphics. Instead, DSM tools help small organizations make simple, customized tools that draw the graphical diagrams using any set of icons, shapes, arrows, or other conventions that make sense to that particular organization. In an example mentioned often by the authors at conferences, the diagrams that are intuitive to a team that designs railroad stations might not look anything like the diagrams that are intuitive to a related team that designs the railroad network.

  This book lays out the Domain-Specific Modeling approach and introduces the MetaEdit+ tool for creating such focused end-user modeling tools.

Appendix C – About the Author

David loves languages. He speaks Japanese and German fluently as well as some Chinese and Spanish. He passed the Japanese Language Proficiency Test (日本語能力試験, Nihongo Nōryoku Shiken or JLPT), Level N2 examination in December 2011.

David is a member of:

- IEEE – Institute of Electrical and Electronics Engineers
- INCOSE – International Council on Systems Engineering
- SAE – Society of Automotive Engineers

Figure C-1 – David J. Hetherington

David has a BA in Mathematics from the University of California San Diego and an MBA from the McCombs School of Business at the University of Texas.

Appendix D – References

- **[AgileM]** *Agile Manifesto* http://www.agilealliance.org/the-alliance/the-agile-manifesto/

- **[Beatty]** Beatty, Joy and Anthony Chen – *Visual Models for Software Requirements.* Microsoft Press, 2012
  See the entry for this book in *Requirements Engineering Books* on page 372 for more information.

- **[CMS17th]** The University of Chicago Press Editorial Staff – *The Chicago Manual of Style, 17th Edition.* University of Chicago Press, 2017
  The Chicago Manual of Style is the primary source of style and formatting conventions used in this book.

- **[Cockburn]** Cockburn, Alistair – *Writing Effective Use Cases.* Addison-Wesley, 2001
  See the entry for this book in *Books on Use Cases* on page 372 for more information.

- **[Delligatti]** Delligatti, Lenny – *SysML Distilled: A Brief Guide to the Systems Modeling Language.* Addison-Wesley Professional, 2013
  See the entry for this book in *SysML Books* on page 371 for more information.

- **[Douglass]** Douglass, Bruce Powel, Ph.D. – *Agile Systems Engineering.* Waltham, MA, USA:Morgan Kaufmann, 2015
  See the entry for this book in *SysML Books* on page 371 for more information.

- **[Friedenthal]** Friedenthal, Sanford and Alan Moore, Rick Steiner – *A Practical Guide to SysML, Third Edition: The Systems Modeling Language.* Morgan Kaufmann, 2014
  See the entry for this book in *SysML Books* on page 372 for more information.

- **[INCOSE]** *The International Council on Systems Engineering* https://www.incose.org/

- **[InSilicoMedicine]** *Advancing In Silico Medicine at FDA* http://www.omgwiki.org/MBSE/lib/exe/fetch.php?media=mbse:patterns:incose2018--morrison.pdf

- **[IoT]** *Internet of Things* http://en.wikipedia.org/wiki/Internet_of_Things

- **[Leffingwell]** Leffingwell, Dean – *Agile Software Requirements: Lean Requirements Practices for Teams, Programs, and the Enterprise.* Pearson Education, Inc., 2011
  See the entry for this book in *Requirements Engineering Books* on page 373 for more information.

- **[MetaEdit]** *MetaEdit+ Modeler* http://www.metacase.com/mep/

- **[Peak]** *Simulation-Based Design Using SysML, Part 1: A Parametrics Primer* http://eislab.gatech.edu/pubs/conferences/2007-incose-is-1-peak-primer/

- **[Pohl]** Pohl, Klaus – *Requirements Engineering: Fundamentals, Principles, and Techniques.* Springer, 2010
  See the entry for this book in *Requirements Engineering Books* on page 374 for more information.

- **[Rechtin]** Rechtin, Eberhardt and Mark W. Maier – *The Art of Systems Architecting, Second Edition.* CRC Press, 2000

- **[SysML]** *Systems Modeling Language* http://sysml.org/

- **[SysML1.5]** *OMG System Modeling Language Specification™ Version 1.5* https://www.omg.org/spec/SysML/1.5/PDF

- **[SysML1.6]** *OMG Systems Modeling Language (OMG SysML™) Version 1.6* https://www.omg.org/spec/SysML/1.6/PDF

- **[UML]** *Unified Modeling Language* http://www.uml.org/

- **[Unicode]** *a standard that aspires to assign a unique number to every character of every human written language* http://unicode.org/

- **[UTF-8]** *Unicode Transformation Format 8. See section 2.5 on page 36 of the Unicode standard.* http://www.unicode.org/versions/Unicode7.0.0/ch02.pdf

- **[Visio-SysML]** *Visio Stencil and Template for SysML 1.0* http://softwarestencils.com/sysml
  Note that at the time of the publication of this book, the currently approved version of the SysML standard is 1.5. As such, some parts of the stencil/templates might not reflect current SysML usage.

Appendix E – Glossary

- **Agile** – an umbrella term for a set of frameworks and practices for managing product development based on short cycles, frequent delivery, and continuous replanning. The concept was originally articulated for software development – see [AgileM]. Currently, the term is used in a wide variety of engineering and management disciplines.

- **codepage** – a table that maps the characters in one or more languages to a set of numerical values. [UTF-8] can be considered to be a codepage of [Unicode].

- **containment tree** – the hierarchical tree of packages within packages in a SysML model.

- **INCOSE** – The International Council on Systems Engineering See [IN-COSE].

- **MBSE** – See "Model-Based Systems Engineering"

- **Model-Based Systems Engineering** – an approach to systems engineering that uses a model database to keep track of the relationships between elements in the system. Model-Based Systems Engineering (MBSE) usually combines the database of relationships with diagramming tools that allow an arbitrary number of diagrams to be created showing different combinations of model elements and their relationships. These diagrams are used to allow different stakeholders to understand and comment on the aspects of the system that are within their area of expertise without becoming confused by the detail of the other aspects of the system.

- **namespace** – In SysML (and UML) a namespace is defined by the node path, starting from the root node and including all the elements down to the current element. For example, using full namespace notation a *door handle* might be shown in a diagram as a *vehicle::body::door::door handle*.

- **requirements traceability** – The process of proving that a system fulfills its requirements by establishing links all the way from the initial marketing requirements down to the actual components that are involved in fulfilling each requirement.

- **SoC** – System on Chip. A highly integrated semiconductor device that combines one or more processing cores with multiple specialized accelerators and peripheral interfaces.

- **SysML** – Systems Modeling Language. See [SysML].

- **system** – INCOSE refers to [Rechtin] in offering this definition of a system: "A system is a construct or collection of different elements that together produce results not obtainable by the elements alone. The elements, or parts, can include people, hardware, software, facilities, policies, and documents; that is, all things required to produce systems-level results. The results include system level qualities, properties, characteristics, functions, behavior and performance. The value added by the system as a whole, beyond that contributed independently by the parts, is primarily created by the relationship among the parts; that is, how they are interconnected".

- **toolchain** – a set of software applications, often provided by different suppliers, that are used in sequence to produce a product.

- **UML** – Unified Modeling Language. See [UML].

- **Unicode** – a standard that aspires to assign a unique number to every character of every human written language. See [Unicode].

- **UTF-8** – an encoding scheme for [Unicode] that uses 1 to 4 bytes of information to represent every character. See [UTF-8].

- **Waterfall** – traditional development project flow. Phases start with customer requirements, moving to architecture, moving to high-level design, then to low-level design, and so on. A chart of the project phases resembles a left-to-right waterfall.

End Notes

Chapter 1 – Introduction

- [1] – For more information on these books, see the *SysML Books* section on page 371.

- [2] – The *Kindle Cloud Reader* is available here: https://read.amazon.com/

Chapter 2 – Quick Start

- [3] – In versions of *Enterprise Architect* previous to version 14, Sparx used the file type "*.EAP". In version 14, Sparx introduced the new filetype: "*.EAPX".

- [4] – Note that part names are actually "roles" from a UML point of view. We will discuss this in more detail in the chapter about internal block definition diagrams.

- [5] – Actors do not need to be human. In fact, SysML provides an alternate box notation for actors such as cloud server processes that are not humans.

- [6] – An early reader has reported that in version 15 of the tool, the requirements id and text can now be entered directly in the properties panel for the requirement. The steps described here are for version 14 of the tool.

- [7] – The observant reader will notice that we have just created the beginnings of a "user story" for our system. User stories are an important part of almost any design methodology.

Chapter 3 – Take a Deep Breath

- [8] – In versions 1.0.0 and v1.0.1 of this book, the term used here was: "Single Version of the Truth". That term was widely used in the MBSE community until around 2020. However, the understanding of the community has evolved to recognize that the "truth" is the superset of all information of the system – not something you would want stored on your laptop! The updated term is a more accurate representation of the goal for the content of the system model.

- [9] – It is actually worse than this. The SoC alone may require as many as 20 different kinds of specialized design engineer. Also, I have not considered the verification and validation teams or the teams that would handle all of the automotive qualification testing. However, as we will soon see, even this modest underestimate of the number of stakeholders is difficult enough.

- [10] – This goal – making diagrams that everyone can understand – sounds rather obvious. However, it is easy to get carried away and produce diagrams that your stakeholders don't actually understand.

- [11] – The three major tools also provide some options to directly import each other's models, including diagrams. However, having tested all three, in my experience only the very simplest SysML diagrams port successfully from tool-to-tool.

Chapter 4 – Block Definition Diagrams

- [12] – This discussion is going to seem very familiar to anyone who has ever done any object-oriented programming in a language like Java or C++. That similarity is not a coincidence. SysML 1.5 is a profile on top of UML and the "block" is a stereotype of the UML "classifier" which is used to model classes in object-oriented languages.

- [13] – See Figure 2-19 on page 22 for the basics of dragging the composition arrow.

- [14] – If this description of names versus roles is making your head spin, you are in good company. This unusual naming philosophy is related to object-oriented programming and SysML's origins in UML.

- [15] – As we can see in Figure 4-11, after we set a specific multiplicity for a part, a notation: "{unique}" appears in the *parts* compartment. This notation was introduced in the SysML 1.4 standard and pertains to the question of whether given a multiplicity > 1, each part would be unique with no duplicates. In any case, for this sort of detail setting to be usable, a lot more support would be needed to support the configuration of different aspects of this part. In an email on 8 August 2018 Sparx support identified the appearance of "{unique}" in this case as a bug that will be fixed in a future release.

- [16] – You may need to click once or twice or adjust the sizing a bit to get the diagram to resize itself properly.

- [17] – Note that *Enterprise Architect* displays the part names with a leading caret symbol. (^) SysML 1.4 was retargeted to UML 2.5 and picked this symbol usage up in the process. The caret indicates an inherited member. For ":Wing", ":Engine", ":Body", and ":Tail" the caret symbol notation is correct. However, ":Entertainment System" is owned directly by "Passenger Plane", not inherited from "Airplane". As such, there should not be a caret in front of this member. Sparx support has acknowledged this as a defect which will be fixed in a future release.

- [18] – Strictly speaking, the table is responsible for arranging for the destruction of its top, legs, brackets, and bolts as it is going up in flames itself. This detail, however, is usually only relevant for software objects.

- [19] – See: https://sparxsystems.com/enterprise_architect_user_guide/15.2/modeling/proptab.html

- [20] – The sharp-eyed reader will notice that the operations we have just defined are somehow related to the value properties we defined in the previous section.

Chapter 5 – Internal Block Diagrams

- [21] – See Figure 4-10 on page 79 for the procedure to set multiplicities.

- [22] – Note that *Enterprise Architect* displays this part with a leading caret symbol. (^) SysML 1.4 was retargeted to UML 2.5 and picked this symbol usage up in the process. It is supposed to indicate an inherited member. However, ":Child" is an owned member, not an inherited member. Sparx support has acknowledged this as a defect which will be fixed in a future release.

- [23] – Personal computer "Do-It-Yourself" enthusiasts will notice that the following model is not actually quite right – current PC cases have a cutout which allows the power supply to present its AC power interface directly. However, we will gloss over that detail for the purposes of illustration.

- [24] – See *Value Properties* on page 93 for the procedure to set up value properties.

- [25] – Right-click on the block in the project browser and use the context menu to add the internal block diagram to the element.

- [26] – **Note:** on a real project you would probably keep the entire model and just make additional diagrams that showed only the elements and the attributes of the elements relevant to the particular discussion at hand. That is the key point of the model-based systems engineering (MBSE) approach. However, this is an instructional text, so I want the example model itself to be as simple as possible. As such, we will just create a new version of the model with only the relevant elements.

- [27] – "JSRP" stands for "Juicer Status Reporting Protocol". Someday you are going to build up a large international standards organization to discuss revisions to this important protocol.

- [28] – The need to make the link bi-directional is not mentioned in the SysML standard. This seems to be an internal requirement of *Enterprise Architect*.

Chapter 6 – Package Diagrams

- [29] – An "Executive Model" would be a model scrubbed of annoying, messy detail.

- [30] – The behavior of this relationship in *Enterprise Architect* was not quite what I expected. A block definition diagram created in the garden package still shows tree types as external blocks.

Chapter 7 – Activity Diagrams

- [31] – The standard suggests that control flow should be represented with a dashed arrow. *Enterprise Architect* does not show a dashed line by default. However, if you select "Configure" from the top menu bar, select "Options" from the ribbon, and then select the "General" tab, you will find an option to show a dashed line for control flow in a SysML model.

- [32] – Since there is no flow that leads to an activity final node, the activity remains alive as a "ghost", even though there are no longer any flows in it – probably not a good design for a real product. However, in the early stages of modeling a real system, you would probably just add a note to the diagram about this concern and come back later to add more detail to take care of that problem.

- [33] – https://en.wikipedia.org/wiki/Google_Books

- [34] – I happen to be partial to MongoDB. https://www.mongodb.com/

- [35] – The exact implementation of this step varies from tool-to-tool. With *Enterprise Architect*, you have to match the name manually.

- [36] – See [SysML1.5] section 11.3.1.1 on page 118.

Chapter 8 – Sequence Diagrams

- [37] – *Sparx Systems* significantly altered the behavior of actors between versions 14 and version 15.2 of the tool, no longer allowing actors to be part of reference associations, but still allowing them as properties on a block. The procedure in this section was updated to work with version 15.2 of the tool.
- [38] – If you double-click the self-message without first selecting it you will open the properties dialog box for the diagram rather than for the self-message.
- [39] – "float" = "real"
- [40] – In order to get the ":Customer" reference to show up in the *references* compartment of the ATM system block and in the project browser, you may need to make an internal block diagram of the ATM system, right-click on the internal block diagram, and select "Synchronize Structural Elements".
- [41] – Refer to *Operations and Receptions* on page 108 for instructions on adding an operation to a block.

Chapter 9 – State Machine Diagrams

- [42] – If the informal notation is a problem for your project, one alternative is to use opaque notation to insert statements from an actual formal programming language. See *Further Study* on page 300.
- [43] – One of the applications of a self-transition is to cause the entry behavior to be executed over again. See *Further Study* on page 300.
- [44] – Frankly speaking, the function of *Enterprise Architect* is a bit awkward here.
  1) If you do not enter a name in the features panel, nothing will be shown for the behavior in the project browser.
  2) If you do enter a name in the features panel, and also select "Show Behavior in Diagram" the diagram will show both.

Chapter 10 – Use Case Diagrams

- [45] – If you have somehow jumped directly to this chapter without reading anything else in the book and do not yet understand how to drag icons to diagrams, you may want to review *Quick Start* on page 9.

Chapter 11 – Requirements Diagrams

- [46] – **Note:** Here we are talking about creating a limited scope "Single Version of the Truth" within the "Shared Vision for the System". The goal is to create just enough clarity so that a specific set of stakeholders can do their jobs without making mistakes. We are *not* attempting to turn the SysML model into the universal repository of all data for the system.

- [47] – *Enterprise Architect* does not provide a function to select which tags get displayed. Turning off tags turns off both ID and text.

- [48] – In fact, when I design this sort of system, I often end up making a UML profile of specialized stereotypes of the «block» and the «requirement» elements. I add the ID tag to all of these elements so that I can make a consistent end-to-end numbering scheme.

Chapter 12 – Parametric Diagrams

- [49] – I have used an internet search for "Unicode pi" to find, copy, and paste the " π " character and a similar search for "Unicode squared" to find, copy, and paste the " ² " character into the tool. See Figure 4-37 on page 101.

- [50] – You may find it easier to expand the size of the symbol in the diagram before adding the value properties to it.

- [51] – You might need to close and reopen the model to make the parametric diagram display the updated formula.

Chapter 13 – Challenges Ahead

- [52] – In the 1980s when I was developing software for IBM, these sorts of behaviors were often referred to as "Feechurs", as in: "That's not a bug, it's a *Feechur*".

- [53] – See [Visio-SysML] on page 380.

- [54] – See: [InSilicoMedicine]

- [55] – Yes. I have had exactly this experience.

- [56] – One of the early leaders in the UML arena is said to have taken the position that models should be produced on whiteboards and that the whiteboards should be erased at the end of each discussion.

- [57] – The level of enthusiasm in the programming language community for object-orientation seems to have dropped off considerably in recent years.

Appendix A – Ordering and Installing

- [58] – Website edition information as of 8 October 2018

- [59] – Text from end user license agreement for version 14 as of 13 May 2018

- [60] – Feedback from Sparx Systems indicates that newer versions of *Enterprise Architect* default to JET4.0 support. Sparx also recommends using one of the DBMS options as all current databases support Unicode. Use of a DBMS is out of scope for this book, but Sparx support will be happy to help you set this up.

- [61] – UTF-8 is a method of encoding that preserves 7-bit ASCII compatibility for plain English and punctuation at the cost of using two bytes per special European character and three bytes per East Asian character.

- [62] – If you have a significant number of legacy JET3.5 models that need to be converted for use with Unicode text, contact Sparx support for assistance.

- [63] – The emoji "fingers crossed" is Unicode Ü. See: https://emojipedia.org/hand-with-index-and-middle-fingers-crossed/

Appendix B – Further Reading

- [64] – Requirements elaboration is a very basic topic that gets surprisingly little treatment in some of the other larger books on requirements.

- [65] – Many of these disillusioned modeling experts were key early founders of the Agile movement and now resist documentation in any form, especially any sort of modeling.

Index

Note: in electronic versions of this book, the numbers shown are sequentially numbered hotlinks to the area containing the related information in the main text, not page numbers.

W

Waterfall – 382

X

XMI –
Unicode support – 369

Z

zooming in and out – 37

www.ingramcontent.com/pod-product-compliance
Lightning Source LLC
Chambersburg PA
CBHW080657220326
41598CB00033B/5241